JAPANimals

Michigan Monograph Series in Japanese Studies
Number 52

Center for Japanese Studies
The University of Michigan

JAPANimals:

History and Culture in Japan's Animal Life

Edited by
Gregory M. Pflugfelder
and
Brett L. Walker

Center for Japanese Studies
The University of Michigan
Ann Arbor 2005

Published by the Center for Japanese Studies,
The University of Michigan
1085 Frieze Building, 105 S. State St.
Ann Arbor, MI 48109-1285

Library of Congress Cataloging in Publication Data

JAPANimals : history and culture in Japan's animal life / edited by Gregory M. Pflugfelder and Brett L. Walker.
p. cm. — (Michigan monograph series in Japanese studies ; no. 52)
Includes bibliographical references.
ISBN 1-929280-30-0 (cloth : alk. paper) — ISBN 1-929280-31-9 (paper : alk. paper)
1. Human-animal relationships—Japan—History. 2. Animals—Japan—History. 3. Animals—Japan—Folklore. 4. Japan—History. I. Pflugfelder, Gregory M., 1959– II. Walker, Brett L., 1967– III. Title. IV. Series.

QL85.J37 2005
591.952—dc22

2005047044

This book was set in Palatino Macron.

This publication meets the ANSI/NISO Standards for Permanence of Paper for Publications and Documents in Libraries and Archives (Z39.48—1992).

Printed in the United States of America

For Conrad Totman

CONTENTS

PREFACE

Confessions of a Flesh Eater: Looking below the Human Horizon

Gregory M. Pflugfelder

I am not, by practically anyone's definition of the term, an animal lover. I keep no pets, eat meat with gusto, and feel no particular urge to commune with fauna in the wild. Nevertheless, in recent years a number of developments have prompted me and many others to think more deeply about the place of nonhuman animals in the world, and more specifically about their role in the history of the Japanese archipelago, which is my academic specialty. Leaving the latter question for the individual chapters that follow, the task of this preface is to recount the origins of the *JAPANimals* project from which the present book derives, and so to allow a more accurate assessment of the volume's contributions.

A few words about the book's title are necessary at the beginning. It is possible that some people may find it contrived, or mistake it for an attempt to profit from the popularity of so-called Japanimation (more commonly known now as anime). There are compelling reasons, however, that led the editors of this volume to choose *JAPANimals* for the name of our undertaking, and they have little to do with cuteness or pop culture. Rather, they center on a common dissatisfaction among the contributors to this book with the way that academic discourses conventionally construct Japan, that is, as a human community that interacts only with other human communities—for example, with "the West," which is all too often similarly imagined in purely human terms. In recent decades, such new disciplines as environmental studies and such philosophical formations as ecofeminism and various calls for "animal rights" have led scholars to reconsider—or perhaps to consider for the first time—the substantial yet complex ties that link human beings with other living creatures on this planet. Although the writers here do not all necessarily identify with these intellectual perspectives, we do all share the view that Japan is more than the sum of its human parts. By merging the toponym *Japan* with the word *animals* in the title, we seek to represent in graphic fashion our common belief that animals—and not only human ones—have played an integral role in determining the history of the archipelago and of the planet.

The *JAPANimals* project had its origins not as an intellectual manifesto, but in the practical arena of pedagogy. It began as a graduate seminar at Columbia University in the spring of 2000. At the time, none of the participants, including myself, who was nominally the instructor, could claim much expertise on the topic, which the syllabus identified ambitiously, if none too helpfully, as "Exploring Animal History in Japan." The vagueness was in fact deliberate, one of the chief rationales behind the course being to encourage original thinking and to stimulate innovative research on the part of participants. The assumption was that by tackling a subject about which a secondary literature did not exist or had barely come into being, students would be forced to step out of the "digest and critique" mode of many graduate seminars and themselves become creative scholars. It was therefore helpful to address a topic that earlier generations had tended to overlook or even belittle.

Since the scholarly silence on nonhuman animals in Japan was practically deafening, it seemed an ideal if initially arbitrary choice. Over the course of four months, participants surveyed the limited secondary literature, identified topics for investigation ("pet projects," we called them), and by the end of the semester had produced research papers of uncommonly high quality. Three of those essays—by Abel, Miller, and Skabelund—are included here.

The work of the seminar did not end there, however. One of the secondary goals of the course was to "hone a range of practical skills that are indispensable for professional historians and other scholars," including "writing grant proposals" and "organizing conferences." Toward that end, the second phase of the *JAPANimals* project began in the fall of 2000. The result was a symposium titled "Animals / History / Japan," which took place under the auspices of the Donald Keene Center of Japanese Culture in April 2001. The editors are grateful to the Keene Center, as well as to the Weatherhead East Asian Institute of Columbia University, for providing the funds that made possible this memorable event. Six new participants joined the project, and contributed chapters to the collection. We were fortunate also to have the participation at the symposium of three prominent historians of the environment and of human-animal relations—Richard Bulliet, Kathleen Kete, and Conrad Totman—whose comments are summarized later in this preface.

None of the original seminar members anticipated that the *JAPANimals* project would have a third stage, namely, the publication of this book. That it did was due largely to the resourcefulness of my coeditor Brett Walker, who visited the seminar as a guest speaker in March 2000, and later served as a presenter and commentator at the "Animals / History / Japan" symposium. As one of few North American scholars to have devoted sustained attention to the history of human-animal relations in Japan, Brett has provided indispensable inspiration for this project from its earliest stages, through his research, his presence, and (dare I say it) his animal magnetism. Through his initiative we located a welcoming publisher in the Center for Japanese Studies at The University of Michigan, after two other presses declared the proposal interesting but not likely to be commercially profitable. We are grateful to the Center for Japanese Studies, and especially to Bruce Willoughby, for their confidence and encouragement.

At each stage of our project—thinking, organizing, and writing—the decision to encompass nonhuman animals within our intellectual purview raised new and intriguing questions. To begin with, in the original graduate seminar, the issue of how to describe and conceptualize the enterprise demanded considerable attention. What the syllabus initially termed "animal history" was not a nomenclature that all could agree upon, and was ultimately abandoned. More than one student preferred to view the interrelationship among different living species as a part of "environmental history." Other alternatives included pluralizing the phrase as "animal histories," coining a new term such as "interspecies history" or "multispecies history," or resorting to a wordy locution such as the "history of human-animal relations." The very absence of an established vocabulary reflected the paucity of existing scholarship. By the same token, the flexibility of available language hinted at the creative potential of the inquiry and enabled seminar members to carry out the research of their choice.

Further complicating the issue of definition was the fact that the category of "animal" itself is a historical and cultural artifact, rather than a biological given, as high-school science might lead us to believe. For someone like myself, who grew up in the 1960s and 1970s, it is mildly disconcerting to realize that younger generations no longer assume that all living beings fall neatly into one or the other of the "plant" or the "animal" kingdoms. Simpler organisms—monera, protista, fungi, and, according to some taxonomies, archaebacteria—young people now learn, enjoy sovereign realms of their own. The reason, of course, is not that the biota themselves have evolved in the span of a few decades, but that the classificatory practices of humans, or more specifically those of contemporary biologists, have changed.

Nor does the now less populous category of "animal," it is important to recognize, possess an exact equivalent beyond the historical sphere of European cultural influence. In the case of Japan, people spoke commonly of animals in a zoological sense only after the nineteenth-century introduction of Western biology, and had to invent a new term, *dōbutsu*, in order to translate the concept. To do so, they combined two Chinese characters, meaning "moving" and "thing," thereby conveying at least one of the root associations of the European classification, as reflected in the words "animated" or "animation."[1] In earlier centuries, Japanese had been less likely to distinguish among living beings according to the presence or absence of motility in them than according to their peculiar mode of locomotion. The earliest extant myths on the archipelago, recorded in the eighth century of the common era (C.E.), speak, for example, of "creeping things" (*ha[f]u mushi*) as a distinct category of living creature, different from both birds and beasts.[2] Contemporary zoologists would dismiss such a category as an illogical mishmash of "unrelated" insects, reptiles, and amphibians. Even ordinary Japanese, who are today taught such scientific taxonomies in school, tend to reserve the term *mushi* for insects alone. Another common ancient term is *kemono*, or "furry thing," which focuses on criteria of appearance, but which by no means encompasses all creatures that biologists today define as "animals."

During the second half of the first millennium, continental notions enriched and complicated Japanese understandings of life on earth. They brought with them into the vocabulary of the islands such classical Chinese compounds as *kinjū*, "birds and beasts," as well as such Buddhist-inflected notions as *shōrui* ("living things") and *chikushō* (roughly, "beastly existence"). As the last word in particular demonstrates, the new vocabulary came coupled with new understandings of the relationship between humans and other sentient beings. According to the Buddhist doctrine of the "six realms of existence" (*rokudō* in Japanese), a person who accumulated bad karma in the present life might be reborn in a subsequent incarnation into the realm of beasts, two levels below that of humans in a six-tier cosmic hierarchy. By the same token, Buddhist ontology linked humans as well as beasts in a karmic continuum with creatures to whom biologists today do not give much credence, ranging from the inhabitants of heaven (*ten*) above to hungry ghosts (*gaki*) and the denizens of hell (*jigoku*) below, with a bellicose race of titans (*shura*) sandwiched in between. Even the distinction between flora and fauna was not always so rigid in Japan as was traditionally the case in Europe. Some Japanese authorities held that plants, too, harbored a soul of sorts, in contrast to Europe, where the possession of a motivating will, or *animus*, in addition to motility itself, is what uniquely marked the "animal." As William LaFleur has shown, a lively debate took place among Japanese Buddhists as to whether plants, or to use the traditional vocabulary, "grasses and trees" (*sōmoku*), could attain enlightenment.[3]

Faced with these lexical complexities, it seemed counterproductive to impose strict limitations on the objects of our research, living or otherwise. The chapters in this volume nonetheless focus on relations through the centuries among some of the more complex and visible life forms on the archipelago, belonging chiefly to the zoological categories of insects, reptiles, birds, and mammals.[4] All are creatures who have attracted considerable notice historically among Japan's human inhabitants. Their prominence on the cultural landscape is reflected, among other things, by their inclusion in a 1713 reference work known as *Wakan sansai zue* (Illustrated Japanese-Chinese encyclopedia), which is the source of the illustrations that precede each of the individual chapters as well as the introduction.

The anthropologist Claude Lévi-Strauss long ago observed that (nonhuman) animals are good not only to eat, but also to think with.[5] This dictum holds true for historians, although few have taken full advantage of its utility. As my colleague Henry Smith aptly put it, our field of vision inevitably changes when we look below the human horizon and take into account happenings closer to the ground (or in the case of birds, above us in the sky, not to mention life beneath the waters). Greater attention to other living creatures frequently reveals cultural and historical processes at work that directly implicate our human concerns, but are not necessarily so conspicuous if we limit our scholarly investigations to human-eye level. In many instances, such considerations challenge received scholarly wisdom, with its longstanding humanist biases. Without going so far as to call for a "posthumanist" or even a "posthuman" mode of understanding history and culture, each of the following chapters demonstrates the intellectual importance of thinking about nonhuman animals in a concrete way.[6]

As the *JAPANimals* project entered the conference stage in the spring of 2001, questions of a more practical nature came to the fore. The symposium offered an opportunity for the original members of the seminar, along with new participants in our project, to step out of the closed confines of scholarship and to interact with broader social constituencies. The event drew a diverse crowd, including not only other academics, but pet therapists, journalists, and even a group of schoolchildren. Each was interested in nonhuman animals from a different perspective, although meaningful conversation was possible among all. Nevertheless, the multiplicity of political and professional agendas that surround the issue of human-animal relations presented the organizers of the conference with some unique challenges. I like to think of one of these episodes as the egg-salad caper, in homage to *What's Up, Tiger Lily?* Woody Allen's "Japanese" spy spoof of the 1960s. In that comic classic, director Woody Allen superimposed his own made-up dialogue on a run-of-the-mill Japanese spy film, spinning an exhilarating yarn about the search for a top-secret recipe for the perfect egg salad.

In North America, some of the most vociferous recent calls for greater attention to nonhuman animals have emanated from political movements such as animal-rights activism and ecofeminism. These movements drew historical inspiration, in turn, from nineteenth-century European predecessors, including antivivisectionist campaigns and the philosophical organization of what became known in the 1840s as vegetarianism.[7] Given these circumstances, even the issue of what kind of food to serve at a conference on human-animal relations assumed an unaccustomed degree of delicacy. To the organizers of the symposium, it seemed reasonable not to risk offending sensibilities by heaping the refreshment table with plates of meat. But what about egg salad? the caterers asked. One branch of contemporary vegetarianism, known as "vegan," abstains not only from once-living flesh, but from all animal products. In the end, it was decided that egg salad would remain one of the lunch options. But the episode underlined the fact that a variety of human-animal relations occur daily even at an academic conference in a big city. To turn Lévi-Strauss on his head, nonhuman animals not only give us food for thought, but they can make us give thought to our food.

Three distinguished discussants at the conference brought to the table further intellectual fodder. The three drew upon their areas of scholarly expertise to help place the topic of "JAPANimals" within a larger historical context. Their observations are briefly summarized in the following paragraphs, which draw not only upon their remarks at the symposium, but upon commentary that they kindly provided in response to the finished chapters.

It was only appropriate to have present at the symposium Conrad Totman, who for many years championed the study of environmental history nearly singlehandedly among scholars of Japan in North America. Totman freely admitted in private conversations that he was a "plant man," much of his earlier work having dealt with the exploitation of forests and the organization of the lumber industry.[8] Nevertheless, the cultural interaction of humans with other animals, he acknowledged, provides valuable information for thinking about the long-term history of human relationships with the biosystem as a whole. For Totman, the larger picture is not a cheery one, human capacity for inflicting damage on other living things having grown dramatically, particularly over recent centuries, and being all too readily employed by those who wield it. As a practical matter, Totman pointed out, when we try to understand the dynamics of human-biosystem relations, it is well to bear in mind that how we humans think about other animals (or about plants) carries little weight when compared to the level of our capacity to manipulate or otherwise affect the world around us. If we need or want something badly enough, and have the capability to obtain it, it seems, we will soon enough devise a rationale to justify doing so. Sadly, the record of human history suggests that it is a matter of little consequence whether any other members of the biosystem—including weaker humans—are inconvenienced by the enterprise.

A different kind of historical perspective was provided by Richard Bulliet, who pointed out that human-animal relations in Japan are "unique among complex literate societies." For Bulliet, a specialist on the Middle East and Islam, a critical factor lies in the domestication of nonhuman animals, which in Japan played far less conspicuous a historical and cultural role than in the West and other parts of the world.[9] The philosophical and psychological gulf between humans and other animals that opened up in societies based on animal husbandry, Bulliet argued, never came to dominate Japanese cultural thinking. In this historical difference, Bulliet detected a glimmer of hope for the future. "By sharing so weakly in the domestic mentality, Japanese have preserved the capacity to recover a spiritual aspect of human-animal relations that may someday offer an alternative to the imaginative narrowness and stultifying humanization that postdomestic culture has so far produced."

Looking from the vantage point of modern European history, Kathleen Kete commented on the "powerful connection between specific behaviors towards nonhuman animals and definitions of modernity." Whether in nineteenth-century France or Japan, such everyday practices as petkeeping and zoogoing became an integral part of the fabric of modern life, subtly sustaining the apparatuses of state power, class control, and imperial dominion.[10] Nevertheless, Kete noted, the implication of notions of animality with the wielding of political power is not purely a modern phenomenon. Rather, the usefulness of the human-animal "divide" derives precisely from its fluidity, which allows it to be channeled in various directions according to historically specific political and cultural needs. For Kete, the promise of incorporating nonhuman animals into our work as historians lies not in constructing new narratives of progress toward modernity, but rather in forcing us to reconsider the "very definition of what history is and does."

Finally, at the third stage of our project—namely the preparation of this volume—nonhuman animals posed new questions for the authors and editors. Although each chapter of this book pursues a different topic, we hope that the chronological organization of the volume and an abundance of cross-references among its chapters will paint a broader picture of changing human-animal relations in Japan over the centuries. The historical invisibility of nonhuman animals, the work of editing constantly reminded us, is subtly embedded in, and indeed reinforced by, the very structure of our language. To give an example, conventional English usage reserves the relative pronoun "who" for human beings, thus assuming implicitly that people alone possess the sort of individuality and agency that make historical accounting possible in the first place. Only children and pet lovers are accustomed to talking about the "dog who lives next door," and in traditional historiography, it is Hannibal's soldiers "who" invaded Rome and not his elephants. The present volume departs from convention by assigning the relative pronouns "who" and "whom" to cultural and historical actors of both the human and the nonhuman variety. It is not our intent to recommend a change in general English usage. Rather, we hope that this linguistic quirk will, by its very idiosyncracy, help to underscore one of the conceptual premises of the volume, which is that nonhuman animals have played a role in the history and culture of Japan, as in other places.

Similarly, in the English vernacular, the designation "animals" customarily excludes people. In fact, one often finds "human" and the "animal" used as if they were antonyms. Most of us carry around in our heads this oppositional sense of humans versus animals, and practice it in our daily speech, even as we accept biologists' taxonomic inclusion of our species in the animal kingdom. The human animal is indeed a walking paradox. For the record, "animal" and "animals" in this volume should be understood to include the creature *homo sapiens*. In those cases where the difference between nonhuman and human species is significant, the authors and editors have tried to make that distinction explicit. Only one chapter, by Ian Miller, diverges from this basic editorial principle, since the very historical process by which "human" and "animal" came to be understood as antonymic lies at the heart of its analysis, and is most easily apprehended by resorting to the idiom of the period in question.

Throughout the volume, the editors have favored the use of such locutions as "human-animal relations" as a way to describe people's interaction with other animal species in diverse historical and cultural contexts. The hyphen in the phrase should be understood not to reinforce a supposed categorical distinction between "humans" and "animals," but rather as a reminder that the two elements are closely linked. So, too, with our title, *JAPANimals*, we hope to foster a vision of Japan that incorporates the historical experiences of living creatures above and below the human plane. Our horizons are enriched when we take into account the history that happens at our feet as well in the seas and skies, and not just at our eye level. The creatures that await discovery have, of course, been there all along; it is we who need to make the effort to see and learn from their stories.

Finally, the editors would like to thank Abby MacBride for her contribution to the index, and the Vice President for Scholarship, Creativity, and Technology Transfer, the College of Letters and Science, and the Department of History and Philosophy at Montana State University for their generous financial contributions to this project.

Uffing am Staffelsee, Bavaria
August 2003

NOTES

1. The seminal Latin category is *animal*, which is fundamentally related to the notion of breath (*anima*) as an indicator of life. Connotations of spirit and of movement followed from this basic meaning.

2. See, for example, W. G. Aston, trans., *Nihongi: Chronicles of Japan from the Earliest Times to A.D. 697* (1896; reprint, Rutland, Vt.: Tuttle, 1972), xv. One twelfth-century work of prose fiction memorably describes an unconventional young noblewoman who plays with such lowly creatures as caterpillars, toads, and snakes, and dubs her "The Lady Who Admired Vermin [i. e., *mushi*]." See Robert L. Backus, trans., *The Riverside Counselor's Stories: Vernacular Fiction of Late Heian Japan* (Stanford: Stanford University Press, 1985), 41–69.

3. William LaFleur, "Saigyō and the Buddhist Value of Nature," in *Nature in Asian Traditions of Thought: Essays in Environmental Philosophy*, ed. J. Baird Callicott and Roger T. Ames (Albany: State University of New York Press, 1989), 183–209; William LaFleur, "Sattva: Enlightenment for Plants and Trees," in *Dharma Gaia: A Harvest of Essays in Buddhism and Ecology*, ed. Allan Hunt Badiner (Berkeley: Parallax, 1990), 136–44. See also Donald H. Shively, "Buddhahood for the Nonsentient: A Theme in No Plays," *Harvard Journal of Asiatic Studies* 20 (1957): 135–61.

4. In historical times, Japanese considered the whale a rather large species of fish, instead of a close relative of land mammals, so that Abel's chapter in this volume may be seen, in addition, as addressing the piscine realm—or as the conventional epithet had it, "things broad of fin and things narrow of fin" (*hata no hiromono hata no samono*). In the traditional, rather than zoological, taxonomy, insects and reptiles would be classed together as creeping things or *mushi*.

5. Claude Lévi-Strauss, *Totemism*, trans. Rodney Needham (Boston: Beacon, 1963), 89.

6. See Cary Wolfe, *Animal Rites: American Culture, the Discourse of Species, and Posthumanist Theory* (Chicago: University of Chicago Press, 2002).

7. For more historical background, see Richard D. French, *Antivivisection and Medical Science in Victorian Society* (Princeton: Princeton University Press, 1975); Coral Lansbury, *The Old Brown Dog: Women, Workers, and Vivisection in Edwardian England* (Madison: University of Wisconsin Press, 1985); Nicholaas A. Rupke, ed., *Vivisection in Historical Perspective* (London: Croom Helm, 1987); Colin Spencer, *The Heretic's Feast: A History of Vegetarianism* (London: Fourth Estate, 1993); James Turner, *Reckoning with the Beast: Animals, Pain, and Humanity in the Victorian Mind* (Baltimore: Johns Hopkins University Press, 1980).

8. See the following works by Conrad Totman: *The Green Archipelago: Forestry in Preindustial Japan* (Berkeley: University of California Press, 1989); *The Lumber Industry in Early Modern Japan* (Honolulu: University of Hawaii Press, 1995); *The Origins of Japan's Modern Forests: The Case of Akita*, Asian Studies at Hawaii, no. 31 (Honolulu: Center for Asian and Pacific Studies, University of Hawaii, 1985). An environmental approach also characterizes the author's two recent survey histories, *Early Modern Japan* (Berkeley: University of California Press, 1993) and *A History of Japan* (Malden, Mass.: Blackwell, 2000), as well as the forthcoming *Preindustrial Korea and Japan in Environmental Perspective* (Leiden: Brill).

9. Richard W. Bulliet's many writings include *The Camel and the Wheel* (Cambridge: Harvard University Press, 1975) and *Hunters, Herders, and Hamburgers* (New York: Columbia University Press, 2005).

10. For Kathleen Kete's provocative historical research on human-animal relations, see "Animals and Ideology: The Politics of Animal Protection in Europe," in *Representing Animals*, ed. Nigel Rothfels (Bloomington: Indiana University Press, 2002), 19–34; *The Beast in the Boudoir: Petkeeping in Nineteenth-Century Paris* (Berkeley: University of California Press, 1994).

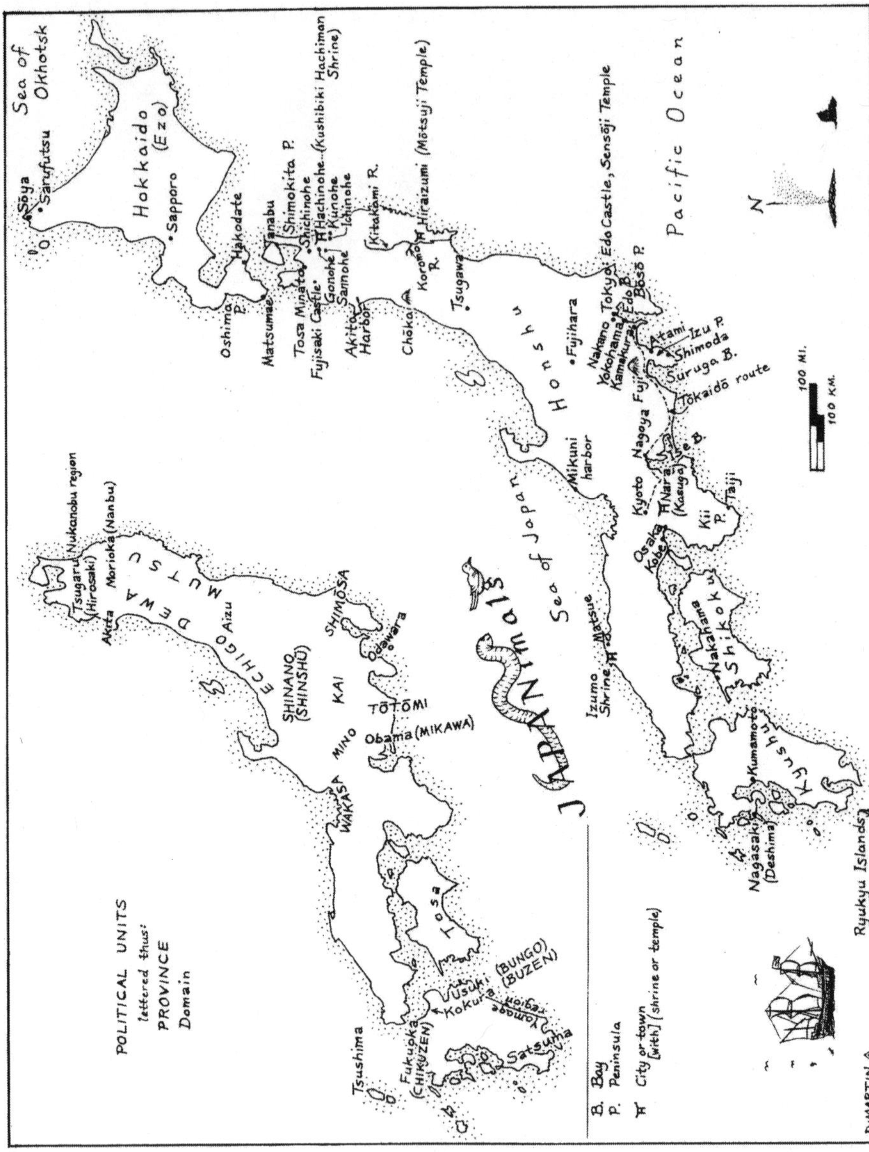

Selective political geography of Japan (pre-1868).

From *Wakan sansai zue*. Courtesy of the C. V. Starr East Asian Library, Columbia University.

INTRODUCTION

JAPANimals: Entering into Dialogue with Japan's Nonhuman Majority

Brett L. Walker

Whenever I think of "JAPANimals," I think of the marvelous "Operation Ghosts" scene in Takahata Isao's animated film *Heisei tanuki gassen ponpoko* (Heisei badger wars; 1994).[1] The main protagonists of the story are badgers or "raccoon-dogs," in Japanese called *tanuki* (the Linnaean classification is *Nyctereutes procyonoides*). These animal heroes live in the Takaga and Suzuka forests on the outskirts of Tokyo and are battling over their shrinking habitat, encroached on by the sprawling Tama New Town construction project. Eventually, faced with certain local extinction because of the destruction of their once-pastoral mountain home, the badgers meet in the dead of night at the abandoned Manpuku shrine. There they decide, clandestinely, to unite in a struggle against human expansion.

As part of their elaborate defense strategy, the badgers vow to "study humans" (*ningen kenkyū*) in order better to understand their villainous behavior. Their research leads them also to resurrect the ancient practice of "shape shifting" (*bakeru*). Sadly, not all badgers are *henge tanuki*, or "transforming badgers," but many are indeed so gifted. Under the spiritual guidance of three elders from Shikoku island—where, the film would have it, badgers still regularly practice shape shifting in order to defend their habitat against humans—the latter plot a ghostly war against the inhabitants of Tama New Town by frightening people away using their ability to transform into ghosts, goblins, and other creatures, actual and fantastic. While passing as humans—a shape maintained, incidentally, only through the consumption of large quantities of overpriced energy drinks—the badgers learn at a local municipal library that the early-modern or Tokugawa period, extending from 1600 to 1868, witnessed frequent episodes of badger metamorphosis, but that the phenomenon had since declined.[2] That is, badgers who shifted shapes were supposedly part of Japan's preindustrial past; modern badgers, of course, scavenge for garbage, rob chicken coops, and die underneath the wheels of speeding cars.

Once "Operation Ghosts" gets underway, hundreds of monsters and other creatures from Japan's historical culture invade Tama New Town, and the scene develops into a visual feast for anyone interested in traditional Japanese lore, religion, ceremonies, and monster tales. Spiritually united and mustering all of their shape-shifting energies, the badgers consume Tama New Town and its human inhabitants by manifesting as eerie, floating images of Chinese dragons who transform into Shinto priests, priests who transform into tigers, tigers who transform into wind deities, wind deities who transform into Buddhist demons, demons who assume the form of a giant "beckoning cat" (*maneki neko*), a beckoning cat who transforms into frolicking fox and rabbit characters from the twelfth-century picture-scroll *Chōjū jinbutsu giga* (Playful pictures of anthropomorphic birds and beasts), and so forth.[3] By the time the scene concludes, the metamorphic badgers have nearly exhausted the Japanese cultural repertory of monsters and other creatures of fantasy, including even some grotesque modern icons, such as walking high-voltage power pylons. Utterly spent, one of the Shikoku elders, Inugami Gyōbu, lies dead, a casualty of the Heisei badger wars.

Such pyrotechnic spectacle notwithstanding, the ghostly cultural images are all but lost on the human residents of Tama New Town. Japanese farmers in the hinterlands of Shikoku might still fall for *tanuki no waza* or "badger tricks," but the meaning of the eerie procession is, for the most part, lost on those living in the suburbs of Tokyo. One quick-thinking capitalist even has the audacity to claim the ghoulish parade as his own invention on the television news, part of the grand opening of his Wonderland Theme Park.

The story ends with the badgers losing their mountain home. Those badgers who are able to shift shape join up with foxes—for, according to longstanding Japanese lore, the latter creatures can also transform themselves at will—and live as humans among humans.[4] Those unable to do so seek their livelihood in garbage pails and chicken coops—that is, if they are lucky enough to avoid being squashed as they cross Tama New Town's many busy intersections. City workers routinely collect the crushed bodies of the less lucky with rubber gloves and place them in garbage bags to be unceremoniously tossed away. Not only badgers, but all the other animals who once called the mountains home also die or are dislocated, replaced by the ecologically monotonous and culturally sterile life of suburban New Town.

In another splendid scene, those badgers who perished during the badger wars enter the afterlife, where they pass their time playing traditional Japanese instruments and singing and dancing. In order to reach the Buddhist Western paradise, they board a fantastic "treasure ship" whose sails consist of the billowed-out folds of one badger's characteristically large scrotum. Even today, storefront Shigaraki-style ceramic badgers on the streets of Japan's towns and cities display exceedingly generous testes. Typically, these ceramic "beckoning badgers" (*maneki tanuki*) wear straw hats, hold a flask of rice wine in one hand, and a neglected promissory note in the other, an ensemble that conveys a folksy invitation from the proprietor to "come on in" and leave your worries behind. In Japanese (which is to say, human) cultural terms, sizeable gonads have long symbolized good fortune; but biologists also point out that "raccoon-dogs" in the wild do in fact have large testes, an evolutionary endowment that is the product of intense competition for females among eligible males and is designed for repeated copulation.

After their ultimate defeat at the hands of the Tama New Town inhabitants, those badgers who decide to live as people suffer under the intensely mundane conditions of modern existence. At least one badger, Shōkichi, decides one night to return to his mountain home. Finding it converted into a golf course, he joins the badgers who remain there in dancing and singing, making carefree merriment as only badgers can do. They play their traditional instruments, drink rice wine, and sing songs, harkening back to a lost Arcadia, a nostalgic bit of paradise on earth.

What should one make of this filmic celebration of Japan's animal diversity and its critique of changing relations between Japanese people and their nonhuman neighbors? The filmmaker, Takahata Isao, clearly seeks to direct the sympathies of the audience toward Shōkichi and the badgers crooning on the nighttime golf course, creatures mourning all too idealistically the loss of an earlier, preindustrial state of human-animal relations. As a historian, I would direct my attention elsewhere, while still remaining sympathetic to Shōkichi's plight. The effects of industrialization on the relationship of humans and other animals—like those of many other modern processes subsumed in "-tion" words, ranging from commercialization to urbanization to environmental pollution—has been vast and largely deleterious to both parties, whether the setting is Japan or places closer to home. But nostalgization is itself a "-tion" word, and the way that filmmakers like Takahata imagine their own history is often less a reflection of the past that they hope to reproduce than a mirror of the present, part and parcel of our own invention of modernity and its consequences. Add to the inherent wishful thinking of nostalgia the more peculiarly Western penchant for imagining East Asian societies, in particular that of Japan, as existing in a closer harmony with nature than their counterparts in Euro-America, and Takahata's animated fable assumes another level of complication.[5]

For all these caveats, Takahata's vision remains compelling. Not only does the film entertainingly dramatize some of the historical processes that have impacted human-animal relationships over recent centuries, but it speaks also to the significant and changing role of nonhuman creatures in defining the limits of human communities and ethnic identities in Japan, as elsewhere, over broad spans of time. Animals such as badgers and foxes represent more than simply biological species within Japan's diverse array of zoological life. They have long played an important role, for instance, in Japanese religion and folklore. Foxes are conventionally identified with the Shinto deity Inari, mischievous beings only to be dissuaded from working their divine magic with offerings of sushi rice wrapped in pickled bean curd. Even if they are not necessarily endowed with supernatural powers, as Takahata's film portrays them, such creatures have in their own ways shaped the behavior and thinking of people living on the Japanese archipelago. Modern humans may have, with greater or lesser degrees of violence, expelled fellow animals from our, and their, physical habitats, yet we have not been able to expunge them from our symbolic imaginations—as the very popularity of Takahata's film attests. The ceramic badger, or for that matter the "beckoning cat," on the streets of Tokyo or Osaka today conveys no less cultural meaning than its red-blooded relative did two hundred years ago. To the would-be patrons of the establishment it says, "Come inside, and be reassured that what you will find in this place is 'traditional' and 'Japanese.'"

Any dialogue between human and nonhuman animals must remain in the end metaphorical rather than literal, insofar as humans, mired in language, cannot really "hear" what their fellow inhabitants of this planet are "saying." Nevertheless, even the possibility of such a dialogue has grown more difficult in modern times. Takahata suggests as much when he has the desperate ploy of his shape-shifting badgers fall largely on deaf human ears. It is to a theme park or to a zoo—and then only on relatively rare occasions—where the contemporary Tokyoite goes in order to engage in meaningful, if largely one-sided, interaction with other animal species (unless, of course, he or she owns a pet, who is most likely to be regarded as another member of the household). Modern life not only clears our streets of fellow living creatures (and even more so dead ones), replacing them with simulacra like the ceramic badger, but tends to erase them from our daily consciousnesses, focusing our eyes and ears almost exclusively on human things. One of the chief aims of this volume is to resensitize readers, including scholars of Japan, to the intimate relationship between human and nonhuman creatures that has existed throughout history, not only in the centuries before industrialization, but, if less conspicuously perhaps, in the modern world as well. Shedding the blinders of our accustomed humanism (note that the term does not always connote praise) and bringing back into earshot a dialogue with nonhuman animals offers an opportunity to refocus and to enrich our received understandings of Japanese history and culture, as each of the following chapters strives to demonstrate.

THE CLASSICAL AND MEDIEVAL PERIODS (710–1600)

The three opening essays of this volume help flesh out what has mostly been a skeletal understanding of the cultural, political, and ethical role of nonhuman animals in classical and medieval Japanese history. In chapter 1, Hoyt Long explores the initial political and cultural impact of the wedding of Buddhist teachings regarding the treatment of deer and other wild creatures with preexisting Japanese spiritual attitudes. He asks new and intriguing questions specifically of Buddhist tales of gratitude, or *ongaeshi*. Challenging the assumption that the transmission of Buddhism to Japan was a smooth process, Long uses tale literature to resurrect a significant clash that took place during the seventh and eighth centuries of the first millennium between Buddhist teachings, which admonished animal sacrifices and the killing of living creatures more generally, on the one hand, and earlier animistic ("Shinto") perceptions of wild animals, especially deer, on the other. Long points out that pre-Buddhist belief systems in Japan placed the deer in the position of mediator between the spiritual and secular worlds. Native ritualists, for example, used the shoulder blades of deer in the practice of scapulimancy, a form of divination. The overlap of the life cycle of deer and early Japanese agricultural rhythms also led to the practice of sacrificing deer in various provinces.

Weaving elements of continental legend together with local lore, Buddhist-inspired *ongaeshi* tales expounded the doctrine of karmic retribution, portraying human and nonhuman animals as part of a single continuum of being. Yet paradoxically, they also served to authenticate a fundamental distinction between the moral categories of the human (or humane) and the beastly. Such a delineation, Long shows, had profound political implications for early state formation under the Yamato confederacy (ca. 300–710) and the Nara imperium (710–784). Buddhist categories of animality allowed elites at the imperial center to wield a new kind of cultural power over both commoners and provincial rulers. Herein lies one of the less appreciated ways in which Yamato and Nara leaders adopted Tang Chinese political principles and the new magic of Buddhism in order to create an imperially centered bureaucratic polity along continental lines. From the vantage point of continental statecraft, based in agrarian principles, the ancient hunting-and-gathering cultures that remained scattered throughout the Japanese archipelago could be cast as religious and political "barbarians" because their way of life did not acknowledge *ongaeshi*, or gratitude toward animals.

In chapter 2, Ria Koopmans-de Bruijn shifts the discussion regarding nonhuman animals in classical and medieval Japan from religious and political history to the arena of folklore studies. Like Long, Koopmans-de Bruijn focuses on the role played by certain animals, in this case snakes or serpents more broadly, in formulating early Japanese communal norms. Didactic fables functioned as key cultural texts in creating a folkic moral order on the archipelago, as they did in many places around the globe. Although the serpents of Japanese folklore shifted shapes—something they rarely did in Western fables—Koopmans-de Bruijn shows that they were more than simply supernatural spirits. Rather, like the deer of *ongaeshi* tales, serpents performed a symbolic role in narratives designed to set the parameters of human kinship and sexual relations. In short, nonhuman animals replaced people in such tales so as more persuasively to convey their moral imperatives. Serpents offered a particularly effective symbolic vehicle because, over the centuries, the inhabitants of the archipelago regarded snakes as among the most potent of living creatures. Early Japanese associated snakes, like deer, with fertility and the harvest, all the more so because of their obvious phallic connotations.

As Koopmans-de Bruijn notes, serpents, unlike many other symbolic animals around the world, can equally represent good and evil, female and male, land and water, medicine and poison. Sociobiologists have paid considerable attention to this fact. Edward Wilson, for example, has highlighted the complex relationship of humans (and of other primates) with snakes in articulating his theory of "gene-culture coevolution." According to Wilson, the "innate tendency to react with both fear and fascination toward snakes" is a prime example of culture and genetics working together, and human culture "draws on that fear and fascination to create metaphors and narratives," often in the form of didactic tales.[6] In the case of Japan, such fables may be found even in the oldest written texts, dating from the early eighth century. Not unlike the story of Adam and Eve, tales of ill-advised human-serpent liaisons contributed, Koopmans-de Bruijn argues, to the early formation of a collective moral code on the archipelago.

In a closing chapter on classical and medieval Japan, Alexander Bay explores the relationship between nonhuman animals and state formation in northeastern Honshu, one of the "barbaric" peripheries left relatively untouched by Buddhist tales of gratitude. Rather than focusing on animals as symbols of religious difference, Bay investigates the economic and political consequences of horse-raising practices in the medieval Kita Ōu region. He argues that animal husbandry on the northeastern frontier shared more in common with Eurasian steppe cultures than it did with the wetland rice agronomy of south-central Japan, where the earlier Yamato and Nara states were centered. When viewed from this perspective, northeastern Honshu, at least until the late medieval period, formed not so much a part of Japan proper as an authentic and semi-independent frontier culture. To lose sight of this fact, Bay cautions, is to misunderstand the far-reaching impact of the sixteenth-century wars of unification.

Although the volcanic-ashen soil of the Kita Ōu region was poorly suited for wetland rice agriculture, it provided more than adequate pasture for horses. The "swift horses of Nukanobu," breeds of Central Asian origin, thrived in these pastures, and may have been transported to the Japanese archipelago along trade routes extending through Hokkaido, Sakhalin, and on into Manchuria and Central Asia. Such steeds set apart the human inhabitants of Japan's far northeast from those who participated in the wetland rice agronomy of the classical and medieval Japanese state. Because of the demand for superior mounts among the archipelago's samurai elite, horses, like their human owners, served as what Bay refers to (borrowing a phrase of Jeffrey Mass's) as "bridging figures," linking the central and peripheral worlds of the medieval Japanese polity. The northeast's horse-raising culture also proved a powerful source of regional identity. The hereditary ruler of Nanbu domain, for instance, was referred to as the "lord of the horse" (*uma no ryōshu*), and the Nanbu breed remained famous well into modern times.

The emergence of a distinct horse-raising culture and ecology in northeastern Honshu provides fodder for Bay's most striking claim, one that goes against the grain of conventional historiography. Bay argues that the "unification wars" that Japan underwent under the late sixteenth-century warlord Toyotomi Hideyoshi (1537-1598) were none other than a colonial conflict. Until armies under Toyotomi control were dispatched to the northeast, the region remained a frontier zone, basically independent of the cultural and ecological hegemony of the medieval Japanese polity. Both Long and Bay train their gazes on nonhuman animals in order to refashion our conventional understanding of early Japanese state formation and expansion. Long's investigation of Buddhist tales involving deer reveals some of the ways in which the Yamato political elite used nonhuman creatures as symbols with which to label those outside the Nara core as religious and political outcasts. Bay focuses on the cultural and ecological outcasts themselves, namely, the horse farmers of the northeast, in order to demonstrate that even in the face of powerful Buddhist symbols, frontier cultures embraced their position outside the reach of the central polity, celebrating a lifestyle that was distinct from that of wetland rice agriculturalists. Deer served as a potent symbol of barbarism and civility for those establishing a new, agriculturally based bureaucratic polity in south-central Japan; horses provided a source of local identity for those contesting that political order in the north. Nonhuman animals, it appears, were at the center of the battle over the creation of classical and medieval Japanese ethnicity, religion, and statehood.

THE EARLY-MODERN PERIOD (1600–1868)

From the seventeenth century onward, Japan began to experience extensive pockets of commercialization and eventually, as some historians characterize it, protoindustrial growth. The rapidly changing economic and ecological landscape of the archipelago would in turn transform the relationship between Japanese people and their animal neighbors. Early-modern attitudes toward living creatures were complex and regionally diverse, making generalization difficult and further research imperative. The two essays on early-modern Japan in this volume touch on issues of cultural representation and of environmental change, while seeking to resituate their significance within broader geographic and historiographic contexts.

One of the most enduring debates regarding early-modern Japan is whether its Tokugawa rulers were able, or even intended, to create a "closed country" (*sakoku*) after expelling Christian missionaries from their realm by the 1640s. Some argue that the purging of Europeans from the archipelago (with the conspicuous exception of the Dutch, who were permitted to trade at their island enclave of Deshima in Nagasaki harbor) meant that Japan had shut its doors to the outside world. Others maintain that this Eurocentric vantage point obscures the commercial, diplomatic, and cultural exchanges that continued unhindered between Japan and its more immediate Asian neighbors. Martha Chaiklin takes the debate to a new level in chapter 4 by exploring the vibrant economics and popular fashions that surrounded early-modern aviculture.

The early-modern commerce in exotic birds, whether for the ornithological studies of shoguns or the avicultural amusement of wealthy merchants, integrated Japan into a global bird trade that brought sparrows from Java; pigeons from Bengal; parrots, parakeets, lorries, and cockatoos from the tropical and subtropical worlds; peacocks from India; cassowaries from the forests of northern Australia and New Guinea; and turkeys from North America. The expansion of European trade networks resulted in no less than an avian diaspora. When viewed from the perspective of the exotic-bird trade, Tokugawa Japan's windows, if not its doors, were wide open; and, over time, many birds flew in and became an enduring part of the natural landscape of the Japanese archipelago and the cultural imagination of Japanese artists and litterateurs. On their frail wings, birds carried a surprisingly heavy burden of economic, cultural, and scientific capital.

The burden was ecological as well. In a manner reminiscent of Alfred Crosby's influential study *Ecological Imperialism*, Chaiklin illuminates the thriving—and ecologically consequential—demand for exotic pet birds that developed during a period when Japan appears in the eyes of many to have been a "closed country."[7] Like the "wild-boar famine" discussed in the following chapter, the interspecies conflict that resulted from the release of certain exotic birds into Japan's early-modern environment centered on competition over food resources. Whether the nonhuman animal involved was a wild boar or a Java sparrow, the human search for commercial profit produced significant environmental changes, which in turn generated ecological conditions fraught with new tensions between humans and other animal species. In the case of the "wild-boar famine," the focus of chapter 5, cash cropping by eighteenth-century farmers altered the rural landscape and economy in such a way as to invite increased predation upon human agriculture by boar and other ungulate creatures. With exotic birds, it was the expanding market for luxury goods that generated consumer demand for the importation of previously unknown living species, whose acclimatization would eventually affect the livelihoods of rural cultivators as well as their city cousins. Significantly, the human factor that initiated ecological change was in both instances a rapidly commercializing economy, which stands as a hallmark of the Tokugawa period as a whole, thus predating the modern industrial process that we more commonly associate today with environmental destabilization.

In the northeastern domain of Hachinohe, swidden and other forms of slash-and-burn farming birthed a landscape that facilitated what Elinor Melville, in her study of the colonization of Mexico, calls an "ungulate irruption."[8] It is crucial to note that the "ungulate irruption" Melville writes of occurred in the context of Spanish colonial expansion. Significantly, if one follows Bay's line of argumentation, the "wild-boar famine," too, occurred in a colonial context, namely, the aftermath of Toyotomi expansion. The irruption of wild boars that plagued the northeastern domain of Hachinohe in the eighteenth century provides suggestive evidence of the residual economic and ecological impact of the colonial conquest theorized in chapter 3. Once robbed of their horse-raising frontier culture, the farmers of Hachinohe, through deforestation and upland rotation farming—essential for early-modern Japan's political agronomy—replaced northeastern forests with fallow plots of thick brush. Typically, these tracts were littered with tuberous plants such as wild yams, bracken, and arrowroot. Wild boar thrived on the starchy tubers, while the brush provided safe habitat. Under such enviable conditions, native boar populations exploded.

On a less enviable human plane, the mid-eighteenth-century Little

Ice Ages, or Neo-Boreal, led to poor harvests, forcing peasants in northeastern Japan into the mountains in search of wild plants in the particularly harsh year of 1749. There, chronicles from Hachinohe reveal, they competed with wild boar for badly needed calories. To combat the proliferation of boar, domain officials ordered systematic hunts throughout Hachinohe, and professional hunters slaughtered thousands of ungulates. Boar killed thousands of peasants, too, not merely through their consumption habits but by reportedly mauling people. Even in a predominantly Buddhist culture, the struggle between human and nonhuman animals may assume deadly proportions. Ironically, some historians have speculated that the increase in boar populations resulted in part from Buddhist-inspired "laws of compassion," promulgated by the fifth Tokugawa shogun, Tsunayoshi (r. 1680–1709), who prohibited, among other things, the hunting of wildlife. It is likely, however, that the more relevant human factor was widespread cash-crop farming, a relationship no less illustrative of the intersection of cultural values and ecological change.

Collectively, the five essays that make up the first half of the volume reveal the interrelation of human and nonhuman animals in preindustrial times to have been neither historically stable nor, especially from the point of view of the latter party, always benign. The badgers of Takahata's film may look back nostalgically upon the early-modern period, yet history shows that human encroachment upon the habitats of other species—as well as the defensive responses of those who have been encroached on—was well underway by the Tokugawa era. Modern processes such as commercialization and (proto)industrialization are not the only culprit, since even the animistic traditions of pre-Buddhist times involved violence against other species. The point is not to idealize an edenic past. Rather, we must learn better to understand the ways in which all historical and cultural contexts presuppose a particular mode of interrelation not just between certain people (classes, if you will) and others, but also between human and nonhuman creatures.

THE MODERN PERIOD (1868–PRESENT)

Introducing the *JAPANimals* chapters that tackle the modern period requires that we once again return to the badger wars being waged in the paved streets of Tama New Town. Toward the end of the memorable "Operation Ghosts" scene, two older gentlemen sit at an outdoor kiosk, heartily drinking hot saké and snacking on stewed side dishes, when suddenly a young boy runs by and points excitedly to the phantoms floating in the sky. "It's a ghost parade!" the lad exclaims. So drunk are the two old men that they do not even notice the ghoulish scene unfolding behind them. But prompted by the boy's shouting, they begin reminiscing about the phenomenon of ghost parades in the old days.

Specifically, the two men's conversation turns to the practice of "fox marriages" (*kitsune no yomedori*) and "fox lantern-parades" (*kitsune no chōchin gyōretsu*), which used to mark the coming of spring in certain rural communities. According to one fox-marriage tradition, Kirin Mountain, near the town of Tsugawa in Niigata prefecture, was home to many foxes who, in former times, were occasionally heard yelping and crying in the night. Townspeople could also detect "fox fires" (*kitsunebi*), or will-o'-the-wisps, that appeared to burn brightly on its nearby slopes. Many of the locals associated such fox fires with the promise of favorable crops, and in time a fertility festival developed, featuring as its symbolic centerpiece the "marriage" of a beautiful woman of the town to a fox. Actual human wedding ceremonies in some rural areas incorporated a related custom. Since marriage festivities frequently lasted well into the night, it was common for the bride to be escorted to the home of the groom through the darkness while accompanied by a parade of paper lanterns that revelers thrust high above their heads on poles. Because these lanterns appeared to float, they came to be associated with fox fires.

"Those sure were the days," one of the gentlemen sighs nostalgically, resting his chin on the palm of his hand. To which his drinking companion responds, "Do you really think that foxes can do all that?" Suddenly, as if both men remember who and where they are, they begin to laugh, blaming their foolish memories on the powers of the human imagination. This wistful conversation between the two men, played out against the background of a portentous spectacle to which they are entirely oblivious, offers a striking metaphor of the missed opportunities for dialogue that have all too often characterized human-animal relations in the modern age. Only in the realm of the imagination, or alternatively of an increasingly commodified "tradition," can the suburbanites of Takahata's film partake in a sense of community with animal species who are in fact neighbors. Amid the probing science, rampant capitalism, and frighteningly destructive technology of the contemporary world, fox marriages have little place outside the commercialized theme park or the imaginative space of celluloid.

The opening chapters of *JAPANimals* offered ample proof that changing perceptions of the natural world in general and violence toward nonhuman animals in particular were not peculiar to the modern age. Nevertheless, it is clear that from the nineteenth century onward, Japan witnessed ever more dramatic shifts in attitudes toward nonhuman creatures, coupled with a greater technological ability to visit them with harm. After the change in political leadership of 1868, conventionally termed the Meiji Restoration, the archipelago's human community mobilized itself en masse around the task of building a modern, industrialized, and militarily powerful nation-state, a goal expressed in such official slogans as "civilization and enlightenment" (*bunmei kaika*) and "rich country, strong military" (*fukoku kyōhei*). This political and cultural mission not only impacted the lives of other animal species in real and largely destructive ways, but also was predicated on a new imagined relationship between human civilization and the natural environment. From the standpoint of "civilization and enlightment," any totemistic endowing of nonhuman creatures with a meaningful cultural significance, as exemplified by the fox wedding, stood only to relegate Japan's status within the global community to that of a "primitive" or only "semi-civilized" society. Scientific and technological mastery of the natural world, by contrast, evidenced the advance of civilization and modernity in the evolutionary trajectory of history.

Under the influence of enlightenment ideology, humans on the archipelago began to consign earlier modes of relationship with other forms of animal life to a newly constructed realm of "tradition," which in turn anchored a sense of the distinctiveness, and implied superiority, of modern civilization. This reordering of nature unfolded not only on an imaginary level, but also on a material one. In some cases, earlier human-animal relations were not abandoned or forgotten so much as they were physically erased. The turn of the century witnessed, for instance, the eradication of Japan's two subspecies of wolf.[9] Other creatures, such as the short-tailed albatross (killed by the millions as part of a domestic as well as export-based feather industry), the Japanese crested ibis (also hunted for its feathers), the white stork, the Iriomote wild cat, the Tsushima wild cat, the Japanese otter, and the Japanese serow, teeter today on the brink of extinction.[10] Moreover, new technologies have endowed human destructive capabilities with a global reach, as reflected in the worldwide controversy over whaling. Conversely, modern society has actively fostered new modes of human-animal interaction, such as zoo-going and pet-keeping, which reinforce the premises of civilized order from within, rather than threatening it from the outside. The final essays of the volume address this complex of modern issues and contradictions from four different perspectives.

In chapter 6, Aaron Skabelund traces Japan's transition into the modern age along a refreshingly unconventional canine trajectory. The centerpiece of his analysis, and of what might be termed nineteenth-century "canine imperialism," was a figure whom Skabelund describes as the "colonial dog." With the establishment of treaty ports dominated by Westerners, the Euro-American dog breeds who accompanied their colonial masters to nineteenth-century Japan became living exemplars of discipline and docility, no less emblematic of thoroughly domesticated enlightenment than the coiffed Parisian poodles of Kathleen Kete's path-breaking study *The Beast in the Boudoir*.[11] The loyalty and obedience of these canines embodied, for many humans on the archipelago, the very civility of Western civilization. By contrast, the raucous howls and errant habits of wolfish local breeds served only to dramatize Japan's "primitive" or "semi-civilized" ways. Before the Restoration, local dogs led semi-feral lives closer to their wolf cousins than to the pet canines of Europe and North America. Meiji attempts to "civilize" indigenous dogs proceeded in tandem with efforts directed at a similarly "unenlightened" human populace, and were likewise filtered through the lenses of class prejudice. What "civilization" could not master, it sought to eliminate. Dog- and wolf-hunting campaigns followed close on the heels of the Restoration, often rationalized through a fear of rabies. As Harriet Ritvo has shown in *The Animal Estate*, hydrophrobia was the bogey-bear of civilization and a cipher for class anxieties around the Victorian world.[12]

When Westerners wrote about "native" dogs of the colonial periphery, Skabelund demonstrates, they transcribed their prejudices toward "Other" people around the globe into a more oblique—and for that reason all the more revealing—register. The creation of the English and American kennel clubs was one institutional manifestation of the symbolism inherent in the figure of the "colonial dog," and resulted in the canonization of certain breeds as icons of national prestige. It was only a matter of time before Japanese sought themselves to enter the larger kennel club of dog-eat-dog imperialist nations. Once the Japanese empire began to expand from shortly before the turn of the century, the long disparaged "native" dogs of the archipelago gradually found new opportunities to bark. By the 1920s and 1930s, nationalist rhetoric would hail them as "Japanese dogs" (*Nihonken*), revered for their loyalty and other qualities deemed worthy of an imperial land. Skabelund rightly notes that the price of this bark involved another sort of bite—in this case, a vicious grip on the aspirations of colonized subjects, including their canine companions and symbols.

In chapter 7, David Lurie examines the changing landscape of modernity through the microscopic lens of what he calls "Orientomology." Cultural studies of insect life on the archipelago by Lafcadio Hearn/Koizumi Yakumo (1850–1904), who made his home in Japan from the 1890s, reveal the complexities of the writer's position as both an Orientalist Western observer of Japan and a naturalized "Oriental." As Lurie shows, Hearn/Yakumo was central to the process of preserving and popularizing existing lore surrounding insects on the Japanese islands, but only at the cost of encapsulating this knowledge, cocoon-like, within a quaint and miniaturized realm of "tradition"—the very definition of which fated its disappearance as a vital aspect of the modern world. For Hearn/Yakumo, Japan was practically synonymous with a heightened cultural sensitivity to "nature." Thus, his writings helped to foster a popular attitude, prevalent in the West even today, that might loosely be termed "green Orientalism."

Paradoxically, the industrial technologies of the new age played an inspirational role within Hearn/Yakumo's imagination. As if to imply that the inexorable currents of modern life need not alienate humans from the world of insects, the author infused his descriptions of that world with its new rhythms. To Hearn/Yakumo's ears, the cry of the cicada sounded like a "sewing-machine in full operation," and the chirping of crickets resembled the "tiniest electric bells." Such references reveal the writer's ambivalence about the relationship of modernity and tradition, and in turn mirror his complicated personal history, since it was modern technology and knowledge that had brought Hearn/Yakumo to the "traditional Orient" in the first place. The author's fascination with the process of insect metamorphosis may likewise be read as a form of autobiographical exegesis, pointing to the deeply self-referential nature of his "Orientomological" project.

In chapter 8, Ian Miller describes another mode of civilizing "nature" in the nineteenth century, one embodied not in the private garden or the homely cricket cage, but in the eminently public spectacle of the zoo. It is widely known that Meiji advocates of "civilization and enlightenment" such as Fukuzawa Yukichi (1835–1901) praised such Western institutions as the public school, the museum, and the penitentiary, which aimed explicitly for the edification and reform of human society. Less often noted is their interest in the intrinsically multispecies institution—at once school, museum, and prison—of the zoological park. Within five years of the Meiji Restoration, the predecessor of the Ueno Zoological Garden opened its gates; within another century, it had become the most frequently visited zoo in the world. Over that span of time, Japanese became less likely to encounter the archipelago's living fauna in the latter's natural habitat, which such human factors as urbanization, commercial exploitation, and population expansion (all symbolized in Takahata's film by the Tama New Town project) subjected to far-reaching ecological changes. It was not the untamed wilderness beyond the city, but rather the zoo nestled within the very heart of the metropolis, that provided an archetype for the "civilized" relationship of humans and other animals in Japan after the nineteenth century.

As in the case of dog ownership, the zoo took mastery of nature literally. Its history provides a vivid object lesson in power, all the more poignant for its blood-and-guts materiality. Modern disciplinary mechanisms required not only certain kinds of humans but also many kinds of nonhumans to live and die in cages. As Miller relates, these creatures served a variety of social and political concerns, the least of which was their own welfare. The creators of the modern zoo objectified the human-animal "divide" through a variety of architectural and rhetorical devices; yet paradoxically, the very nature of its disciplinary apparatus meant that brutality could not ultimately be confined to one side of the bars. The success of its spectacle depended as much on what was displayed for public consumption as on what zookeepers—though not necessarily historians—managed to keep out of view.

In the final chapter, Jessamyn Abel links Meiji modernization with more contemporary developments. In the context both of nineteenth-century dog-eat-dog imperialism and of late twentieth-century "green imperialism," the whaling industry played a crucial role in shaping perceptions of Japan in the world community. Prior to the Restoration, the American whaler's spyglass projected a view of Japan as a dangerous land beyond the pale of international law and civilized humanity, unwelcoming even of the hapless castaway. As Abel points out, this vision circulated broadly through such popular texts as Herman Melville's *Moby Dick*. More than a century later, an image of Japan as a cultural renegade and scofflaw once again came to dominate international perceptions, not because of any mistreatment of foreign whalers, but rather because of continued Japanese hunting of the animals who were their prey. The whaling industry, which to nineteenth-century Japanese had appeared as a beacon of modern civilization, represented in the eyes of a new generation of environmentally minded Americans all that was "barbarous" and "inhumane."

Ironically, as Arne Kalland and Brian Moeran have argued, whaling before the mid-nineteenth century played only a minor role in Japan's maritime economy, so that its contemporary prominence is a kind of "invented tradition."[13] This irony is lost on Westerners ignorant of the historical role of pelagic whaling in furthering Euro-American imperialist expansion and cultural hegemony, as well as on Japanese who defend its practice as an ageless repository of the nation's cultural identity. In Japan as elsewhere, modernity thrives and transforms people's lives by identifying, through the labeling of "tradition," what it is not. Yet paradoxically, it hungers to make sense of its present by imagining, and often fabricating, connections with that same "traditional" past. History, one might say, is the whipping boy of the modern age.

The nine chapters in *JAPANimals* are chronologically and thematically diverse, spanning the seventh through the twentieth centuries, and probing subjects ranging from the formation of early political orders and communal identities to the emergence of modern disciplines, interstate relations, and ecological transformations. The chapters nevertheless form an integrated whole in that all of the authors strive to articulate a dialogic relation among humans, nonhuman animals, and our shared history. Together, they offer a cohesive vision of Japan as the collective site of historical and cultural processes that have been informed at every stage by both human and nonhuman actors. It is important to recognize that the Japanese archipelago is no different in this respect than other places. Everywhere, the clicking and clacking of the modern age and its human-centered concerns has overwhelmed Takahata's metaphorical badgers and all their voiceless neighbors. To fail to heed the crooning and merrymaking of the badgers at the golf courses of Tama New Town is thus not only to disregard an important part of Japan's history, but to risk ignoring valuable lessons regarding the common fate of all life on earth.

NOTES

1. Heisei refers to the reign name of Emperor Akihito, who assumed the throne after the death of his father Hirohito (or the Shōwa emperor) in 1989.

2. For more on badger lore and cultural symbolism in Japan, see Nakamura Teiri, *Tanuki to sono sekai* (Tokyo: Asahi Shinbunsha, 1990). For a general treatment of animal symbolism in Japanese culture and history, see the same author's *Dōbutsutachi no reiryoku* (Tokyo: Chikuma Shobō, 1989). For a more recent treatment of wildlife "wars" and animal symbolism in general, see John Knight, *Waiting for Wolves in Japan: An Anthropological Study of People-Wildlife Relations* (Oxford: Oxford University Press, 2003).

3. For selected plates from *Chōjū jinbutsu giga*, see *Genshoku Nihon no bijutsu*, vol. 8: *Emakimono*, ed. Akiyama Terukazu (Tokyo: Shōgakkan, 1968), 42–47.

4. For more on transforming foxes and Inari worship in Japan, see Nakamura Teiri, *Kitsune no Nihonshi* (Tokyo: Nihon Editā Sukūru Shuppanbu, 2001); Karen A. Smyers, *The Fox and the Jewel: Shared and Private Meanings in Contemporary Japanese Inari Worship* (Honolulu: University of Hawaii Press, 1999).

5. Julia Adeney Thomas discusses the Western tendency to overstate dramatically Japanese people's benign relationship with the natural world in *Reconfiguring Modernity: Concepts of Nature in Japanese Political Ideology* (Berkeley: University of California Press, 2001).

6. Edward O. Wilson, *Consilience: The Unity of Knowledge* (New York: Vintage, 1998), 210.

7. See Alfred W. Crosby, *Ecological Imperialism: The Biological Expansion of Europe, 900-1900* (Cambridge: Cambridge University Press, 1986).

8. Elinor G. K. Melville, *A Plague of Sheep: Environmental Consequences of the Conquest of Mexico* (Cambridge: Cambridge University Press, 1997).

9. On wolf extinction in Japan, see my *The Lost Wolves of Japan* (Seattle: University of Washington Press, 2005).

10. Fujiwara Eiji, "Wildlife in Japan: Crisis and Recovery," *Japan Quarterly* 35, no. 1 (January-March 1988): 26–31.

11. Kathleen Kete, *The Beast in the Boudoir: Petkeeping in Nineteenth-Century Paris* (Berkeley: University of California Press, 1994).

12. Harriet Ritvo, *The Animal Estate: The English and Other Creatures in the Victorian Age* (Cambridge, Mass.: Harvard University Press, 1987)

13. Arne Kalland and Brian Moeran, *Japanese Whaling: End of an Era?* Scandinavian Institute of Asian Studies Monograph Series, no. 61 (London: Curzon, 1992).

From *Wakan sansai zue*. Courtesy of the C. V. Starr East Asian Library, Columbia University.

CHAPTER ONE

Grateful Animal or Spiritual Being? Buddhist Gratitude Tales and Changing Conceptions of Deer in Early Japan

Hoyt Long

Of all the places where one encounters nonhuman animals in history and culture, it is perhaps in literature where some of the strangest and most bewildering breeds are discovered. Take, for instance, the thirteenth-century tale of the heroic warrior Minamoto Yorimitsu (948–1021) and his battle with enormous "dirt spiders" (*tsuchigumo*). In a Muromachi-period (1392–1573) picture scroll that depicts the major events of the dirt-spider narrative, one image shows Yorimitsu and his fellow warriors slaying a mammoth, anthropophagous spider who towers over the men with a body nearly ten times their size.[1] It is a ghastly scene, to say the least, but all the more compelling for its grotesque exaggeration and misrepresentation of what is tacitly known to be a much smaller terrestrial creature.

One is certainly tempted to disregard such an abnormal and seemingly false representation as exactly that, relegating it to the realm of mere fantasy and historical curiosity. To do so, however, ignores the fact that the textual and visual representations are linked to a real biological creature, a creature who inhabited the same physical space as the human animals who created these representations. Indeed, the dirt spiders would have been meaningful to Japanese readers and viewers only because the name and image drew them into immediate association with the living creatures they tacitly knew as *kumo* (spiders). There is, of course, a gap that comes between the living animal and the various cultural representations affixed to it, but this should not force us to think of those representations as any less a part of reality. Humans, nonhuman animals, and the symbolic representations of animals that humans create are forever engaged in a complex dialogue, a dialogue that, in one way or another, is the concern of every chapter in this volume. Each essay will inquire into the complexities of this dialogue in a Japanese context. The present chapter begins the inquiry by considering an early genre of Buddhist tale literature and the way in which that genre reflected a fundamental transformation of human-animal relationships in seventh- and eighth-century Japan.

This chapter seeks also to encourage further inquiry into Japanese literary representations of nonhuman animals in general, a subject that has until recently received little scholarly attention. As anyone familiar with the corpus knows, Japanese tale literature is filled with an abundant array of intriguing animals. More common than spiders are the foxes, turtles, badgers, serpents (to be discussed in the next chapter), and other familiar creatures who have played an integral part in Japanese folklore through the ages. Considering the extent to which human cultures throughout history have relied on other animals to create their fables, folklore, and myths, the significance of nonhuman animals in a Japanese context comes as no great surprise. Yet, as abundant as these representations are, scholars have been reluctant to consider their symbolic meaning in ways that problematize and foreground their origins in specific social, religious, and ecological contexts. All too often, these "symbolic animals" are simply dismissed as inconsequential or irrelevant to the larger significance of the tales and the ideological contexts from which they arose.

Rather than dismiss them, however, we must interrogate their origins and see what they reveal about the people and societies who gave life to them in the first place. What do the animals of tale literature tell us about how their creators understood themselves as distinctly human? Considering the transcultural nature of so many animal tales, imported as they were from the Asian mainland, we must ask what happens when the representation of an animal rooted in a particular environmental and cultural context is transported to a different setting. How might such representations have altered the way in which people on the receiving end perceived that animal? How might they have altered the way in which the real biological animal was treated? Additionally, how might previous notions of what it meant to be "animal" or "human" have thereby been problematized?

Answers to these questions will naturally differ with historical context, medium of transference, and the animal under discussion; hence, one must shy away from totalizing responses. However, in the hope of offering some partial answers, the present chapter examines the specific time and place of seventh- and eighth-century Japan and the particular medium of Buddhist *ongaeshi* (gratitude) tales, especially those tales that relate to deer. After laying some of the theoretical groundwork for the ensuing discussion, it outlines the essentials of the *ongaeshi* tale and its historical connection to animal representation in early classical Japan. A subsequent section will explore a particular *ongaeshi* tale about a deer and consider the ways in which its representation of the animal existed in potentially tense discord with the conception of deer in more "native," that is, non-Buddhist, beliefs and practices of the period. By doing so, it highlights in a new way the cultural diversity of classical Japanese society, calling attention to the links between that society's development and the ideologically charged dialogue among humans, nonhuman animals, and their various symbolic representations.

TRACKING THE SYMBOLIC ANIMAL

One of the fundamental themes with which all the essays in this collection are concerned is how the nonhuman animal functions symbolically within human societies. Why have nonhuman animals played such a popular and enduring role in human attempts to express ideas about, and to come to terms with, our own identity? Social anthropologists, cultural historians, and philosophers alike have grappled with the question, but one of the most compelling answers comes from the anthropologist Roy Willis:

> The crux of the explanation of the apparent universality of animals as images of profoundest symbolic significance would seem … to lie in the fact that 'the animal' is both within us, as part of our enduring biological heritage as human beings, and also, by definition, outside and beyond human society. The image of the symbolic animal is therefore necessarily a dualistic image, structurally homologous with the duality in human society and the human self between the real and the ultimate ideal, the actual and the longed for, even if subconsciously.[2]

While modern industrial societies have increasingly widened the gap between the lives of humans and other animals, opening up a space for machines and other objects to serve equally profound symbolic functions, Willis's comment is just as relevant for today's technological world as it is for the nonurban, preindustrial African societies that Willis originally researched. Certainly, there were places and times when a closer proximity to other animals, whether through hunting or agricultural practices, made humans keenly aware of the traits that they shared with fellow creatures, among them the quality of being animate and alive. Despite similarities, however, the degree to which we humans reside in our own languages, modes of experience, and societal rules makes it impossible, both then and now, for us to relate to other animals in the same way that we relate to other humans. Human culture, in particular the use of complex language, has perennially forced a cleavage between our world and the world of nonhuman animals. This separation from, and inability to converse with, the animal world has contributed to a sense of "otherness" so profound that it has allowed for various kinds of difference to be imagined by historical and contemporary societies alike. And as the animal "other" has not the means to voice any objection, at least linguistically, it has proved all the more useful for the acquisition and reinforcement of stable notions of the human "self." The image of the nonhuman animal has provided a means for humans to delineate and define their own place in the world, making the animals in question, as the anthropologist Claude Levi-Strauss long ago noted, not just good to eat, but also "good to think" with.[3]

By using the term "other" here, I do not mean to oversimplify the human experience of nonhuman animals and the use of those animals as potent cultural symbols. It is important to recognize that in any society, there always exists a wide variety of ways in which the idea of "human" is defined in opposition to the idea of "animal." And for every individual animal species that has attained symbolic significance within a particular society, many more symbolic variations of that same animal have likely been generated over the course of the society's history. One way in which to understand the vast array of cultural responses toward animals that may exist in any given society is to regard them as products of residual, dominant, and emergent cultural formations.[4] Residual formations are those based in older or more traditional practices, for example, the animistic attitudes of many Native American groups. Dominant formations are those practices or ideas supported by the prevailing political and social order, such as the contemporary treatment in North America of certain animals as household pets. Emergent forms are those practices or ideas that have recently been introduced into or created within a society, for example, the notion that some animals, particularly primates, should be legally protected under the same rights afforded to humans.

Ongoing interaction among residual, dominant, and emergent elements—interaction often driven by politically powerful groups and individuals—effectively rearranges the positions of the elements over time even as it produces new cultural forms to add to the mix.[5] The idea that residual, dominant, and emergent representations of animals continually vie for cultural prominence or truth value is significant for my argument because it belies the very cultural constructedness of those representations. Visual or textual representations of nonhuman animals should never be mistaken for transparent or unmediated depictions of the animal itself. Rather, they must be seen as standing apart from their real-world counterparts as symbolic animals rooted in complex social and historical contexts—symbolic animals who evolve and transform within a network of interacting cultural and ideological forces.

For this reason, the symbolic animal is best thought of as a multilayered sign that to some extent derives its meaning from phenomenological encounters with actual animals but which, as a sign, is always open to a wider variety of meanings articulated and understood at the discursive level. For example, the Walt Disney character of Bambi may point to what we know to be a four-legged forest animal with antlers and a penchant for plants, but at the same time he is imbued with a host of cultural meanings that have little relation to the biological animal itself.[6] Bambi's connection to the real-world animal is not irrelevant, of course. Indeed, the symbolic meaning given to most animals generally reflects the predominant material and physical relations that exist between a group of humans and the animal in question.[7] However, the inability of the nonhuman animal to represent itself guarantees that its symbolic representation will be overdetermined by discursive factors. These factors include the various cultural associations that circulate within a society, the visual or textual uses of the symbol that are developed by certain groups of people, and the ways in which individual "readers" imbue the symbols with their own interpretations.

Symbolic animals are by no means disconnected from their real-world counterparts, however, and should not necessarily be construed as "false." On the contrary, as Steve Baker notes, the "representational, symbolic, and rhetorical uses of the animal must be understood to carry as much conceptual weight as any idea we may have of the 'real' animal, and must be taken just as seriously."[8] Indeed, symbolic animals exert a strong influence over the way in which humans interact with the living creatures whom the symbols represent. In the case of Bambi, for instance, the story of the persecuted deer has created generations of ardent animal lovers who view deer in the wild as living manifestations of the "innocent" and "adorable" fictional character, interacting with them in a way that befits the moral message of the story. Such a perception of deer has entailed significant political consequences in North America, bolstering the messages of animal-rights activists who feel that hunters should relate to deer in the same way that they themselves do. It is not that one group understands the proper relationship of humans to deer and that the other group does not, but that both modes of relating to the living animal are determined by conceptions of deer created and maintained at the discursive level. Simply put, "animals," as humans know them anyway, are necessarily culturally mediated symbols that circulate discursively, eventually becoming effective instruments of ideology when they acquire a certain level of cultural authority. Additionally, these representations come to reflect and embody the various understandings of the human-animal divide—that is to say, what it means to be on either side of that supposed line—that a society produces. It is for these reasons, then, that the symbolic animals inhabiting literary and artistic texts warrant close attention. Among other things, they tell us a good deal about how the relationships between human and nonhuman animals were both configured and contested during the historical moments in which the symbols circulated.

BUDDHIST *ONGAESHI* TALES AND THEIR ANIMAL INHABITANTS

While it is true that the symbolic animal with which this study concerns itself is the deer, it is a deer far removed, both culturally and historically, from Walt Disney's Bambi. The deer of the present inquiry is, in its various manifestations, loosely tied to the historical period extending from the early seventh century to the later years of Japan's Nara period (710–784). This particular historical juncture is significant because it brackets a time when locally based and in that sense more "native" conceptions of the deer were confronted with the alternatives of Buddhist thought and practice—alternatives that were gradually gaining acceptance among the ruling political elite. Previously dominant conceptions of deer and other nonhuman animals were, in effect, confronted and transformed by newly emergent cultural forms transplanted from the continent. These emergent conceptions were imported and diffused by Buddhist practitioners in a number of ways, one of the most popular being the Buddhist animal tale. A wide variety of these tales circulated in some form by the Nara period, and one of the most prominent motifs within the genre was that of *ongaeshi*, literally, "returning a favor." It is a motif that, for a number of reasons, proves useful in discussing symbolic animals of Japan's early classical period and the representations of the human-animal divide that they embodied.

First, the basic plot structure of the *ongaeshi* tale depends on interaction between human and nonhuman animals. Consequently, the two share not only language but also moral principles within the narrative. Thus, they provide an important window into the nature of specifically Buddhist symbolic animals. Second, the didacticism present in all of these tales, relying as it does on the rhetorical manipulation of "animal" and "human" categories, foregrounds uniquely Buddhist conceptions of the human-animal divide. Later sections of this chapter will demonstrate the affront that such conceptions presented to more "native" attitudes toward deer and other nonhuman animals—attitudes based in the animistic practices and traditions of Japan's pre-Buddhist communities. First, however, it is necessary to discuss the *ongaeshi* tale and its relation to orthodox Buddhist ideas about nonhuman animals.

The concept of *ongaeshi* is semantically equivalent to the notion, in English, of "gratitude." Arguably, one of the key components in the organization of all social life is a belief in the moral importance of expressing gratitude for acts of kindness. Indeed, scholars of ethics have gone so far as to claim that gratitude constitutes a fundamental element out of which all human societies are formed—that it is both the first source of morality and one of the distinguishing characteristics of the human species.[9] Its importance is proved by the fact that cultures all over the world have made gratitude a prominent theme in their folktales, proverbs, and unwritten moral codes. The ancient cultures of South and East Asia are no exception. In the case of India, various schools of Buddhism, which had emerged in the centuries prior to the Common Era, made gratitude a primary component of their respective belief systems and helped to codify the concept through didactic tales and doctrinal teachings. Known by the Sanskrit term *kṛta* (also *upākarā*), which carried both the passive meaning of feeling indebted to others and the active meaning of doing something to repay an obligation, gratitude became an important moral code of conduct in early Indian society.[10] Incorporated into numerous sutras of the Mahāyāna (Greater Vehicle), a northern school of Buddhism that achieved orthodox status in East Asia, the Buddhist-inflected notion of gratitude made its way into China where it was represented by the character *en* (恩). While this ideograph connoted the "blessing of Heaven" within more native Chinese philosophical traditions, its meaning grew increasingly worldly as more and more Buddhist texts were translated. Eventually, it came to represent a blessing or favor received from, or owed to, another person. Early Buddhist practitioners in Japan, working as they often did within the world of Chinese script, adopted the same character, in Japanese pronounced as *on*, to express an equivalent meaning. They also borrowed a two-character Chinese compound that referred to the specific action of repaying a favor (Ch.: *baoen*; J.: *hōon*), an expression that then became the basis for the more colloquial term *ongaeshi*. Both *hōon* and *ongaeshi* were used interchangeably to signify the general notion of showing gratitude toward someone or something that treated you kindly, whether human or nonhuman.

Although it is difficult to trace the exact movement of Buddhist notions of gratitude from India into East Asia, and harder still to assess their wider ideological impact, the prevalence of such terms as *en* and *baoen* in Chinese translations of Mahāyāna texts is evidence that it was a primary concern for those involved in the production and transmission of doctrinal knowledge.[11] In fact, *baoen* was a concept of such importance that it merited its own sutra, known in Chinese as *Dafangbian fo baoen jing* (Sutra of the Buddha's requiting a favor by great expedient means).[12] Translated into Chinese from Sanskrit around 220 C.E., the sutra expounds the doctrine of *baoen* from a Mahāyānist perspective. It presents a counterargument to the controversial idea that the historical Buddha Shakyamuni's act of leaving home to become an ascetic constituted an act of ingratitude toward the blessings (*en*) of his parents. From a perspective that accounts for dependent origination and the transmigration of souls from one life to the next, all sentient beings become potential parents of Shakyamuni, and he in turn becomes a parent to all sentient beings. From the latter vantage point, Shakyamuni's quest to save all sentient beings through the teachings of Buddhism may thus be construed as one of the highest forms of gratitude possible.[13] When nonhuman animals are included in the category of sentient beings, as they sometimes were, then the sutra points us to an understanding of *baoen* as a moral code that transcends the human-animal divide.

The association of Buddhist notions of gratitude with the realm of nonhuman animals is made more explicit in another significant doctrinal reference. It comes from *Dazhi dulun* (Numerous treatises on great wisdom), a seminal commentary on the Mahāyāna sutras of Perfect Wisdom (*Mahāprajñā-pāramitā-sūtra*) attributed to the Indian Buddhist Nāgārjuna (ca. 100–200 C.E.) and translated into Chinese by the Indian scholar Kumārajīva (350–409 C.E.). An encyclopedic work that discusses the many philosophical systems contained within Indian Buddhism of the early Common Era, the commentary contains the following passage, which espouses the virtues of knowing gratitude:

> Knowing *en* is the essence of great compassion and the first gate to establishing good deeds. People will love and respect you and your name will be praised far and wide. Upon death you will attain rebirth in Heaven and in the end you will become [a follower of] the way of the Buddha. Those who do not know *en* truly are beasts [Ch.: *chusheng*; J.: *chikushō*].[14]

The passage reveals quite explicitly the link between the Buddhist discourse of gratitude and ideas about what it means to be "human" or "beast"—a link established in Buddhist doctrine at least as early as Nāgārjuna's time. Similar didactic comments in which one's status as human or nonhuman animal is defined solely on the basis of whether or not gratitude is properly expressed appear over and over again in the Chinese and Japanese *ongaeshi* tales of later centuries.

In fact, the passage from *Dazhi dulun* has a direct connection to *ongaeshi* literature and doctrine, as it is cited in the introduction to chapters on *baoen*, or returning a favor, in two influential Chinese collections of Buddhist tales. The Chinese monk Dao Shi (d. 683) assembled both *Zhujing yaoji* (Essentials of the various sutras; 659) and *Fayüan zhulin* (Forest of pearls in the garden of the Dharma; 668), and both collections proved influential for later compilers of Buddhist tales in Japan. The former was transmitted to the Japanese archipelago at an undetermined point during the eighth century, while the latter entered around the time of the compilation of *Kojiki* (Record of ancient matters; 712). As the two collections contained a foundational set of themes, stories, and doctrinal content upon which to draw, it was relatively easy for Japanese proselytizers and compilers of Buddhist tales to appropriate the content for their own interpretations of *ongaeshi* doctrine. Indeed, in two of the most prominent tale collections of the classical period, *Nihon ryōiki* (Strange and miraculous stories of Japan) and *Konjaku monogatari* (Tales of times now past), one finds a sizeable amount of *ongaeshi* tales and didactic commentary on the importance of showing gratitude.[15] For instance, *Nihon ryōiki*, a late eighth-century text known as the first extant Japanese collection of tales, contains several *ongaeshi* narratives that draw from both Chinese and more "native" Japanese sources. The stories offer a glimpse of how *ongaeshi* doctrine took shape within Japanese Buddhism during the early years of its development in the sixth to eighth centuries. Similarly, *Konjaku monogatari* contains many *ongaeshi* stories originating from around the same period, if not earlier, even though the collection was not compiled until around 1100. Despite their historical distance from one another, then, it is important to recognize that the *ongaeshi* tales within both collections served to transmit orthodox Buddhist conceptions of gratitude from the continent to Japan. To the extent that these tales were told with animal characters, as was often the case, they also brought to Japan a distinctively Buddhist understanding of the nonhuman animal.

That animal characters had such a prominent place in Buddhist *ongaeshi* tales should come as little surprise. Folklorists have shown that in cultures all across the globe, tales of gratitude have long been told with nonhuman actors.[16] Chapter 2 of this volume introduces similar motifs in connection with serpent folklore. But while such use of nonhuman animals may not be unique, there are certain characteristics specific to the medium of the *ongaeshi* tale. First, nearly all such tales are based on a shared narrative structure: a human rescues from death, or shows kindness toward, another member of the animal kingdom, and is then rewarded by that animal with some jewel or treasure that serves as a token of gratitude. There are, of course, many variations on the theme. People of every social stratum, ranging from court aristocrats to common peasants, fill the human role. A wide array of creatures, including cranes, turtles, sparrows, and crabs, play the part of the grateful animal. And various types of treasure may substitute for the jewel, such as magical powers, long life, prosperity, and food.[17] Second, and most important, the standard narrative pattern is rooted in the Buddhist concept of *hōjō* (liberation of living beings), an act of kindness that often serves as the motivating force behind the animal's display of gratitude. It is primarily because of this concept that the symbolic animals of *ongaeshi* tales take on a distinctively Buddhist air.

Hōjō has its doctrinal origins in two canonical texts known in Japanese as *Bonmyōkyō* (Sutra of Brahma's net) and *Konkōmyōkyō* (Sutra of golden light). The former, translated into Chinese by Kumārajīva in 406 C.E., belongs to the precepts of the Mahāyāna school and contains a list of forty-eight commandments to be followed by all disciples of the Buddha. Commandment twenty admonishes those who do not practice the liberation and rescue of living beings:

> As a [child] of the Buddha, one must with a compassionate heart practice the work of liberating living beings. All men are our fathers. All women are our mothers. All our existences have taken birth from them. Therefore, all the living beings of the *rokudō* [six realms of existence] are our parents, and if we kill them, we kill our parents and also our former bodies; for all earth and water are our former bodies, and all fire and wind are our original substance. Therefore, you must always practice liberation of living beings (since to produce and receive life is the eternal law), and cause others to do so; and if one sees a worldly person kill animals, one must by proper means save and protect them and free them from misery and danger.[18]

Basing its argument on the Buddhist notion of transmigration, the passage effectively unites all sentient beings as products of the four original substances. If all living creatures are interconnected, giving birth to and being born from one another, then killing another living being becomes tantamount to killing one's own parents and destroying in part the very source of one's own life. This precept effectively transforms the Buddhist belief in transmigration into an absolute truth and reifies that truth through a law that encourages all pious followers to show mercy toward all animals at all times. We know that Buddhist adherents in Japan were familiar with this law by at least the late eighth century because the monk Kyōkai, compiler of *Nihon ryōiki*, implicitly alludes to it in the first volume of his tale collection. "How swift and immediate is the penalty for evil actions. We cannot but believe in the law of karmic causality. Though they may appear to us as merely beasts [*chikushō*], these creatures may have been our parents in a previous life.... Therefore we must show them mercy."[19]

While *Bonmyōkyō* incorporated the act of *hōjō* into Buddhist law, *Konkōmyōkyō* established a mythic basis and model for the performance of *hōjō* as a rite through which one could acquire this-worldly benefits. In the fourth chapter of the sutra, translated into Chinese around 420 C.E. by Dharmaraksha II, one finds a *jātaka* tale (birth story of the Buddha) in which a previous incarnation of the Buddha rescues ten thousand fish from certain death. Reincarnated as a rich man named Rūsui, the Buddha happened upon a dried-up pond where fish were struggling to stay alive and, feeling compassion for their plight, he had twenty elephants carry water to the pond so that the fish would survive. Thereafter, he held a banquet for the fish at which he gave them spiritual nourishment by preaching the *dharma* (Buddhist Law), in particular the doctrine of dependent origination. But just as the banquet ended, a large earthquake struck the region and all ten thousand fish perished. All were reborn, however, in the Tōriten heaven, and in order to show their gratitude to Rūsui not only for saving their lives but also for giving them an opportunity to escape their bestial existence, they returned as angels and offered him jewels and other wonderful treasures.[20] This story from *Konkōmyōkyō* influenced Buddhist practice in Japan as early as the late seventh century, when it became the basis for the popular and long-lasting ceremony of *hōjōe*, an observance involving the release of living creatures in mass numbers as a ritual means of acquiring spiritual merit.[21] The sutra was popular among emperors of the seventh century, who ordered that it be recited extensively in regional Buddhist temples. Again, we know that Kyōkai was familiar with the text because he refers to it in story five of the second volume of his compilation.[22]

Providing legitimacy to the act of freeing living beings (*hōjō*), then, is a pair of scriptural references—references that also help to support the act as the key motivational element in *ongaeshi* tales. However, while the two scriptures may operate in tandem, the last section of this chapter will show that underneath them lay two seemingly contradictory ideas about the place of the nonhuman animal in human society. On the one hand, *Bonmyōkyō* calls into question the rigidity of the human-animal divide by asserting the innate interconnectedness of all beings. On the other hand, *Konkōmyōkyō* implicitly functions to assert an essential difference between the two categories of "beast" and "human." Both ideas are closely intertwined in *ongaeshi* tales, and they ultimately work together to create the uniquely Buddhist symbolic animal previously alluded to. For now, it is enough to say that both ideas are integral to the *ongaeshi* tale and that Buddhist practitioners and the ruling elite knew of them from the seventh century onward. Their presence in the following gratitude tale about a magnificent nine-colored deer provides a clearer picture of how they function generally in the *ongaeshi* tale and how they produce in this particular narrative a symbolic deer who conforms to orthodox Buddhist conceptions.

THE DEER'S TALE

> At a time now past, there stood a mountain in India [Tenjiku] upon which lived a deer with white horns and nine-colored fur. The people of the kingdom knew nothing of the animal's existence. At the base of the mountain there was a large river. The deer shared its mountain home with a crow and the two of them passed the time as the best of companions.[23]

Here, at an isolated mountain haven, the tale of the magnificent deer begins. It is a tale that, in its Japanese manifestation, is known by the title "Story of the Nine-Colored Deer of the Mountains Who Saves a Man Beside the River." Contained within the India section of *Konjaku monogatari*, the tale serves as a focus for the ensuing discussion about changing conceptions of deer and other nonhuman animals during the period of Buddhism's integration into Japanese society. The origins of the story can be traced back to the standard Pāli collection of *jātaka* tales, into which it was incorporated under the title *Ruru-jātaka* (Tale of the Buddha's birth as a deer).[24] Later, Buddhist practitioners singled out the story and it became a sutra of its own. It was then translated into Chinese during the Wu dynasty (222–280 C.E.) by the scholar Zhi Qian and given the name of *Foshuo jiuselu jing* (Buddha's preaching of the nine-colored deer sutra).[25] After its incorporation into the Chinese Buddhist canon during the third century, the story gained popularity among Buddhist priests and scholars, as evidenced by the fact that Zhi Qian's translation was reproduced in the chapters on gratitude (*baoen*) of the aforementioned Chinese tale collections *Zhujing yaoji* and *Fayüan zhulin*.

Knowing that these compendia had a profound influence on the compiler of the *Nihon ryōiki*, we can date the tale's entry into Japan sometime prior to that text's completion in the late eighth century. As is always the case with texts of this early period, however, it is much harder to determine how widely the deer tale circulated before its eventual incorporation into *Konjaku monogatari* in the early twelfth century. It undoubtedly passed through the hands or mouths of some Buddhist practitioners between the late eighth and early twelfth centuries, because a comparison of the Chinese version and the *Konjaku monogatari* rendering reveals the presence of minor alterations in the narrative. Regardless, I have selected this particular story for analysis not because it was verifiably popular or widely read at the time, but rather because it accurately represents the themes and motifs of the *on-*

gaeshi genre as it existed during the historical period in question. So, having historicized the story, let us return now to the solitary depths of the deer's mountain abode.

All was peaceful at the Indian mountain until a man appeared one day and tried to cross the large river, only to be swept up in its strong current. On the verge of drowning, he called out to the mountain gods, the forest gods, the heavenly gods, the dragon god, and anyone else who might possibly rescue him from certain death. Just then the deer passed by, and hearing the man's cries for help, it jumped into the river and told the man to grab onto its antlers so that the two could swim together to safety. Once they reached the bank of the river, "the man, overjoyed that his life had been saved, turned to the deer with tears in his eyes and his palms together in thanks. 'It is because of you, deer, that today my life is still with me. What ever can I do to repay this debt of gratitude [*on o mukuiru*]?'"[26]

In turn, the deer's response was simple: "Do not tell anyone of my existence here, for if people ever find out my whereabouts, they will return to hunt me down for my valuable antlers and fur." Swearing to keep the deer's secret, the man returned home and managed to keep his promise until one night when the queen of the realm had a dream about the magnificent nine-colored deer. On waking, she became so desperate to acquire its beautiful pelt and antlers that she feigned sickness and demanded that the king capture the deer for her. The tale continues:

> Thereupon the king sent out the following proclamation: "If there is anyone who can search out and present this magnificent deer to me, I will bestow upon that person gold and silver treasures and anything the person desires." The man who had been rescued by the deer heard the king's proclamation and was quickly overcome by greed, forgetting all about the deer's favor [*on*].[27]

Leading the king and an army of soldiers, the man returned to the mountains where the deer was sleeping peacefully in its cave. There was no time for the deer to escape, and, resigned to its fate, the creature prepared to sacrifice itself to the king's army. Just then the king cried out: "Hold off a moment before you shoot this deer. Take a look and you will see that this is no ordinary deer." Thereupon the deer asked the king how it was that he knew where to find it, and the king immediately pointed to the man standing beside him. The deer was quick to reproach the ungrateful man for having forgotten a favor (*on*) despite the fact that the deer had risked its own life to save him. After hearing the whole story, the king decided not to kill the deer, and instead declared that from that time onward, no deer should be killed in his kingdom; any man who did so would be, along with his entire family, promptly executed.[28] The story continues:

> Having made this proclamation, the king and his army returned to court and the deer went home in a joyful mood. After that the rain fell at the appropriate times in the kingdom and no wild winds ever blew. Within the kingdom there was no more sickness, the five grains grew in abundance, and there was not a poor person in the land. So it is that those who forget favors [*on*] are of the human realm and those who help humans are of the realm of beasts [*kemono*].[29] This is true now just as it was long ago. At that time the nine-colored deer was I, Shakyamuni. The crow was Ananda, the king was Sondari, and the man who fell into the water was Devadatta....[30]

For early Japanese encountering this story, the biological animal signified by the word deer (Ch.: *lu*; J.: *shika*) would have been immediately recognizable. Although there are regional variations in the species even on the Japanese archipelago, deer are common throughout East Asia, and anyone living in the area we now call Japan would have been familiar with the animal. And yet, even if the biological animal were recognized underneath the coat of nine-colored fur, the deer's status as a discursive representation, as a symbolic animal embedded within Buddhist ideology and doctrine, means that it would have evoked a specific set of meanings unknown in more "native" animistic symbolic systems. In representational terms, it was a deer of an entirely different breed. While the signifier for deer was easily translated between societies familiar with the biological creature, cultural meanings associated with the animal could not be so readily transferred from one ideological system to another. The following sections will describe the most immediately relevant of these systems—locally-based animistic conceptions of deer on the one hand and orthodox Buddhist conceptions on the other—in the hope of revealing their points of intersection and contestation. With the entrance of *ongaeshi* animal tales like the nine-colored deer story into a Japanese political and religious milieu, the stage was set for an ideological clash of symbolic animals that would take centuries to work itself out.

THE SYMBOLIC DEER OF "NATIVE" ORIGIN

The task of describing locally based and more "native" conceptions of the deer—conceptions that either predated Buddhism's entry into Japan or rested beyond the purview of its influence during the religion's rise to prominence—remains complex and problematic for a number of reasons. First of all, the presence of a diverse array of communities on the archipelago long before, and well into, the period in question makes it difficult to talk about an overarching belief system in which deer held a single symbolic meaning. Add to this the mounting evidence that immigrants from different parts of the Asian continent formed many of these communities, and the situation becomes increasingly complex.[31] Even with the emergence of a fairly stable central polity in the Kinai region by the sixth century, and the further consolidation of its power in 672 with the introduction of an elaborate system of civil codes (*ritsuryō*), communities outside the central polity's domain—like Kita Ōu, to be discussed in chapter 3—retained a good degree of cultural autonomy. Second of all, it is difficult to define the deer's "native" or "pre-Buddhist" symbolic role in Japan because many of the resources that provide information about this role were created at a time when Buddhism was already well on its way to establishing itself as a powerful religious institution. As much as one might like to draw a distinct dividing line between some "pre-Buddhist" historical moment and a new societal configuration in which Buddhism reigned supreme, the reality is that the historical shift was a complicated and messy affair. Although Yamato political elites actively adopted Buddhism as a state religion and promoted its dissemination into the provinces, commoners and elites living within those provinces maintained their traditional religious practices and beliefs for some time. Changes occurred more rapidly in some regions because of their proximity to the capital or to the Korean peninsula, but for other areas it was several centuries before Buddhist doctrines and ethical codes permeated deep enough to bring about significant cultural change. Even within the political center, diachronic change occurred unevenly and Japanese religious life became syncretic in nature, leaders promoting Buddhist ideas at the same time they preserved older practices that brazenly contradicted those same ideas.

It would appear, then, that "native" is a term of little critical value for the context with which this essay is concerned. In a recent study on the genesis of East Asia as a geographical region and cultural sphere between

221 B.C.E. and 907 C.E., Charles Holcombe insightfully argues that when looking at emerging local societies like those of Japan, "it sometimes becomes almost meaningless to attempt to distinguish 'native' from imported."[32] Nonetheless, Holcombe consistently advocates a conceptual model that recognizes shared "universal" East Asian core elements that overlap with local cultural peculiarities at multiple levels. It is exactly these local peculiarities that are of interest here and to which it is still useful to ascribe the term "native," albeit with a healthy dose of qualification (and hence the slightly awkward use of quotation marks). Thus, when I use the term to describe certain conceptions of nonhuman animals or certain systems of belief, I do not do so in any strict chronological sense. Rather, the term indicates that those things had their origins in non-Buddhist practices, even if they were loosely woven into the same social fabric of which Buddhist beliefs were also a part. As for where the "native" conceptions and beliefs were actually native to, it has already been noted how difficult it is to talk about any sort of unified indigenous community. However, there is reason to believe that even before the consolidation of Yamato political power in the sixth and seventh centuries, the relatively small size of the Japanese islands led to the formation of shared cultural practices among diverse human communities scattered about the region. Just as the agricultural techniques of wetland rice agriculture moved rapidly across southern and central Japan during the Yayoi period (300 B.C.E.–300 C.E.), so too must have various other cultural practices, including practices related to deer and other animals. My subsequent use of "native," then, is meant to acknowledge the presence of cultural variance, but also to indicate the existence of commonalities, prime among them the absence of Buddhist influence, that ultimately outweighed the differences. Finally, it is important to point out that "native" is not to be confused in the present context with what is today called Shinto. While there was certainly some overlap between the two during the historical period dealt with here, Shinto was just beginning to come into its own as an institutionalized religion, and its development was heavily influenced by continental religious systems such as Daoism (known more popularly in the West as Taoism).[33] Thus, any conflation of the two terms does more to confuse the historical picture than to clarify it.

Let us turn now to the biological deer and its symbolic manifestations in the "native" or "pre-Buddhist" cultural world of early Japan. The animal known today as *Cervus nippon* or Sika deer and divided up into several subspecies (*Cervus nippon centralis* on the main island, *Cervus nippon nippon* in Kyushu, *Cervus nippon yesoensis* in Hokkaido, and so on) has flourished on the islands for millennia, securing for itself a prominent niche in the regional ecosystem when larger mammals became extinct around 12,000 years ago. As was the case with other mammals native to the area, such as the Asiatic Black Bear and the wild boar (the latter to be discussed in chapter 5), the deer's abundant numbers made it an invaluable source of clothing and sustenance for communities of hunters and foragers living on the archipelago. Strict dependence on hunting and foraging activities gradually declined, however, around 400 B.C.E., when wetland rice cultivation was introduced into the southern island of Kyushu. From there it spread throughout much of the south and even into northern areas of Japan's main island, Honshu, marking the start of the Yayoi period and signaling a major shift in methods of utilizing the environment to meet human needs.[34] Although one might expect the move to agriculture to prompt a waning in the deer's cultural significance, in actuality such decline did not occur. Part of the explanation lies in the fact that hunting remained an important source of food and livelihood for many, especially in regions less suited to paddy agriculture. The lack of decline can also be attributed, ironically, to the formation of a unique relationship between deer and those very same agricultural practices.

Archaeological evidence provides much of what we know about the deer's symbolic status during the Yayoi period. Of the roughly 160 examples of Yayoi pottery that contain some sort of decorative drawing, about 40 percent have pictures of deer; such pictures are prevalent on bronze pieces as well.[35] In his study of the cultural history of deer in Japan, Hirabayashi Akihito hypothesizes that because the images of deer were so often combined with other images to depict an elaborate, agriculturally based religious ceremony, deer must have played a key role in ritual. As their blood was a symbol of growth and rebirth, the deer were most likely used as sacrificial offerings to those gods who could grant agricultural prosperity. Several accounts from *Fudoki* (Records of wind and earth; compiled beginning in 713), in which deer blood is used as a substitute for water to encourage the growth of newly planted rice seedlings, attest to the likelihood of Hirabayahi's supposition.[36] Why this close link between deer and agriculturally centered rituals? One explanation is that the biological changes that Japanese deer undergo in the course of a year, such as fawning, growth of antlers, molting of fur, and dropping of antlers, coincide with major points in the growing cycle of rice. Just as rice seedlings are being planted in early summer, fawns are born, the antlers of male deer start to develop, and the deer's coat gradually molts from a darker brown to a white-speckled beige. When rice is harvested in the fall, the fur turns thick again in preparation for the winter months, and the mating season reaches its peak. By the time the harvest is completely over, male deer begin the process of shedding their antlers. The life cycles of deer and rice are also intertwined in a more concrete way: to this day, deer are fond of eating young rice seedlings in the spring and mature grains in the fall.[37]

Another reason for the deer's continued importance as a cultural symbol was that for centuries it had been considered an animal of great totemic significance, an animal that in various ways offered access to the realm of the gods. Archaeological and textual evidence reveals that a number of religious and hunting-based rituals asserted and reinforced the deer's connection with the spiritual realm. For example, it has been shown that the shoulder blades of deer were used in oracle-bone divination practices beginning in the Yayoi period, and that they remained the animal bone of choice until the late seventh century, when the use of turtle shells, long favored in China, grew more common.[38] (Chapter 4 will describe how early-modern Japanese used songbirds, too, in certain divination practices.) Drawings on the pottery of the period also tell us that deer antlers were a key component in shamanistic rituals, as they were used to adorn the headdresses of shamans who served as mediums between gods and local rulers.[39] During the Kofun period (300–710 C.E.), a time when tribal chieftains were venerated by burial in large tombs, deer skins and antlers were used as items of tribute to deceased leaders. The practice of using deer antlers, hides, and meat as tribute items for deceased leaders and current rulers, including the emperor, as well as for offerings in religious ceremonies at Shinto shrines, continued well into the subsequent Nara period.[40]

Textual evidence from *Fudoki* and *Nihon shoki* (Chronicles of Japan; 720) also supports the argument that deer served an essential symbolic role as mediators between the secular and spiritual worlds. For example, *Fudoki* incorporates numerous accounts of toponymic origins that involve an encounter with a deer as the impetus for naming a location, an indication that deer were seen as intimately linked to local land gods.[41] Other stories portray deer as exceptional listeners, so exceptional in fact that their ears are thought to be a means by which a person's prayers could be heard by the gods.[42] We also know that deer, as manifest symbols of regional land gods, were closely connected to the power of local chieftains. This power was reaffirmed through ceremonial hunts in which a chief symbolically usurped the power of the local gods by killing a deer. There are also many stories in *Fudoki* and *Nihon shoki* of emperors who go out to hunt deer either for pleasure or for ceremonial purposes, although most of the accounts are probably fictional and adapted from regional sources in ways that pay homage to a fabricated imperial lineage. Hirabayashi is careful to point out that underneath such representations lay an implicit discourse of Yamato's centralizing political power asserting itself over regional competitors.[43]

Despite the seemingly disparate ways in which the symbolic status of the deer was culturally and ritually reinforced, in every case the deer was treated as an animal of great spiritual significance. While the structure of the relationship between humans and deer probably varied among groups of different status positions and among communities in different regions, there is every indication that in the more "native" animistic cultural world of early Japan, the symbolic deer served as a link to a hidden spiritual realm. Even if the deer's spiritual potential was most often realized when human inhabitants of the Japanese archipelago sacrificed the animal, whether living or dead the deer was construed as an important mediator with, and messenger to, the gods. In order for this symbolic construction to take place, the same human inhabitants had necessarily to imagine the deer as inherently different from themselves. They did so in two seemingly contradictory, yet mutually supportive, ways. On the one hand, deer were imagined as nonhuman in a way that justified or legitimated the taking of their lives; they had to be seen as inherently different creatures whom one could kill for the sake of one's livelihood or for religious purposes. On the other hand, deer had to be imagined as possessing a spiritual connection to the gods that humans inherently lacked or had somehow lost over time. In short, they had to be made divine. While this is not the place for a lengthy discussion of the nature of animism in pre- and early classical Japan, the important point is that the symbolic construction of deer as spiritual rapporteurs consisted of a dual imaginary process. It is a point that will be returned to shortly.

Though the more "native" animistic meaning of deer remained highly influential well into, and even after, the Nara period, especially in Japan's hinterlands, members of the Yamato ruling elite began to challenge it during the late seventh century under the new symbolic order of Buddhism. Following the introduction of the continental creed to Japan in the late sixth century, Buddhist monks and nuns struggled for several decades to establish the new belief system as the dominant state religion. After some time, however, doctrinal and organizational means were found to combine the imported sacred order with older cultural forms. Due to the constant influx of continental cultural influences, Buddhist institutions and liturgical activity expanded rapidly enough to become an integral part of elite life as early as the 640s.[44] Once Buddhism was adopted and supported by those in power, it became an effective political tool, and elite members of the Yamato state incorporated it into imperial mandates and into the bureaucratic structure that helped to maintain their control over the provinces. Yet political life was not the only thing affected by Buddhism's rapid institutional growth and its association with elite power; social life, too, soon began to feel an impact. After those in power had converted, at least in part, to the worldview and moral order promoted at Buddhist temples and monasteries, it was only a matter of time before they expected others to do the same. One part of this moral order that rulers took a keen interest in was the way in which it defined "proper" interactions between human and nonhuman animals. As mentioned earlier, the moral precepts of orthodox Buddhism had long admonished the practice of animal sacrifice and the killing of other living beings (*sesshō*). By the late seventh century, emperors saw these precepts not just as guidelines for members of the monastic order, but as applicable to all in the empire.

Beginning in the late seventh century and continuing throughout most of the eighth, Yamato rulers issued numerous proclamations calling for restrictions to be placed on hunting, animal sacrifices, and the consumption of meat during certain ritual periods. Some of the more significant and far-reaching injunctions include a decree promulgated by emperor Tenmu in 675, which called for a restriction on the use of certain hunting devices (pitfalls, spear-traps, fishtraps, and so forth) and on the consumption of cows, horses, dogs, monkeys, or fowl. The prohibitions did not extend to other kinds of animal meat. In the following year, 676, Tenmu, influenced perhaps by political practices on the continent and by *hōjō* doctrine itself, ordered that various provinces take it upon themselves to liberate living things. The practice of issuing injunctions related to the treatment of nonhuman animals proved so popular that subsequent generations of emperors (and shoguns, as shall be seen in chapters 4 and 5) adopted it.[45] Emperor

Shōmu, who reigned from 724 until his death in 756, was perhaps the most prolific when it came to issuing these kinds of injunctions, promulgating at least ten over the course of twenty years. Some of them called for an end to hunting deer and boar, some ordered prohibitions against hunting and fishing on Buddhist fast-days of the month, and others demanded an end to killing any living thing at all.[46] That Shōmu issued so many prohibitions may well be a testament to their ineffectiveness, but this in no way detracts from the eagerness with which the monarch pursued the political and spiritual aims of transforming the state's moral order. Other important proclamations made after Shōmu's reign include one from 764, recorded in *Shoku Nihongi* (Continued chronicles of Japan; 797), which attempted to alleviate the emperor's illness by calling for a five-month moratorium on the killing of living things and on the use of deer or wild boar as sacrificial tribute items. It was followed by a similar proclamation in 780, which demanded an end to any use of animal meat or fish as a ritual offering.[47]

To summarize, Buddhism brought with it a radically foreign conception of the proper relationship between human and nonhuman animals, a conception that initially took root in the Japanese centers of Buddhist learning before merging with imperial policy during the seventh and eighth centuries. Evidence of the conception's growing presence and influence may be found in Buddhist tales circulating during the period, some of which were later included in *Nihon ryōiki*.[48] Several of the stories leave little doubt that members of the monastic order were strongly opposed to having contact with nonhuman animals and that people who took part in killing the latter were considered the most immoral and deserving of punishment in the eyes of Buddhist monks like Kyōkai.[49]

The shift in attitude toward the place of nonhuman animals in religious ritual, social practice, and daily life was by no means immediate and definitive, and it is important to understand the historical juncture as a transitional period rife with contradictions. Although imperial injunctions and didactic messages ultimately filtered outward through government offices or temple networks to reach commoners and provincials, those whose lives depended on hunting and killing animals probably carried on with their activities much as before. Until they became devout Buddhist followers themselves, the new East Asian moral order being thrust on them by the ruling elite would have meant very little. Change was slow to come even among the ruling and religious elite. At the same time that emperors such as Tenmu and Shōmu issued injunctions against slaughtering animals, they and their successors carried on the tradition of accepting deer and other meat for the New Year's celebration at least until the tenth century. They also continued to accept offerings of animal flesh from provincial leaders, since the practice had long been a way for rulers at the center to reaffirm their positions of power.[50] In the nineteenth and twentieth centuries, the presentation of living animals to the Imperial Zoo, both from distant prefectures and from Japan's expanding colonial empire, may be seen as an echo of this tradition of animal tribute and will be examined in detail in chapter 8 of this volume. To return to the classical period, however, emperors and courtiers alike hunted for ceremonial purposes and for general recreation long after the introduction of Buddhism, as may be seen in references from *Nihon shoki* and other well-known literary collections, such as *Man'yōshū* (Collection of ten thousand leaves; 759) and *Konjaku monogatari*. Not only the court but also state-supported Shinto shrines built prior to and during the Nara period served as a haven for more "native" animistic practices, accepting offerings such as deer skins and antlers as tribute items according to rules detailed in *Engishiki* (Book of rites; 905). It is significant, however, that such rituals were not carried over to Shinto shrines built after the imperial capital moved to Heian in 794, an indication that a major political and ideological shift was indeed underway.[51]

Despite the contradictions inherent in the age, there is little doubt that Buddhist-based conceptions of the nonhuman animal were finding a home in elite circles during the seventh and eighth centuries, providing their members an opportunity to say things about animals that would have been culturally incomprehensible just a century or two before. How did orthodox Buddhism articulate its particular understanding of the human-animal divide and why exactly was that understanding at odds with more "native" animistic attitudes? Returning to the *ongaeshi* story of the nine-colored deer and the doctrinal elements that provided its ideological foundation will help us to explore these questions in greater depth.

THE MOULTING OF A SYMBOL

Although it is true that the deer story represents only a small part of the Buddhist symbolic order as it was articulated in Japan during the historical period in question, it provides an important window into Buddhist conceptions of the nonhuman animal. To say so is not to imply that the story itself had any direct causal effect on the ideological shift that was taking place in religious and social practices involving nonhuman creatures. It does, however, reveal the theology that underlay attempts by the Yamato elite to replace once-dominant local and "native" cultural formations with newly emergent Buddhist ones. The new theology makes itself most apparent in the manner by which the magnificent nine-colored deer is represented in the tale. While the text would have the reader or listener believe that in form and movement the animal retains the characteristics of a deer, its ability to communicate and interact with people according to human-based linguistic and moral codes indicates the extent to which the deer has been anthropomorphized. Whatever ties the textual representation of the nine-colored deer might once have had to the human encounter with deer in the wild, those ties have become rather tenuous. Indeed, the nine-colored deer is surrounded by a mythical and otherworldly aura, an aura further enhanced by the text's acknowledgment of the deer as a previous incarnation of the Buddha. Such a mode of animal representation is typical of much *jātaka* literature, and though it bears similarities to anthropomorphic representation in other cultures, in a Buddhist context it is specifically linked to notions of karma and transmigration through the six realms of existence. As John Garrett Jones notes,

> The talking animal in an Indian context has the added significance that, granted belief in rebirth, all men (including the bodhisattva) will actually have lived in a multiplicity of animal bodies in the past and may well do so again in the future. If, as an animal, one is to gain promotion in a future birth, there has to be the possibility of gaining merit as an animal. One therefore has a vested interest in believing, as an existential possibility, not merely a mythological convention, that an animal is capable of moral choice and virtuous conduct.[52]

Depending on the level of one's karmic merit, a human can be reborn into one of six realms of existence: the realm of hell, the realm of hungry ghosts, the realm of beasts, the realm of the titanlike Asuras, the realm of humans, or the realm of heaven. Implicit in this idea of fluid movement between different forms of existence is the notion that all forms are closely interrelated, especially human and beastly forms since they exist on the same physical plane. Beasts may occupy a lower place than humans in the karmic hierarchy, but they are generally thought to be of the same essence and of the "same chain of becoming."[53] Humans can be reborn as beasts and beasts can be reborn as humans in a veritable wheel of karmic fortune that blurs the boundaries between the human species and other living creatures. This blurring of boundaries is evident in the deer tale, where the animal simultaneously plays the role of a deer and a reincarnated Buddha whose associations with the human body of Shakyamuni further complicate attempts to fix firmly the deer's identity. This sort of blurring may be found in other Buddhist stories as well, including one from the India section of *Konjaku monogatari* in which a doe becomes impregnated with a human-deer child after licking the sweat of a mountain hermit from a well.[54] In contrast to the more "native" animistic representations examined earlier, in which deer were construed as distinct spiritual entities and in which boundary-blurring anthropomorphic representation was far less common, differences between deer and humans in these two Buddhist stories are practically denied.[55] But if there is theoretically no ultimate distinction between humans and nonhuman animals such as the deer, why is it still necessary for the *ongaeshi* tale of the nine-colored deer to rely on a character of a different species? And why does the didactic message conveyed in the tale, which implies that only beasts understand the meaning of gratitude, depend on the very bestiality of the character?

Perhaps the nine-colored deer presents an enduring trace of a much older tale that existed before the rise of Buddhism in India. Or perhaps the deer was incorporated into the story intentionally so as to reinforce the notion that people and nonhuman animals are interconnected beings. Regardless, it is important to recognize that the deer's bestial status is necessary to maintain the logic of the text's didacticism and even its narrative progression, since it was ultimately the deer's antlers and fur that made it an object of desire in the first place. The deer is both a supplement to the story in the sense of an addition, a superfluous costume for the reincarnated Buddha, and an absolutely essential component of the narrative. Thus, at the same time that the text blurs the boundaries between deer and humans, it also reinforces differences by demanding that the deer retain its bestiality and hence its "otherness"—an otherness made more permanent by deer's status as lower than humans in the karmic hierarchy. The deer is seemingly human in its actions and even morally superior to certain human characters, but it is also different enough that it must return to the mountains—that is, to the place where it belongs—at the end of the tale.

These seemingly contradictory views of deer operate alongside each other to form what might be called a dual view of animality—a view that serves as a key structural element in this and other *ongaeshi* tales. Such a dual view is present also in doctrinal material supporting the ritual of *hōjō* (freeing living beings), which, as a previous section discussed, constitutes the very reason that gratitude is expressed in *ongaeshi* animal tales. It bears recalling that the *Bonmyōkyō* sutra emphasizes the relative sameness and interconnectedness of all sentient beings, while the narrative of the *jātaka* tale from *Konkōmyōkyō* relies on the fact that fish are animals undergoing a form of suffering inherent to their position as such. Here again one may detect the two sides of a dual view: in the first instance there is a religious ideal asserting the essential sameness of humans and other animals, and in the second instance there is a tendency to reinforce the otherness and inferiority of nonhuman animals who sit lower in the karmic hierarchy of existence. Richard Tapper hints at the universality of the dually conceived symbolic animal when he describes two competing perspectives quite similar to what is found in Buddhist tradition. He explains,

> Animals, or rather cultural constructions of them, are used as metaphors for moralizing and socializing purposes in two rather different, even contradictory, ways. Sometimes certain animals are idealized and used as models of order and morality, in animal stories and myths. The animals are treated as agents and social beings, with motives, values and morals; and differences between them and people are implicitly denied. By contrast animals are sometimes represented as the Other, the Beast, the Brute, the model of disorder or the way things should not be done.[56]

It was earlier noted that the conception of the deer in the more "native" symbolic order also operated according to a dual structure, and so its presence in Buddhist *ongaeshi* tales does not signal a remarkable difference. However, when one compares the two poles of each duality, it becomes apparent that the Buddhist view must have represented a radical departure from local cultural formations. On the side of the dual view that idealized nonhuman animals as moral exemplars or spiritual mediators, we find in the Buddhist symbolic order a conception of them as sentient beings who, because of their interconnected relationship with human existence, are to be shown great compassion. Naturally, this precludes the hunting or killing of animals such as deer, an act tantamount to killing one's own parents, one's own kind, or quite possibly the Buddha himself. It is a point made all too clear in an early thirteenth-century Buddhist tale concerning a sage who wishes to change the ways of a friend who loves to hunt. He tries to dissuade the friend by disguising himself as a deer. But, as fate would have it, he is killed with an arrow when that same friend mistakes him for the real animal.[57] Reflected in this story, as well as in countless *ongaeshi* tales, is the Buddhist prohibition against killing animals that was propagated through imperial injunction and religious doctrine from classical times onward. Knowing what we do about the more "native" symbolic order, in which rituals reinforced the deer's link to the spiritual world through acts of ceremonial hunting and sacrifice, it is doubtful that a Buddhist approach to nonhuman animals could have symbolized anything other than a radically alien attitude. For in effect, to admonish the act of killing was to undercut potentially the very foundations of the "native" animistic relationship between deer and humans. A deer seen through the eyes of Buddhist theology could not, at least on ethical grounds, be treated in the same way as a deer understood within more traditional belief systems.

On the opposite pole of the dual view of animality, we find a tendency to mark nonhuman animals as ontologically different from humans in a way very much to the former's detriment. Within the Buddhist *ongaeshi* tale, this negatively defined difference is organized around the idea that beasts are morally inferior to humans and that they occupy a lower place in the karmic hierarchy. The pejorative sense of the animal as a lowly beast is not so strong in the deer story as it is in other Buddhist tales, but there is throughout an implicit emphasis on the deer's animal "otherness." Indeed, until the king recognizes the deer as an extraordinary being, it has meaning only as a rare and valuable commodity needed to satisfy the desires of the queen. Other stories in *Nihon ryōiki* demonstrate that the symbolic animal of early Japanese Buddhism was additionally seen as an immoral beast with whom one should have limited contact or else risk spiritual and physical defilement. Those characters who have intimate dealings with nonhuman animals immediately become targets of contempt.[58] Similarly, the conclusion to our deer story warns that continued contact with animals through hunting will lead to scorn in the deadly form of public execution. More than just a moral injunction, then, improper interaction with nonhuman animals was potentially construed as an appropriate object of religious and political punishment.

Within the more "native" symbolic order, on the other hand, it would be difficult to find deer who are marked as different from humans due to their moral corruptness or innate impurity. Deer were certainly dehumanized in a way that justified their being hunted and killed, but rather than representing them in a way that discouraged interspecies contact, early inhabitants of Japan promoted the formation of intimate and visceral relationships with the wild creature. By contrast, Buddhist-based conceptions often conflated the nonhuman animal with beastliness and immorality, encouraging a strict division between the human and nonhuman realms. It is a division symbolized by the king's decision to provide the deer a protected environment of its own at the tale's conclusion. With the clear demarcation of boundaries, the deer comes to be seen as an animal whose only appropriate place in human society is as an object of preservation. The king's final act suggests again how great must have been the ideological divide between Buddhist conceptions of the nonhuman animal and the various local conceptions with which they competed.

Now, let us blur further the lines between literature and history, between religious idea and social fact, by asking how the king's order to create a protected haven might have been received by those who encountered the story in seventh- and eighth-century Japan. Little evidence exists to suggest that an actual deer park similar to those found in India was established at the time. Although Japan's most famous deer park, which today surrounds the Kasuga shrine in Nara, was conceptualized as early as the shrine's founding in 768, it did not become an institutional reality until many decades later.[59] Nevertheless, the deer park's presence in the story must have allowed for the once inconceivable—if not absurd—notion of creating a protected area for deer to enter the social imaginary of the religious and political elite. And, as this chapter has shown, the notion would have been part of a much larger symbolic constellation making its way into certain levels of society in the form of proclamations, precepts, and *ongaeshi* tales. Though one suspects that few rulers at the time would have been willing to follow in the king's footsteps, the idea that his realm would prosper in succeeding generations ultimately establishes his compassion toward the deer as the "natural" and morally superior stance. He is the ideal "human," the one who does not forget to honor a debt of gratitude and thus the one whom others should look up to.

This last point draws attention to a fact that has been implicit throughout the foregoing analysis: any recasting of what it means to be "animal" usually goes hand in hand with a recasting of what it means to be "human." A change in the meaning of either of the two categories forces the human-animal divide to shift. For Japan's Buddhist practitioners in the seventh and eighth centuries, it meant that those who piously upheld Buddhist laws and beliefs, just as the king did, were to be considered the most ideal of humans. And so, ironically, as early Japanese Buddhists defined nonhuman animals in ways that associated the killing of them with barbarity, those people who continued to kill animals came themselves to be seen as "inhuman beasts." In other words, the symbolic recasting of animals made it possible for those with religious and political authority to dehumanize people who did not fall in line with Buddhist teachings and thereby to legitimate the assertion of power over those same humans.[60] The king's creation of a deer park not only made him an ideal human in the eyes of Buddhism, but it also gave him a profound new means of control; he had now the moral authority to restrict access to the deer to any who might wish to treat it, by hunting or otherwise, in an "inhuman" way.

The clearest example of how the emergent Buddhist symbolic order was actually used to create a religious and political "other" out of those who hunted may be found in early eighth-century references to the Emishi people, to be discussed again in chapter 3. Living on the northern edge of Japan's main island, the Emishi had for some time maintained a degree of cultural autonomy from the Yamato population who came to dominate central and western Japan. Though they appear to have adopted many elements of Yayoi agrarian culture as it moved up the archipelago, they continued to depend much more on hunting and fishing than their neighbors to the south, and probably spoke a language of their own well into the Nara period.[61] After consolidating control of the Kinai region in the seventh century, however, Yamato rulers increasingly felt the need to extend their domain northward, leading to a long series of military actions against the Emishi beginning in 709. As the resistance of the Emishi was formidable, subjugation wars continued throughout the eighth century before ending in the so-called pacification era (774–811), a period of large-scale and largely ineffective military engagements.[62] It is significant that the compilation of *Nihon shoki* (720) was taking place just as this century of conflict got underway. The text purported to chronicle the history of the Yamato court from the legendary emperor Jinmu's accession to the throne in 660 B.C.E. up to the year

697 C.E., but it is less a reliable source of historical fact than it is a reflection of elite Yamato culture as it wished to see itself in the early 700s. Tellingly, the Emishi appear many times in *Nihon shoki*, and a number of these references clearly demarcate them as "savages" who are no better than beasts. They are variously described as having "by nature the hearts of beasts," as being "very hairy men" (it bears noting that *kemono*, a traditional word for beasts, literally means "hairy [or furry] things"), as having a propensity "to live upon animal food," and as dwelling under trees in the recesses of the mountains.[63]

The most striking account may be found in a section claiming to represent events of the seventh month of 110 C.E., when the emperor Keikō supposedly described the Emishi in the following manner to an imperial prince who offered to quell the Emishi disturbances.

> We hear that the Eastern savages [*azuma no hina*] are of a violent disposition, and are much given to oppression: their hamlets have no chiefs, their villages no leaders, each is greedy of territory, and they plunder one another.... Amongst these Eastern savages Yemishi are the most powerful, their men and women live together promiscuously, there is no distinction of father and child. In winter they dwell in holes, in summer they live in nests. *Their clothing consists of furs, and they drink blood.... When they receive a favor* [*on*], *they forget it*, but if an injury is done them they never fail to revenge it.[64] (Long's italics)

The passage was likely written in the early 700s, and it is quite clear that its authors manipulated the image of the Emishi (or Yemishi) effectively in order to justify their subjugation. Not only do Emishi commingle with nonhuman animals on a level that orthodox Buddhist beliefs would deplore, but they also do not understand what it means to repay a favor, something about which any decent human—or for that matter, any decent beast, according to *ongaeshi* rhetoric—would be fully aware. The circulation of such images around this time surely made it easier for the devoutly Buddhist emperor Shōmu, who issued so many injunctions against the killing of nonhuman animals, to justify the deployment of a large military campaign in 737 for the purpose of pacifying the "beastly" people to his north.

The case of the Emishi provides a concrete example of how Buddhist attitudes toward nonhuman animals might have provided an ideological rationale for the spread of Yamato hegemony. If we turn our focus back to the

Kinai region, however, such obvious examples become scarce. Is it possible that similar ideological strategies may have been used to assert control over disloyal regional elites or members of lower classes who practiced more "native" animistic forms of interaction with animals? Were imperial proclamations that prohibited certain forms of hunting an attempt to undermine the authority of local rulers who hunted deer in order to reaffirm their own connection with local land gods? Consider the issuance of imperial decrees in 730 and 741 calling for restrictions on large-scale traditional hunting practices carried out by ruling chiefs in outlying provinces. Hirabayashi Akihito argues that the political motivations behind such edicts were twofold: not only did hunting interfere with agricultural work at a time when central authorities desperately needed food for a growing city population, but the ruling elite also needed a way to restrict the activities, and standardize the religious practices, of those who might challenge its authority.[65] Once again, we see the potential for Buddhist attitudes toward nonhuman animals to be used as justification for the political expansion of the Yamato state.

CONCLUSION

Further research will likely turn up other archaeological and textual clues from the classical period evidencing a clash of antlers between the Buddhist symbolic deer and its more "native" rivals. It may not be an easy task, however, to uncover the material and discursive sites—such as the hunting grounds of regional elites—where such struggles took place. More challenging still is assessing the actual effects of changes at the symbolic level on the attitudes and practices of Japan's seventh- and eighth-century inhabitants. Nevertheless, even if the full social effects of the Buddhist view of nonhuman animals are difficult to reconstruct, it is important to recognize the potential for that view to enter into a tension-filled dialogue with more "native" animistic animal practices. Such a drastic redefinition of the human-animal divide at this historical juncture, promoted as it was by elites invested with great political power, must have had a significant impact on the lives of those who still inhabited the confines of an older symbolic order. Although standard narratives typically portray the rise of Yamato hegemony as an exclusively human historical drama, it should be apparent by now that the role played by Buddhist symbolic animals, and by extension their real-world counterparts, in the rise of this new political and religious order can no longer be overlooked.

The animal characters of early Japanese tale literature are not so innocent and insignificant as they may first appear.

Which brings us back to the larger issue of animal representation and the ideologies embedded in the seemingly innocent symbolic animals circulating within a society. These symbolic animals, rooted as they are in historical and cultural context, greatly determine the shape of the dialogue in which they, the humans who create them, and their real-world animal counterparts are engaged. As this chapter has attempted to show, the decision to view a biological creature like the deer as a grateful animal or a symbolic being, as a polluted beast or a sacrificial offering, can have real social and political consequences in the human realm. When symbolic animals are manipulated by politically powerful groups or individuals who attempt to establish just one vision of the animal as universally true, the effects on those who do not see things in the same way can be particularly invasive or devastating. The same political and ideological forces that shift the positions of symbolic animals among residual, dominant, or emergent cultural formations can turn them into highly charged sites of contention and contestation. And as our deer, symbolic and otherwise, cross paths with different systems of human meaning, their encounters, like those of Bambi, do not always have a happy ending.

NOTES

1. The tale is commonly known as *Tsuchigumo zōshi* (Tale of the dirt spiders). A reproduction of the scroll may be found in Okudaira Hideo, ed., *Otogizōshi emaki* (Tokyo: Kadokawa Shoten, 1983), 2–6.

2. Roy Willis, *Man and Beast* (London: Granada, 1974), 9.

3. Claude Lévi-Strauss, *Totemism*, trans. Rodney Needham (Boston: Beacon, 1963), 89.

4. I borrow the terms *residual, dominant*, and *emergent* from Raymond Williams in order to emphasize the idea that the meanings and practices associated with nonhuman animals are always multiple within a society and always evolving in a diachronic fashion. Although Williams uses the terms to discuss cultural forms in modern societies, they are also useful for examining premodern contexts. Specifically, they allow us to avoid framing historical analysis in terms of synchronic shifts from one absolute cultural form to another. See Raymond Williams, *Marxism and Literature* (Oxford: Oxford University Press, 1977), 121–27.

5. For an interesting discussion of how power and politics play a role in fixing the meaning of animals in northern India, see Paul Robbins, "Shrines and Butchers: Animals as Deities, Capital, and Meat in Contemporary North India," in *Animal Geographies: Place, Politics, and Identity in Nature-Culture Borderlands*, ed. Jennifer

Wolch and Jody Emel (London: Verso, 1998), 218–40.

6. For a discussion of the history of the Bambi character and its changing cultural significance in the United States, see Matt Cartmill, *A View to Death in the Morning: Hunting and Nature through History* (Cambridge, Mass.: Harvard University Press, 1993), 161–88.

7. This point is made by Tim Ingold in his introduction to *What is an Animal?* ed. Tim Ingold (London: Unwin Hyman, 1988), 12. In the same collection of essays, see also the article by Richard Tapper titled "Animality, Humanity, Morality, Society," 47–61. Tapper offers a fascinating discussion of how human and animal relations of production (such as hunting and gathering, pastoralism, agriculture, and urban-industrial production) influence greatly the social constructions of animality and humanity.

8. Steve Baker, *Picturing the Beast: Animals, Identity, and Representation* (Manchester: Manchester University Press, 1993), 10. Although Baker is primarily concerned with visual representations, the first chapter of his book provides a theoretical look at the processes by which nonhuman animals circulate within human societies as cultural representations.

9. One scholar who has made this claim is Joseph Anthony Amato II. See his *Guilt and Gratitude: A Study of the Origins of Contemporary Conscience* (Westport, Conn.: Greenwood, 1982), 28. Of particular relevance is the first chapter on gratitude and its changing role in the conscience of premodern and modern humans.

10. See Mibu Taishun, "On the Thought 'kṛtajñā' or '知恩' in Buddhism," *Indogaku bukkyōgaku kenkyū* 14 (1966): 960. In this article, Mibu discusses in detail the concept of *kṛta* (meaning either a benefit conferred by others or a sense of feeling obliged) and its evolution within the Mahāyāna and Tibetan Buddhist traditions. One of his primary interests is with the way in which the Indian Buddhist concept was integrated into Chinese and Tibetan societies.

11. See Mibu Taishun's article above for a more thorough examination of these texts.

12. The original text may be found in Takakusu Junjirō and Watanabe Kaigyoku, eds., *Taishō shinshū daizōkyō,* 85 vols. (Tokyo: Taishō Issaikyō Kankōkai, 1922–1933), 3 [cat. no. 156] (hereafter *TSD*). All subsequent citations to *TSD* list the volume in which the specific text appears, the catalog number of the text in square brackets, and, if relevant, the page number, in that order.

13. Sōka Gakkai, ed., *Shinpan bukkyō tetsugaku daijiten* (Tokyo: Seikyō Shinbunsha, 1985), 1557.

14. The text may be found in *TSD* 54 [cat. no. 2123]: 67c. Unless otherwise noted, all translations are my own.

15. Kyoko Nakamura tells us that Kyōkai, the compiler of *Nihon ryōiki,* was profoundly affected by *Zhujing yaoji* and that he used the Chinese collection as a model for his own work. See her *Miraculous Stories from the Japanese Buddhist Tradition* (Cambridge, Mass.: Harvard University Press, 1973), 36.

16. See the well-known motif index of folk literature compiled by folklorist Stith Thompson. Under the entry for "gratitude" in Thompson's index, only a handful of tales have just humans in them. The rest rely on interaction between human and nonhuman animals in which the latter are generally the ones who show gratitude for an act of kindness. See Stith Thompson, *Motif-Index of Folk-Literature,* 6 vols.

(Copenhagen: Rosenkilde and Bagger, 1955), 1: 428–32. Interestingly, tales grouped under the category of "ingratitude" are more likely to contain just human characters, and when there are ingratitude stories with both human and nonhuman actors, it is almost always the human who plays the role of the ingrate. For the latter type of tale, see Thompson, *Motif-Index*, 5: 494–96. While such characterizations may seem overly general, they are at least consistent with the extensive body of folk literature from which Thompson drew, a literature that includes tales from such far-flung places as Arabia, China, Greece, India, Ireland, Japan, Malaysia, the Philippines, Spain, and western Africa.

17. Shimauchi Keiji discusses this basic narrative structure in his analysis of the well-known Urashima Tarō legend. See Shimauchi Keiji, *Otogizōshi no seishinshi* (Tokyo: Perikansha, 1988), 21.

18. The original text may be found in *TSD* 24 [cat. no. 1484]: 1006b. The translation comes from Jane Marie Law's "Violence, Ritual Reenactment, and Ideology: The *Hōjō-e* of the Usa Hachiman Shrine in Japan," *History of Religions* 33 (1994): 325–26.

19. All citations from *Nihon ryōiki* are from Akiyama Ken et al., eds., *Nihon koten bungaku zenshū*, 51 vols. (Tokyo: Shōgakkan, 1970–1976), 6: 106 (hereafter cited as *NKBZ*).

20. The complete text of this tale may be found in *TSD* 16 [cat. no. 663]: 352b–53c.

21. According to *Nihon shoki*, the first *hōjōe* were held in the fifth year of Emperor Tenmu's reign (676). There is evidence from archaeological digs to help support this claim. See Okada Shōji, "Iwashimizu *hōjōe* no kōsaika," *Kokugakuin daigaku daigakuin kiyō* 24 (1992): 3. Other scholars have argued, however, that the first instance of the ritual did not occur until 710, when a *hōjōe* was held at the Usa Hachiman shrine in the northeast corner of Kyushu. Whatever the case may be, we can be certain that the story and the ritual itself were well known in Buddhist circles by the early eighth century. For more on the history of the *hōjōe*, see Law, "Violence, Ritual Reenactment, and Ideology"; Duncan Ryūken Williams, "Animal Liberation, Death, and the State: Rites to Release Animals in Medieval Japan," in *Buddhism and Ecology*, ed. Mary Evelyn Tucker and Duncan Ryūken Williams (Cambridge, Mass.: Harvard University Press, 1997), 149–62.

22. See *NKBZ*, 6: 160. For a discussion of the sutra's popularity among the political elite in the seventh century, see Conrad Totman, *A History of Japan* (Malden, U.K.: Blackwell, 2000), 72. "[Emperor] Tenmu lavished gifts on immigrant monks and promoted especially the reading of sutras that offered protection to rulers, notably the *Konkōmyō-kyō* or Sutra of Golden Light."

23. The tale of the deer is number eighteen in the fifth volume of *Konjaku monogatari* and is reproduced in Satake Akihiro et al., eds., *Shin Nihon koten bungaku taikei*, 100 vols. (Tokyo: Iwanami Shoten, 1989-), 33a: 438–442 (hereafter cited as *SNKBT*). The passage just cited appears on p. 438.

24. The story is conventionally listed as Pāli *jātaka* no. 482. A translation may be found in E. B. Cowell, ed., *The Jātaka or Stories of the Buddha's Former Births*, 6 vols. (Cambridge: Cambridge University Press, 1895–1907), 4: 161–66. Over five hundred *jātaka* were preserved in the Pāli language of the Southern Buddhists. Their official incorporation into the Buddhist canon as a single collection occurred sometime

between the fourth and fifth centuries C.E. For more on the history of the *jātaka* tales, see John Garrett Jones, *Tales and Teachings of the Buddha: The Jātaka Stories in Relation to the Pāli Canon* (London: Allen and Unwin, 1979), 3–7.

25. The text of the sutra may be found in *TSD* 3 [cat. no. 181]: 452–53. Considering the differences between the Chinese translation and the *Ruru-jātaka*, it appears either that changes were made in the process of translation or else that the tale as it arrived from India was already a variant form of the Pāli version.

26. *SNKBT*, 33a: 438–39.

27. *SNKBT*, 33a: 439. It is interesting to note that in the Chinese version of the sutra, the man justifies his greediness through a particular understanding of "animal" that is embodied in the following comment. "With this deer I could acquire great wealth; besides, this deer being a beast (*chikushō*), what does it care of death?" See *TSD* 3 [cat. no. 181]: 452c.

28. In the original *jātaka* tale, it is worth noting that the king pronounces that all birds and beasts should be allowed to live unharmed. The idea that all living things, and not just deer, deserve protection does not appear to have carried over into Chinese and Japanese versions of the tale.

29. It should be noted that the didactic commentary in the Pāli and Chinese versions of the tale does not make such a generalized distinction between humans and beasts. Instead, both make reference to an old proverb averring that it is better to haul a log than an ungrateful man out of a torrent.

30. *SNKBT*, 33a: 441.

31. See Charles Holcombe, *The Genesis of East Asia, 221 B.C. - A.D. 907* (Honolulu: University of Hawaii Press, 2001), 185. As Holcombe points out, "Mounting Japanese archaeological evidence increasingly supports the theory that the early Jōmon hunter-gatherer Stone Age culture had some roots in the Yue cultural sphere of prehistoric southern China and Southeast Asia, while the subsequent Yayoi revolution in Japan was inspired by new waves of immigrants arriving through Korea from the north, beginning about 400 B.C."

32. Ibid., 211.

33. Holcombe (ibid., 196) notes that some recent historical revisionists have come to see premodern Shinto belief as merely a local brand of Taoism.

34. See Totman, *History of Japan*, 23–31.

35. See Hirabayashi Akihito, *Shika to tori no bunkashi* (Tokyo: Hakusuisha, 1992), 33. Much of the discussion that follows draws from Hirabayashi's work, which provides the most complete and thorough analysis of the deer's cultural history in premodern Japan.

36. Ibid., 89. The origins of *Fudoki* can be traced to 713, when the emperor Genmei requested that officials in all outlying provinces (*kuni*) compile a record of their particular areas. This record was to include a list of all goods produced in the region; an account of soil-fertility levels; information on the origins of place names for mountains, rivers, and fields; and recordings of local customs and orally transmitted tales. Officials were also told to assign two-character Chinese compounds to the provincial, district, and town place-names. Only five provinces (Harima, Bungo, Izumo, Hizen, and Hitachi) complied with the initial request, and their records were put together into the original *Fudoki*. It is primarily from the records of Harima province (in present-day Hyōgo prefecture) that we learn of deer blood being used in

agricultural rituals.

37. See Okada Seishi, "Kodai denshō no shika," in *Kodaishi ronshū*, ed. Naoki Kōjirō Sensei Koki Kinenkai, vol. 1 (Tokyo: Hanawa Shobō, 1988), 139.

38 For more detailed information on the use of deer shoulder blades as oracle bones, see Hirabayashi, *Shika to tori no bunkashi*, 55–57. Accounts of such divination practices appear even in *Kojiki*.

39. Tatsumi Kazuhiro, *Fudoki no kōkogaku: Kodaijin no shizenkan* (Tokyo: Hakusuisha, 1999), 163–64.

40. Evidence may be found in *Engishiki* (Book of rites; 905), a text that describes in detail the type and quantity of offerings to be made at different shrines and ceremonies. Although other animals besides deer were used as offerings, deer antlers and deerskins were by far the most prevalent items listed. See Okada, "Kodai denshō no shika," 129–33.

41. Okada, "Kodai denshō no shika," 141.

42. Tatsumi, *Fudoki no kōkogaku*, 160.

43. Ibid., 174–76. See also Hirabayashi, *Shika to tori no bunkashi*, 94–100.

44. Totman, *History of Japan*, 54. For an excellent discussion of how the institution of Buddhism drew Japan into a larger East Asian cultural and ideological sphere, see Holcombe, *Genesis of East Asia*, 94–108.

45. The first two injunctions by emperor Tenmu are recorded in *Nihon shoki*, chapter 29. The original text of the injunctions may be found in Kojima Noriyuki et al., eds., *Shinpen Nihon koten bungaku zenshū*, 88 vols. (Tokyo: Shōgakkan, 1998), 4: 362, 372. English translations appear in W. G. Aston, trans., *Nihongi*, 2 vols. (1896; reprint, Rutland, Vt.: Tuttle, 1972), 2: 328–29, 334. For more information on the injunctions, see Christopher Chapple, "Nonviolence to Animals in Buddhism and Jainism," in *Inner Peace, World Peace: Essays on Buddhism and Nonviolence*, ed. Kenneth Kraft (Albany: State University of New York Press, 1992), 57.

46. See Yagi Tsuyoshi, *Nihon ryōiki no kenkyū* (Tokyo: Kazama Shobō, 1976), 168.

47. For more on these later injunctions, see Hirabayashi, *Shika to tori no bunkashi*, 79–80. For a detailed historical account of the many proclamations issued during this period, see also M. W. de Visser, *Ancient Buddhism in Japan: Sutras and Ceremonies in Use in the Seventh and Eight Centuries A.D. and Their History in Later Times*, 2 vols. (Leiden: Brill, 1935), 1: 204–11. It is interesting to note that King Asoka of India issued similar proclamations after his conversion to Buddhism. He established several laws requiring the kind treatment of beasts, including laws that restricted meat consumption, curtailed hunting, and established hospitals and roadside watering stations for nonhuman creatures. The trend continued in parts of China and Korea, where the influence of Buddhism encouraged political leaders to call for an end to the killing and sacrifice of nonhuman animals. See Holcombe, *Genesis of East Asia*, 95–96.

48. Although there is some debate among scholars regarding the date of compilation—some arguing that Kyōkai wrote the preface in 787 and others contending that the work was compiled during the Kōnin era of 810–824—the stories had presumably been circulating in some form several decades prior to their inclusion in the collection. A more detailed discussion of the historical debate may be found in Nakamura, *Miraculous Stories*, 9–14.

49. In several of the tales, venerable priests intentionally avoid or show an aversion to nonhuman animals. In story 7 of the first volume of *Nihon ryōiki*, Master Gusai decides to free several turtles caught by a fisherman. Rather than liberating them himself, however, he orders someone else to do it so as to avoid having direct contact with the animal. In story 29 of the second volume, Master Gyōgi criticizes and then expels a woman from his religious service because he notices that she wears animal oil in her hair. Additionally, it should be noted that very little mercy is shown those who violate the precept against killing living things and that their actions usually throw them into a veritable hell-on-earth from which they rarely escape alive. In story 11 of the first volume, a man finds himself consumed in flames one day as a penalty for a lifetime of catching fish in a net. In story 16, a man who enjoys killing living beings contracts a fatal disease after skinning a rabbit alive. A man in story 21 loses his eyes for working his horses to death. Finally, in story 10 of the second volume, a young boy finds himself in a field of fire because he has made a habit of hunting bird eggs to boil and eat.

50. Hirabayashi, *Shika to tori no bunkashi*, 105–7.

51. Okada, "Kodai denshō no shika," 133.

52. Jones, *Tales and Teachings of the Buddha*, 188–89.

53. The argument that there is no ultimate distinction between the various forms of existence is made by James P. McDermott in his article "Animals and Humans in Early Buddhism," *Indo-Iranian Journal* 32 (1989): 270. Interesting comparisons may be drawn between this notion of a "chain of becoming" and the Christian cosmological idea of *scala naturae*, or the Great Chain of Being, which depicted the world as a vast filigree of lower and higher forms. See Arthur O. Lovejoy, *The Great Chain of Being: A Study of the History of an Idea* (Cambridge, Mass.: Harvard University Press, 1936), 67–98.

54. The story is number 5 in the fifth volume of *Konjaku monogatari.*

55. One example of boundary-blurring representation with non-Buddhist origins may be found in the sixteenth volume of *Man'yōshū*. In it appears a poem in which a deer "talks" about the various medicinal uses of its own body parts.

56. Tapper, "Animality, Humanity, Morality, Society," 51.

57. The story is number 7 in the first volume of *Uji shūi monogatari* (Collection of tales from Uji; ca. 1200). A variant of the tale appears in the seventh-century Chinese tale collection *Fayüan zhulin*.

58. In several *Nihon ryōiki* stories, the mark of scorn is literally affixed to protagonists who, after failing to adhere to Buddhist precepts, are reborn into the bodies of nonhuman animals. See story 10 in the first volume, and stories 9 and 32 in the second volume.

59. There is still some debate as to whether the deer park at Nara was modeled after those established in India, but it is hard to imagine that the idea would have come about without any Buddhist influence from the continent. What is interesting about the Kasuga shrine's deer park, however, is that its origins are rooted not only in Buddhist belief, but also in "native" practices and Shinto mythology. The shrine's mythical founder is said to have arrived on a white stag, and the shrine was linked from an early time with rituals that involved the sacrifice and offering of deer. The association is likely a result of the fact that it was the family temple of the Fujiwara clan, which had for centuries prior to the shrine's founding been respon-

sible for carrying out imperial divination practices using deer bones. The topic of the deer park at Nara requires further research in order to elucidate how "native" and Buddhist conceptions of the deer competed for meaning at the time of the shrine's founding and in the ensuing centuries. The following works provide an excellent starting point: Allan Grapard, *The Protocol of the Gods: A Study of the Kasuga Cult in Japanese History* (Berkeley: University of California Press, 1992); Susan Tyler, *The Cult of Kasuga Seen through Its Art* (Ann Arbor: Center for Japanese Studies, University of Michigan, 1992), 67–73.

60. For further discussion of the political and social ramifications of Buddhist attitudes toward nonhuman animals, see Yagi, *Nihon ryōiki no kenkyū*, 166. Although I question the vehemence with which Yagi asserts that the imperial proclamations of the Nara period were motivated entirely by political concerns, his argument helps us to look beyond religious doctrine and into the political sphere.

61. See Karl F. Friday, "Pushing beyond the Pale: The Yamato Conquest of the Emishi and Northern Japan," *Journal of Japanese Studies* 23 (1997): 4. According to Friday, references to interpreters attached to the Yamato court's eight-century subjugation armies provide evidence of the Emishi's use of a distinct language.

62. For the best English-language introduction to the history of the conflict between the Yamato and the Emishi, see Friday, "Pushing beyond the Pale."

63. These passages from *Nihon shoki* correspond, putatively, to the eighth month of 121 C.E. (chapter 7), the second month of 582 C.E. (chapter 20), the fourth month of 658 C.E. (chapter 26), and the seventh month of 659 C.E. (chapter 26), in that order. See Kojima et al., *Shinpen Nihon koten bungaku zenshū*, 2: 388; 3: 478; 4: 21; 4: 226. The English quotations are from Aston, *Nihongi*, 1: 212; 2: 96; 2: 252, 2: 262.

64. Aston, *Nihongi*, 1: 203. For the original, see Kojima et al., *Shinpen Nihon koten bungaku zenshū*, 2: 370.

65. Hirabayashi, *Shika to tori no bunkashi*, 75–76.

From *Wakan sansai zue*. Courtesy of the C. V. Starr East Asian Library, Columbia University.

CHAPTER TWO

Fabled Liaisons: Serpentine Spouses in Japanese Folktales

Ria Koopmans-de Bruijn

> Of all the animals in Japanese folklore, the serpent plays perhaps the greatest part....
>
> —Masaharu Anesaki, "Japanese Mythology" (1928)[1]

Animals have left their tracks in Japanese tale literature since at least the earliest extant works written on the archipelago, such as *Kojiki* (Records of ancient matters; 712), *Nihon shoki* (Chronicles of Japan; 720), and the local gazetteers known as *fudoki* (compiled from 713 onward). Throughout the classical and medieval periods, an abundance of nonhuman animals populated literary narratives, including the deer stories that Hoyt Long introduced in the previous chapter. Many, if not all, such animal tales harbor meanings that go much deeper than the surface plot might suggest, provoking human reactions ranging from awe at the fantastic to religious enlightenment to the subtle inculcation of various forms of social knowledge. They conform to the general pattern of the fable, which the *Oxford American Dictionary of Current English* defines as a "story, esp[ecially] a supernatural one, not based on fact," or a "tale, esp[ecially] with animals as characters, conveying a moral."[2]

The present chapter analyzes Japanese animal tales not as literary expressions, but rather from the perspective of folklore studies. It is necessary therefore to begin by presenting a broad outline of folklore studies as a discipline, in particular as it applies to Japan and its animal life. A later section will narrow the focus of discussion to a particular subgroup of animal tales, chiefly from classical and medieval Japan, namely, those dealing with snakes and other serpentine creatures. It will be argued that the motif of the serpent who develops, or attempts to develop, conjugal relations with a human being usefully highlights the didactic functions of Japanese serpent folklore, and of animal folklore in general. Warning less of the dangers of human-serpent contact than of the risks involved in forming certain types of human-human relations, such folktales encode a set of structuring norms that have, over the course of history, helped to regulate prevailing social hierarchies. They therefore illustrate the observation of anthropologist Paul Shepard that "myth"—and I would argue folktales, including fables, in general—far from removing us from the world of the everyday, instead "informs our individual lives with exemplary models" and "our relationship to others in standards of conduct."[3] In order to illustrate this point, the chapter will draw heavily on specific fables, whether in the form of tale summaries drawn from so-called type and motif indexes or else in the form of translated extracts. In so doing, it is hoped that it may also convey some of the distinctive flavor of serpent folklore in Japan and elsewhere in the world.

THE STUDY OF FOLKLORE

Folklore refers in the context of this inquiry to the entire body of (originally orally) transmitted tradition. As broad as such a definition might be, however, it by no means exhausts the range of objects addressed by the discipline known today as folklore studies. Since at least the second half of the nineteenth century, folklore studies has become an institutionalized scholarly discipline in various parts of the world, including the Japanese academy, which heavily adopted Western disciplinary models during the Meiji period (1868–1912). Nevertheless, folklore studies remains a complex discipline with numerous branches, and interpretations of the word "folklore" itself differ significantly among its many scholars. Under the heading "What is Folklore?" for example, the website of the American Folklore Society cites eight different definitions of the term, together with its cognate "folklife."[4] The 1984 edition of *Funk and Wagnall's Standard Dictionary of Folklore, Mythology, and Legend* gives no less than twenty-one definitions of the same concept.[5] Adding to the complexity of the matter are the porous borders that folklore studies shares with a large number of other academic disciplines, including anthropology, history, literature, psychology, religion, and sociology. All in all, it is no exaggeration to say that the only thing folklorists seem to agree upon in defining the character of their own work is that it is, indeed, difficult to define.

Nevertheless, certain terms and concepts recur in most definitions of folklore, among them "tradition," "transmission," and "orality." To give an example, the serpent narratives to be examined in this chapter are "traditional" in the sense that they have been handed down over the course of centuries, in many cases from before the adoption of writing systems, which is to say, the beginnings of historical time. "Tradition" simultaneously implies "transmission," which is to say that it is the communication of folklore from one person or persons to another person or persons that makes it an object of "folk" knowledge. Hence, to folklorists, the particular origins of a tale are frequently of less interest than its subsequent dissemination over time and space, as well as the continuous transformations that occurred during the process of its being adapted and interpreted within ever-changing cultural and historical contexts. Until the printing boom of Japan's early-modern or Tokugawa period (1600–1868), the transmission of folktales typically took place by oral/aural means, whether through the medium of traveling storytellers or through the mouths of household or community elders.

Folklorists conventionally credit Yanagita Kunio (1875–1962) with the foundation of Japanese folklore studies, or as he lastingly dubbed it, *minzokugaku*, the "study of [Japanese] folkways." An inveterate collector of folktales and prolific writer on many aspects of Japanese culture, Yanagita worked together with a diversity of other researchers, including such luminaries as the literary scholar and poet Origuchi Shinobu (1887–1953), the biologist Minakata Kumagusu (1867–1941), and the art historian and exponent of the folkcraft (*mingei*) movement Yanagi Muneyoshi (1889–1961). During the early twentieth century, Yanagita cofounded a string of folklore-related journals, and, in 1947, he established the Folklore Research Institute (Minzokugaku kenkyūjo). The monumental influence that Yanagita exerted on the subsequent development of folklore studies in Japan has not been without its critics, who see his imprint as an "ideological and emotional lodestone" that has, for many years, handicapped the development of original theories and new methodologies.[6] Nevertheless, Yanagita's pioneering efforts in developing a systematic methodology for the collection, classification, and comparative analysis of folklore in Japan, as well as the actual data collected through survey-based fieldwork conducted by him and his colleagues, have made an enduring contribution to the modern study of the Japanese folktale.

Given the tremendous numbers of folktales in existence, some form of arrangement and classification is not only helpful but even necessary in order to find one's way around. In folklore studies around the world, two complementary forms of classification prevail: by tale type and by motif. According to Stith Thompson (1885–1976), a pioneer in the classification of folklore, the "principal use of a motif-index is to display identity or similarity in the tale elements in all parts of the world so that they can be conveniently studied."[7] Motif indexes classify those elements in folktales that identify them as belonging to a specific culture. Type indexes, by contrast, classify the universal elements of folktales. They furnish a "basis for the survey of traditional narrative in an area having a large common store of tales," and assume that "all versions of a type have a genetic relationship."[8] In other words, tales of a certain character may be found anywhere in the world; these are the tale types. However, every culture fills these shared tale types with local or regional detail; these are the motifs that turn the variants of a given type into native tales.

In 1948, Yanagita published *Nihon mukashibanashi meii*, which was later translated into English as *The Yanagita Kunio Guide to the Japanese Folk Tale* by former disciple Fanny Hagin Mayer (1899–1990).[9] The *Guide* introduced a classification system apparently developed from scratch by Yanagita and his coworkers, and it is based on the folktales collected by them over the course of several decades. Although Yanagita was certainly familiar with, and influenced by, the work of certain European folklorists, he was evidently unaware of the classification work already performed by Finnish folklorist Antti Aarne (1867–1925) and the American Stith Thompson. The former's type index of folktales, the first of its kind, appeared in 1910. It was expanded, edited, and translated into English by Thompson, and has since come to be affectionately referred to by folklore scholars as the *Aarne-Thompson Index* (or simply the *Aa-Th Index*).[10] During the 1930s, Thompson unveiled a complementary motif index, which, along with Aarne's index, he subsequently expanded and revised.[11]

Since the 1940s, folklorists have used Aarne and Thompson's magna opera, which attempted an overview of the folktales of the entire world, as a basis for more localized indexes, including those compiled by former Yanagita associates in Japan. Among the earliest examples in Japan, onetime Yanagita collaborator Seki Keigo (1899–1990) published a six-volume "Anthology of Japanese Folktales," *Nihon mukashibanashi shūsei*, between

1950 and 1958, dividing some 8,600 examples into 700 types (*kata*).[12] While acknowledging his indebtedness to the *Aa-Th Index* scheme, the author did not follow its classification practices in all respects. Rather than dividing each tale type into motifs, Seki chose rather to focus on each individual type and its characteristics. Far closer to the *Aa-Th Index* in its organization is the 1971 *Type and Motif Index of Japanese Folk-Literature*, by Hiroko Ikeda, a former disciple of Yanagita, who subsequently studied in the United States under the supervision of Stith Thompson.[13] Because not all Japanese tales that Ikeda collected fit into the existing types of the *Aa-Th Index*, she created several new classifications, yielding a total of 439 types. Students of the Japanese folktale thus have three important classified compendia on which to draw, each differing significantly in its method of presentation. Yanagita's *Guide* quotes a representative version of a tale for each type; Seki's "Types of Japanese Folktales" (based on the final index volume of his "Anthology") provides a summary of the plot; and Ikeda's *Index* offers a schematic tale analysis following the Aarne-Thompson pattern. The discussion and analysis below draws upon all three of these resources, yet favors Ikeda's principle of economically sketching out both plot and motif.

Every culture possesses unique folktales, yet at the same time certain folktale motifs, including those involving serpents, appear in a variety of cultures. We find examples of such motifs on all continents, often without any direct historical relationship among one another. All humanity shares certain characteristics in common, such as the need to eat, to sleep, to find shelter against the elements, as well as the more distinctively human need to explain phenomena by which we are surrounded. Such common characteristics of the human species account in part for the universality of certain folklore motifs around the globe. Furthermore, it is in the nature of all human cultural groups to seek, or actively to construct, a knowledge of their own beginnings, as is attested by the worldwide prominence of creation myths, which constitute another form of folklore. Whether as myths, legends, fairy tales, or fables, the tales that people tell and pass on to future generations constitute an oral literature that functions to record the collective memory of, as well as implicit and explicit behavioral guidelines for, particular cultural groupings. Only at a relatively recent point in time did such tales come to be preserved and disseminated in writing, even as oral transmission continued to be widely practiced.

Although they are more often cited as the first written works of history in Japan, the eighth-century *Kojiki* and *Nihon shoki* are simultaneously its oldest extant sources of folklore. *Kojiki* in particular is an excellent example of recorded oral literature. According to tradition, it was a male court scholar, Ō no Yasumaro (?–723), who set down the narrative in writing from the dictations of one Hieda no Are (650–?), likely a female member of a hereditary clan or guild of reciters (*kataribe*). Whereas the responsibility for transmitting history resided with such professionalized storytellers until the introduction of Chinese script, once writing practices were adopted, that duty shifted into the hands of a similarly organized collectivity of scribes (*fubitobe*). Yet, even though writing may have been in use in court circles as early as the fifth century, literacy was a skill that only a small percentage of society possessed until the modern era. For well over a millennium, the written word remained unavailable as a communication tool for most. Although Herbert Passin has estimated an impressive overall literacy rate of 39 to 47 percent by the end of the Tokugawa period, that is to say, in the mid-nineteenth century, it must also be taken into account, in the words of Marshall Unger, that "what constituted literacy varied greatly, from a bare knowledge of the elements of the *kana* syllabaries to productive facility in several socially prestigious and functionally distinct styles of Japanese and Sino-Japanese writing."[14] For much of society then, the oral skills of storytellers remained the chief medium through which to receive social information, moral instruction, and textual entertainment for many centuries after the introduction of a writing system in Japan.

Whereas *Kojiki* proclaims itself to be the written record of an originally oral narrative, the much longer *Nihon shoki* was in all likelihood based to a greater extent on existing writings, of which, unfortunately, none except *Kojiki* survive. The content of the two works was considered "history" by the ruling elite, even if much of what is included in them would not accord with our current conception of what that term designates. The pioneering Western translator of *Nihon shoki*, William George Aston (1841–1911), went so far as to assert that the "earlier part [of *Nihon shoki*] furnishes a very complete assortment of all the forms of the Untrue of which the human mind is capable, whether myth, legend, fable, romance, gossip, mere blundering, or downright fiction."[15] By the same token, for folklorists, the issue of "Truth"—at least as Aston understood it—or historical accuracy is at best of secondary importance, and it is much more significant that the texts preserve a wealth of the earliest known versions of folktales, some of which survived in one form or another to the present day.

Stith Thompson points out that the single most important aspect of folktales lies in their plot structure.[16] While the actual words with which the storyteller elaborates the plot depend on the linguistic skills, style, and eloquence of the individual, as long as the plot structure remains intact, the tale type remains the same in classificatory terms. Cultural context, too, plays an important role in the presentation of folktales. A plot told as a myth explaining the origin of a cultural group or some aspect of that group tends to be told in a very different vein and using very different language than if that same plot were told for the purpose of whiling away the hours as entertainment. A set of reptile-related narratives that have been transmitted in Japan over the course of more than a millennium furnish a convenient illustration of the folktale's inherent mutability. In *Nihon shoki* we find the following brief tale:

> Autumn, 7th month [supposedly, in 478 C.E.] A man of Tsutsukaha in the district of Yosa in the province of Tamba, the child of Urashima of Midzunoye, went fishing in a boat. At length he caught a large tortoise, which straightway became changed into a woman. Hereupon Urashima's child fell in love with her, and made her his wife. They went down together into the sea and reached Hōrai San, where they saw the genii. The story is in another Book.[17]

Kojiki does not incorporate the same narrative, but it does feature a lengthy story about two brothers, one a hunter, the other a fisherman. One day the brothers agree to exchange roles and the fisherman goes into the mountains to hunt, while his brother takes the fisherman's hook and goes out to sea. The hunter, however, loses his brother's fishhook. Thereupon, he meets a certain "Deity Salt-Possessor" who takes him to the underwater palace of the "Deity Ocean-Possessor." The hunter marries the Ocean-Possessor's daughter and stays with her in her father's palace for three years. Then one day, the hunter tells his father-in-law about the lost fishhook, and the sea deity assembles the fishes who are his subjects to help find it. Once it is located and returned to the hunter, he is escorted back to his own land, carrying a "tide-flowing" and a "tide-ebbing" jewel received from the sea deity, which he uses to control his brother.[18]

Both the *Nihon shoki* and the *Kojiki* narratives embody the characteristics of myth and legend, even if their written format, as well as the imperial court's sponsorship of their compilation, endowed them, at least for their limited audience of eighth-century readers, with the aura of official history. Folklore scholars generally divide folktales into a number of subcategories, prime among them, at least for our purposes, myths, legends, fairy tales, and animal tales. Among these, a myth is defined by folklorists as a traditional story associated with religious beliefs, in which the principal actors are deities, supernatural beings, or superhumans. Myths are typically origin narratives—stories explaining how certain phenomena arose. Legends, like myths, are traditional stories; however, unlike myths, legends generally focus on human beings rather than on divine subjects, and the events in them are often explicitly identified with a particular locality. The stories related in legends are told as truth, as historical fact, although these facts are not (and cannot be) authenticated. The line between myth and legend is vague, however, and both the *Nihon shoki* and the *Kojiki* tales just discussed could arguably be considered as belonging to either group. Indeed, Stith Thompson points out that none of the subcategories of folktale sustains too rigid a definition, and that they easily blend one into another.[19]

Folklorists define fairy tales as stories relating supernatural events, usually located in an imaginary environment, and in which we find magical elements and occurrences. To this day, one of the most popular Japanese fairy tales remains that of Urashima Tarō, a young fisherman who one day saves a tortoise. In gratitude, the tortoise takes Urashima to the palace of the dragon king "beyond the sea," where he meets and marries Princess Otohime. After a while the fisherman remembers his parents and prepares to go back home. Before his departure Otohime presents him with a bejeweled box (*tamatebako*) as a keepsake, but she warns him never on any account to open it. When Urashima returns to the site of his former home on land, he finds everything changed. After a time, it becomes clear that instead of just a few days, no less than three centuries have elapsed since his departure. In his despondency, he ignores Otohime's warning and opens the box, whereupon his hair turns white. Urashima grows very old in just a few moments, and finally drops dead.[20]

This fairy tale, as can easily be recognized, shares basic elements with the *Kojiki* and *Nihon shoki* accounts, yet along the way the story has received a different ending. We saw that the *Kojiki* and *Nihon shoki* versions fall into the folkloric categories of myth (because they involve divine characters) and legend (because, particularly in the *Nihon shoki* example, they relate to specific localities). The Urashima Tarō story, on the other hand, is a typical fairy tale, set in an imaginary place and filled with magical events. In short, a single tale or plot structure has over time been adapted into a variety of categories, and its style as well as content details have been adjusted in each case.

In addition to possessing the characteristics of myth, legend, and fairy tale, the above stories are at once animal tales, that is to say, traditional narratives featuring nonhuman animals as principal characters—for example, fishes, tortoises, and dragons. Even the sea deity's daughter in *Kojiki* is described as a *wani*, a term that in an eight-century context signified something akin to a dragon or a serpent, but today has come to refer to the crocodile (not an animal indigenous to Japan). Animal tales proper usually explain animal characteristics, such as how the leopard came by its spots. They are chiefly meant to entertain. By contrast, the fable is a special kind of animal tale with a didactic and moralizing character. As Stith Thompson puts it, animal tales prove that the "world of the human and the animal are never far apart."[21] Ambiguity is at the core of many of these tales, which "show animal actors in all sorts of distinctly human situations," with animals talking and acting like humans, and in which the line between human and nonhuman animals is often hard to define.[22]

ANIMAL SYMBOLISM AND SYMBOLIC ANIMALS

It is remarkable how important a role nonhuman animals—both real and imaginary—play in the symbolism of most cultures. The range of different things animals can represent as symbols is likewise vast. All of us are familiar with such examples of animal symbolism as the dove who serves as a messenger of peace, or the black cat who signals foreboding. But symbolic animals are not limited to such traditional icons, or even to actual inhabitants of the biological realm. Human societies are constantly generating new species of fantastic beings, just as they continually find new symbolic uses for existing animals.

What generally go by the name of monsters—typically, creatures with a distinctly nonhuman appearance, but with many remarkably human behavioral characteristics—furnish a ready example of the latter phenomenon. In today's mass-mediated society, animal-like monsters of an increasing variety parade before us in film, television, and in literature. Television cartoons and children's movies produced by such companies as Walt Disney offer an ongoing array of monsters and other nonbiological creatures, as do the video games so popular among adolescents. These latter-day beasts of the imagination differ from many traditional symbolic creatures in that they have been developed chiefly for entertainment purposes. The vast majority of humanity does not attribute to them any material reality, let alone fear or worship them. However, in their own way they incorporate, as well as serve to impart, a distinct set of contemporary cultural and moral lessons, just as the creatures of folktale did long ago.

A wide variety of nonhuman animals appear in traditional Japanese folktales, both real and imaginary. One of the best known of the latter type is the *tengu*. Often rendered in English as a "mountain goblin," it is conventionally imagined as a half-human, half-avian creature, and is typically depicted with wings, a long nose or beak, and (particularly in noh-theater masks) a red face. Sometimes, the *tengu* is portrayed as an evil abductor of Buddhist priests, whose minds it is said to pollute with thoughts running counter to Buddhist principles. At other times, the *tengu* is revered as a benign guardian of certain mountains, and is associated with mountain spirits (*yama no kami*) and mountain ascetics (*yamabushi*).[23] An equally conspicuous yet quirky creature of folklore is the *kappa*, an aquatic sprite or demon with a saucerlike skull filled with water from which its vital powers derive. It is commonly said to prey upon humans and other animals who approach the rivers and ponds where it makes its lair, and to rip out their livers or other organs.[24]

Somewhat more familiar to Western audiences, perhaps, is the dragon, which was introduced into Japan from China around the same time as Buddhism, in the sixth century. Continental descriptions of dragons looked and sounded to Japanese of the time very much like the native serpent-monsters who had theretofore variously been referred to as *mizuchi*, *okami*, *orochi*, *wani*, and *watatsumi*. The above indigenous categories defined serpentlike creatures in a rather loose manner, and could refer to beings ranging from water snakes to sea gods. Upon the introduction of the new reptilian icon from the continent, the Chinese character for dragon (pronounced in Sino-Japanese as *ryū*, and in Japanese as *tatsu*) was adopted specifically to refer to a dragon in the Chinese image. Nevertheless, earlier images of serpents survived in folklore, as did the preexisting designations.[25]

The example of the dragon helps illustrate the fact that folkloric serpents, both in Japan and elsewhere, bear varying degrees of resemblance to the biological animals we call snakes (or *hebi* in Japanese).[26] It is primarily for this reason that the present chapter employs the generic term "serpent," except when referring to the biological snake and some of its more straightforward representations. Although dragons may at times have been imagined in a relatively snakelike form, they might also display attributes that set them apart from the everyday snake with respect to size, shape, color, and other features. For example, the "eight-forked serpent" (*yamata no orochi*) who is slain by the culture hero (or antihero) Susanoo in *Nihon shoki* is described as extending "over a space of eight hills and eight valleys," possessing fiery eyes, and having eight tails.[27] Quite commonly, however, folktales offer little or no physical description of their serpent characters, leaving such details up to their listeners' or readers' imagination.

Besides snakes, the biological animals who appear perhaps most frequently in Japanese folktales are the fox and the *tanuki* (Lin.: *Nyctereutes procyonoides*; commonly translated as badger or raccoon-dog).[28] Both have long been viewed as crafty creatures with supernatural powers. In historical times, foxes (*kitsune*) were widely deemed capable of bewitching people, and, like many creatures of Japanese folklore, demonstrated the capacity to transform themselves at will. The fox also fulfilled a religious function as the messenger of the Shinto god Inari, and was itself sometimes regarded as a transformation of that deity.[29] By comparison, the *tanuki* was somewhat less feared in folk culture, although it was no less fond of crafty tricks and shape shifting, as the introduction to this volume has already discussed.[30] Its image may still be seen at the entrance of restaurants and other commercial establishments, often in a beckoning pose and with a set of noticeably oversized testicles.

Another recurrent biological creature in the folklore of Japan is the Japanese monkey or macaque (Lin.: *Macaca fuscata*), of whom large numbers still inhabit the archipelago. The anthropologist Emiko Ohnuki-Tierney describes the monkey as the "animal considered [by Japanese] to be most similar and therefore closest to humans," and she has explored in considerable detail its function as a scapegoat and as a symbolic "threat to the human-animal boundary." Although her claim may be overbroad even from the perspective of a folklorist, she suggests that "we can tap a significant part of the Japanese structure of meaning by examining the transformations of the meaning of the monkey."[31]

The above creatures by no means exhaust the repertory of nonhuman animals who inhabit Japanese folklore. Their much greater variety is suggested, for example, by the art historian Tijs Volker's estimate that no less than eighty-five different beings are depicted in the ornamental purse toggles known as *netsuke* alone.[32] Nevertheless, there are few animals who represent as wide a range of symbolic functions as does the serpent, and unlike most other animals it does so consistently throughout the world. In virtually all cultures, including Japan's, the serpent is recognized as a powerful symbol, even though its symbolic meanings may differ from one culture to another.[33] No doubt the single best-known example of serpent symbolism in the Western world is the biblical serpent of the Garden of Eden, yet it is far from unique in its cultural centrality. The indigenous mythology of Australia centers on the rainbow serpent, whom Aboriginals traditionally considered to be the creator of all things. The Maya and Aztec people of Central America likewise placed great stock in Quetzalcoatl, their plumed serpent god. And in Africa, abundant archaeological proof may be found of the importance of serpent symbolism in Zimbabwe.[34]

Apart from the deadly *habu* (Lin.: *Trimeresurus flavoviridis*) of Okinawa, virtually the only poisonous snake indigenous to Japan is the less-than-lethal *mamushi* (Lin.: *Agkistrodon halys*; generally translated into English as a viper or adder). Yet fear of snakes within the Japanese archipelago has always been widespread, and in fact reflects a universal phenomenon. E.O. Wilson, citing the work of biologist Balaji Mundkur and others, explains this fear as an aspect of gene-culture coevolution. The belief of Wilson and other sociobiologists is that humans, and indeed all higher primates, possess an innate fear of snakes, one whose evolutionary roots lie in the physical dangers that they pose to primates, but which has, by the same token, developed (at least among humans) into cultural fascination and metaphor.[35] Mundkur, in his groundbreaking study *The Cult of the Serpent*, dedicates an entire chapter to the question of the historical development of ophidiophobia and "the symbol-making potential latent in it."[36]

Although the fear factor certainly forms an important part of the serpent's potency as a cultural symbol, other aspects of snakes' perceived behavior and appearance clearly contribute as well. Not only are some snakes capable of poisoning and killing, but the snake's habit of occasionally shedding its skin suggests eternal life, its glare hypnotizes, and the unpredictability and seeming speed of movement of the limbless body startle.

Such characteristics can inspire awe, which in turn leads to an exaggeration of these traits in the serpent narratives that humans create. Thus, many of the serpent's symbolic functions are connected with the true behavior and physiological attributes of biological snakes only in a fairly distant way.

Whether in Japan or elsewhere, the most consistent characteristic of the serpent as a symbol is found in its ambiguity. The treachery of the snake in the Garden of Eden is made possible in a sense by this symbolic inconstancy, but it constitutes only one example. Serpents can represent both good and evil; they can be gods or demons; they are both male and female; they are associated not only with land but with water; they represent death as well as eternal life, poison and medicine, deceit and wisdom. Furthermore, as will be discussed below, the serpent provides a conspicuous example of phallic symbolism, and as such is often associated with fecundity.[37]

JAPANESE SERPENT FOLKLORE

In her *Index*, Hiroko Ikeda distinguishes five types of Japanese folktale involving conjugal liaisons between serpents and humans.[38] The unions portrayed in all of them, it will presently be argued, stand in symbolic terms for inappropriate or risky human-human relationships, with a nonhuman serpent replacing one of the implied human partners so as more effectively to convey and to emphasize the story's cautionary lessons. Ikeda's typology provides a convenient framework for surveying the tales because it permits one not only to make broader observations regarding the "serpentine spouse" tale in general, but to identify distinctions among its variants. The summary narratives and quotations below are intended to convey a representative sense of the basic plot structure and characteristics of each type of tale. It must be kept in mind that many variants exist, depending on locality, period, mode of transmission, and other factors. Indeed, Ikeda cites from twenty-one to one hundred and thirty variants for each of the tale types. While these figures are by no means exhaustive, they nevertheless offer a suggestive indication of how widespread the tales actually were.

Stork's Eggs

The tale type identified by Ikeda as "Stork's Eggs" has the fewest number of recorded variants.[39] It involves a man who promises to marry a serpent provided she will spare the life of a frog she is about to swallow. The serpent agrees, and the marriage takes place. However, after the wedding the man becomes ill. A fortuneteller—who is really the grateful frog in disguise—appears at the home and divines that the man is in need of medicinal stork's eggs. The serpent wife reverts to her original form so that she can climb with greater ease into a nearby tree where storks have built their nest. When she reaches the nest she is pecked to death by the storks, whereupon the man becomes well again.

The Japanese folk serpent can be either male or female, and some tale types—particularly those represented by the largest number of variants—are gender specific and tend to involve male serpents.[40] In the case of the "Stork's Eggs" tale type, however, it is female serpents who are in the majority, although variants featuring a male serpent do exist. In the latter cases, some adjustments are made in order to account for the asymmetries that were considered normative between human males and females within the cultural context of the story's original audiences. For instance, instead of offering himself as spouse, the man promises the serpent that he may have the man's daughter as a bride. Furthermore, the fortuneteller—or rather, the grateful animal—appears on the scene not when the bridegroom falls ill, but rather when the bride becomes pregnant. It is noteworthy that after the serpent's death, the young woman's pregnancy is miraculously terminated, relieving her of the responsibility to bear and raise the serpent's offspring. There are other tale types, however, such as those of the "Snake Wife" and the "Snake Paramour," in which bearing the offspring of a serpent is not necessarily deemed a negative development.

F. J. Daniels has remarked on a number of other aspects of gender difference in Japanese serpent folklore.[41] When one considers the five tale types to be examined here, female serpent characters are more often presented in a positive light: they more frequently act out of gratitude, for instance. They also tend to be more successful in winning over their chosen mate, even if the union does not last. Male serpents, on the other hand, are more frequently frustrated in their efforts to enter into a relationship. This is particularly the case in tales of a more recent date. Serpent deities in such early texts as *Kojiki* and *Nihon shoki* generally manage to maintain their intimacy with a human at least for a while, although secrecy is required in order for the relationship to endure. Even gods, it would seem, are not permanently able to overcome the problems associated with "otherness."

Grateful Crabs

The tale type labeled "Grateful Crabs" in Ikeda's *Index* may be seen in many respects as a variation on the previous plot. The gender of the serpent in this case is usually male, and the grateful animal generally a crab rather than a frog.[42] The early ninth-century tale collection *Nihon ryōiki* (Strange and miraculous stories of Japan), compiled by the monk Kyōkai (dates uncertain) offers two heavily Buddhist-infused variants of the tale. One of them appears under the title "On the Immediate Reward of Being Saved by Crabs for Saving the Lives of Crabs and a Frog."[43]

In it we find the story of a devoutly observant woman. At the outset of the tale, she saves eight crabs from some cowherds who are about to roast and eat them.

> Afterwards she was in the mountain and saw a large snake swallowing a big toad. She implored the large snake, "Please set this frog free for my sake, and I will give you many offerings." The snake did not respond. Then, she collected more offerings and prayed, saying, "I will consecrate you as a kami [i.e., a deity]. Please give it to me." Still without answering, the snake continued to swallow the toad. Again she pleaded, "I will become your wife in exchange for this toad. I implore you to release it to me." Raising its head high, the snake listened and stared at her face, then disgorged the toad. The woman made a promise to the snake, saying, "Come to me in seven days."[44]

When a holy man, "Most Venerable Gyōgi," hears the woman's plight, he advises her to "just keep steadfast faith in the Three Treasures."[45] She follows his advice, locking herself in her house and praying, even as she hears the serpent outside knocking on the walls with its tail, searching for a way in. The serpent finally succeeds in tearing a hole in the thatched roof, but once inside, it is cut to pieces by the eight crabs who had been saved by the woman at the tale's beginning.

Several of the motifs visible in the "Stork's Eggs" tale type may be recognized here as well. Once more, we find a human making a serpent a generous offer in return for the life of another, nonhuman creature. Significantly, however, in the case of "Grateful Crabs," the human is able to avoid consummation of the liaison—a pattern that we will shortly see again in the "Snake Husband Killed" tale type. A further shared motif is that of the trickster. In "Stork's Eggs," the disguised frog tricks the serpent into behavior that will lead to its death. In "Grateful Crabs," the trickster element is somewhat weaker, although not entirely absent. The woman has promised herself in good faith—if no doubt unwisely—to the serpent. Nevertheless, she hides herself in her house when the serpent comes to claim her, rather than welcoming him, and thus maneuvers her prospective spouse, albeit perhaps unwittingly, into putting himself at the mercy of the crabs' claws. The other factor that leads to the serpent's demise is, of course, the intervention of the holy man, and implicitly of the Buddhist law as accessed through prayer, a twist that accords well with the religious coloring of Kyōkai's collection as a whole.

The central motif in both the above tale types is that of the grateful animal. As Hoyt Long has noted in the preceding chapter, the Buddhist doctrine of *hōon* or *ongaeshi*—both roughly meaning gratitude or the repayment of favors—was a motif often expressed through nonhuman-animal characters in tale literature. As the *Nihon ryōiki* version of the "Grateful Crabs" tale puts it, rhetorically: "[E]ven an insect which has no means of attaining enlightenment returns a favor. How can a man ever forget kindness he has received?"[46] Nevertheless, although the "Stork's Eggs" and the "Grateful Crabs" tale types conform to the general pattern of the grateful-animal tale, they also complicate that motif in certain respects. In it simplest variation, the basic plot of the grateful-animal tale requires only two characters, of two different species: a human being who performs an act of kindness, and a nonhuman creature (whether deer, turtle, frog, bird, or something else) who benefits from that favor and later repays it. The "Stork's Eggs" and "Grateful Crabs" tale types, significantly, introduce another nonhuman actor centrally into the picture in the figure of the serpent.[47]

Ironically, the gratitude of the animal who has received a favor results, in both tale types, in the death of another sentient being, namely, the serpent who in one way or another poses a threat to the human character. In other words, the act of repaying kindness, encouraged by the Buddhist doctrine of *hōon*, leads, seemingly without censure, to the contravention of another Buddhist principle, that which admonishes the taking of sentient life in any form. To quote the *Bonmyōkyō* sutra: "all the living beings of the six *gāti* [realms of existence] are our parents, and if we kill them, we kill our parents and also our former bodies."[48] Indeed, it was the act of liberating an animal life (*hōjō*), rather than allowing its destruction, that initiated the story's circle of gratitude in the first place. Does the life of a harmful serpent, one is tempted to ask, count for less in the cosmic hierarchy and in the karmic cycle than that of a grateful crab or frog?

The question allows of no simple answer. For one thing, the apparent contradiction in the tale's moral stance regarding the sparing of animal life may be, at least in part, an effect of the various narrative transformations and conceptual accretions that characterize folktales in general, as texts that have been transmitted, and continually adapted, over the course of centuries. Indeed, when one strips away the Buddhist elements of gratitude and respect for sentient beings that Kyōkai has layered onto his rendering of the "Grateful Crabs" tale, one is left with a much simpler narrative centering around a human's quelling, through trickery, of a menacing serpent foe. The same is likewise true of the "Stork's Eggs" tale type. It is possible that the original form of both tales followed the simpler foe-quelling pattern, and that later Buddhist-inflected versions retain some of the earlier elements. It should be noted, furthermore, that Buddhist lore itself is replete with ambivalent references to serpents, not only as benevolent creatures and indeed as protectors of the faith (one need only think of the *naga*, or hooded cobra, sheltering the Buddha while meditating under the *bo* tree), but as spiteful spirits from whom humans need to seek protection by means of charms—metal being particularly effective—or through reciting mantras to ward off any harm that serpents might potentially cause. [49] Perhaps ophidiophobia and the "symbol-making potential latent in it" places the serpent at a disadvantage vis-à-vis other nonhuman creatures in the human cultural imagination. In the final analysis, it appears that the serpents of tale literature have a distinct tendency to be treated at times as somehow less, or other, than fully animal, even as they play an important role in policing the boundaries of appropriate human behavior.

Snake Wife

In the tale type Ikeda calls the "Snake Wife," the killing of the serpent character is averted by having the creature bring harm upon itself.[50] The serpent here invariably appears as a beautiful woman who comes to a certain man's house and insists on becoming his wife. The marriage is a happy one—or so it seems—and soon the woman finds herself pregnant. When the time comes to deliver the child, the woman follows customary practice and ensconces herself in a parturition hut, but not until she has made her husband promise not to look at her while she is inside. However, the husband is too full of curiosity to keep his word, and when he peeps into the hut he sees a large serpent coiled around a baby. Once the woman finally emerges from the hut she is very sad and tells her husband that she cannot stay with him now that he knows her true form. She leaves the infant with its father and gives him one of her eyeballs to nourish the child. The eyeball soon gets lost, however, and, not knowing what to do, the man goes to the pond where his former wife resides in order to ask for her help.[51] She entrusts him with her second eyeball, but exacts from him a promise to toll a bell for her regularly so that she will still be able to tell night from day despite her blindness.[52]

Fanny Hagin Mayer, the early disciple of Yanagita, relates a more recent variant of this tale. No significant differences occur in the Mayer variant between the arrival of the woman and the scene in which she gives up her second eyeball and asks for the bell to be rung. Thereupon, however, according to Mayer's version:

> The father realized how helpless his great snake wife was now. He placed a bell in the mountain temple by the bank of the pond. He struck it six times at dawn and six times at sunset to let her know the time. Bōtarō [the child] gradually grew up, nourished by the eyeball. He heard that his mother was in the pond. One day he went to its bank and called, "Bōtarō's mother, please come out! Bōtarō's mother, please come out!"
>
> His mother came out then in her human form. She could not see her son because she was blind, and she had to feel his face to know it was he. He put her on his back and took her home. There he built her a room and gave her whatever she wanted to eat every day. He was a good son to her.[53]

Mayer's variant, which does not appear in Ikeda's typology, was recorded some time in the early twentieth century.[54] Some of its elements surely represent the accretion of motifs that are historically recent, at least from the folklorist's perspective. The last paragraph, for example, seems to reflect, as well as to reinforce, Confucian moral teachings about the virtue of filial piety. Although Confucianism was not previously unknown in Japan, it widely permeated popular culture only in the Tokugawa period, when it received the official patronage of the early-modern shogunate. The virtue of filial duty continued to be emphasized also under the civic ideology promoted by the late nineteenth- and early twentieth-century imperial state. This motif of the "good son" would thus seem to be a Tokugawa or even later accretion. It is absent in variants of an earlier date, which generally end when the child is still an infant and which allocate him no further role in the plot.

Snake Paramour

"Snake Paramour" is one of the best-known folktales in Japan, and possesses many variants. Seki Keigo, in an article published in 1940, counted sixty-seven different versions, while Ikeda's *Index* includes no less than a hundred.[55] Depending on the variant, the serpent in this tale type may represent either good or evil. In brief, the tale relates the story of a young woman who is secretly visited every night by an anonymous lover who disappears in the morning before dawn and never shows himself by daylight. When the young woman finds herself pregnant, someone—in most accounts, her mother—advises her to pin a threaded needle into the suitor's robe when he leaves. The next morning they find that the thread leads through a small hole in the door, out of the house, and into a pond, grove, or other natural habitation. Here a conversation is overheard between a serpent, on the verge of death because of iron poisoning, and his mother, who scolds him for getting involved with a human being at the cost of his life. The serpent son replies that he is content with the situation since the young woman is carrying his offspring. However, the mother explains that human beings are clever enough to know methods of preventing serpent-babies from being born, such as imbibing certain drinks or taking special baths, usually on specific festival days. The tale often ends with the young woman ridding herself of the unwanted fetus by precisely such means.

In some variants of the tale, the liaison actually produces a child. The descendants of such human-serpent unions, according to the latter renderings, are apt to bear distinguishing physical characteristics, such as scales on their backs or elsewhere on their bodies.[56] In its *Kojiki* version, the earliest recorded, the tale is told as the story of the birth of the divine child Ōtataneko during the reign of the emperor Sujin.[57] Whereas the *Nihon shoki* account does not concern itself with Ōtataneko's birth, it does record that he was later called upon to assist in pacifying the country through worship of his father, whom it identifies as the deity Ōmononushi.[58] Both *Kojiki* and *Nihon shoki* relate another tale involving Ōmononushi in which the latter deity visits his wife, Yamato-toto-hime, only at night. When she asks him to stay until daybreak so that she might have a glimpse of him, he instructs her to look into her toilet-box on the following morning. When she does so, she is startled to discover a comely little snake curled up in the toilet-box, whereupon she emits a shriek. The snake—her husband—then changes into human form and tells her that her behavior has disgraced him, and that he now can no longer stay with her. After his departure, Yamato-toto-hime, overcome by shame, commits suicide.

These tales from *Kojiki* and *Nihon shoki* highlight yet another factor related to Japanese serpent symbolism, namely, its deep religious associations. A serpent-worshipping tradition existed throughout known history in Japan, and Ōmononushi was one of Japan's earliest-known serpent deities. Japanese widely believed snakes to possess eternal life, because of their habit of shedding their skin and thus appearing rejuvenated. They were also regarded as guardians of the rice paddy, in part because of their fondness for consuming mice and other pests, and were venerated over the centuries by farmers. The religious associations of serpents may be found in both Shinto and Buddhist contexts. On visiting Shinto shrines even today, one occasionally comes across devotees of serpent-gods, although many Shinto priests tend to disapprove of the practice. Alternatively, serpents served as the reincarnation of Buddhist divinities, or functioned as their messengers. For example, specifically Buddhist associations are quite pronounced in certain variants of the preceding "Snake Wife" tale type that account for the location of a particular temple bell.

In Japanese folk culture, as elsewhere, serpents also function as potent symbols of fertility. This characteristic appears to have arisen not only from their aforementioned associations with rejuvenation and with agriculture, but from snakes' conspicuously phallic appearance. Strongly phallic depictions of snakes may be found even today in Japan's rural areas, often sitting alongside the fields. Their cultural association with fecundity offers one reason that serpents may have provided a popular motif in folktales concerning human conjugal relations. Nevertheless, serpent symbolism in folklore is seldom purely sexual, and the emphasis of the tales lies on the consequences of inappropriate reproductive liaisons in a social sense, and not on specific sexual acts.

Snake Husband Killed

According to Ikeda's *Index*, "Snake Husband Killed" is the serpent-mate tale type that has the greatest number of variants.[59] Several motifs already encountered reappear in this type, including a farmer rashly promising his daughter in marriage to a serpent. Depending on the variant, a number of different things may subsequently occur. Most commonly, the liaison is never consummated because the prospective bride tricks her serpent mate-to-be into courting his own demise. For example, in one particular variant, the girl requests a dowry of one thousand needles and one thousand gourds. When she arrives at the pond where the serpent lives, she asks him to do her one favor before she can join him. She requests that he try to sink the gourds and make the needles float.[60] While the serpent is busy attempting this impossible task, the girl flees, and the suitor ultimately dies of exhaustion.

The didacticism of this tale type focuses less on Buddhist notions of gratitude, or on Confucian ideas of filial piety, than on such practical issues as the importance of due reflection before one speaks or acts. What might have happened, the listener or reader cannot help but wonder, had the serpent been able to fulfill the girl's request? The implicit answer, of course, is a liaison between two socially inappropriate partners, that is to say, the very theme that all five tale types above share in common, and implicitly warn their audiences against. The following section will draw some general conclusions about the social lessons that serpent-spouse tales convey.

THE MORAL OF THE STORY

The foregoing discussion has highlighted the substantial role played by both real and imaginary animals in the world's folklore, Japan standing in this respect as no exception. Whether serpents or other creatures, nonhuman animals are beings familiar enough to people to make for intelligible and engaging storytelling, but at the same time different enough to be endowed with a strong symbolic potency.[61] This symbolism sows a deeper meaning between the lines of the tales, and often functions in a didactic way. Not only entertainment value but also a heavy element of moral instruction thus characterizes Japanese folktales about serpent spouses, as it does the folkloric genres of fable and animal tale more generally. As we have seen, the narrative in each of the five tale types analyzed above centers around a liaison—or in some cases a thwarted attempt to form a liaison—between a human and a serpent character. Yet in terms of didactic function, the serpent character may be read more accurately as a symbolic representation of another human or, more specifically, a human mate who is unsuitable for partnership from the point of view of prevailing social and communal norms.

At the most basic level, serpent-spouse tales reinforce a normative understanding that social alliances, and especially conjugal ones, must take place between members of the same species. Often, an awareness of this taboo forms an integral part of the tales' plot structure: it implicitly motivates both the reluctance of many of the human characters to enter into a marriage across species lines, and the perceived need of the serpent characters to disguise themselves in human form. Yet it is unlikely that the primary purpose of such tales was to discourage sexual relations between humans and nonhuman animals per se. Indeed, a concern for what Europeans variously called "bestiality" or "sodomy" rarely surfaces in Japanese cultural texts until the nineteenth or twentieth century. Rather, the taboo against interspecies liaisons functions, in the context of the serpent-spouse folktale, to convey the lesson that human-human unions, too, must be formed in accordance with various communal and social norms, and that ill-advised pairings bear significant social consequences. Humans are replaced within the narrative with nonhuman animals, in this case serpents, in order to permit the tale's listeners to distance themselves more easily from the situation in question, thus allowing them to observe and to absorb its lessons with less resistance and in an entertaining fashion.

Across the corpus of serpent-spouse tales, the particular forms of normative transgression that the relations between the partners represent are numerous and varied, nor do they break down neatly according to tale type. Nevertheless, some general observations can be made. For example, one of the central lessons that many of the tales serve to reinforce is a normative understanding that a marked disparity in social origin or in individual characteristics between potential mates can lead to unfortunate results. The story of "Snake Husband Killed," for example, not only admonishes implicitly against trying to marry outside one's social category, but also suggests, arguably, that a woman clever enough to engineer her would-be husband's demise would hardly be likely to make a good wife in the first place. Similarly, while Urashima Tarō may have enjoyed his luxurious sojourn in the undersea palace of his reptilian bride, it is equally significant that the storyteller returns him ultimately to his home on dry land, and that his fate there is hardly enviable.

The business of mate selection within the tales, as well as among their audience, thus involves issues of congruity and compatibility, not only of individuals but of the households to which they belong. Evaluation of these criteria in actual social practice becomes further complicated when a potential spouse hails from a different locality, as is often the case in an exogamous society. The inherent risks of incorporating into one's kinship network an unfamiliar outsider, and the importance of verifying his or her origins, serve as an important theme in many folktales of the serpent-spouse variety. Here, the foreignness of the potential mate in terms of community membership takes the symbolic form of a creature belonging to a different species, in this case one whose alien nature is magnified by an underlying substratum of ophidiophobia. To a certain extent, the fear that it might in fact be a serpent who would enter undetected through the conjugal door was embedded not only in the plot of certain folktales, but metaphorically in the thoughts of many humans facing the prospect of marriage, particularly in an age where social information did not travel easily from one community to another.

Some of the tales hint further at a practice called *yobai*, which remained in existence, particularly in some rural regions, well into the twentieth century. *Yobai*, often translated rather ungracefully into English as night-crawling, was for centuries a commonly accepted practice whereby a young man would visit a prospective marital partner at night in the form of a trial marriage. Since such a relationship was unofficial and unacknowledged, it could be broken off by either partner at any time. In many cases, the liaison would eventually be recognized, particularly once the young woman became pregnant, as occurs in the example of the "Snake Paramour." The nightly visits by a male suitor of unknown provenance do not become a problem until the young woman finds herself pregnant with his offspring and societal norms demand that the suitability of the partner be verified.

Finally, serpent-spouse tales provided concrete—if intentionally exaggerated—examples of the importance of careful scrutiny and honest disclosure in negotiating social alliances. On the one hand, the misfortunes of the human spouse, or intended spouse, serve as a warning of the dangers of entering into a relationship without properly informing oneself of the partner's credentials. On the other hand, the experiences of the serpent, too, have lessons to teach. Those who are tempted to pretend to be what they are not in order to win a preferred partner are put on notice that such actions have consequences, that the truth will come out, and that one will not escape unscathed from such behavior. No matter how dutiful a parent, few would envy the fate of the abandoned and blind serpent dwelling in a pond.

In the end, folktales are notoriously oblique. They do not spell out their message or moral code explicitly, but refer to it through symbolism and suggestion. That lesson is culturally determined, and understanding it requires familiarity on the part of the audience with the cultural background from which the tale derives. At the same time, because the tale is not explicit with regard to the lesson it conveys, there is room for the message or code to evolve, as we have seen reflected in the abundance of variants of the tale types discussed in this chapter. This evolution may occur in the style in which the tale is presented, for example, whether it is a fairy tale for children or a fable for adults. It also registers itself in the gradual change of encoded norms over time. Societal issues that were important in the eighth century did not necessarily have the same relevance in the nineteenth century, and yet a variant form of a tale already presented in *Kojiki* could nonetheless still function quite suitably as a vehicle for nineteenth- and twentieth-century concerns. In the inherent mutability of the folktale lay its remarkable utility as a bearer of social knowledge, and the secret of its longevity.

NOTES

1. Masaharu Anesaki, "Japanese Mythology," in *The Mythology of All Races*, ed. Louis Herbert Gray, 13 vols. (1916–1932; reprint, New York: Cooper Square, 1964), 8: 331.

2. *The Oxford American Dictionary of Current English* (New York: Oxford University Press, 1999), 277. Definitions 1 a) and 1 b).

3. Paul Shepard, *The Others: How Animals Made Us Human* (Washington, D.C.: Island, 1996), 7.

4. See http://afsnet.org/aboutfolklore/aboutFL.cfm.

5. "Folklore," in *Funk and Wagnall's Standard Dictionary of Folklore, Mythology, and Legend*, ed. Maria Leach (San Francisco: Harper and Row, 1984), 398–403.

6. J. Victor Koshmann, "Introduction," in *International Perspectives on Yanagita Kunio and Japanese Folklore Studies*, ed. J. Victor Koschmann, Ōiwa Keibō, and Yamashita Shinji, Cornell University East Asia Papers, no. 37 (Ithaca, N.Y.: Cornell University, China-Japan Program, 1985), 1.

7. Stith Thompson, *The Folktale* (Berkeley: University of California Press, 1977), 416.

8. Ibid.

9. Kunio Yanagita, *The Yanagita Kunio Guide to the Japanese Folk Tale,* trans. and ed. Fanny Hagin Mayer (Bloomington: Indiana University Press, 1986).

10. Antti Aarne and Stith Thompson, *The Types of the Folk-Tale: A Classification and Bibliography*, 2nd rev. ed., FF Communications, no. 3 (Helsinki: Suomalainen Tiedeakatemia, 1964).

11. Stith Thompson, *Motif-Index of Folk-Literature: A Classification of Narrative Elements in Folktales, Ballads, Myths, Fables, Mediaeval Romances, Exempla, Fabliaux, Jest-Books, and Local Legends,* rev. ed. (Bloomington: Indiana University Press, 1955).

12. Seki Keigo, *Nihon mukashibanashi shūsei,* 6 vols. (Tokyo: Kadokawa Shoten, 1950–1958). See also Keigo Seki, "Types of Japanese Folktales," *Asian Folklore Studies* 25 (1966): 1–220.

13. Hiroko Ikeda, *A Type and Motif Index of Japanese Folk Literature,* FF Communications, no. 209 (Helsinki: Suomalainen Tiedeakatemia, 1971).

14. Herbert Passin, *Society and Education in Japan* (New York: Kodansha International, 1982), 56–57; J. Marshall Unger, *Literacy and Script Reform in Occupation Japan: Reading Between the Lines* (New York: Oxford University Press, 1996), 25. To illustrate his point about multilayered literacy (and illiteracy), Unger cites a study by Richard Rubinger on the statistics of a literacy test conducted among all males of Tokiwa village in Nagano prefecture in 1881. Unger concludes that if "literacy is defined as the ability to read at least ordinary materials and fill out simple forms," male literacy in this village in the 1870s came to a mere 8 percent.

15. W. G. Aston, trans., *Nihongi: Chronicles of Japan from the Earliest Times to A.D. 697* (1896; reprint, Rutland, Vt.: Tuttle, 1972), xv.

16. Thompson, *Folktale,* 10.

17. Aston, *Nihongi,* 368.

18. Basil Hall Chamberlain, trans., *The Kojiki: Records of Ancient Matters* (1882; reprint, Rutland, Vt.: Tuttle, 1981), 145–54. For another rendering, see Donald L. Philippi, *Kojiki* (Princeton: Princeton University Press, 1969), 148–55.

19. Thompson, *Folktale,* 10.

20. Although a large number of variants of this tale exist, the outline given here is representative of the core plot shared by most of them. For an English-language version (one of many that are available), see Yei Theodora Ozaki, *The Japanese Fairy Book* (Rutland, Vt: Tuttle, 1970), 26–42.

21. Thompson, *Folktale,* 217.

22. Ibid.

23. As early as 1908, the Dutch scholar M. W. de Visser published a detailed study of "The *Tengu*" in *Transactions of the Asiatic Society of Japan* 36, pt. 2 (1908): 25–99. Carmen Blacker deals memorably with *tengu* abduction stories in her classic *The Catalpa Bow: A Study of Shamanic Practices in Japan* (London: Allen and Unwin, 1975), 181–85.

24. The *kappa* has received substantial scholarly attention. An interesting recent treatment of the subject, in both its traditional and its modern-day incarnations, may be found in Michael Dylan Foster, "The Metamorphosis of the Kappa: Transformation of Folklore to Folklorism in Japan," *Asian Folklore Studies* 57 (1998): 1–24.

25. M. W. de Visser, *The Dragon in China and Japan* (Amsterdam: Johannes Mueller, 1913).

26. For a recent cross-cultural study of dragon lore, see David E. Jones, *An*

Instinct for Dragons (New York: Routledge, 2000).

27. Aston, *Nihongi*, 53. Susanoo's feat has been compared with dragon-slaying tales from other cultures, such as the myth of Perseus and Andromeda and the Saint George legend.

28. M. W. de Visser's "The Fox and the Badger in Japanese Folklore" (*Transactions of the Asiatic Society of Japan* 36, pt. 3 [1908]: 1–159) is one of the earliest, and remains one of the most comprehensive, Western-language studies of folklore surrounding both of these animals.

29. For a useful study of the Inari cult, see Karen A. Smyers, *The Fox and the Jewel: Shared and Private Meanings in Contemporary Japanese Inari Worship* (Honolulu: University of Hawaii Press, 1999).

30. On *tanuki* folklore, see U. A. Casal, "The Goblin Fox and Badger and Other Witch Animals of Japan," *Asian Folklore Studies* 18 (1959): 1–93; Violet H. Harada, "The Badger in Japanese Folklore," *Asian Folklore Studies* 35 (1976): 1–6; de Visser, "The Fox and the Badger."

31. Emiko Ohnuki-Tierney, *The Monkey as Mirror: Symbolic Transformation in Japanese History and Ritual* (Princeton: Princeton University Press, 1987), 6–7.

32. T. Volker, *The Animal in Far Eastern Art and Especially in the Art of the Japanese Netsuke, with References to Chinese Origins, Traditions, Legends, and Art* (Leiden: Brill, 1975).

33. On serpent symbolism in Japan, I have found particularly useful the following works: Abe Shinji, *Hebigami denshōron josetsu* (Tokyo: Dentō to Gendaisha, 1981); Ōmori Shirō, *Yamata no orochi* (Tokyo: Gakuseisha, 1970); Takada Mamoru, *Onna to hebi: Hyōchō no Edo bungakushi* (Tokyo: Chikuma Shobō, 1999); Yoshino Hiroko, *Hebi: Nihon no hebi shinkō* (Tokyo: Hōsei Daigaku Shuppankyoku, 1979).

34. On the Aboriginal rainbow serpent, see, for example, Helen F. McKay, "Lumerai, the Mother Snake: A Rainbow Serpent Creation Story from the Northern Territory," in *Gadi Mirrabooka: Australian Aboriginal Tales from the Dreaming*, ed. Helen F. McKay (Englewood, Colo.: Libraries Unlimited, 2001), 41–42. Neil Baldwin dedicates an entire volume to the various incarnations of Quetzalcoatl in his *Legends of the Plumed Serpent: Biography of a Mexican God* (New York: Public Affairs, 1998). On the Zimbabwean archeological findings, see Thomas N. Huffman, *Snakes and Crocodiles: Power and Symbolism in Ancient Zimbabwe* (Johannesburg: Witwatersrand University Press, 1996).

35. E. O. Wilson, *Consilience: The Unity of Knowledge* (New York: Knopf, 1998), 78–79.

36. Balaji Mundkur, *The Cult of the Serpent: An Interdisciplinary Survey of Its Manifestations and Origins* (Albany: State University of New York Press, 1983), 209–54 (the quotation appears on p. 254).

37. I have relied most heavily on two studies in my thinking about the cross-cultural aspects of serpents and their symbolic meanings. One is Balaji Mundkur's work cited in the preceding note. The other is Hans Egli, *Das Schlangensymbol: Geschichte, Maerchen, Mythos* (Olten, Switzerland: Walter-Verlag, 1982). Both volumes adopt an interdisciplinary approach and are broad in geographic scope but devote relatively little attention to Japan's serpent folklore.

38. The Aarne-Thompson numbers for Ikeda's five types are 312B (Snake Husband Killed; *Hebi muko*), 411A (Stork's Eggs; *Kō-no-tori no tamago*), 411B (Grate-

ful Crabs; *Kani hōon* or *Kanima dera*), 411C (Snake Paramour; *Miwayama*), and 413C (Snake Wife; *Hebi nyōbō*).

39. Ikeda, *Type and Motif Index*, 102.

40. F. J. Daniels comments on gender difference in Japanese serpent folklore in "Snakes as Wives and Lovers in Japanese Myth, Legend, and Folk-Tale," *Japan Society of London Bulletin* 4, no. 20 (February 1975): 19–20.

41. Ibid.

42. Ikeda, *Type and Motif Index*, 102–3.

43. I have adopted the title of the story from Kyoko Motomochi Nakamura, trans., *Miraculous Stories from the Japanese Buddhist Tradition: The* Nihon Ryōiki *of the Monk Kyōkai* (Richmond, U.K.: Curzon, 1997), 176–78. The original version may be found in *Nihon ryōiki*, vol. 30 of *Shin Nihon koten bungaku taikei*, ed. Izumoji Osamu (Tokyo: Iwanami Shoten, 1996), 79–80. The work is generally referred to by its abbreviated title; the full title is *Nihonkoku genpō zen'aku ryōiki* (Strange and miraculous Japanese stories of revelation, retribution, good, and evil). Subsequent quotations are from Nakamura. For another variant of the story in the same collection, see Kyōkai, *Nihon ryōiki*, 74–75; Nakamura, *Miraculous Stories*, 171–73.

44. Nakamura, *Miraculous Stories*, 177.

45. The Three Treasures of Buddhism are the Buddha, the Buddhist law (*dharma*), and the monastic community (*saṃgha*). The character of Gyōgi is based on an actual historical figure, a monk of the Hossō sect of Buddhism, who lived from 668 to 749.

46. Nakamura, *Miraculous Stories*, 178.

47. In the case of "Stork's Eggs," there is a third nonhuman actor, namely, the stork, but this figure's actions bear relatively little moral weight in the story.

48. M. W. de Visser, *Ancient Buddhism in Japan: Sūtras and Ceremonies in Use in the Seventh and Eighth Centuries A.D. and Their History in Later Times*, 2 vols. (Leiden: Brill, 1935), 1: 198.

49. See M. W. de Visser, "The Snake in Japanese Superstition," in *Mitteilungen des Seminars fuer Orientalische Sprachen zu Berlin, Erste Abteilung, Ostasiatische Studien* 14 (1911): 267–322 (especially p. 317).

50. Ikeda, *Type and Motif Index*, 106–7.

51. Even today, various communities claim that their local pond was the home of the serpent from this tale.

52. Another tale involving a serpent woman in association with a temple bell is the legend of Dōjōji temple. The plot of this legend also fits the human-serpent liaison pattern. It is particularly famous in its noh-theater interpretation, which is still regularly performed. In it, a young woman has set her sights on a young Buddhist priest. He is not responsive to her advances, and in fact flees her pursuit, while her rage over being thus slighted transforms her into a huge serpent. The priest hides under a temple bell at Dōjōji temple in Wakayama prefecture, but the serpent woman coils herself around the bell and turns it white hot with the heat of her fury before disappearing into a nearby pond. When the bell is later lifted, nothing is left of the young priest but his ashes. The tale is told in the context of a larger story about the history of the erection of a new bell at the Dōjōji temple. For a translation of the noh play, see Kanze Kojirō Nobumitsu, "Dōjōji," in *Twenty Plays of the Nō Theatre*, ed. and trans. Donald Keene (New York: Columbia University Press, 1970), 237–52.

53. Fanny Hagin Mayer, *Ancient Tales in Modern Japan: An Anthology of Japanese Folk Tales* (Bloomington: Indiana University Press, 1984), 37.

54. Mayer indicates (ibid., 37) that the variant in question was collected by Yanagita's collaborator Sasaki Kizen (1886–1933) in Esashi county, Iwate prefecture. A precise recording date is not provided, but the variant is included in Sasaki's 1931 collection *Kikimimi sōshi* (Tokyo: Sangensha), 182–86.

55. Ikeda, *Type and Motif Index*, 103–4; Seki Keigo, "Hebi mukoiri dan no bunpu," *Minzokugaku kenkyū* 6, no. 4 (December 1940): 1–34.

56. This belief has lasted into quite recent times. While working as a Community Analyst at the Manzanar War Relocation Center in California during the early 1940s, the anthropologist Morris Opler (1907–1996) interviewed interned Japanese Americans who told him about families or individuals they knew—or had heard of—who "had power over snakes" and reportedly could be recognized by the scales on their bodies. See Moriss Edward Opler, "Japanese Folk Belief Concerning the Snake," *Southwestern Journal of Anthropology* 1 (1945): 249–59.

57. Chamberlain, *Kojiki*, 218–19 (Philippi, *Kojiki*, 203–4). According to legend, Sujin reigned from 97 to 30 B.C.E.

58. Aston, *Nihongi*, 152–54.

59. Ikeda, *Type and Motif Index*, 74–75.

60. The gourd motif in this example appears as early as the eighth-century *Nihon shoki*, although not in connection with a human-serpent liaison. See Aston, *Nihongi*, 298–99.

61. Boria Sax makes the same observation in the context of another animal when he writes: "The fox is human enough to inspire a limited degree of identification. At the same time, it is enough of an animal to create a psychic distance, thus removing the action from the realm of every day." See Boria Sax, *The Parliament of Animals: Anecdotes and Legends from Books of Natural History, 1775-1900* (New York: Pace University Press, 1992), 6.

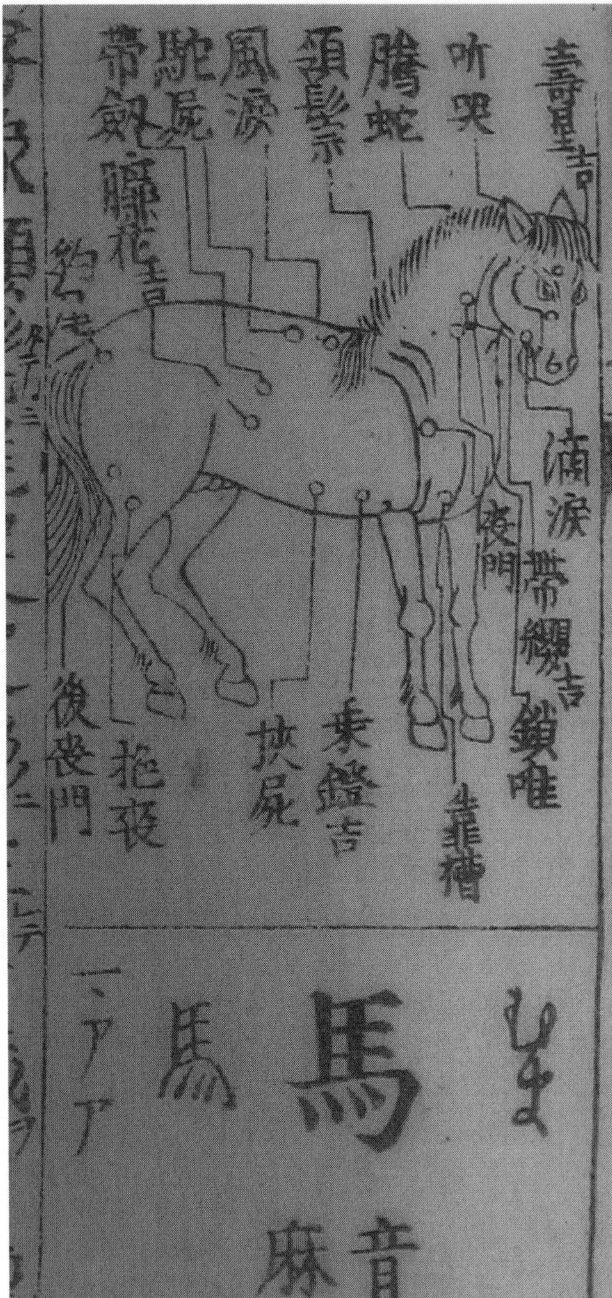

From *Wakan sansai zue*. Courtesy of the C. V. Starr East Asian Library, Columbia University.

CHAPTER THREE

The Swift Horses of Nukanobu: Bridging the Frontiers of Medieval Japan

Alexander Bay

During Japan's classical and medieval periods, between the seventh and the sixteenth centuries, the cold and rugged region in the north of the provinces of Mutsu and Dewa, referred to at the time as Kita Ōu, constituted the vast frontier land of Honshu, Japan's main island.[1] Throughout these periods, the region was politically and culturally distinct from south-central Japan, or the Yamato core. Linked to the Eurasian continent by extensive seaborne trade routes, Kita Ōu was part of the transmarine world of Northeast Asia, which also encompassed Ezo (modern Hokkaido), Karafuto (Sakhalin), and the Amur River Basin on the Asian mainland. The peoples living in Kita Ōu participated in seaborne trade networks, exchanging goods with various continental peoples across ethnic and political lines.[2] Archaeological remains of high-quality Chinese porcelain, for example, dating from the medieval period, have been unearthed in Aomori prefecture and southern Hokkaido, revealing a regional economy dependent on trade with Chinese posts in Northeast Asia.[3] The establishment of such trade routes allowed Kita Ōu to provide Yamato elites with a number of important commodities, such as horses, hawks, salmon, kelp (*konbu*), and the skins of sea otters, marine mammals not native to Japan proper.[4] It also dictated that northeastern Honshu would maintain a distinct culture and economy, a world apart from the Sinocentric order concurrently developing in the Yamato core.

Such circumstances have led some scholars to argue that Japan's far northeast should not be considered part of the Yamato polity, but rather as part of a Northeast Asian transmarine cultural sphere. Indeed, the social and economic practices of horse farming, iron working, and seaborne trading in Kita Ōu had more in common with transmarine Northeast Asia than they did with Yamato society, which was centered increasingly on paddy-based cereal cultivation and organized according to Confucian humanistic ideals.[5] Just as deer and the human practices surrounding them, discussed in chapter 1, helped to define the nature of civility for seventh- and eighth-century Yamato elites, the multispecies activity of horse farming served as an important aspect of the far northeast's cultural identity throughout Japan's medieval period.

Cultural identity proved critical in Kita Ōu because the region was not separated from the Yamato polity by any natural or ethnic boundaries. For this reason, medieval Kita Ōu should be seen as a frontier zone, a region of integration between distinct cultural and political worlds. That is to say, the far northeast spawned its own culture by incorporating various communities of peoples and their practices, as well as nonhuman actors. It did not necessarily embrace, and sometimes even rejected, both the Sinocentric social and political institutions prevalent in Yamato Japan and the transmarine Northeast Asian culture to its north.

The present chapter stresses two points. The first is that historians need to develop a more nuanced sense of space in medieval Japanese history and that, consequently, Kita Ōu should be seen as a frontier culture, not a line that marked the northernmost borders of the Yamato polity. To use the language of recent geographers, the region is best understood as a "zone of integration" between Yamato Japan and transmarine Northeast Asia. This chapter pays special attention to the role that horses played in the construction of the far northeast's frontier culture. Perhaps even more than the human inhabitants of Kita Ōu, horses served as "bridging figures," creatures that galloped between the cultural spheres of Kita Ōu and Yamato Japan.[6] Testimony to this fact may be found in the archipelago-wide celebration of the "swift horses of Nukanobu" throughout the classical and medieval periods.

A second point is that Ōu remained a frontier zone—neither Yamato Japan nor transmarine Northeast Asia—until fully colonized (not reintegrated or reunited) by the armies of Toyotomi Hideyoshi (1537–1598) in the late sixteenth century. Only when the colonizing warlord Hideyoshi ordered his forces into the northeast in 1591, inscribing his authority onto the region politically and culturally, did Kita Ōu become truly integrated into the polity of south-central Japan. Significantly, it was by cutting the region off from its traditional seaborne trade routes, and hence the ability to conduct commerce with Northeast Asia, that Hideyoshi was able to deny the region's inhabitants the ability to maintain their independence from the political and cultural hegemony of the Yamato core. At this point in the late sixteenth century, on the eve of what historians conventionally, if misleadingly, term the reunification of Japan, Kita Ōu became what Mark Hudson refers to as an "attached periphery" to the burgeoning Japanese realm (*tenka*).[7]

Focusing on Kita Ōu forces us to reconsider the geographic and political extent of the "Japanese realm" during the medieval period.[8] Instead of reunifying a hitherto recognized archipelago-wide "nation" torn apart in the upheaval known as the era of Warring States (1467–1568), which is to say, by civil war, Hideyoshi constructed through conquest and colonization a realm that for the first time in Japanese history extended to the northeastern reaches of Mutsu and Dewa. Indeed, Hideyoshi did not unify Japan in the late sixteenth century; he created it.

FRONTIERS IN JAPANESE HISTORY: GEOGRAPHY AND HISTORIOGRAPHY

Geographers argue that frontiers must not be seen as synonymous with linear boundaries or national borders, but rather as "zones in which the characters and influences of two or more different regions or states come together."[9] They are zones where separate social and cultural entities interact, but where one party to the interaction does not fully dominate the other. Instead, there is "mutual interpenetration and sway" between the two sides.[10] By contrast, boundaries establish or demarcate the limits of well-defined political bodies. For this reason, according to geographers, it is hard to justify the use of the word "boundary" to characterize the land that divides, say, two kingdoms, at least before the rise of early-modern states. Without a political center that can establish and enforce precise political borders, the term "frontier" ought to be used to describe such regions.

In general, historians have only slowly adopted a zonal understanding of frontiers. Consequently, scholars focusing on northeastern Japan in the medieval period have been reluctant to think in anything but linear terms. Authors such as Saitō Toshio, Mimi Yiengpruksawan, Irumada Nobuo, and Ōishi Naomasa perceive a topographic border dividing Kita Ōu from Yamato Japan, relegating the former region exclusively to a transmarine Northeast Asian sphere defined by cultural and economic practices.[11]

According to their view, this boundary extended from Mount Chōkai, on the coast of Dewa, to the Koromo River, which runs through Mutsu to the Pacific coast. North of this boundary, the Emishi—non-Yamato peoples living in the far northeast—shared more in common with the seminomadic, iron-working, and horse-raising peoples of the Amur River Basin than with the paddy agriculturists of south-central and western Japan. In short, scholars to date have generally concurred that Emishi culture, with its seaborne trade and horse farming, belonged to a world whose boundaries extended from the Amur River Basin and Sakhalin Island to Hokkaido and Kita Ōu.

Historian Bruce Batten is one of few scholars who have approached Japan's frontiers in zonal terms. Iconoclastically, he posits that the evolution of northern Japan followed the "classical zonal form of a frontier."[12] According to this model, no clear distinction between inner and outer zones of the Yamato polity existed and, instead of a single area, overlapping zones of control and influence formed the frontier region. Throughout the ancient period, the central government—that is, the Ritsuryō state—slowly extended land division practices northward, establishing frontier military bases, villages, and, finally, areas mapped and delineated into districts. By the beginning of the medieval period, the northern boundary of Japan extended to and encompassed Sotogahama in the Tsugaru region.

Neither the Yamato state nor the ethnic groups of Northeast Asia proved capable of erecting boundaries around Kita Ōu, however. Thus the area remained a frontier, not a boundary or a border. The example of the powerful Ōshū Fujiwara and the Tsugaru Andō families—both descended from Emishi—will presently illustrate how cultures hailing from Northeast Asia and Yamato Japan intermingled to create a distinct frontier culture in Kita Ōu. Before proceeding, however, it is necessary to point out an important distinction between the Emishi and the Ainu peoples of the far northeast. Contrary to a common misconception, the Emishi did not evolve over time into the Ainu; rather, the former were most likely descendants of Yayoi-period (300 B.C.E.–300 C.E.) settlers who remained outside the cultural and political reach of the Yamato core.[13] Indeed, historians such as Mark Hudson argue that the designation Emishi was political in nature and referred to any and all northeastern "barbarians"—that is, all non-Yamato peoples. He contends that since the term was a political and, therefore, an artificial construct, "Emishi" did not in fact refer to any specific ethnicity at all.[14]

While the label Emishi may not have signified a particular ethnicity, the far northeast was nonetheless populated by various groups of people, whom today we might see as ethnically, though not racially, different from one another. For example, between the twelfth to fourteenth centuries, people of the Satsumon archaeological culture inhabited the Tsugaru and Shimokita peninsular regions.[15] The Emishi, consequently, were probably influenced by Satsumon culture to the north as well as by Yamato culture to the south. Instead of assimilating into either the southern Yamato culture or the northern cultures emanating out of Ezo, the Emishi developed a distinctive frontier lifestyle. For example, they were horseriders; but on occasion they also served as civil and military officials for Yamato elites.[16] While in certain instances Emishi may have shared characteristics with Yamato peoples, they also incorporated the cultural practices of the proto-Ainu or, as they were known after the twelfth century, the Ezo. (Readers should take note that, by convention, the term "Ezo" refers to both a geographical region and a cultural community.)

Because proto-Ainu groups maintained strong ties to Sakhalin Island and the Amur River Basin, the remains of Ezo cultural artifacts in northeastern Honshu testify to the penetration of transmarine Northeast Asian culture into Kita Ōu. One telling example may be found in what archaeologists call the *naiji tetsunabe* (literally, "inner-ear iron pot"), a relic of early Ainu culture. Used to cook meat and fish, this type of vessel was a product of the hunting and fishing culture of proto-Ainu groups.[17] The archaeological record shows that the pot entered northeastern Honshu in the medieval period and then moved southward. Digs in Aomori and Iwate prefectures have produced twenty-two of these pots, including the three oldest, revealing the southerly flow of Ezo artifacts which in turn influenced the culture of Kita Ōu.[18]

As these artifacts illustrate, the various Emishi groups of the far northeast were frontier peoples, shaped by their place between transmarine Northeast Asia and Yamato Japan, neither fully Tungus nor fully Yamato. One can turn for illustration to the history of the Ōshū (or Hiraizumi) Fujiwara family. Originally, the Ōshū Fujiwara descended from an Emishi chieftain family, the Kiyohara. By the beginning of the twelfth century, they had established a semi- or, arguably, a fully autonomous kingdom in the far northeast. Recalling the strategy of early Yamato kings, the Ōshū Fujiwara used Buddhism to create a sacred realm in their capital of Hiraizumi. They deployed the Buddhist faith, and particularly its pageantry, in order to legitimate their presence in, and rule over, the region of the Kitakami River Basin, in a manner reminiscent of their predecessors in the Yamato core, already discussed in chapter 1.[19]

The massive amount of Buddhist iconography commissioned by the Fujiwara vividly records the replication of central, and centralizing, practices in distant provinces. Nevertheless, it is important to remember that the Fujiwara were not simply mimicking the rituals of Yamato elites. The artwork within Hiraizumi temples suggests a reworking of Buddhist practices into what might be called a frontier Buddhism. Intermixed with Buddhist iconography on temple walls are scenes of the hunt and of the slaughter of animals (decidedly not Buddhist in origin) that reflect the presence of a nonagrarian, non-Buddhist lifestyle in Kita Ōu.[20] Frontier funeral rites also prevailed in the region. For example, the Fujiwara merged mummification practices from Sakhalin with the burial-robe styles of Ezo chieftains as well as Buddhist imagery borrowed from Yamato. Three daises within the Konjikidō temple hold the mummified bodies of the Fujiwara leaders Kiyohara (d. 1128), Motohira (d. 1157), and Hidehira (d. 1187). Motohira wears a vest with designs similar to those worn by Ezo (or proto-Ainu) chieftains.[21]

The combination of Yamato Buddhist iconography with Northeast Asian hunting scenes and mummification practices records for us the intermingling of two cultural spheres. Pointing to the Ōshū Fujiwara's frontier culture, Mimi Yiengpruksawan has persuasively argued for the recognition among scholars of an autonomous cultural and political sphere in northern Mutsu and Dewa during the eleventh and twelfth centuries.[22] The Fujiwara used Buddhism to create and rule a sacred realm—a realm that nevertheless lay, in geopolitical terms, beyond the Yamato polity and its Japanese kings and emperors.

Yiengpruksawan focuses on the Buddhist iconography at Hiraizumi, pursuing her investigation chiefly from the perspective of art and architectural history. In addition to the social and political authority of religion, the Fujiwara also relied upon the economic power of trade to consolidate their rule over the Kitakami River Basin. By controlling Kita Ōu's commerce with transmarine Northeast Asia, they enriched themselves and strengthened their position vis-à-vis Kyoto. Through the established trade routes of Japan's far northeast, the Fujiwara procured various luxury items that acted as potent forms of cultural capital when presented to Kyoto as gifts. For example, Fujiwara Motohira sent, among other items, one hundred Chinese coins, one hundred eagle feathers, sixty seal-skin pelts, and fifty Nukanobu chargers to the monk Unkei as payment toward a statue for the Mōtsūji temple.[23] Such acts of largesse demonstrated Fujiwara cultural and political mastery over the northeastern frontier. Indeed, Yiengpruksawan claims that the ability of the Fujiwara to forward large quantities of luxury goods to Kyoto reflected its, not the Ritsuryō state's, lordship over Kita Ōu.[24]

The historian Amino Yoshihiko has similarly asserted that, in the northeast, the Fujiwara "set up a state separate from the [Yamato state of the] Kantō and the Chūbu [regions]," and that these Kita Ōu lords manipulated personal relations with Yamato elites in order to retain autonomy. Amino makes the important point that even if Yamato Japanese believed the northeast was part of their realm, those living in the region did not necessarily share that view.[25]

While Yiengpruksawan does not explicitly invoke frontier theory, she clearly demonstrates that the Ōshū Fujiwara constructed a middle-ground-like polity, manipulating the "cultural forms" of Kyoto aristocrats as well as of the Emishi nobility.[26] Yiengpruksawan maintains that the Fujiwara were both inside and outside the Yamato polity, being Emishi chieftains at the same time that they were Yamato elites.[27] Similarly, Ōishi Naomasa claims that the Ōshū Fujiwara and Tsugaru Andō based their regional political and cultural authority as Emishi lords on ties with both Northeast Asia and the Yamato polity. Straddling the frontier, the two families penetrated the world of the Emishi and Ezo as well as that of their neighbors to the south, drawing "frontier political authority" from their unique positions in the far northeast.[28] Facing both directions, their political authority was oriented toward both Ezo and Kyoto, and according to Ōishi, enjoyed "currency" on both sides.

Ōishi insists that in order to trade with the Emishi or Ezo, the Fujiwara and Andō had to be, at least in the local context, ethnically Emishi or Ezo themselves. That is, the two families presumably needed to play up their Emishi genealogy in order to deal with non-Yamato peoples. At the same time, they could act as the northernmost outpost of ancient court or medieval shogunal authority in Kita Ōu, claiming affiliation to and status within the Yamato polity.[29] However, there is a teleological problem with Ōishi's thesis. It presumes that similar ethnicity was necessary for economic exchange across the far northeastern frontier, including with Hokkaido. Such an assertion goes against the growing consensus among scholars that it was interaction among different peoples that led to Ainu ethnogenesis in the first place. Emori Susumu argues that contact among various groups, especially with Yamato from the south, brought about the creation of a new ethnic Ainu identity between the twelfth and fourteenth centuries.[30] Mark Hudson, too, asserts that it was through their dealings with Yamato peoples in Kita Ōu that the inhabitants of the far northeast fostered a distinct Ainu ethnos.[31] In short, the manner in which Ōishi characterizes the Fujiwara and Andō is not congruent with current scholarship on the early Ainu. One could even speculate that if the Fujiwara and the Andō had hailed from entirely the same cultural sphere as prevailed on the island of Ezo, there might have been no Ainu ethnogenesis at all.

Evidence suggests that the Fujiwara and Andō were not historical fence sitters. We should not simply imagine them as donning their Emishi hats to enjoy "currency" when crossing into Ezo, while reverting to Yamato hats in order to deal with Kyoto. Whereas Ōishi posits that these northern lords had "dual, frontier identities," they did not in fact have dual natures: they were not from both Ezo and Yamato. The point, rather, is that they were from neither and both at the same time.[32] They borrowed from each culture and integrated it into what became a new and distinct culture and polity of their own. Ample empirical and archaeological evidence buttresses the argument for a Kita Ōu-centered frontier culture between Yamato and transmarine Northeast Asia, including the history of horses and horse trade in the region.

Yiengpruksawan concludes her book by recounting the destruction of the Ōshū Fujiwara and with them, supposedly, the frontier autonomy of Kita Ōu. She sees an "epoch [coming] to an end" when Minamoto Yoritomo (d. 1199), the first Kamakura shogun, rode with his army into the Kitakami River Basin in 1189. "A land of mystery and obsession for many a Kinai ruler had finally been incorporated into the mainstream nearly four centuries after Tamuramaro."[33] Yiengpruksawan thus places the end of an autonomous enclave in Kita Ōu in the late twelfth century. In contrast, this chapter argues that up until the end of the medieval period, as late as the 1590s, the region remained outside the political mainstream as a distinct frontier culture and polity, tucked between Yamato Japan and the transmarine Northeast Asian world.

THE ANDŌ: A FRONTIER FAMILY

The history of the Tsugaru Andō family helps to illustrate Kita Ōu's continuing status as a frontier well beyond the time of the fall of the Ōshū Fujiwara and the rise of the Kamakura shogunate. The Andō descended from the Abe, a powerful Emishi family who served on and off as peacekeepers in the northeast for the Yamato court. During the late thirteenth century, the Andō policed the Tsugaru region and controlled trade between Ezo and Kita Ōu through the office of *Ezo no sata* (also known as *Ezo kanrei* or Ezo Governor). Itō Kiyoshi points out that the Andō received their investiture from the Hōjō family, the second clan, after the Minamoto, to dominate the Kamakura shogunate.[34] Yet, as it turns out, the *Ezo no sata* office may only have legitimated the Andō's de facto position as overseers of trade between Tsugaru and Ezo, because the Andō additionally held another title, that of *Hinomoto no shōgun*. Kaiho Mineo suggests that the label *Hinomoto* (which would appear literally to mean "Sun's Origin") referred to the geographic area of Kita Ōu and the southern tip of the present-day island of Hokkaido. The exact derivation and significance of the designation *Hinomoto no shōgun* remain unclear, but the term most likely referred to the position of the Andō as controllers of trade and relations between the far northeast and Ezo. Although Hōjō authority came to an end with the destruction of the Kamakura shogunate in 1333, the Andō were able to maintain their status as controllers of Kita Ōu, as well as of trade and relations with Ezo, using the *Hinomoto no shōgun* title throughout the medieval period.[35]

The Andō oversaw trade with Ezo from their base in the port town of Tosa Minato. Numerous documents reveal that ships based out of Tosa Minato sailed between Ezo and Yamato ports. For example, an entry in *Daijōin monjo* (Records of the Daijō temple) states that in the ninth month of 1306, twenty ships arrived in the Echigo harbor of Mikuni. One of them contained northern sea products, including salmon and *kosode,* which could either mean Chinese silk-embroidered cloth or a kind of Ezo vest. The vessel most likely was an Andō carrier, transporting goods between Ezo and Echigo.[36]

Archaeological evidence in northeastern Honshu and southern Hokkaido, dating from between the thirteenth and the fifteenth centuries, serves to highlight the once booming seaborne trade flowing through Kita

Ōu. Relics such as large quantities of Chinese porcelain and coins expose a vibrant commercial economy. It appears that Chinese items constituted a substantial proportion of the goods that circulated in transmarine Northeast Asia.[37]

While there are few sources detailing the specifics of northeastern trade networks, *Suwa daimyōjin ekotoba* (Picture scrolls of the Suwa deity; 1356) offers a tantalizing glimpse into the multicultural and multiethnic world of Kita Ōu. In compiling the scrolls, the monk Enchū (1295–1365) drew upon old stories, legends, folklore, and other materials already in circulation.[38] The inclusion of the *tōi hōki* or "eastern barbarian revolt" of 1326 and related information on the various peoples of the far northeast make this portion of the scroll, as one historian has put it, "priceless as a medieval Ezo source."[39]

The Suwa scrolls document that three groups of people were active in trade between Kita Ōu and Ezo. The first to be described, the Wataritō (or Watarishima; literally, "group who crosses over"), hailed from the Usorikeshi and Matoumai regions, the names of which possibly represent early designations for Hakodate and Matsumae, towns in present-day southern Hokkaido.[40] The Wataritō

> come and go in large numbers, trading on the Sotogahama coast. The second and third groups, the Hinomoto and the Karako, come from foreign countries. Their appearance is similar to a female demon.... As a people, they eat the meat of fish, beasts, and birds, not knowing the five grains. Communication is difficult even if one translates numerous times. The Wataritō look similar to the peoples of Yamato, but they have large sideburns and hair all over their bodies. Their speech is rustic, but generally translates.... They do not ride horses.... The person called Andō Futoshi is the *Ezo kanrei* [Ezo Governor].[41]

According to Kaiho Mineo, the picture scrolls do not describe the world of the early-modern Ainu, but a truly medieval, in-between world, where Wataritō (probably Satsumon people, whose culture flourished in 700–1200 C.E.) and other proto-Ainu groups (such as the Okhotsk people of northern Hokkaido, 600–1000 C.E.) mixed and intermingled with the Emishi cultures of Kita Ōu. For example, they record that the Wataritō looked like Yamato people and basically spoke the same language, but in addition to being "hairy" (a common East Asian trope to describe barbarism), the text explains that they did not ride horses.[42]

The Karako and Hinomoto (possibly Okhotsk people or, by the fourteenth century, actual Ainu), however, were different from Yamato people. They were meat eaters, spoke undecipherable languages, looked and dressed like "demons," and did not cultivate rice, an important sign of Yamato civility. The Karako (literally, children of Kara or Tang China) were probably Sakhalin Ainu, Nivkh, Uilta, or Yukagir peoples living on Karafuto who had contact with the Mongols in northeastern Manchuria or, later, Ming Chinese. The influence of Mongol and Chinese peoples—Karahito—became associated with the geographic area of Karafuto, and merged into the single appellation "Karako."[43] The Hinomoto reference is probably to early Ainu living in southeastern Ezo. Kaiho posits that the peoples known as the Karako and Hinomoto in medieval documents developed into the Ainu sometime around the fourteenth century.[44]

THE POLITICS OF WARHORSES AND SEABORNE TRADE

Having laid the groundwork for a reconceptualization of Kita Ōu as frontier zone rather than as Japan's medieval border, this chapter now turns its focus to the rhythms of politics, economics, and daily life in the region during the second half of the medieval period, roughly from the fourteenth to sixteenth centuries. At this time, two warrior families, the Nukanobu Nanbu and the Tsugaru Andō, maintained prominence in the region. Significantly, they did so by basing their economic power upon horses and seaborne trade.

The Nanbu originated from Kai province in the south, claiming genealogical ties with the Minamoto family. They supposedly descended from the younger brother of Minamoto no Yoshiie (1039–1106), namely, Minamoto no Shinrasaburō Yoshimitsu (1045–1127).[45] Later genealogies state that the fifth-generation family chieftain, Nanbu Mitsuyuki, was the first to establish a Nanbu presence in the far northeast, but the historicity of this northward move is not clear.[46] The Nanbu had overseen horse farms in the Nanbu, Hagii, and Takeno areas of Kai in central Honshu, and most likely Mitsuyuki, like the Kudō and Soga families who originally worked horse farms on the Izu perninsula, relocated from the Kantō region to Mutsu in order to raise warhorses for the powerful Hōjō family.[47]

Mitsuyuki probably moved into the Mutsu district of Nukanobu during the late thirteenth century, there staffing the Nukanobu horse farms and raising chargers for his Hōjō patrons. Later, his offspring established a number of cadet families throughout the region. They spread to different locales to raise horses themselves at such sites as Sannohe ("third door") and Kunohe ("ninth door"), and took on the names of their respective proprietorships. By the beginning of the medieval period, the Ichinohe, Sannohe (who eventually became the Nanbu main line), Yonnohe, Shichinohe, Hachinohe (Nejō), and Kunohe Nanbu families lived in the broader Nukanobu region.[48]

The Nukanobu region had long been famous for its horse farms. In fact, the stoutest warhorses of the classical and medieval periods hailed from Nukanobu, and chargers raised at Nukanobu carried many renowned warriors into battle. In military chronicles such as *Genpei jōsuiki* (Chronicle of the rise and fall of the Minamoto and Taira families; latter half of the fourteenth century), we read of Minamoto no Yoshitsune riding down the Hiyodori cliffs at the epic battle of Ichi-no-tani on a steed from Sannohe, and of Sasaki no Takatsuna fording the Uji River to attack the Taira on a charger from Shichinohe. Minamoto no Yoritomo provides another example of a famous warrior who bestrode a Nukanobu mount, for his two most treasured horses, Surusumi ("Black Ink") and Ikezuki ("Indiscriminate Biter"), came from Nukanobu farms.[49] These so-called *Nukanobu no shunme*, or "swift horses of Nukanobu," were larger and more powerful than the breeds of ponies found in south-central Japan. Historians trace their origins to central Asian or Korean stocks, speculating that the Emishi imported and introduced the breed into Kita Ōu. Scholars also posit that the Emishi or Ōshū Fujiwara later established nine horse farms—Ichinohe through Kunohe—in Nukanobu to raise these warhorses.[50]

During the fourteenth century, the Nanbu took over the Nukanobu farms, and became known for supplying Yamato elites with chargers of the highest quality.[51] For example, Prince Sadanari recorded in his dairy, *Kanmongyoki* (Record of things seen and heard; 1416–1448), that in the eighth month of 1418, a Nanbu lord traveled from the northeast and presented shogun Ashikaga Yoshimochi (r. 1394–1423) with one hundred horses and one thousand pieces of gold.[52]

Above all else, the "swift horses of Nukanobu" bring into relief the frontier status of Kita Ōu and its strong ties to Northeast Asian trade routes. It is quite possible that these horses did not all come from Nukanobu farms, and that the Nanbu may have imported some from the continent. It was not at all unheard of for northeastern warriors to import horses into Kita Ōu from as far away as central Asia. According to Satō Yūjirō, author of the little known *Nanbu bashi* (History of Nanbu horses; 1918), Kakizaki Kurando, whose stronghold was located on the Shimokita peninsula, brought over one hundred chargers from Mongolia, Manchuria, and Russia for his war against the Nanbu in 1455. In 1605, Date Masamune (1567–1636) imported a number of horses from Persia through a northern route, and in order to avoid the shogun's suspicion, he hid them on a farm in Shichinohe.[53] Albeit disparate, these records suggest that Nukanobu was part of an international horse trade that extended not only south to Kyoto, but also north to continental Northeast Asia and beyond.

Horses played a pivotal role in the Nanbu family's integration into the northeastern frontier zone, acting as what Jeffrey Mass has described in other contexts as "bridging figures." High-quality warhorses were important to medieval warrior society, as well as to the economy of Kita Ōu. The Nukanobu farms were originally part of the Emishi landscape, where both animal husbandry and seaborne trade remained important to human livelihoods. Being originally Kantō horse raisers, the Nanbu were able quickly to adapt to the culture and economy of Kita Ōu with their valued horse-raising expertise. When the Nanbu family moved from their horse farms in the Kantō region to the pastures of Nukanobu, they shed their Yamato identities and became enmeshed in the frontier culture of Kita Ōu.

Although extant documentary sources reveal little about actual living conditions in the far northeast, a number of factors surely influenced the Nanbu's daily lives. To start with, they inhabited a northeastern frontier region that was agriculturally distinct from south-central Japan. Instead of managing rice fields, the Nanbu maintained horse pastures. Since they broke and trained warhorses, the Nanbu were excellent cavalrymen. In addition, as a family of horseriders, they were highly mobile, not unlike the seminomadic peoples of North Asia. Indeed, there are numerous examples of Nanbu cavalry drives south from Nukanobu deep into enemy territory during the Nanbokuchō Wars (1336–1392) fought between the rival northern and southern imperial courts.[54] Although the Nanbu established forts and castles as home bases, they retained a certain "hordelike" quality. While Japanese warrior culture in the fourteenth century was based on very different principles from that of nomadic Mongol hordes, the Nanbu evinced seminomadic traits that resembled, if only slightly, horse-based cultures on the continent. Such a characterization accords with the opinion of many scholars who argue that northeastern Japan had more in common with Eurasian steppe cultures than with life on the alluvial plains of south-central Japan. The Nanbu, like the Mongols, resided in a frontier region, raised horses for their livelihood, and hence spent most of their lives "in the saddle."

At the same time, the Nanbu retained their Yamato cultural traits and their contacts with the Yamato polity, playing a pivotal role on behalf of the southern court during the Nanbokuchō Wars. For example, in 1334, under the authority of Emperor Go-Daigo (r. 1318–1339), Kitabatake Akiie (1318–1338) charged Nanbu Moroyuki (d. 1338) with the administration of Tsugaru.[55] Because of the ambiguity of this investiture, we can only speculate that the office was similar to that of *Ezo no sata* held by the Andō, and consisted largely of policing the Tsugaru region. It may also have entailed overseeing trade with Ezo.[56] Although the *Ezo no sata* title possibly shifted to the Nanbu, the Andō maintained their *Hinomoto no shōgun* status, remaining entrenched in the region. If the Nanbu's charge to administrate included not only policing but commercial matters as well, then consistent Nanbu aggression against the Andō in the fifteenth century may indicate regional competition over control of trade networks connecting Kita Ōu with Northeast Asia.

In order to strengthen further their position in the northeast vis-à-vis Kyoto, the Nanbu and Andō competed to establish personal relations with the Muromachi (or Ashikaga) shogunate (1336–1568). Prefiguring the sort of quasi-tributary giving of birds and other animals to be discussed in chapter 4, in 1418 the Nanbu brought one hundred horses and one thousand pieces of gold to the Ashikaga shogun. In 1423, the Andō sent the shogun salmon, kelp, sea-otter pelts, and other items harvested from northeastern waters. Evidencing the ability of the Nanbu and Andō to provide Yamato Japan with commodities procured through trade with the far northeast, these gifts, as forms of tribute, were intended to solidify relations between northeastern families and Kyoto. For the Andō, salmon and kelp were rarities procured through trade circuits in the north. By contrast, large warhorses and gold were goods that could be obtained only through Nanbu trade networks, and both were valuable to the warriors who now dominated Yamato politics. The presentation of such objects solidified personal relations—critical to medieval politics in general—that in turn formed the basis for political and cultural ties between Yamato Japan and Kita Ōu.[57] As mounts for cavalrymen or gifts between warriors, horses again served as bridging figures, enabling frontier magnates in the far northeast to establish links with Kyoto. As trade items, horses were crucial to the Kita Ōu economy; as tribute they were valued by Yamato elites.

With such bridging figures at the ready, the Nanbu maintained ongoing ties with Kyoto throughout the fifteenth century. In 1422, for example, the court awarded Nanbu Mitsutsune, tenth Hachinohe Nejō chieftain, the honorific title of *Satsuma no kami,* making him nominally the governor of Satsuma province at the southwestern end of the archipelago.[58] According to *Mansai jugō nikki* (completed 1435), the journal of Sanpōin Mansai, chief abbot of Daigo temple, Nanbu Nagayasu (eleventh Hachinohe Nejō chieftain) was invested with the title *Tōtōmi no kami* or governor of Tōtōmi province in the tenth month of 1432, and his sons were honored with police-attendant positions.[59] Through such largesse, the Muromachi shogunate, which requisitioned the titles from the imperial court, extended its reach, however nominally, into the north, and established personal connections with the Nanbu that promised to bring northeastern goods into shogunal coffers and, conversely, new forms of legitimacy to Nanbu lords. The shogunate succeeded in cementing personal relations with the Nanbu from the latter half of the fifteenth century. In 1465, Nanbu Nobunaga received an order requesting his services in Kyoto. Once in the capital, Nobunaga spent eleven years in courtly and shogunal circles, being entertained at the shogun's palace and playing the flute for the future emperor Go-Tsuchimikado (r. 1500–1526).[60]

Although the Nanbu benefited from contacts with Kyoto, they remained autonomously entrenched in the frontier zone. The Nanbu family's hereditary lands lay in the Nukanobu region. The family slowly extended its holdings into Tsugaru throughout the fifteenth century, despite numerous shogunal cease-and-desist orders.[61] First, they attacked the Andō in Fujisaki in 1421.[62] Fujisaki castle lay at the confluence of the Iwaki, Hira, and Asei'ishi rivers and was an important site for Tsugaru trade. Endō Iwao has referred to this locale as a "center for northern trade" among the "mountain, river, and sea peoples" of the far northeast.[63] After driving the Andō from Fujisaki, the Nanbu attacked the Andō at their base in Tosa Minato in 1432, solidifying control over the entire Tsugaru region. Indeed, the *Mansai* journal records that the Nanbu drove the Andō into Ezo at this time.[64] The Andō later resettled in Akita on the main island, but never returned to the Tsugaru region; they left the Nanbu in possession of Tosa Minato.

As this brief overview of Nanbu activity suggests, the family came to covet trade with Ezo, and so attempted to take over the major hubs of trade in the Tsugaru region. Ultimately, they intended to usurp the Andō's position within Ezo trade networks. After the Nanbu drove the Andō from Kita Ōu, the region still remained attached to the shipping lanes that ran between Ezo and northeastern Honshu. Even as late as 1669, the lucrative trade between Ezo and the Tsugaru region was within living memory of certain Ainu chiefs.[65]

Simply put, throughout the medieval period, Kita Ōu lay snugly contained between the Yamato and transmarine Northeast Asian worlds. The livelihoods of horse farming and seaborne trade tied the region to the larger transmarine sphere of Northeast Asia, allowing Kita Ōu to remain autonomous within northeastern Honshu. When investigating this medieval frontier culture, Japanese historians generally focus on differences between the two families in Kita Ōu. For example, Irumada Nobuo depicts the Andō as *umi no ryōshu* (lords of the sea) and the Nanbu as *uma no ryōshu* (lords of the horse), claiming their lifestyles to be "diametrically opposed."[66] Likewise, Itō Kiyoshi divides the north into distinct land- and sea-based worlds.[67]

However, some important sources suggest otherwise. *Nochi kagami* (Mirror of a latter age; 1853), a history of the Muromachi shogunate, records that in 1423 the Andō presented shogun Ashikaga Yoshikazu (r. 1423–1425) with various trade items obtained through northern sea lanes, including horses, but also fowl, Chinese coins, sea-otter pelts, and kelp.[68] It is important to note that the Andō, not just the Nanbu, traded horses. Like the Nanbu, the Andō possessed horse farms in the Tsugaru region. In a will dating from 1325, Andō Munesue bequeathed the title of *Ezo no sata* and his *maki* or pasture lands in Nakahama to his only son.[69] While this document does not specify the kind of pastures deeded, it is probable that they belonged to a horse farm similar to the ones overseen by the Nanbu family in the Nukanobu region.

We should not assume that once the Nanbu forced the Andō out of Kita Ōu, the Tsugaru region, especially Tosa Minato, stopped serving as a hub for the transmarine Northeast Asian trade, or that the Nanbu family lacked an interest in seaborne commerce.[70] Recent archaeological digs at the historical site of Tosa Minato have uncovered the remains of earthen walls and moats, suggesting that warriors inhabited the port town and even fortified it in the fifteenth century. The completion of these earthworks dates from between 1425 and 1450, indicating that even after the Andō fled southward to Akita, the Nanbu built up and maintained the Tosa harbor for trading purposes.[71]

While the evidence of Nanbu involvement in trade itself is scarce, we know that the Nanbu possessed an interest in the geographical centers of trade and even went to war to take Tosa Minato from the Andō. Documents reveal that Tosa Minato continued to serve as a major port for northern trade up until the early-modern period. A source dated 1463 details a dispute in the domain of Obama, located in the southerly province of Wakasa, between a vassal of the Takeda family and a vassal of the Ishiki family over the contents of a vessel named the Tosa-maru. The document also refers to the *shugo* or military governor of Buzen, a post occupied by the Ōuchi family.[72] The name of the ship—Tosa-maru—would seem to imply that it was a vessel based out of Tosa Minato. The embroilment of the Buzen governor suggests Ōuchi involvement in the southern end of trade networks that ran from Tosa Minato to Kyushu, passing through Wakasa ports. Amino Yoshihiko has cited the document as an illustration of the far-reaching extent of shipping lanes emanating out of Tosa Minato during the Muromachi period.[73] According to *Kaisen shikimoku* (Record of ship navigation), a Muromachi source, Tosa Minato ranked among the most important harbors in all of Japan.[74] The work is nominally dated 1223, but Amino believes that it is actually a late Muromachi text.[75]

Archaeological and written records point to the continued importance of Tosa Minato in linking Ezo and the transmarine Northeast Asian sphere to trade routes that ran as far south as Kyushu and beyond even during the period of Andō administration. Because the Nanbu usurped the Andō's centers of trade at Fujisaki and Tosa Minato, the Nanbu likely appropriated the Andō's commercial authority as well, overseeing trade routes that linked Tsugaru and Ezo. Since the documentary and archaeological evidence suggests a culture dependent on both horse raising and seaborne trade—and one that extended well into the medieval period—it is fair to view the Andō and Nanbu as having shared lifestyles and livelihoods within the northeast's late-medieval frontier culture.

A more nuanced understanding of Japan's northeastern frontier emerges when we recognize that both the Nanbu and the Andō were "lords of the sea" as well as "lords of the horse." The Andō, identified by Irumada as lords of the sea, owned horse farms and traded in horses; the Nanbu, putatively lords of the horse, possessed a harbor of major importance to seaborne trade. Instead of a region characterized by separate land and sea spheres, terrestrial and aquatic worlds overseen by two warrior families with diametrically opposed economic agendas, the frontier zone of Kita Ōu offered the inhabitants of the northeast both landborne and seaborne forms of economic opportunity.

CREATING JAPAN: HIDEYOSHI'S COLONIZATION OF KITA ŌU

By the early sixteenth century, the Nanbu family had emerged as masters of Kita Ōu and controlled a diverse range of lands. They held excellent horse farms in Nukanobu, and, having driven off the Andō, they oversaw the Tsugaru region. In the Senboku area, also in northeastern Honshu, the Nanbu even possessed rare alluvial lands capable of producing rice. In terms of present-day prefectures, the Nanbu controlled all of Aomori, the northern half of Iwate, and the area surrounding the Yoneda River in Akita.[76] This situation changed drastically in the 1570s, however, when a bitter succession dispute broke out within the Nanbu family, weakening their ability to administer their holdings. A Nanbu vassal, Ōura Tamenobu (1550–1607), used the dispute as a pretext to rebel in Tsugaru. He formed an *ikki* or armed league among various Nanbu captains and local elites, and solidified his control over the area during the late 1570s and early 1580s.[77] Sometime before 1586, Tamenobu traveled to Kyoto and submitted to Toyotomi Hideyoshi. Hideyoshi, by this time undisputed hegemon of the realm, made Tamenobu his vassal and confirmed the latter's proprietorship over the Tsugaru region. With Hideyoshi's vermilion seal and its implied investiture, Tamenobu could claim Tsugaru as a hereditary holding.

There can be no mistake that the above developments threatened all the Nanbu's holdings in Kita Ōu. In order to secure their standing, the Nanbu in 1586 sent a representative to Maeda Toshiie (1538–1599), a powerful ally of Hideyoshi, asking him to arbitrate between Hideyoshi and the Nanbu leadership. The Nanbu submitted to Hideyoshi through Toshiie in the following year with an oath sealed in blood.[78] They undoubtedly hoped that future negotiations with Hideyoshi would bring Tsugaru and its access to Ezo trade back into Nanbu holding. The Nanbu, though vassals of Hideyoshi, did not heed Hideyoshi's 1587 *sōbuji* declaration ordering the cessation of fighting across the archipelago. Indeed, after the Nanbu family's longstanding succession dispute died down in the latter half of the 1580s, the Nanbu sent a punitive force against Tamenobu in late 1589. They may have reckoned that after retaking Tsugaru, they could claim rightful proprietorship over the region. However, they did not have time to pursue their war to any conclusive end. In the second month of 1590, a messenger from Maeda Toshiie arrived in Nukanobu carrying orders to join Hideyoshi's Odawara campaign. The Sannohe chieftain, Nanbu Nobunao (1546–1599), had no choice but to call back his troops and travel south to join Hideyoshi's army.[79]

Although the Nanbu had submitted to Hideyoshi earlier, in 1586, they had not met him personally or received his official seal—which the hegemon considered realmwide law—confirming their domain holdings. Nobunao reached Odawara in the fourth month of 1590. He finally met with Hideyoshi on the twenty-seventh day of the seventh month and obtained a vermilion seal recognizing the Nanbu family's domain.[80] Nonetheless, the Nanbu were not able to convince Hideyoshi to rescind his recognition of Tsugaru independence, and they lost that territory to Tamenobu. Hideyoshi did, however, award the Nanbu an additional four districts south of Nukanobu—Waka, Hienuki, Shiwa, and Hei.[81] While seemingly an act of largesse, this measure had troubling consequences for both the Nanbu family and the fate of Kita Ōu.

In the late sixteenth century, Hideyoshi spread his influence throughout the archipelago, offering a new source of political legitimacy to warrior lords on the periphery or even outside of the Yamato polity. Hideyoshi succeeded in extending his political power over all four of the large islands, save for much of Ezo/Hokkaido, and was able to displace Nanbu authority over Kita Ōu. Since investiture from Hideyoshi was now a critical factor in legitimating local rule, the Nanbu were no longer the only source of authority in the far northeast. These circumstances gave Tamenobu the chance to seek out another patron and secure his personal lordship over the Tsugaru region.

Hideyoshi, then, did not simply absorb northern warlords into his federation of daimyo. Rather, he altered the very fabric of frontier life in Kita Ōu. By examining Hideyoshi's Kunohe campaign of 1591, we may see how Hideyoshi displaced the medieval power structures in Kita Ōu, erasing its frontier status and irrevocably changing the nature of the region.

After a decade-long internal clan struggle, Nanbu Nobunao became the twenty-sixth chieftain of the Sannohe Nanbu sometime in the early

1580s.[82] Nobunao faced two important tasks from the beginning of his tenure. The first was to establish his authority over the Nanbu vassal corps. The second was to pacify the Tsugaru region, in effect reestablishing Nanbu control over the area. In order to assert his own standing as their collective military commander and overlord, Nobunao demanded that all major vassals take oaths of loyalty.[83] He arranged a meeting between himself and the most powerful Nanbu vassals. Nobunao ordered Hachinohe (Nejō) Nanbu chieftain Masayoshi to a gathering at the Kushibiki Hachiman shrine, an undated letter records.[84] Another letter, this one also undated, reveals that at this meeting Masayoshi pledged faithfully to serve Nobunao.[85] Indeed, we may safely assume that all major vassals there assembled gave Nobunao their oaths of loyalty.

Attempting to retake Tsugaru, Nobunao sent Masayoshi to subjugate the rebellious Tamenobu. However, as we have already seen, before the Nanbu could pursue their Tsugaru campaign, a messenger from Maeda Toshiie arrived, conveying orders for the Nanbu to join Hideyoshi's armies at Odawara. Hideyoshi's command prompted the Nanbu to consolidate their cadet families and to rationalize their vassal corps. Throughout the medieval centuries, the Nanbu clan had comprised various semiautonomous branch families like the Hachinohe Nanbu, who might presumably now have sought independent daimyo status from Hideyoshi. Instead, Nobunao hoped to rally a subordinated and loyal group of warrior followers around a single warlord chieftain—namely, himself.

In order to adapt to Hideyoshi's new political order, Nobunao forced Masayoshi to dissolve the Hachinohe Nanbu family and take on the clan name of Hachinohe, becoming a vassal of the Sannohe Nanbu. Nobunao then placed Masayoshi's lands and warrior followers under his own control. After Nobunao reorganized his military strength, he left Masayoshi in charge of the Nanbu holdings and traveled south to join Hideyoshi's Odawara campaign. This consolidation effectively destroyed the autonomy of the Hachinohe Nanbu.[86]

After the Odawara campaign, Hideyoshi set out to extend his authority over the only part of the realm that he had yet to pacify: the far northeast. In the eighth month of 1590, Hideyoshi traveled as far as Aizu, while his generals Asano Nagamasa (1547–1611) and Gamō Ujisato (1556–1595) advanced farther north into the territories of Kasai and Ōzaki.[87] Soon after Nagamasa's penetration of the far northeast, armed leagues sprang up in

Kasai, Ōzaki, Waka, and Hienuki. Nagamasa ordered the Nanbu to engage the *ikki* forces at Toriyuzaki, but harsh winter snows forced the Nanbu to retreat. Ultimately, the Date and Gamō armies entered the foray and put down the rebellions. The sudden outbreak of violent resistance to Hideyoshi's pacification campaigns extended as far north as Nukanobu. In the second month of 1591, Kunohe Masasane, employing masterless samurai from the defunct Kasai and Ōzaki *ikki,* along with other vassals of the Kushibiki, the Shichinohe, and the Ichinohe, began open warfare against the Nanbu.[88]

Disgruntlement among rebellious vassals centered on the preceding succession dispute and the consolidation of the Hachinohe and Sannohe lines. First of all, a Kunohe heir had been passed over when the Nanbu chose Nobunao to inherit the chieftain position. Second, when the Hachinohe Nanbu submitted to Nobunao, the Kunohe clan also forfeited some private properties in the Kunohe area. The Shichinohe and the Ichinohe, both former vassals of the Hachinohe Nanbu, could well have lost their independent holdings along with the Kunohe, and this prospect drove them to risk rebellion. These families may have hoped to establish an independent hold over their hereditary proprietorships, after which they could have petitioned Hideyoshi to recognize as legitimate their claims to the Kunohe, Shichinohe, and Ichinohe areas. Hideyoshi, however, did not have a separatist vision for Nanbu lands.

Following Hideyoshi's orders, Nobunao's forces had been deployed in the Shiwa, Iwate, and Hei districts, and proved unable to respond forcefully to the Kunohe rebellion. Left with no choice, Nobunao requested reinforcements. In response, Hideyoshi sent an army of over 60,000 men into northern Mutsu. Hideyoshi conveyed an order on the fifteenth day of the sixth month of 1591 to stop all fighting and to await the arrival of Tokugawa, Date, Asano, and Toyotomi forces.[89] By the ninth month of 1591, Hideyoshi's army had destroyed the Ichinohe fortress and was besieging Kunohe castle. According to a letter written by Asano Nagamasa, the siege army bombarded Kunohe castle with flaming arrows and arquebus fire, and after two days of continued attacks, the castle surrendered.[90] When Hideyoshi put down the Kunohe rebellion, he brought Kita Ōu firmly into his grasp.

INTERNAL COLONIZATION: CHALLENGING THE REUNIFICATION PARADIGM

Hideyoshi's colonization of the north did not necessarily have, as some scholars argue, a stabilizing effect on the region.[91] Indeed, Hideyoshi's conquest and colonization of Kita Ōu changed the power structure of the Nanbu clan in a number of disruptive ways. For example, in order to participate in Hideyoshi's daimyo federation, the Nanbu consolidated their branch families, thereby destroying the longstanding frontier autonomy—based in part on the administration of vast horse farms—of the Hachinohe and Kunohe families. Hideyoshi's new social and political order fundamentally changed the nature of the Nanbu family in Nukanobu. Local warrior houses resisted and rebelled against Hideyoshi's attempt to colonize the area, which elicited a full conquest by Japan's new hegemon. The Nanbu were forced to call on Hideyoshi to fight their battles, because under the new government the Nanbu were not able to keep peace in their own domain. Ultimately, Hideyoshi not only rearranged local proprietary lordships and the source of their legitimacy but fundamentally changed the cultural and economic relationships between Kita Ōu and transmarine Northeast Asia. Once more, horses provide a revealing lens through which to examine this change.

In 1593, Hideyoshi awarded the Kakizaki family in Matsumae, located at the southern tip of modern Hokkaido, the exclusive right to trade with the Ainu.[92] This move had two effects on Kita Ōu. First, it cut the region off from its culturally and economically defining connection with transmarine Northeast Asia, one that, as we have seen, dated back to the classical and medieval periods. Seaborne trade no longer linked Kita Ōu to Northeast Asia.[93] After Hideyoshi, the Matsumae family became integrated into a continental trade that originated at Ming, and later Qing, posts at Deren on the Amur River. Second, Hideyoshi's conquest and colonization rearranged the internal geopolitical landscape and political economy of Nanbu domain. In the wake of the massive dearmament at the beginning of the early-modern period, the Nanbu were forced to destroy thirty-six out of forty-eight forts, including the one at Hachinohe. The Nanbu then established their castle town in Morioka to the south.[94] Because the Nanbu lost the Tsugaru region, but gained rich agricultural lands to the south, Mori Kahee asserts that they "naturally" shifted the center of their cultural and economic activity from the horse-farming region of Nukanobu to the rice-farming belt running through the flood plains of the Kitakami, Nakatsu, and Shizukuishi rivers.[95] In short, the region's political, economic, and cultural *raison d'ētre*, all centered in horses, ended at the onset of early modernity.

In response to Hideyoshi's move northward, the Nanbu family were forced to alter radically their spatial worldview, reflecting the larger geopolitical changes that swept Kita Ōu in the late sixteenth century. The shift to rice farming, and the loss of trade with Northeast Asia, heralded the end of Kita Ōu's frontier culture and, for the first time, the near-total consolidation of the Japanese realm. Without the Tsugaru region, the Nanbu lost control of Tosa Minato, which in effect cut them off from seaborne trade with Ezo. Once denied access to the Northeast Asian transmarine trade, the Nanbu had no choice but to adapt to the political economy of the early-modern period, making a difficult transition from horse farming to paddy agriculture and cash cropping. The domain monopolies of the Tokugawa period (1600–1868) in northeastern Honshu provide evidence of this change. Horses were no longer the main livelihood of the Nanbu's traditional branch-family territories; instead, domains in the area monopolized the sale of salt, fish products, rice and other simple grains, soybeans, safflower, copper, saltpeter, and lumber.[96] Hachinohe domain, once the center of the Nukanobu farms, monopolized the region's iron, soybean, oil cake, fish oil, and salt sales, but not the trade in horses.[97] Tsugaru domain, too, was cut off from commerce with Northeast Asia. As Mark Ravina has shown, despite the domain's efforts to develop agriculture and industry, Tsugaru had a difficult time adapting to the agrarian political economy of the early-modern era.[98]

John Hall once characterized Hideyoshi's unification of Japan as "straight-forward." Defeat in battle, he implied, led to political submission and the acceptance of Hideyoshi's hegemony. In short, Hall saw unification as a fairly uniform process. "Since the unification process resulted from the ascendancy of one daimyo coalition over the nation and not from the reemergence of a central monarchial authority, the new hegemony, rather than destroying daimyo rule, extended it uniformly upon the people of the entire nation."[99] This explanation may hold true for campaigns in Kyushu and the Kantō—the very regions on which historians have focused most of their attention—but not with regard to the far northeast.[100] Hideyoshi did not spread his hegemony over Kita Ōu in a straightforward or uniform manner. Rather, his conquest and colonization severed the region from its historic ties to Northeast Asia, destroyed its unique frontier culture, and changed the very fabric of life in Kita Ōu for those who resided there. Unification transformed not only political alliances but also the culture and livelihood of the region.

For all these reasons, Hideyoshi's conquest and colonization of the far northeast conforms strikingly to Michael Hetcher's model of "internal colonialism." Rather than viewing the process of national development as one in which integrated and institutionalized center-periphery relations metamorphose into a homogenous national culture and create social and economic equality across regions, the internal-colonization model submits that the core culturally and politically dominates the periphery by exploiting its resources. Through internal colonization, peripheral regions become just that, rather than independent frontier zones. They come to depend economically on the center, and structural inequalities among the regions increase rather than decrease.[101] As the periphery grows dependent on trade with the center, peripheral protoindustrialization develops around what are essentially export markets, much like third-world economies that emerged in the aftermath of Western imperialism.[102] Although absorption of former frontier zones into a central polity creates economic links, it does not necessarily translate into effective political integration.[103] The massive famines that the far northeast experienced during Japan's early-modern period serve as cruel testimony to this harsh fact. In short, through internal colonization, nations such as Japan did not develop uniformly, but rather through a process of marginalizing hinterlands and creating peripheries.[104]

Endemic famines in the northeast represent one of the symptoms of internal colonization and third-world-style economic dependency on domains' export trade to the center. Brett Walker's analysis of the Hachinohe wild-boar famine of 1749 in chapter 5 will further demonstrate that the process of integrating Hachinohe domain into the political and economic networks of early-modern Japan fundamentally changed the environment of the region, down to the ecological level. The famines in Hachinohe and elsewhere in the northeast bare the disruptive dynamic by which Kita Ōu became enfolded into south-central Japan, destroying those frontier characteristics that once defined the region. The process so often called "reunification" did not bring peace and stability to a preexisting "nation"; rather, it actually created such a nation for the first time. Before the 1590s, a cohesive social, political, and cultural entity extending from the southern tip of Satsuma to the Oshima peninsula on Hokkaido simply did not exist.

CONCLUSION

As has been stressed repeatedly throughout this essay, pre-Tokugawa Kita

Ōu must be understood not as a transborder region but as a frontier, a zone of integration between transmarine Northeast Asia and the Yamato core. The Ōshū Fujiwara mixed Northeast Asian and Yamato cultures in Hiraizumi during the twelfth century, creating a frontier culture and polity. The temples in Hiraizumi evinced this syncretism, bearing hunting motifs on their walls and housing the mummified bodies of the Hiraizumi Fujiwara chieftains while at the same time displaying Buddhist iconography adapted from more southerly sources. In this frontier region, lifestyles and livelihoods depended in part on maritime trade. During the succeeding centuries, the Andō and Nanbu, the two primary clans dealt with in this chapter, tied themselves to trade circuits that ran from the Eurasian continent through Tosa Minato and Nukanobu, and on into Yamato Japan. Prosperity in the region also depended on horse farming. The "swift horses of Nukanobu" were the economic and cultural pillars of the Nanbu's identity and economy throughout the classical and medieval periods. As horse traders, the Nanbu presented the Ashikaga shoguns with the finest warhorses on the archipelago. They may even have acquired a number of these chargers from continental stocks, buying from Mongol and Tungus horse dealers active in Northeast Asian transmarine trade routes.

The nature of politics in Nukanobu reflected the distinct and local forms of power and political organization in Kita Ōu. The Nanbu yoked their economic power, based on horse farms and trade, to Yamato elites. Through these connections, the Nanbu solicited court titles for themselves and their followers. Henceforth, their political power and legitimacy stemmed from an amalgam of local and central practices, and the Nanbu succeeded in controlling a large portion of what are today Aomori, Iwate, and Akita prefectures.

In the late sixteenth century, however, Hideyoshi destroyed the various geographical, economic, and political characteristics that had distinguished Kita Ōu fundamentally from south-central Japan. It is not as simple a matter as Hideyoshi bringing peace and stability to Kita Ōu. Rather, his campaigns aimed for the conquest and colonization of frontier lands, a process that irreversibly changed the culture and ecology of the region. At the critical onset of early modernity, Hideyoshi cut off Kita Ōu from the northern sea trade, and the Tokugawa shogunate followed suit by forcing the region to adapt to a political economy based on paddy agriculture, for which it was not environmentally suited. The extension of the early-modern state into the far northeast destroyed ancient trade routes and compromised the economic vitality of the region. Subsequently, crop failures, famine, pestilence, ungulate irruptions, and economic immiseration in general plagued northeastern Japan and Ezo throughout the early-modern period.[105]

Thus, Kita Ōu, a frontier region once populated by horse-raising peoples of various cultural backgrounds, a region of international trade and contact, was to become one of the poorest and most isolated regions in Japan in the early-modern period and beyond. Ironically, one of the few legacies of Kita Ōu's rich past that remains today is a famed *meibutsu* or regional specialty. The town of Gonohe, an area famous since the classical period for producing the "swift horses of Nukanobu," is now renowned for its *basashi*—horsemeat sashimi.

NOTES

The author wishes to thank Ethan Segal, Kären Wigen, Brett Walker, and Gregory Pflugfelder for their much needed suggestions, and to acknowledge that a Japan Foundation Japanese Study Fellowship supported the final stages of research and writing. The chapter is dedicated to the memory of J. P. Mass, master historian, in whose seminar the project had its origins, but whose untimely passing prevented him from seeing its completion.

1. Contrary to the conventional chronology that frames this volume, I categorize the Nara (710–790), Heian (792–1185), and Kamakura (1185–1333) periods as Japan's "classical" era. The subsequent Kenmu (1333–1336) and Muromachi (1392–1568) periods are, by contrast, "medieval." For the growing consensus among pre-1600 historians that the medieval age began with the destruction of the Kamakura shogunate in 1333, not with its founding in 1185, see Andrew E. Goble, *Kenmu: Go-Daigo's Revolution* (Cambridge, Mass.: Harvard University Press, 1996); Jeffrey P. Mass, "Of Hierarchy and Authority at the End of Kamakura," in *Origins of Japan's Medieval World*, ed. Jeffrey P. Mass (Stanford: Stanford University Press, 1997), 17–38.

2. Irumada Nobuo, "Nukanobu no shunme," in *Tōhoku kodaishi no kenkyū*, ed. Takahashi Tomio (Tokyo: Yoshikawa Kōbunkan, 1986), 621, 630; Mimi Hall Yiengpruksawan, *Hiraizumi: Buddhist Art and Regional Politics in Twelfth-Century Japan* (Cambridge, Mass.: Harvard University Press, 1998), 16–17, 33, 35.

3. Kaiho Mineo, *Chūsei no Ezochi* (Tokyo: Yoshikawa Kōbunkan, 1987), 164.

4. Ōishi Naomasa, "Tōgoku: Tōhoku no jiritsu to 'Nippon no kuni,'" in *Nihon no shakaishi*, vol. 1, *Rettō naigai no kōtsū to kokka*, ed. Asao Naohiro et al. (Tokyo: Iwanami Shoten, 1987), 243; Yiengpruksawan, *Hiraizumi*, 35.

5. Ōishi, "Tōgoku," 241–43; Yiengpruksawan, *Hiraizumi*, 14–17, 47. Although Amino Yoshihiko has sought to debunk the myth of a monolithic agrarian Japanese society extending back into prehistory, I think we can still make a meaningful generalization that south-central Japan was relatively oriented toward agriculture and northeastern Japan was not.

6. Here I use Jeffrey P. Mass's term "bridging figures" to describe the role that horses played between Yamato Japan and Kita Ōu. Mass first used the term to

describe the role of late-Heian warrior elites in connecting provincial warriors to the capital and to court circles, as in the following example. "The leaders of the Taira and Minamoto need to be appreciated in this light [as provincial "trouble-shooters" for the highest central elites]. They were not, as they are usually depicted, regional chieftains chafing under courtier dominance. Rather, they were bridging figures—military nobles in the truest sense—between the great central aristocrats, who were their patrons, and the great provincial warriors, who were their followers. These leaders' dual character, born out of service to two constituencies, is essential to an understanding of ... warrior development." See Jeffrey P. Mass, "The Kamakura Bakufu," in *The Cambridge History of Japan*, vol. 3, *Medieval Japan*, ed. Kozo Yamamura (Cambridge: Cambridge University Press, 1990), 49–50.

7. An "attached periphery" is connected to the core by economic and political ties, but suffers exploitation; an "autonomous periphery" interacts with the core through trade and exchange without compromising its autonomy. In his discussion of twelfth-century Ainu ethnogenesis, Mark Hudson argues that the northeast was an "autonomous periphery" to the Kinai while Ezo was an "attached periphery" of the northeast. See Mark J. Hudson, *Ruins of Identity: Ethnogenesis in the Japanese Islands* (Honolulu: University of Hawaii Press, 1999), 219.

8. Bruce Batten makes the important point that we cannot associate the geographical limits of modern Japan with those of the premodern archipelago in "Frontiers and Boundaries of Pre-Modern Japan," *Journal of Historical Geography* 25 (1999): 166–82.

9. C. B. Fawcett, *Frontiers: A Study in Political Geography* (Oxford: Clarendon, 1918), 17–18, 24.

10. Ladis K. D. Kristof, "The Nature of Frontiers and Boundaries," *Annals of the Association of American Geographers* 4 (1959): 269–82. It is worth quoting Kristof at length. "The *frontier* is an *integrating factor*. Being a zone of transition from the sphere (ecumene) of one way of life to another, and representing forces which are neither fully assimilated to nor satisfied with either, it provides an excellent opportunity for mutual interpenetration and sway. Along the frontier life constantly manipulates the settled patterns of the pivotally organized socio-political and cultural structures. It is precisely this watering down of loyalties and blurring of differences that the central governments attempt to forestall by substituting the semi-autonomous frontiers with a controlled and exact borderline." (Emphasis in original.) See Kristof, "Nature of Frontiers," 269–73.

11. Irumada, "Nukanobu no shunme," 590–631; Ōishi, "Tōgoku," 241–43; Saitō Toshio, "Kyōkai toshi Hiraizumi to Kita Ōu sekai," in *Tōhoku kodaishi no kenkyū*, 474–75; Yiengpruksawan, *Hiraizumi*, 14–17, 47.

12. Batten, "Frontiers and Boundaries," 170.

13. On the prickly issue of Emishi ethnicity, see Karl F. Friday, "Pushing Beyond the Pale: The Yamato Conquest of the *Emishi* and Northern Japan," *Journal of Japanese Studies* 23 (1997): 1–24.

14. Hudson, *Ruins of Identity*, 198–200.

15. Kaiho, *Chūsei no Ezochi*, 184–85.

16. For more on the horseriding Emishi, see William Wayne Farris, *Heavenly Warriors: The Evolution of Japan's Military, 500-1300* (Cambridge, Mass.: Harvard University Press, 1992); Karl F. Friday, *Hired Swords: The Rise of Private Warrior Power in*

Early Japan (Stanford: Stanford University Press, 1992); Friday, "Pushing Beyond the Pale." For a source attesting to the fact that Satsumon and proto-Ainu peoples did not ride horses, see the following section on the Suwa picture scrolls.

17. The inside hooks or ears enabled its users to suspend the pot over an open fire without burning the material used to elevate it.

18. Ōishi Naomasa, "Hiraizumi Fujiwara-shi to Tsugaru Andō-shi," in *Tsugaru Andō-shi to hoppō sekai*, ed. Oguchi Masanaka (Tokyo: Kawade Shobō Shinsha, 1995), 198–99.

19. For more on early Yamato monarchs, see Joan Piggott, *The Emergence of Japanese Kingship* (Stanford: Stanford University Press, 1997).

20. Yiengpruksawan, *Hiraizumi*, 183, 197–98.

21. Ibid., 131–33.

22. Yiengpruksawan reiterates Saitō's conception of a *fushū* nation—a nation of "assimilated" Emishi chieftains. See ibid., 199–201.

23. *Azuma kagami*, vol. 1 of *Shintei zōho kokushi taikei*, ed. Kuroita Katsumi (Tokyo: Yoshikawa Kōbunkan, 1988), 353.

24. Yiengpruksawan, *Hiraizumi*, 94–96.

25. Amino Yoshihiko, "Deconstructing Japan," *East Asian History* 3 (1992): 128–29, 135. Mark Hudson also asserts that the polity of the Hiraizumi Fujiwara was distinct from that of the Yamato court. See Hudson, *Ruins of Identity*, 204–5.

26. Richard White challenges the "Turnerian" (referring to the theories of historian Frederick Jackson Turner) understanding of U.S. frontiers with his own "middle ground" paradigm, arguing that the frontier of westward colonization was not a simple expansion into barren lands, but that there was interaction between distinct peoples and cultures from the start. White argues that, by adopting and adapting the other's cultural forms to meet their needs, Native Americans and Europeans constituted the middle ground, merging elements of the other's culture into "something quite different from the Algonquin, Iroquian, and French cultures that gave them birth." See Richard White, *The Middle Ground: Indians, Empires, and Republics in the Great Lakes Region, 1650-1815* (Cambridge, Mass.: Harvard University Press, 1991), 55–56.

27. Yiengpruksawan, *Hiraizumi*, 205. Other historians are reluctant to consider Kita Ōu a region distinct from south-central Japan. The notion that the Hiraizumi rulers were not a part, however peripheral, of Japan seems to make some scholars nervous, and most are reluctant to integrate such alien-seeming practices as mummification, along with northern burial garbs, into standard narratives of Hiraizumi history. See Yiengpruksawan, *Hiraizumi*, 133. For a skeptical view of Yiengpruksawan's thesis, see Robert Borgen's review of *Hiraizumi* in *Journal of Japanese Studies* 27 (2001): 227–31.

28. Ōishi, "Hiraizumi Fujiwara-shi to Tsugaru Andō-shi," 176–77.

29. Ibid., 180–81.

30. Emori Susumu, "Ainu minzoku to Andō-shi," in Oguchi, *Tsugaru Andō-shi to hoppō sekai*, 222–23.

31. Hudson, *Ruins of Identity*, 206–32.

32. Ōishi, "Hiraizumi Fujiwara-shi to Tsugaru Andō-shi," 176–77.

33. Yiengpruksawan, *Hiraizumi*, 205. In his capacity as *seii taishōgun* (Great Barbarian-Subduing Generalissimo), Sakanoue no Tamuramaro (758–811) led the

first successful campaign to pacify the Emishi of Mutsu and Dewa during the late eighth and early ninth centuries.

34. The sources are scarce, but in 1325 Andō Munesue willed his *Ezo no sata* title (which appears as *sato* in the document) to an unnamed offspring. See Iwate-ken Kyōiku Iinkai, ed., *Iwate-ken chūsei monjo,* vol. 1 (Tokyo: Kokusho Kankōkai, 1983), 32 (doc. 85). This dispensation ignited fighting between Munesue's two sons, Hidenaga and Hidehisa. The succession dispute grew into a more generalized disturbance known as the *Ezo hokki,* roughly translatable as Barbarian Rebellion. See Itō Kiyoshi, "Muromachi no Nanbu no uji," in *Hokuhen no chūseishi: He no machi no kigen o saguru,* ed. Aomori-ken Rokunohe-chō (Tokyo: Meicho Shuppansha, 1997), 131–32.

35. Kaiho, *Chūsei no Ezochi,* 134–35; Brett L. Walker, *The Conquest of Ainu Lands: Ecology and Culture in Japanese Expansion, 1590-1800* (Berkeley: University of California Press, 2001), 26–27.

36. Kaiho Mineo, *Chūsei Ezo shiryō* (Tokyo: San'ichi Shobō, 1983), 74–75 (doc. 183); Miyazaki Michio, *Aomori-ken no rekishi,* Kenshi shirīzu, no. 2 (Tokyo: Yamakawa Shuppansha, 1970), 85.

37. Kaiho, *Chūsei no Ezochi,* 164, 186.

38. Zoku Gunsho Ruijū Kanseikai, ed., *Gunsho kaidai,* vol. 6 (Tokyo: Heibunsha, 1962), 450–59.

39. Ibid., 458.

40. Kaiho suggests these possible readings in *Chūsei no Ezochi,* 168–69.

41. *Suwa daimyōjin ekotoba,* in *Nihon shomin seikatsu shiryō shūsei,* vol. 26, ed. Tanikawa Ken'ichi (Tokyo: San'ichi Shobō, 1983), 63.

42. Kaiho, *Chūsei no Ezochi,* 158–59.

43. Ibid., 161.

44. Ibid., 162–63.

45. Miyazaki, *Aomori-ken no rekishi,* 70.

46. Itō remarks that medieval sources relating to the Nanbu are few, but that early-modern family histories and genealogies are useful for filling in the gaps. See Itō, "Muromachi no Nanbu," 128.

47. Miyazaki, *Aomori-ken no rekishi,* 70–73.

48. Ibid., 98. The Shichinohe were *ichizoku* (cadet family) vassals of the Hachinohe from the time of Nanbu Masanaga, the fifth-generation Hachinohe Nejō chieftain. A number of Sannohe Nanbu scions broke off from the main line and founded cadet lineages. The younger brothers of nineteenth-generation chieftain Yasunobu all started cadet families: Takanobu founded the Ishikawa, Nagayoshi the Minami, Nobufusa the Ishikame, and Nobutsugi the Kemanai. See the genealogy in Mori Kahee, *Iwate-ken no rekishi,* Kenshi shirīzu, no. 3 (Tokyo: Yamakawa Shuppansha, 1972), 71. The Kita were also a cadet family, but it is not known when they broke off from the main line or who their founding patriarch was. See Matsuoka Kōichi, ed. *Aomori-ken hyakka jiten* (Tokyo: Tōō Nippōsha, 1981), 244. In the late sixteenth century, these vassal chieftains maintained relative autonomy from the main branch, residing in castles on their hereditary proprietorships. For example, the Kita inhabited Ken'yoshi castle, the Minami occupied Asami castle, the Shichinohe maintained Shichinohe castle, and the Kunohe held Kunohe castle. Koida Yukiya, *Hachinohe Nejō to Nanbu-ke monjo* (Tokyo: Kokusho Kankōkai, 1986), 360 (hereafter cited as *HNNM*).

49. Mori, *Iwate-ken no rekishi,* 49; Satō Yūjirō, *Nanbu bashi* (Hachinohe: Nan-

bu Bashi Hakkōsho, 1918), 33.

50. The origins of horse farms in Nukanobu are not clear. There are basically three possibilities. The first is that Emishi created these farms during the latter half of the eighth century, and that the farms became an integral part of the Emishi's horseriding culture. Alternatively, the provincial governors of Mutsu may have established a system of farms in the early Heian period from which they could secure a yearly supply of "tax" horses. A third possibility is that the Ōshū Fujiwara founded horse farms throughout the region in the twelfth century. See Irumada, "Nukanobu no shunme," 594.

51. According to house records of the Nanbu, at some point in the mid-fifteenth century, the Kyoto monk Eigoku requested a light-fawn-colored steed from the Nanbu for Shiba Takehira. In 1590, during Hideyoshi's conquest of Ōu, Asano Nagayoshi (later known as Nagamasa) requested a chestnut-colored horse from the lord of Hachinohe. See Washio Yoritaka, ed., *Nanbu-ke monjo* (Tokyo: Yoshino-chō Shiseki Chōsakai, 1939), 46 (doc. 69), 47–48 (doc. 70), 75–76 (doc. 118; hereafter cited as *NM*).

52. Itō, "Muromachi no Nanbu," 127.

53. Satō, *Nanbu bashi*, 59–61.

54. For the Nanbu during the Nanbokuchō Wars, see Ōikawa Taikei, *Michinoku chūsei gōzoku* (Tokyo: Kokusho Kankōkai, 1976), 195–274.

55. Itō, "Muromachi no Nanbu," 131–33. For Akiie's orders concerning the Tsugaru, see *NM*, 25–26 (doc. 32).

56. Emperor Go-Daigo, no doubt, wanted to bring contact between the Tsugaru region and transmarine Northeast Asia under his administration's control. For more on Go-Daigo, see Goble, *Kenmu*.

57. For the importance of personal relations in late medieval politics, see Mary Elizabeth Berry, "Public Peace and Private Attachment: The Goals and Conduct of Power in Early Modern Japan," *Journal of Japanese Studies* 12 (1986): 235–72.

58. *HNNM*, 281; *NM*, 46 (doc. 69).

59. Itō, "Muromachi no Nanbu," 144–45. For the appointment documents, see *NM*, 49–51 (docs. 71-72).

60. Koida Yukiya believes that Nobunaga did not travel south until after the Ōnin War, returning to Nukanobu in 1488. See *HNNM*, 313. For the order summoning Nobunaga to the capital, see *NM*, 59–60 (doc. 96). A letter that Nobunaga sent home around 1487 recounting his exploits in the capital may be found in *NM*, 60 (doc. 97).

61. In 1432, Mansai recorded in his journal that the Nanbu attacked the Andō at Tosa Minato, subsequently driving them across the Tsugaru straits to Ezo. During the Nanbu attack against the Andō, the shogunate issued a number of cease-and-desist writs. According to Mansai, the Nanbu's lawlessness angered the shogunate for two reasons: first, that uncontrollable warfare might spread throughout all of Mutsu, and second, that the trade lanes between Ezo and Kita Ōu might be disrupted by Nanbu aggression. The Nanbu, however, did not conform to the dictates of central authority. See Itō, "Muromachi no Nanbu," 144; Kaiho, *Chūsei Ezo shiryō*, 113 (doc. 299).

62. Shichinomiya Keizō, *Michinoku no taiheiki* (Hirosaki: Tsugaru Shobō, 1980), 210–11.

63. Endō Iwao, "Andō-shi to Tsugaru no sekai," in Oguchi, *Tsugaru Andō-shi to hoppō sekai*, 88–89.

64. Itō, "Muromachi no Nanbu," 144; Kaiho, *Chūsei Ezo shiryō*, 113 (doc. 299).

65. Walker, *Conquest*, 68–69.

66. Irumada, "Nukanobu no shunme," 620–21.

67. Itō Kiyoshi, *Chūsei kokka to Kantō: Ōu* (Tokyo: Azekura Shobō, 1999), 37.

68. Itō, "Muromachi no Nanbu," 143; Kaiho, *Chūsei Ezo shiryō*, 133 (doc. 298).

69. Iwate-ken Kyōiku Iinkai, *Iwate-ken chūsei monjo*, 32 (doc. 85).

70. Representative of this tendency in Japanese scholarship are two conference volumes on the Andō and Tosa Minato: Kokuritsu Rekishi Minzoku Hakubutsukan, ed., *Chūsei toshi Tosa Minato to Andō-shi* (Tokyo: Shinjinbutsu Ōraisha, 1994); Oguchi, *Tsugaru Andō-shi to hoppō sekai*. None of the articles contained in these collections, however, explore a Nanbu interest in trade.

71. Senda Yoshihiro, "Tosa Minato: Fukushijō no chōsa," in Kokuritsu Rekishi Minzoku Hakubutsukan, *Chūsei toshi Tosa Minato to Andō-shi*, 52–53.

72. "Mandokoro naidan kiroku, 1463," in *Muromachi bakufu hikitsuke shiryō shūsei*, ed. Kuwayama Kōnen, vol. 20 of *Nihon shiryō sensho* (Tokyo: Kondō Shuppansha, 1980), 243–44.

73. Amino Yoshihiko, "Chūsei no Nihon kaikōtsū," in Kokuritsu Rekishi Minzoku Hakubutsukan, *Chūsei toshi Tosa Minato to Andō-shi*, 26–29.

74. The three most important ports were Anotsu in the province of Ise, Hakata in Chikuzen, and Sakai in Izumi; the most important harbors were Mikuni in Echizen, Motoyoshi in Kaga, Wajima in Noto, Iwase in Etchū, Imamachi in Echigo, Akita in Dewa, and Tosa in Mutsu. See Miyazaki, *Aomori-ken no rekishi*, 85.

75. Amino, "Chūsei no Nihon kaikōtsū," 28–29.

76. Mori, *Iwate-ken no rekishi*, 83–85; Hachinohe Shishi Hensan Iinkai, ed., *Hachinohe shishi: Tsūshihen* (Hachinohe: Hachinohe-shi, 1976), 133.

77. Miyazaki, *Aomori-ken no rekishi*, 116. For problems with dating these events, see *HNNM*, 360–62; Mark Ravina, *Land and Lordship in Early Modern Japan* (Stanford: Stanford University Press, 1999), 115–17.

78. Fujiki Hisashi, "Chūsei Ōu no shūmatsu," in *Chūsei Ōu no sekai*, ed. Kobayashi Seiji and Ōishi Naomasa (Tokyo: Tōkyō Daigaku Shuppankai, 1978), 211.

79. *HNNM*, 386.

80. Hachinohe Shishi Hensan Iinkai, *Hachinohe shishi*, 135; *HNNM*, 387.

81. Mori, *Iwate-ken no rekishi*, 102.

82. *NM* sources from this period unfortunately bear no year date. Therefore, scholars such as Koida are forced to speculate on the respective dates of the extant documents.

83. Oaths of loyalty were common during the Warring States period of the fifteenth and sixteenth centuries. Hall asserts that "by this time almost exclusive reliance was placed upon the oath as the mechanism for maintaining loyalty and compliance to authority." See John W. Hall, *Government and Local Power in Japan, 500-1700: A Study of Bizen Province* (Princeton: Princeton University Press, 1966; reprint, Ann Arbor: Center for Japanese Studies, The University of Michigan, 1999), 253.

84. *HNNM*, 380–85; *NM*, 65 (doc. 104).

85. *HNNM*, 380–85; *NM*, 67–68 (doc. 107).

86. Hachinohe Shishi Hensan Iinkai, *Hachinohe shishi*, 136.

87. *HNNM*, 390–92. Nagamasa pushed into Hienuki province and from Toriyuzaki castle requested a chestnut horse from the Hachinohe lord. See *NM*, 75–76 (doc. 118).

88. *HNNM*, 390–97.

89. *NM*, 74–75 (doc. 116).

90. Quoted in *HNNM*, 393–97.

91. Walker, *Conquest*, 29–35.

92. Ibid., 29–35.

93. Hideyoshi's investiture adversely affected not only Kita Ōu but Ezo as well. Kaiho Mineo argues that the early-modern Japanese state fundamentally altered the fabric of life in Ezo, destroying the economic, political, and social independence enjoyed by the medieval Ezo peoples. See Kaiho, *Chūsei no Ezochi*, 169, 200–201. Brett Walker also shows that a number of Ainu chiefdoms had depended on trade with Kita Ōu before the early-modern period. However, when the Matsumae monopolized the trade between Ainu and the Japanese, the Ainu fell to the unfair trading practices of Matsumae officials and their contracted merchants. The new trading arrangements were so unfavorable that many Ainu, such as those from the Ishikari region, fought against Matsumae domain forces during the Shakushain War of 1669 in order to regain the ability to trade freely with Kita Ōu. See Walker, *Conquest*, 68–69.

94. Hachinohe Shishi Hensan Iinkai, *Hachinohe shishi*, 136–38.

95. Hosoi Hakaru, "Morioka-han," in *Hanshi daijiten*, ed. Kimura Motoi, Fujino Tamotsu, and Murakami Tadashi, 8 vols. (Tokyo: Yūzankaku Shuppan, 1988–1990), 1: 57; Mori, *Iwate-ken no rekishi*, 102.

96. Hosoi, "Morioka han," 1: 77.

97. Miura Tadashi, "Hachinohe han," in *Hanshi daijiten*, 1: 95.

98. See Ravina, *Land and Lordship*.

99. John Whitney Hall, "Japan's Sixteenth-Century Revolution," in *Warriors, Artisans, and Commoners: Japan in the Sixteenth Century*, ed. George Elison and Bardwell L. Smith (Honolulu: University of Hawaii Press, 1981), 12.

100. Amino Yoshihiko posits a similar argument for the construction of the "Japanese" nation. "Japan ... began with the *ritsuryō* state, inseparably tied to the appellation *tennō*, which controlled Honshu, Shikoku and much of Kyushu and was based in the small region of Kinai, and which through fierce struggles with subsequent states and with the various societies and regions of the peninsula, gradually became what it is today." Amino, "Deconstructing Japan," 132–33.

101. Michael Hechter, *Internal Colonialism: The Celtic Fringe in British National Development, 1536-1966* (Berkeley: University of California Press, 1975), 81.

102. Hechter, *Internal Colonialism*, 81. In the following quote, the relation between the far northeast and central Japan during the early-modern period is fairly described if we substitute *Ezo and Kita Ōu* for *Celtic*, and *the shogunate-dominated central polity* for *England*. "In general, political incorporation forced the Celtic territories to develop in a manner which complemented, but did not permit competition with, England. This was accomplished in two ways. Incorporation stimulated interregional trade and thereby extended market forces to the Celtic economies. In the periph-

ery, this caused pressures for the evolution of highly specialized export economies. Mass population movements ensued as regional specialization proceeded in each of the Celtic lands.... Therefore, political incorporation indirectly led to the development of economic dependence in the peripheral regions by facilitating the expansion of production for exchange" (81).

103. Ibid., 123.

104. As Kären Wigen argues, national development and centralization should be seen not as a process of standardization, but of differentiation. "Centralization was by nature a differentiating process; creating a new geopolitical cartography meant designating cores and peripheries, elevating certain places at the expense of others. As a result, assimilation into the emerging state had very different implications for different places." Although Wigen is discussing the emergence of the Meiji state here, I believe the same holds true for Hideyoshi's colonization of the north. Kären Wigen, *The Making of the Japanese Periphery, 1720-1920* (Berkeley: University of California Press, 1995), 215.

105. For more on famine, plagues, and poverty and economic immiseration of peoples in northern Japan and Ezo during the early-modern period, see Susan B. Hanley and Kozo Yamamura, *Economic and Demographic Change in Preindustrial Japan, 1600-1868* (Princeton: Princeton University Press, 1977); David L. Howell, *Capitalism from Within: Economy, Society, and the State in a Japanese Fishery* (Berkeley: University of California Press, 1995); Ravina, *Land and Lordship*; Walker, *Conquest*; James W. White, *Ikki: Social Conflict and Political Protest in Early Modern Japan* (Ithaca, N.Y.: Cornell University Press, 1995).

From *Wakan sansai zue*. Courtesy of the C. V. Starr East Asian Library, Columbia University.

CHAPTER FOUR

Exotic-Bird Collecting in Early-Modern Japan

Martha Chaiklin

The Japanese cultural landscape is populated densely with birds. Depictions of cranes may be found on Yayoi period (300 B.C.E.–300 C.E.) bronze bells, and archaeologists have excavated clay roosters from Kofun period (300–710) tombs. Classical Japanese verse reveals an appreciation for birds even in the most ancient sources. The *Man'yōshū* (Collection of ten thousand leaves; ca. 770), for example, includes many celebrated verses about cranes, cuckoos, hawks, wild geese, and other avifauna. Court diaries and other forms of early prose provide similar references, such as a segment on the wonders of avian life in *Makura no sōshi*, the tenth-century "Pillow Book" by Sei Shōnagon.[1] In the pictorial realm as well, birds have provided a favored motif. Indeed, they command an entire genre known as *kachōga*, literally, "flower and bird pictures." Although this style of painting was inspired in part by Song-dynasty (960–1279 C.E.) Chinese conventions, it became so influential in Japan that even artists who typically worked in other genres included *kachōga* in their oeuvre. Among them are such early-modern woodblock-print masters as Andō Hiroshige (1797–1858), known today more widely for his landscapes (*sansuiga*), and Kitagawa Utamaro (1753?–1806), renowned for his portraiture of beautiful women (*jinbutsuga*).

Likewise, birds were deeply ingrained from early times in Japanese spiritual life. For example, a form of divination long existed in which interested parties traveled into the mountains to kill a bird. If the creature had a full stomach, diviners interpreted it to presage the coming of a plentiful and auspicious year; an empty stomach, conversely, portended food scarcity and difficult times. The arrival and departure of migratory birds was carefully marked to track the passing of the seasons. Nesting swallows were considered especially lucky, as was noted by Edward Morse (1838–1925), an American zoologist who taught the natural sciences in Japan during the late 1870s and early 1880s. Morse observed that swallow nests commonly adorned homes and shops in both city and country. Rather than destroying the nests as a nuisance, the residents of these structures often preferred to construct a small shelf underneath the nest to keep the birds from soiling the mats inside.[2] On a more supernatural level, human beings had fused with birds since at least the Heian period in the form of the folkloric creature known as the *tengu* (see also chapter 2). Part human and part avian, *tengu* differ from the Harpies of Greek mythology not only in gender (Harpies are female, *tengu* male), but in a greater variability in the distribution of their human and birdlike parts. Like many other Japanese monsters, *tengu* possessed a dual nature: they could serve both as protectors of the worthy and as corrupters of the weak. *Tengu* were more than the stuff of stories, however, and had deep associations with certain Shinto traditions.[3]

The crane is perhaps the most prominent avian to soar the Japanese cultural horizon, symbolically connoting long life and good fortune. The red and white hues of the crane are even today considered a particularly auspicious color combination, and frequently adorn clothing and accessories used in marriage ceremonies. Many Japanese believe that one thousand origami cranes, laced together on a string, will help to ward off illness. It is not clear when exactly this tradition developed, but the practice of folding paper in prescribed shapes has an ancient connection with Shinto rituals. The 1797 work *Hiden senbazuru orikata* (Secrets of folding one thousand cranes) contains one of the first explicit references to crane talismans.[4] It is likely that the conventional number of folded birds reflects the fact that cranes, according to Japanese lore, reputedly live for one thousand years. During the Tokugawa period, the shogunate explicitly forbade commoners to kill cranes. Tokugawa protocol dictated that the shogun present a crane to the emperor in Kyoto each year to be consumed at the imperial New Year's banquet. Similarly, the shogun provided a New Year's feast of cranes for assembled domain lords, or daimyo, at his castle. As the Tokugawa period progressed, the tradition was in turn adopted by the daimyo, who served crane to their most important vassals. Nevertheless, the eating of crane was, legally at least, reserved for the upper classes.[5] João Rodrigues (1562–1633), a Jesuit missionary who spent over two decades in Japan, claimed that cranes were prized as food even more than pheasants, quails, pigeons, and other game birds.[6]

It was another prominent bird in Japanese culture, the hawk, who helped hunters bag cranes and other prey. Hawking, which is not distinguished from falconry in Japanese practice, is ancient, as pottery figures of humans with hawks perched on their arms excavated from Kofun period sites attest. One of the earliest extant Japanese texts, *Nihon shoki* (Chronicle of Japan; 720), also makes mention of the practice.[7] Both archeological and documentary sources suggest that falconry arose originally as the preserve of the imperial house and its courtiers. The early connections of falconry with the imperial house likely also bear a relation to the practice of ritual hawking at certain Shinto shrines.

When the military elite assumed control of Japan in the Kamakura period (1185–1333), they too adopted hawks as symbols of power, thus establishing a tradition of hawking among the warrior class.[8] The Tokugawa shogunate encouraged falconry among its vassals because it was an effective means of preserving and developing military skills in an era of stability. Regional lords therefore valued hawks as gifts when cementing relations with the shogun and with other lords.[9] As a result of this association with military skill, as well as the innate characteristics of the species, hawks came to symbolize courage and valor. Like the crane, hawks were among the most common of the many birds represented in family crests (*mon*). Other examples of the scores of birds with iconographic meaning were such species as cormorants (symbols of faithfulness to one's master as well as of good eyesight), crows (connoting death and bad fortune), wild geese (evoking the arrival of autumn as well as wedded bliss), and cuckoos (*hototogisu*, representing summer and unrequited love).[10]

EARLY-MODERN BIRD OWNERSHIP

Actual human relationships with birds in early-modern Japan may be seen as falling into three main types. The first is culinary, which is to say the hunting and domestication of birds for food or medicinal use. The second involves service, in which human beings harness avian abilities, as in the case of hawking or fishing with cormorants. But it is a third type, bird collecting, that, because it was not confined to the elite or to members of a particular profession, actually touched the greatest number of people.

One can only speculate as to when the people of Japan began caging birds to keep as pets. There is little doubt, however, that the practice became increasingly widespread during the seventeenth and eighteenth centuries. Peace during Japan's early-modern period led to steadily expanding urban centers and a rising standard of living. By the late 1600s, economic prosperity and increased leisure time had led to a greater measure of disposable income for luxuries, including pets. Although the phenomenon was likely only temporary, bird ownership underwent a decline through edicts issued in 1687 that limited presentations of birds from the provinces to once a year and forbade the ownership of live birds by commoners. Shogunal disapproval probably affected ownership in and around the Eastern Capital, but it is unlikely that the injunctions were rigorously enforced elsewhere. Caged birds were easy to maintain even in the smallest of residential spaces, and made it possible to cultivate a little bit of nature even in the crowded tenements of the city.

By the seventeenth century, an extensive distribution and retail system blanketed much of Japan, facilitated by rapid boat transport. While little is known about the actual mode of distribution of any specific type of bird, these commercial conditions suggest that pet birds did not have to be limited to local species. Indeed, around the city of Edo (seat of the shogunate, today's Tokyo), bird catching was officially prohibited for all purposes except securing hawk fodder, which the shogun and his councilors required in order to raise, as well as to hunt with, their prize falcons. Bird catchers appear to have favored birdlime, but also included snares and nets in their arsenal.[11] Francis Hall (1822–1902), an American merchant who lived in Japan between the years 1859 and 1866, described a bird catcher whom he observed along the Tōkaidō post road as follows:

> He carried in his hand a long bamboo pole, one end of which was smeared with a viscous substance and strongly adhesive. He had a peculiar whistle in his mouth which imitated the chirping of a bird. They hovered about the adjacent roofs attracted by the sound. When the opportunity offered, the bird catcher, with a dexterous snap or push of his pole, struck the birds with it. Which entrapped by the bird lime were easily secured and put into a basket the bird catcher carried on his back like a trout basket. At Yedo [i.e., Edo] these bird catchers are seen daily plying their trade.[12]

Bird catchers like the one described by Hall were known, like their long bamboo poles, as *torisashi*. The "viscous substance," or birdlime, was a paste made by pounding the bark of a type of holly with a small amount of water.[13]

Tokugawa Japanese kept many different kinds of birds as pets. The most popular of caged birds were bush warblers (*uguisu*), two separate types of robin (*komadori* and *ruri*), and quail.[14] Collectors of songbirds (*meikin*)—a designation that in Japan included quail—trained them to compete against one another to see which bird could produce the most beautiful melody. Quail did remain, nonetheless, a game bird, and in more ways than one. Not only were they hunted, but they were sometimes trained to fight matches, like the cockfights of Indonesia. While not as showy as some species, sparrows were also popular as caged birds, perhaps because they were widely available and therefore inexpensive.[15] A famous pet sparrow appears in *Shitakiri suzume* (Tongue-cut sparrow), a folktale of obscure origin. In the tale, a spiteful old woman cuts out the tongue of her neighbors' pet sparrow because it has eaten her laundry starch. After the injured bird flies away, the old man and woman who had cared for the bird search the countryside frantically for their pet. Joyfully reunited with one another on a mountaintop, the sparrow brings the old couple to his mountain home for a feast. When it is time for them to leave, the sparrow offers the couple a choice of two baskets, one light and one heavy. As is the rule in didactic tales, the good old people modestly choose the light one and are surprised to find themselves rewarded with a bottomless trove of riches. Afterward, the wicked neighbor grows envious and seeks out the sparrow. When offered the same choice of baskets, she greedily selects the heavier basket, only to discover devils inside.[16] While the moral of the tale revolves around compassion, greed, and the folk belief that sparrows always repay their debts of honor, the story suggests on a more quotidian level that even a poor old couple could reasonably be expected to keep a sparrow.

As is equally true today, early-modern bird enthusiasts frequently hung their pets in cages outdoors when weather permitted. On one occasion, Francis Hall even witnessed a traveler with canaries dangling from the palanquin.[17] The birdcages that housed feathered pets came in a variety of shapes and sizes. A bird shop pictured in *Jinrin kinmō zui* (Illustrated collection of professions; 1688), one of the oldest sources to depict the various trades practiced in early-modern Japan, shows round and square cage bases with woven as well as barred covers of varying heights. Styles appear to have changed with time, however, as an 1830 miscellany, *Kiyū shōran*

(Lighthearted listing), records that "today's insect cages look like the round bird cages of old." [18] A few decades later, one foreign visitor would observe that Japanese kept nuthatches in "very tall cages, with an upright stick in the middle, at the top of which [was] a crosspiece with a notch, in which the bird [placed] the nut or berry."[19] The birdcages described in these works were typically crafted from woven bamboo or other soft woods. Perhaps because quail fanciers gathered for song competitions, the containers for these birds appear to have been of a different class. The few birdcages from Tokugawa Japan that have survived were elaborate square cages for quail, including some that sported glass bars.[20] According to the late seventeenth- and early eighteenth-century physician and scholar Terajima Ryōan, connoisseurs expended as much effort over quail cages as they did over the birds themselves.[21] While there is evidence of craftsmen specializing in birdcages in Osaka in 1692, it is not clear how widespread the trade was. In any case, the fanciful and opulent bird-palaces found in Europe at the time do not seem to have been very common in Japan.[22]

A variety of shops made it their business to sell pet birds. The 1688 *Jinrin kinmō zui* lists specifically designated stores, called *kotoriya*. It explains that these shops "sell many, many kinds of pet birds. If one brings a bush warbler, quail, or other songbird to the shop, they will teach it to sing."[23] The fact that a guidebook published four years later identified shops selling birds in all three of the great metropolises of the day—Edo, Kyoto, and Osaka—is testimony to the popularity of birds as pets.[24] In 1718, the shogunate issued licenses to ten bird wholesalers and forbade others from practicing the trade. However, dozens of shops retailed birds to pet owners.[25] Only six years later, in 1725, this system was found to be inadequate. The shogunate responded by licensing six wholesalers for waterfowl and eight for other birds, but still forbade any second-tier wholesalers or retail sales. [26] Primarily, the government established this rather strict system of wholesalers in order to control prey and food for their hawks and to clamp down on bird theft.[27]

Regulations on bird sales would remain in place until the middle of the nineteenth century. The 1824 guidebook *Edo hitorimono annai* (A loner's guide to Edo) lists no bird merchants at all, but only two egg wholesalers and three feather wholesalers. Of course, this does not mean that such establishments did not exist. Indeed, records from the early nineteenth century specify that two songbird sellers had obtained shogunal warrants.[28]

Similarly, in Osaka, Jan Cock Blomhoff (1779–1853) noted an entire "street where they only sell birds and other kinds of animals" in his account of a Dutch court journey in 1817. [29] There is plenty of evidence to support the conclusion that bird ownership remained widespread despite restrictive measures on the retail system.

Moreover, only the political capital of Edo was regulated so strictly. In Osaka, for example, a licensed guild of bird wholesalers had formed by the seventeenth century, but by the eighteenth century it had split into separate guilds of dealers and wholesalers.[30] In the 1850s, one street in Yokohama boasted more than twenty "poultry shops."[31] These establishments, according to observers, contained a variety of cages set up around a courtyard, smaller birdcages stacked atop larger ones. They housed storks, ducks, pheasants, doves and pigeons, bantam roosters, swans and geese, along with animals such as dogs, monkeys, goats, and fish.[32] American Francis Hall, mentioned earlier, offered a description of one such store:

> A shop for the sale of the beautiful little Japanese dogs interested me especially. It was a menagerie on a small scale. In the front sales room were the vivacious little fellows in cages, in a back room a whole pack of them was let loose on the floor. A long yard in the rear was appropriated to various animals. There were monkeys from the Straits, a black bear, cranes several feet high, and even goats and sheep were caged up as curiosities. There were a variety of birds, the most beautiful of which were golden and silver pheasants, the latter, with its white plumage bedecked with scallops of silver and the curving plumage of its tail, the most distinguished prisoner of all.[33]

Dutch diplomat Dirk de Graeff van Polsbroek (1833–1916) visited a bird vendor in Osaka on his way from Nagasaki to Edo in 1858. There he noted some three hundred pretty birds enclosed in a single large cage. He and his party purchased them all and granted them their freedom. According to de Graeff van Polsbroek, "As if in thanks, the beasts flew first to the trees in the garden, and lofted their most beautiful song, and then disappeared."[34]

As one might expect in a nation with a high rate of literacy, publishers produced and marketed many books in the eighteenth and nineteenth centuries to satisfy the appetites of the numerous bird fanciers who resided throughout the country.[35] One such work, *Yobukodori* (The cuckoo; 1710), for example, offered information on caring for quail, thrushes, shrikes, bush warblers, and swallows, among other types of bird.[36] Another book with wide circulation was *Momo chidori* (A hundred plovers; 1799), which described the essentials of caring for and raising no less than sixteen avian varieties. Books were also written on how to cultivate singing voices in certain birds, and on how the aficionado should appreciate and praise bird song.[37]

EXOTIC BIRDS AND THE DUTCH TRADE

Although early-modern Japan was composed of semiautonomous domains, in many ways it remained a totalitarian regime. This is apparent in the strict control of foreign trade, which was relegated to Nagasaki. The southern port, although distant from Edo, was usurped by the shogunate and placed under its direct control. After 1641, only Dutch and Chinese merchants were allowed to trade in Nagasaki, making it the hub of foreign trade.[38] Many restrictions were placed upon both trade and the foreign merchants who conducted it over the course of the Tokugawa period. For example, Dutch traders were required to live on a small artificial island in the bay, all foreign women were banned, the kinds and amounts of precious and base metals that could be exported were regulated, and it was forbidden to take Japanese currency or weapons out of the country. Yet this constrictive trade environment was no hindrance to the introduction of exotic birds into what was already a strong tradition of aviculture.

Nonnative species of birds came to Japan long before Europeans had any knowledge of the islands. *Nihon shoki*, one of Japan's most ancient mythohistorical records, notes that a prince from the Korean kingdom of Silla presented a peacock and a parrot to the powerful female emperor Suiko in 598. The nature of ancient records means that such formal political exchanges involving birds are all we have documentation about, but the sporadic character of contact with the rest of the world ensured that exotic presents of this kind remained rare in classical times. Travel abroad and foreign embassies trickled off in the following centuries, so that there was little occasion for the introduction of exotic avian life. Although Japanese pirates terrorized the China seas in the fifteenth and sixteenth centuries, these men were not usually literate, and we do not know what they brought back home with them.

The arrival of Europeans in Japan in the mid-sixteenth century brought a significant increase in the import of exotic birds. Greater contact with the outside world was initiated after three Portuguese mercenaries were blown ashore in a small Chinese junk in 1543. Within five years, Portuguese traders had opened trade with Japanese merchants, which further expanded after Portuguese interests established a base on Macao in 1557. For a time, they enjoyed a monopoly on commerce with Japan, partly on the basis of Pope Alexander VI's 1493 bull *Inter Caetera,* which divided the world among the Catholic powers, allocating the Philippines to the Spanish and Japan to the Portuguese, and partly because the Ming Chinese had prohibited trade with Japan in retaliation for pirate attacks. Eventually, Spanish merchants chose to ignore these restrictions and commenced trading with the Japanese in 1589. Signifying a shift in the balance of global power at the end of the sixteenth century, northern European countries also began to seek profits in East Asia: the Dutch and English set up trading posts, called "factories," in Japan in 1609 and 1613, respectively.

While Europe was in the midst of what is sometimes termed the Age of Exploration, Japanese leaders focused on domestic issues. The end of the tumultuous period known as the era of Warring States (*sengoku;* 1467–1568) was brought about through a series of campaigns led first by Oda Nobunaga (1534–1582) and then, after his assassination, by his general Toyotomi Hideyoshi (1536–1598), concluding with Tokugawa Ieyasu (1542–1616). After Ieyasu was officially named shogun in 1603, both European and Asian dignitaries sought to gain favor with Japan's new rulers by lavishing them with exotic gifts. Such offerings frequently included animals. The Portuguese, for example, presented a pair of peacocks to the retired shogun Tokugawa Ieyasu in 1607.[39] In 1614, Cambodians presented the shogun with two tiger cubs and one parrot, while the Vietnamese (or more accurately, Annamese) offered a parrot and a peacock in the following year. Likewise, in 1624, the Dutch made a present of one bird of an unspecified type, as well as a gold pheasant (one of the pair had died while being transported) and two cranes.[40]

Tokugawa Ieyasu abdicated in favor of his son Hidetada (1579–1632) in 1605, yet the shogunate's approach to foreign policy did not change significantly until the third shogun, Iemitsu (1604–1651), took office in 1623. In that year, the English, having found little financial success in Japan, packed up their factory and left. The following spring, the shogunate expelled all Spanish nationals for what they perceived as seditious activities. Finally, over the course of the 1630s, Iemitsu became increasingly isolationist, permitting only official ships to go abroad (1633), limiting the size of vessels in order to prevent ocean voyages (1635), forbidding travel abroad and exiling all children fathered by foreign nationals (1636), and, ultimately, expelling the Portuguese (1639). Historians have come to call these acts the *sakoku* or "closed country" edicts, based on a nineteenth-century translation of a seventeenth-century German essay on "Whether Japan Should Remain Shut Up."

Throughout the remainder of the Tokugawa period, only the Chinese, Dutch, and Koreans retained official trading privileges with the Tokugawa shogunate. The Dutch and Koreans were required to make a gift-laden journey to receive audience with the shogun in Edo. Korean missions were only sporadic, but the Dutch performed this trip annually until the end of the eighteenth century, when declining trade revenues led them to petition successfully for a reduction in the rather expensive journeys. Nevertheless, gifts still had to be sent. In general, the gifts consisted of textiles and other trade items, but on occasion the visitors bore more exotic presents, especially when Dutch merchants required some special favor. Historians have hitherto paid disproportionate regard to gifts made by the Dutch of certain large land mammals, such as elephants (1813), horses (several times during the eighteenth century), and camels (1646 and 1821). When there was opportunity to see them, these animals sparked the interest of artists. For example, many woodblock prints of the camels brought in 1821 exist because they were rejected as gifts. The Dutch factory head gave them to his Japanese mistress so that she could support herself after he left by charging admission to see them. Gift birds, even large ones, were transported in covered cages, therefore resulting in less visual evidence. Nonetheless, winged creatures were brought more frequently and, as will be discussed later, had a lasting impact on the Japanese landscape.

Dutch merchants brought what is likely the first cassowary to Japan in 1646, although it was not presented to the shogun in Edo until the following year. The cassowary is a flightless, fruit-eating bird that roams the forests of Northern Australia and New Guinea. The reference work *Wakan sansai zue* (Illustrated Japanese-Chinese encyclopedia; 1713) notes that the cassowary is "shaped like a chicken, three or four feet high," that it "frequently eats burning embers and small stones," that its "excrement is ashes or small stones," and that the bird "chases anyone who approaches." The idea that cassowaries eat fire may have been initially introduced to Japan by the Dutch. In 1596, during the first Dutch voyage to Java, a group of indigenous inhabitants brought aboard a four-foot-tall cassowary as a gift when the Dutch were anchored off the northern coast of the island. The Javanese allegedly told the Dutch that it was a rare bird who ate fire. The sailors decided to test the assertion by feeding it some gin. Astonishingly, the bird survived the ordeal and the captain brought it back to Holland in 1597. After several months as a sideshow attraction, the captain presented the cassowary to Prince Mauritz of Nassau.[41] Of course, cassowaries do not actually eat fire, but they do appear to be rather goatlike in what they will consume. Indeed, on one occasion, cassowaries kept as pets in the Dutch castle at Batavia (today's Djakarta) in 1675 ate all the musket balls that had been laid out in the courtyard for distribution to the soldiers. The armorer who had commanded that the ammunition be set there was punished by having to follow the birds around, picking up the balls as they were excreted.[42]

Another one of these quirky birds was brought as a present to the shogun Ietsuna in 1663. By this time, the reputation of the cassowary had apparently preceded it, because the shogun rejected the gift, allegedly on the grounds that the creature was "good for nothing but to devour a large quantity of victuals."[43] It was perhaps a wise decision, for cassowaries can live as long as forty years in captivity.[44] Moreover, larger females sometimes reach a height of six feet and their kicks can be lethal. The Dutch merchants may have kept the rejected bird for themselves rather than sending it back to Batavia, because a Japanese painting of 1699 shows one wandering about the Dutch compound in Nagasaki.[45] Further evidence of a cassowary on Deshima may be found in the encyclopedia *Wakan sansai zue*, which notes not only that the Dutch harbored one in their Deshima factory but that they also presented cassowaries to the shogun.[46] When another cassowary brought in 1735 died, the Dutch failed to obtain permission even to bury it, since interment was a right often refused to foreign men, let alone their birds.[47] Shogun Ienari (1773–1841) refused yet another gift of three cassowaries in 1825.[48]

Modern scholars have sometimes confused historical descriptions of the cassowary with the ostrich, because the word *dachō*, presently the standard Japanese term for an ostrich, referred at the time to cassowaries, who were alternatively called by the name *hikuidori* (literally, "fire-eating bird"). The early-modern term for ostrich was *hōgorō* (from the Dutch word for ostrich, *struisvogel*). Dutch documents tell us that in 1658, a great cage with bamboo bars was dragged by fourteen men into the shogunal castle. The giant ostrich who was housed inside the cage, a gift from the Dutch factory, had miraculously outlived its three companions by surviving the ocean journey from southern Africa and, subsequently, an immense fire in the city of Edo.

By all accounts, shogun Ietsuna (1641–1680) was very pleased with the gift. The poor bird's luck ran out when it ran into a tree during a rainstorm a short time afterward and died.[49] The *Wakan sansai zue* encyclopedia also notes the gift, claiming erroneously that the Dutch used ostriches in place of horses to carry firewood and transport goods.[50] The Dutch factory sent for three other ostriches immediately after the death of the first. The birds departed Africa aboard Dutch ships in 1658, but all perished during the long voyage.[51]

Gifts were not confined to larger, flightless creatures, for Dutch Company servants presented many smaller birds as well. Frequently, the Dutch brought along peacocks, parrots, cockatoos, canaries, and turkeys. Sometimes, as in 1641, too many birds of the same kind were brought; on this particular occasion, shogun Iemitsu opted to refuse a nide of Persian pheasants offered him because he had already received so many.[52] The over-abundance may have been due to the fact that often a few extras were sent to compensate for the high rate of shipboard mortality. It appears that the Dutch brought no more pheasants to Edo castle (the Chinese presented them into the early part of the eighteenth century), but other kinds of birds continued to serve as gifts. In 1735, for example, six turkeys were presented, along with two cuirasses, to shogun Yoshimune (1684–1750) in order to "cajole" him into offering better trading conditions to the Dutch.[53]

Nor was the shogun the only Japanese to receive Dutch gifts of living creatures. Foreign merchants were also required to distribute presents to various officials connected with the trade in Nagasaki. The *sakoku* edicts were only part of an ongoing process of systematizing foreign trade that involved rules and regulations for all parts of the commercial process. As part of the Tokugawa shogunate's seizure of the port, a magistrate (*bugyō*) was appointed in 1603. Two or three officials were regularly delegated to this position within the shogunal bureaucracy, and rotated between service in Edo and Nagasaki. The Nagasaki magistrates oversaw foreign trade as well as general administration of the port city. While officials probably received gifts much earlier, the first specific mention of presents for magistrates in the negotiation journals was in 1738. In 1740, both Nagasaki magistrates, Kubota Tadatō (1674?–1753) and Hagiwara Yoshimasa (1699?–1745), received a veritable aviary of gift birds from the Dutch factory (see Table 1).

No record of the gift of birds to other officials appears until 1753, when the Dutch conferred eight mynahs upon Takaki Sakuemon, the shogunal steward (*daikan*), whose responsibility it was to collect taxes for

Table 1: Gift birds for Nagasaki Magistrates in 1740[54]

	Kubota Tadatō	Hagiwara Yoshimasa
Parakeets	13	2
Mynahs	10	2
Lories	9	5
Java sparrows[55]	15	
Munias [56]	15	2
Finches[57]	4	22
Golden doves[58]	10	2
Canaries	1	

the shogun. He was apparently a bird fancier, because he had received birdcages as gifts in previous years.[59] A few years later, in 1756, the acting head of the city officials of Nagasaki (*nenban machidoshiyori*) accepted from the Dutch a present of four lories.[60] By 1764, the trade journals indicate that many other officials received gifts from the Dutch, including, in that year, a gift of two canaries to one of the city officials (*machidoshiyori*).[61] The birds were sometimes bestowed along with accoutrements: Dutch merchants brought an ivory birdcage to Japan in 1646, for example.[62] This splendid cage is the only one with a physical description in the trade journals, but the Dutch factory also supplied other birdcages to Japanese officials, such as two presented to a city official in 1741.[63] Bird feed was sometimes provided as well.[64]

The growing number of officials who received birds as presents, combined with the fact that avian gifts were brought year after year, suggests that birds were well received by Japanese authorities. Other evidence supports this conclusion. Japanese officials connected with the Nagasaki trade did not have to wait for the Dutch to decide to bring them birds. Instead, they could place special orders (*eisen*) with the Dutch factory.[65] No doubt this system was in place from the earliest days of the Dutch trade, but it was only beginning in 1719 that a fairly continuous record of these requests survives in the Dutch East India Company archive. The earliest *eisen* come from the shogun or his councilors (*rōjū*), but over time the system came to include an expanding range of officials connected with Nagasaki trade. Requests for foreign goods were diverse, ranging from amber to watches to mummies, and everything in between. But birds proved particularly popular, and Japanese officials ordered at least one species of bird every year of the eighteenth century and throughout the first three decades of the nineteenth for which records are extant.

Tokugawa Yoshimune, who was shogun when these records begin, was renowned for his wide-ranging interests. He requested birds during every year of his reign for which the Dutch East India Company archive has preserved a record, except one (1737). In 1719, Yoshimune first ordered two cassowaries, who were dutifully transported to Japan on Company ships.[66] The birds were carried to Edo in a wooden cage covered with nets for safety.[67] Unlike earlier shoguns, Yoshimune must have liked his cassowaries, because two years later he inquired whether the creatures could breed in captivity and was reassured that they could.[68]

Yoshimune also sought to acquire an ostrich. The shogun's interest in this particular bird was not prompted by contact with live specimens, as the only ostrich brought successfully to Japan in early-modern times was the ill-fated one presented to Ietsuna in 1658. Rather, Yoshimune's curiosity about the bird seems to have been academic in origin. He likely acquired his knowledge of ostriches from Jan Jonston's (1603–1675) *Naeukeurige beschrijving van de natuur der viervoetige dieren, vissen en bloedlooze water-dieren, vogelen, kronkel-dieren, slangen en draken* (an English version of which appeared as *An History of the Wonderful Things of Nature, Set Forth in Ten Severall Classes*).[69] First published in Latin in 1650, Jonston's work was one of the earliest books to feature copious plates of birds, along with more fanciful winged creatures such as Harpies and griffins. The work's visual richness contributed to its popularity in Europe, and compensated for the derivative content. Later, it was published in numerous editions and translations, and a Dutch copy was presented to Tokugawa Ietsuna, recipient of the unlucky ostrich, in 1663. The book probably lay untouched for more than a half-century until Yoshimune asked to view it in 1717. From 1722 onward, Yoshimune ordered a pair of ostriches annually for fourteen consecutive years. But try as they might to fulfill his wishes, Company servants were unable to keep these notoriously bad sailors alive during the long voyage from the Cape of Good Hope to Batavia.[70]

Yoshimune also made frequent requests for peacocks, turkeys, mynahs, and munias. In fulfilling these orders, the Dutch enjoyed a greater measure of success. To the modern reader, turkeys may seem out of place in a list of exotic birds, but they were not imported for consumption by early-modern Japanese. Fanciers allowed them to strut about much like peacocks.[71] The Dutch kept some in their factory compound, probably for consumption, as turkeys were already a staple source of protein on ocean voyages by the seventeenth century. These turkeys were often shown to visitors, such as the Nagasaki magistrate in 1699, who observed them along with a peacock and some cows.[72]

None of Yoshimune's successors ordered as many birds as had their ancestor. His son, Ieshige, ordered birds on only three occasions: four mynahs and five cockatoos in 1774; two peacocks in 1778; four munias, four parakeets, two canaries, and three lories in 1784. Even more tellingly, Ieshige's successor, Ienari, never ordered birds at all, although his brothers asked for "forty-six assorted birds" in 1788.[73]

The shogunal steward, another official who could order exotic birds from the Dutch, made such requests only sporadically until 1776. Thereafter, the person in this position placed large and diverse orders every year. Similar orders from the Nagasaki magistrates appear from 1735, and they were the source of the most numerous and varied of such requests to originate from the different officials involved in foreign trade. Nagasaki magistrates asked for birds almost every year after their first order, as did other Nagasaki city officials after 1756. The reason for the particularly high and diverse demand from magistrates, not only for birds but for foreign goods in general, was partly because their position allowed them to make such demands, and partly because Japanese officials' gift requirements were no less onerous than those of the Dutch merchants. Many of the magistrates' demands were probably made to satisfy a need to present gifts that reflected their position to the outside world. Birds were considered important enough as gifts that on one occasion, shogunal officials detained the Dutch in Osaka during their journey to Edo because the "birds which the Magistrate of Nagasaki had ordered for the nobles in Edo had not yet arrived."[74]

THE EXOTIC-BIRD TRADE

In addition to special orders from officials, a speculative trade in exotic birds, conducted by both Dutch and Chinese merchants, thrived in early-modern Japan. Early in the eighteenth century, *Wakan sansai zue* lists several species of birds among Chinese imports, including mynahs, golden pheasants, silver pheasants, partridges, "Nanjing pigeons," fantails, and Korean magpies.[75]

Another source, *Tōransen mochiwatari chōjū no zu* (Illustrations of birds and beasts imported on Chinese and Dutch ships), suggests a much wider range of species. The book spans the years from approximately 1748 to the end of the Tokugawa period. It consists of paintings of imported animals made by official artists at the behest of the shogunal steward. It is believed that these paintings were produced as a sort of mail-order catalogue so that officials in distant Edo could decide what, if anything, they wanted to purchase. The drawings are precise enough to identify species, showing fifty-five different kinds of birds. Some, but not all, of the pictures include the agent from whom the birds were acquired. In addition to the varieties mentioned in *Wakan sansai zue*, one finds many other species of bird identified as having come on Chinese junks. Among them are Chestnut buntings, orioles, and bramblings from China; black-headed munias from Southeast Asia; several kinds of lories and cockatoos from the Moluccas; and even Amazonian yellow-crested parrots, who must have been acquired from sailors in Batavia or elsewhere in Southeast Asia.[76]

Nevertheless, whether due to a high wholesale price in Southeast Asian markets, a lack of knowledge about how to keep exotic birds alive, the smaller size of Chinese junks making transport difficult, or a profit margin insufficiently high to attract interest, the Chinese were never to become as heavily involved in the bird trade as were the Dutch, importing smaller quantities and fewer exotic varieties. Significantly, the Dutch had the advantage of a global trade network.

It is not clear when birds became a staple commodity, as opposed to a rarity, within the framework of Dutch-Japanese trade. The lack of documentary records relating to the exotic-bird trade stems partially from the system under which Dutch trade was regulated. The Dutch East India Company (VOC) did not deal in birds except as gifts or in response to special orders, while private trade by VOC company servants was frowned upon by their employers. Although the shogunate instituted a system that officially recognized the personal dealings of the merchants and ship captains of the VOC in 1685, it was not encouraged by the Company, so that few personal records of such transactions survive.[77]

There is, however, some evidence that the sale of birds on private account was a longstanding tradition. For example, in 1617, English East India Company merchant Richard Cocks (1566–1624) complained of having to buy parrots from a few of his sailors, as visiting Japanese officials had hinted, rather insistently, that they would appreciate the birds as gifts.[78] It is apparent that the sailors had brought the parrots in order to put them up at market. Engelbert Kaempfer (1651–1716), a German doctor resident at the Dutch factory from 1690 to 1692 and author of the later influential essay about Japan being "Shut Up," observed that sailors and other private individuals sold birds on the sly, rather than at the regular auctions, so that they could obtain greater profits.[79] Indeed, one Dutch petty officer allegedly tried to smuggle a parrot in his pocket but was caught because the bird started talking.[80] Further evidence of unofficial trade in birds may be found in Dutch factory records from 1790, which state that the factory head "sent an order to the ship to deliver the birds that have been sent privately."[81] Perhaps to forestall unauthorized profiteering, shogunal officials sometimes presented the Dutch with price lists detailing what they were willing to pay for various kinds of birds.[82]

Confirmation that the Dutch brought birds to Japan on speculation rather than just as gifts or special orders may be found in the factory diaries kept by the *opperhoofd*, or factory head, at Deshima. They suggest that Japanese generally believed that their exotic pets could be readily acquired and, if necessary, replaced. The venture was truly speculative, because birds who died, even after purchase, were sometimes returned, the corpse neatly packed in a box.[83] A case in point is the 1781 request of the Satsuma lord for a black turkey, a peacock, and some canaries. In this particular instance, factory head Isaac Titsingh (1745–1812) apologized for not having the birds on hand, but promised to deliver them when the next ship arrived. Obviously, plans had already been made to bring more exotic birds to Japan without predetermined owners, as Titsingh would have had no way to communicate with Batavia before the next vessel departed for Japan. Similarly, the magistrate of Nagasaki assumed that he would be able to get "five pairs of canaries and four Batavian doves" on demand.[84] Bird trade on Deshima may be seen in another diary entry that complains of heavy losses caused by a careless bird keeper who had left the cage doors open when cleaning them and let all the birds fly away.[85]

The Dutch transported large quantities of birds to Japan each year. In August of 1736, for example, the trading vessel *Abbekerk* arrived in Nagasaki carrying sixty-five Java sparrows, five turtledoves, one white Bengal pigeon, one parrot, a turkey, and two cassowaries.[86] In the same year, two other ships, the *Sint Laurens* and *'t Huijs den Eult,* made the same voyage to

Japan, in all likelihood each similarly laden. It was common Company practice to divide goods among different vessels in order to minimize the loss if one of the ships disappeared at sea. A conservative guess would therefore be that Dutch ships transported upward of two hundred birds in 1736 alone. Because the shogun Yoshimune had only requested fifty munias that year, political gifts or special orders cannot account for the remaining number of birds, so that the remnants of the avian cargo must have been for vending. Throughout the late eighteenth century, missives to Batavia regularly requested that sufficient quantities of birds be sent to Japan.[87]

On the Japanese side, sumptuary regulations support the notion that exotic birds enjoyed a high demand among Japanese consumers throughout the early-modern period. In 1662, for example, Chinese traders were forbidden from importing live animals.[88] The same prohibition was extended to the Dutch in 1668.[89] Sumptuary laws were usually issued in direct response to a perceived crisis. In 1668, it was a large fire in Edo that put such a strain on shogunal finances that even members of the warrior class were forbidden to make new clothing from certain kinds of fabrics. As the crises eased, so did the restrictions. By 1690, "strange birds" appear again in a list of Dutch imports that Engelbert Kaempfer included in his influential *History of Japan*.[90] Another such proscription was issued in 1789, with similarly limited effect.[91] By the middle of the nineteenth century, the bird trade had picked up so much that the shogunate created the post of Commissioner of Birds expressly to handle the Dutch bird trade. The individual who held it was "responsible for the pick-up and delivery and price setting of the strange animals people bring with them."[92]

The birds imported to Japan originated from all over the Dutch trade empire in Southeast Asia. While it is conceivable that the Dutch may have procured some birds, such as parrots, from South America or Africa, the rigors of the ocean voyage probably proved far too great for most other species. One nineteenth-century factory head specifically noted that parrots, lories, cockatoos, and mynahs hailing from the East Indies fetched high prices, suggesting that it was perhaps not worth the additional risk to transport the birds from farther away.[93] The aforementioned catalogue, *Tōransen mochiwatari chōjū no zu*, confirms that birds imported by the Dutch were predominantly Southeast Asian or Australasian. The notable exceptions in that document are guinea fowl, brought in both 1819 and 1829, and an African gray parrot brought in 1832. Almost certainly none were carried directly from Europe. In the mid-seventeenth century, the shogun Iemitsu had inquired whether it was possible to import falcons from Holland, to which the Dutch factory head responded that, "Because Holland was far from Jacatra [Djakarta], these birds could not be transported here alive."[94]

Some European species may have numbered among the cargo of Dutch ships nonetheless, particularly since there is mention of "Dutch doves" in the historical record. However, imported species such as the brambling were shared between Europe and China due to migratory patterns and therefore, although they might be considered European, were not shipped directly from Europe. Thus, the majority of birds undoubtedly originated in the colonial periphery. A large bird market flourished in Batavia, for example, the port from which Dutch and Chinese ships headed to Japan. Calcutta, and later Singapore, also boasted large bird emporia. It was also possible to purchase birds from locals in various smaller ports of call, who would bring birds and other merchandise directly out to the ships.[95] In any case, the Dutch seem to have secured their bird inventory from third-party vendors and proprietors, rather than from any organized system of trapping within the framework of the East India Company trade empire.

Once the birds arrived in Japan, local merchants who had permission to participate in the foreign trade occasionally bought them for purposes of speculation. The novelist Ihara Saikaku (1642–1693) describes what may well have been a familiar scenario in his 1692 work *Seken mune san'yō* (This scheming world). In Saikaku's story, a Kyoto silk merchant, desperate to make more money, decides to invest in exotic birds. He fails, however, because a plethora of exotic species are already glutting the market. In the end, the merchant manages to break even only on peacocks because, even though they are more common than some other birds, their ornamental qualities make them perennially popular. Saikaku no doubt intended for his readers to take away from the story a prudent lesson about merchant morality, yet its greater value for the purposes of the present analysis lies in illustrating the conspicuous extent to which the exotic-bird trade in early-modern Japan had established itself as an element of popular culture.[96]

AVIAN ACCULTURATION

What the preceding history demonstrates is that birds proved not only important political gifts, but also lucrative trade items from the point of view of profiteering merchants looking for new commodities to buy and sell. Visitors to Deshima could see turkeys (presumably to be eaten later), cassowaries, and peacocks.[97] When the painter and scholar of "Dutch learning" (*rangaku*) Shiba Kōkan (1738–1818) toured the factory in 1789, he was entertained to see a white parrot who flew around and boldly sat on the shoulders of visitors.[98]

While not everyone shared Shiba's opportunity to visit Deshima, even the poorest urban resident had access to street entertainment (*daidōgei*). Contemporary accounts reveal that street displays in early-modern cities often featured birds. Although such live exhibits were prohibited in 1691 under Tsunayoshi's policy of "clemency for living creatures" (to be discussed also in the next chapter), they quickly regained their popularity after his successor, Ienobu, repealed the injunction in 1709. To the delight of urban crowds, street performers trained native birds to do such tricks as drag one another around on a toy horse, climb a ladder, pull up a bucket, play miniature instruments, shoot a bow, and draw lottery tickets.[99] Performers also used small imported birds to do similar tricks in at least one large touring show—almost a circus of sorts—that traveled between Edo, Kyoto, and Osaka in the mid-eighteenth century.[100]

Parrots and peacocks were the most common varieties of bird employed in street entertainment. The Dutch transported to Japan many kinds of parrots, parakeets, and cockatoos, originating from throughout the tropical and subtropical worlds. But the majority of the birds probably came from Southeast Asia and Australasia, if for no other reason than these regions' relative proximity. Flower-and-bird prints (*kachōga*) by Hiroshige illustrate several readily identifiable parrots, such as Pennant's Rosella, the Electus Parrot, and the Mustached Parakeet, all native to Australia. Because *Tōransen mochiwatari chōjū no zu* only depicts birds brought for shogunal officials, mass-produced works like these give us some idea of what kinds of birds were known to those outside the government. As previously mentioned, parrots had traveled to Japan since ancient times, but it was only in the early-modern period that these hook-billed creatures became part of the everyday landscape. Records of street shows with parrots date from as early as the middle of the seventeenth century, and continue to appear throughout the Tokugawa period. Of course, facility with language remained the parrot's prime selling point, but these intelligent birds could also be trained to do all manner of tricks.

The peacock (*kujaku*) was another standard street performer. Native to India, the peacock was known early in Japan through the figure of Kujaku Myōō (Sanskrit: Mayura), a Buddhist deity dedicated to the salvation of the human race. The divinity is conventionally depicted on the back of a peacock. By the mid-seventeenth century, peacock handlers (*kujaku tsukai*) appeared in Japanese roadways. These street artists performed a dance together with the auspicious bird.[101] Street performances involving peacocks remained perennially popular, even as they grew more commonplace, not so much for spiritual reasons but because of the birds' striking visual characteristics.[102] Indeed, peacock teahouses (*kujaku jaya*), a forerunner to the menageries and zoos to be discussed in chapter 7, were a familiar landmark in such early-modern cities as Edo, Nagoya, and Osaka. Patrons sat sipping tea while enjoying the sight of peacocks strutting around in cages.[103] As the alternative names *kachō jaya* (flower-and-bird teahouse) and *meichō jaya* (special bird teahouse) would suggest, other birds or animals were also shown in similar circumstances. Sensōji temple in the Asakusa neighborhood of Edo, for example, boasted an entire aviary of birds, including Java sparrows and avadavats, but peacocks remained the most widely known imported species.[104] The extravagant feathers of the peacock added to the bird's cultural appeal: numerous illustrations from the early-modern period show them displayed in a vase or a brush holder.

Although it may not actually have eaten fire, the odd-looking cassowary made a fine sideshow as well. It apparently took little time for Japanese merchants to appreciate the bird's commercial potential, for, after the earlier mentioned incident in which shogun Ietsuna declined his cassowary in 1647, a "rich Japanese" is said to have told its Dutch proprietors that a good deal of money could be made by showing the creature in Osaka.[105] This particular specimen never made it to the western metropolis, but other cassowaries imported in 1779 and 1786 would go on display before curiosity-seeking audiences in Edo.[106]

Although a wealthy Osaka merchant could presumably make money merely by charging admission to see an imported cassowary, the restricted nature of foreign trade meant that, in order to assure a steady supply of birds, street performers and private fanciers would have eventually to depend on more active forms of aviculture, which is to say, the breeding of birds domestically. Japan boasts a long tradition of aviculture, a practice originally connected with falconry. With the rise of the early-modern merchant class, however, the breeding of such birds as chickens and pigeons developed into a common hobby. Books like *Shichō hitsuyōki* (Necessary information to raise birds) and the earlier cited *Momo chidori* mention as species suited for domestic breeding such imported birds as the Java sparrow, the parakeet (*inko*), and the turkey. Notably, *Shichō hitsuyōki* states that further tips for the care of exotic birds could be obtained by asking a Dutchman.[107] Another writer, Hino Kanroku, produced a dozen or so books on birds and aviculture, including one specifically on exotics imported by the Dutch and Chinese.[108] Interestingly, the spread of aviculture in Japan paralleled similar trends in England, where aviculture as a hobby had been the preserve of the aristocracy until the nineteenth century, when raising birds, especially parakeets and canaries, became popular among the new middle classes.[109]

Similarly in Japan, small finches and sparrows, and especially pigeons and canaries, were the most popular choices for hobbyists because they were the easiest to breed. The Dutch contributed to the pigeon stock in Japan as well, importing several varieties. But merchants were not ornithologists. Trade documents do not always precisely define species, and they use names whose meanings sometimes have been lost. It has therefore proven difficult to identify definitively all of these birds. Imports definitely included fantails, golden pigeons from Fiji, rock pigeons from Malaysia, turtledoves, and "Batavian doves," which might signify any one of several kinds of pigeon or dove, but most likely referred to the zebra dove, still a popular caged bird. The *blauwe duif* (blue dove) was probably the Goura crowned pigeon of New Guinea, a spectacular blue species.[110] These blue pigeons were sold along with cassowaries and other rare birds and beasts in Singapore.[111] With the help of imports, Japanese pigeon purveyors purportedly could breed hybrids in any shade or marking that their customers demanded.[112]

By contrast, canaries were unknown outside of Madeira until the Portuguese took possession of the Atlantic island in 1420. Wild canaries are olive-green, and the yellow birds we know today were not bred until the seventeenth century.[113] In Japan, special orders made to the Dutch for canaries concentrate heavily around the mid-eighteenth century and then taper off. Abundant evidence of canaries in Japan even in the nineteenth century suggests not that the birds had become unpopular, but rather that fanciers had started to breed them domestically and no longer needed to rely on imports. In 1849, for example, the lord of the Usuki domain in Bungo (in today's Gifu prefecture) brought back canaries as souvenirs from a stay in

Edo.[114] A decade later, a letter from the wife of the first British consul in Hakodate told of seeing a "great many canaries" soon after the couple's arrival in Nagasaki in 1859. She also spoke of "snow white birds with pink beaks," a description that would seem to indicate that Japanese fanciers had bred canaries or Java sparrows to be albinal.[115]

ORNITHOLOGY AND DUTCH LEARNING

The second half of the eighteenth century brought a new kind of bird collecting to Japan. From around this time, scholars began gathering birds and studying them for scientific purposes rather than keeping them simply as pets, curiosities, or emblems of power. Early-modern Japanese interest in ornithology was tied to the rise of what is generally known in English as "Dutch learning." This literal translation of the Japanese word *rangaku* actually referred to all kinds of Western science, as opposed to science based on native or Chinese traditions. The shogunate's promulgation of *sakoku* edicts during the 1630s had caused an initial avoidance of research on topics related to the West. Nonetheless, from the late seventeenth century onward, there was a gradual resurgence in Japanese scholarly activity concerning such practical aspects of European knowledge as medicine, although the serious study of Western philosophy or literature was inhibited by fears about how the shogunate might interpret existing prohibitions against Christianity. Historians have often credited Yoshimune with fomenting *rangaku* in Japan after he became shogun in 1716, but in fact, his interest was personal and he did little actively to promote study of any sort. It is more accurate to say that he fostered an air of tolerance for it.[116] Throughout the eighteenth century, Japanese engagement with Western science continued to be affected by the ebbs and flows of conservatism in shogunal politics, as well as the progress from theoretical to practical application in the West, which attenuated its theological aspects, making the subject less dangerous to pursue.

The study of Western natural sciences in Japan grew out of the study of pharmacological botany. Until the Enlightenment in the West, the Christian philosophical basis for the natural sciences made it difficult for Japanese intellectuals openly to study any Western works concerning them. Intellectual efforts in natural history, therefore, tended generally toward the compilation of encyclopedic works (such as *Wakan sansai zue*, cited many times in this chapter) rooted in Chinese textual authority as opposed to empirical knowledge based on Western taxonomies. It is also important to keep in mind that ornithology developed in the West more slowly than other natural sciences. Some date ornithology as a discipline back to Aristotle (384–322 B.C.E.), but, despite a brief flowering during the Renaissance, the scientific study of birds remained at the most rudimentary level until the end of the eighteenth century.[117] The fact that rich collectors bought up specimens for their curiosity cabinets hindered the fledgling science by making it difficult for serious students to obtain specimens.[118]

Preservation presented further obstacles. While the difficulties of preserving specimens of living things posed significant technical challenges for all eighteenth-century naturalists, it was a particularly acute problem for ornithology.[119] To preserve smaller animals such as lizards, scientists simply bottled them in an alcohol solution. This process was sometimes used for small birds as well, but the deleterious effect of the liquid on feathers can easily be imagined. Other techniques included drying and stuffing or embalming and dipping birds in varnish, all forms of taxidermy that altered the appearance of the birds as well as making them extremely vulnerable to insect damage. The above factors combined in such a way that, as Paul Farber has written, "if it is true that interest in birds permeated eighteenth-century [European] culture, it did so without much of an awareness of birds as a serious object of scientific research."[120]

From about the mid-eighteenth century onward, the collection and classification of new plants and animals became one of the primary purposes of European voyages of exploration.[121] However, it was not until the combined efforts of Mathurin-Jacques Brisson (1723–1806), who devised a workable system of classification in 1760, and George Buffon (1707–1788), who popularized Brisson's system through such works as *Histoire naturelle des oiseaux* (Natural history of birds; 1770–1785), that ornithology finally assumed the form of a true science.[122]

Despite cultural, geographic, and philosophical barriers, Japan therefore did not lag significantly behind the West when it came to the pursuit of ornithology. While not, strictly speaking, works of natural history, the writings of Ando Shōeki (1703–1762)—who served as a physician in Hachinohe during the "wild-boar famine" to be discussed in the following chapter—signal a developing native concern with ornithology. A doctor by training, Shōeki has been described as a "social and ecological philosopher."[123] Although influential, his works were not widely circulated during his lifetime because of the author's outspoken antishogunal views. Possibly as a result of his having witnessed the ecological upheaval of Hachinohe's "wild-boar famine," Shōeki condemned early-modern Japan's market economy because it promoted social inequality and facilitated the destruction of the natural environment.

Shōeki's contribution to Japan's native ornithological tradition is most clearly embodied in one of his surviving manuscripts, *Hōsei monogatari* (Tales of the world of law). Written around 1760, this Buddhist-inspired philosophical work describes an imagined encounter among the living creatures of the natural world. In the tale, birds, beasts, crawling things, and fish gather together to compare their ways of life with that of humans. Interestingly, Shōeki decided to begin his imaginary discourse from an avian perspective, starting the debate with the pigeon. Other feathered philosophers included the crane (described as "our court noble"), the hawk ("our feudal lord"), the kite, the sparrow, and the dove. All in all, Shōeki represented forty different kinds of birds. Two of his winged creatures are mythological: the *ran*, a legendary Chinese bird with five colors and a cry in five tones, and the *kiba*, with two human heads, which Shōeki clearly identifies as a creature of fancy. At the same time, the characteristics of each actual bird are described in such a way as to suggest that Shōeki incorporated into the account his own empirical observations, thus reflecting the early stirrings of ornithological science.

Significantly, the work awards a prominent role to two exotic birds. One of them, the parrot, compares his facility for imitating human speech to two Japanese monks who in the ninth century traveled to China, one bringing back the Tendai and the other the Shingon creed of Buddhism. The parrot is followed by a bird of paradise, who "eats nothing but air and never defecates but farts continually instead." In Toshinobu Yasunaga's clever translation, the bird of paradise claims that farting brings him closest to "birdahood."[124] One cannot blame Shōeki for his inaccurate description of the bird of paradise, as no record of live specimens being imported to Japan can be found until the Dutch presented six to the Nagasaki magistrate in 1764, two years after Shōeki's death.[125]

The second half of the eighteenth century witnessed an increasingly scientific approach to the study of birds. One of the most famous scholars of "Dutch learning," Hiraga Gennai (1729–1779), organized four exhibitions of useful plants, animals, and minerals, and published the results of his studies under the title *Butsurui hinshitsu* (An appraisal of natural products; 1763). His work relied heavily on Chinese taxonomy, but Gennai later obtained Dutch books, including one by Jonston (like the copy in the shogunal library), and altered his methods to conform to Western practices. Carl Peter Thunberg (1743–1828), a disciple of Linnaeus who spent a year in Japan as factory doctor at Deshima, observed a scientific collection of indigenous Japanese birds in Osaka in 1776.[126] Later naturalists, such as Udagawa Yōan (1798–1846), built upon the earlier achievements of Shōeki, Gennai, and others.

Powerful domain lords, such as Shimazu Shigehide (1745–1833) of Satsuma and Kuroda Narikiyo (1795–1851) of Fukuoka, also pursued interests in natural history in general and ornithology in particular.[127] Both men had close personal contacts with the Dutch, which allowed them access to books and specimens not available to many scholars. In particular, Shigehide was influential in the highest political circles, partly through the marriage of his daughter to the heir to the shogun, and was thus able to obtain permission to place special orders directly from the Dutch. His requests were primarily scientific, but he also indulged in songbirds like the canaries he acquired in 1788. Shigehide also made several requests for ostrich eggs, although it is not clear if they were to be hatched, eaten, or used in scientific study.[128] Ostrich eggs were much easier to obtain than live birds: the Khoisan people of southern Africa brought large quantities of them to the Dutch East India Company castle in Cape Town to trade.[129] It was also simpler to transport eggs than live birds by sea, so that Company servants were able to fulfill Shigehide's requests.

Live specimens like those gathered by Gennai were especially important for the Japanese because many of the preservation methods used in the West were, as already noted, problematic. Drying was always a possibility, but the characteristically high humidity of the archipelago rendered even this simple method ineffective because of the high vulnerability to insect damage of exposed flesh. Glass-production techniques in eighteenth-century Japan lagged significantly behind those of the West, so that specimen bottles proved difficult to come by and often had to be imported. The introduction of sealed glass cases—reputedly the invention of German naturalist Johann Leonhard Frisch (1666–1743)—significantly aided in the preservation of bird specimens, but sheet glass is one of the most difficult of glassmaking techniques to master.[130]

Briefly, glass blowers used one of two methods to produce flat sheets of glass. In one, the crown method, the glass blower created a very large bubble and then used centrifugal force to draw out and flatten the piece. This technique required great strength, and the pieces of glass that could be cut out and used remained fairly limited. To produce glass with the cylinder method a large tube was blown and then snipped and pulled flat. Even though it produced larger sheets of glass, the latter method did not come into widespread use in the West until the nineteenth century. It also required great strength and skill.[131] While production of sheet glass remained essentially beyond the grasp of Japanese artisans until the twentieth century, they do appear to have mastered the technique of drying taxonomic specimens. A. W. Habersham, a lieutenant with the U.S. naval expedition of 1854, noted one such figure for sale at a bazaar in Shimoda:

> One of the objects most worth of admiration was an artificial bird,—an ordinary chicken-hawk; and it was decidedly the most naturally-executed thing that I ever saw. No feather-work specimen of Rio Janeiro [*sic*], Madeira, or any other part of the world, ever excelled it. It was the first thing of the kind that we had seen or heard of; but we were told that they were quite plentiful in Yeddo [i.e., Edo]. This fellow sat upon an ivory perch, to which he was secured by a chain of the same, and was invariably, when first seen, taken for a live bird: everything was perfect.[132]

While Habersham did not specify the material from which the body of the hawk was made, the description sounds like a common form of taxidermy in which dried skin is stretched over a mold. At least one known European example of taxidermy is known to have made its way to Japan, for the Dutch presented an arrangement of flowers and preserved songbirds under a glass cover to the lord of Satsuma in 1822.[133]

EXOTIC BIRDS IN THE JAPANESE ENVIRONMENT

As we are often reminded today, trade involving live animals can have significant ecological consequences. Alfred Crosby has explored the ecological impact of large influxes of European domesticated animals in colonial environments, but ecological upheaval also may occur as the result of traffic in wild animals.[134] *A Field Guide to the Birds of Japan* lists fourteen species of "escapees" who have acclimated to Japan.[135] Most, if not all, of these birds came to Japan originally aboard Dutch or Chinese ships. More than half are paddy birds from Southeast Asia, some of which had acclimatized at least as early as the eighteenth century. The red avadavat, for example, is mentioned in the 1713 *Wakan sansai zue*, which notes that the bird came from a foreign country but was notoriously difficult to raise. By contrast, the same work describes the similarly exogenous Java sparrow as an easy breeder.[136] Although *Wakan sansai zue* is not always the most reliable source of ornithological information, Terajima Ryōan, the encyclopedia's compiler, was correct about at least one thing: once acclimatized, Java sparrows bred easily both in the wild and in captivity, and so they spread quickly throughout the Japanese archipelago.[137]

Three types of munia have also acclimatized in Japan, as have the African finch, the orange-cheeked and black-rumped waxbills, and the pin-tailed whydah. Already in the eighteenth century, *Wakan sansai zue* decribes waxbills as birds who are "raised in cages but are now flying around."[138] Other originally African birds currently found in Japan are the masked weaver, red bishop, and rose-ringed parakeet (which is also found in India). There are many species of parakeets, but the most commonly caged one, the budgerygah came to Japan from Australia. While historical records are not always clear as to the route by which these species reached Japan, Dutch officials and sailors could have bought African and Australian birds either at port or at Southeast Asian bird markets. Only one of the "escapee" birds that have acclimatized, the red-crested cardinal, is South American in origin, and probably a later introduction. As in the case of the nonindigenous animals discussed by Alfred Crosby, Japanese farmers today regard many of the above paddy birds as "pests" because they feast on cultivated grains, primarily rice, intended for human consumption.

CONCLUSION

The early-modern Japanese fascination with exotic birds was not a chicken-and-egg situation, for interest in caged birds, both domestic and exotic, existed long before foreign trade with the Dutch brought regular shipments of them to Japan's shores. The beginning of this chapter divided human interest in birds into three main categories: gastronomy, service, and collection. In the early-modern period, exotic birds fell only into the last category, whether as pets or as specimens. While interest existed in some service birds like hawks, the yearlong voyage from Europe made their importation an impossibility. Similarly, the expense of an imported bird and the limited role of animal proteins in the early-modern Japanese diet meant that the cooking pot was an unlikely destination. Turkeys were the only conventional form of poultry to be imported, but, in the case of Japan, even these birds more commonly were left to strut like peacocks in the yard. Peacocks themselves, although eaten in some parts of the world, were palatable only when young, which made them a relatively inconvenient food source. Not only did exotic-bird enthusiasts find their pets enjoyable to behold in private, but they could also hang them outside in a demonstration of conspicuous consumption.

Pet ownership and aviculture were by far the predominant reasons for the importation of exotic birds. Ornithology, by contrast, developed fairly late, and if science had been the main reason to request birds, many more and different varieties would surely have entered the country. Instead, similar varieties were requested year after year, parrots and songbirds appearing with the greatest frequency. Exotic birds were carried primarily, although not exclusively, by the Dutch, and the distribution of imported species mirrored the extensiveness of the Dutch trade empire. Most birds that found their way to Japan originated in Southeast Asia, but others were brought from New Guinea, Australia, and as far away as Africa and South America. East Indiamen could move large quantities of birds despite less than desirable shipboard conditions because their highly organized trade network moved quickly and efficiently.

The history of the exotic-bird trade also demonstrates that, while isolated from much of the globe throughout the early-modern period, many Japanese of the time enjoyed a surprisingly direct form of contact with a world they were not themselves allowed to visit in person. The pet birds they cherished have perished along with the Dutch East India Company and the shogunate, but the effects of the early-modern trade in exotic birds have proved to be longer lasting. The canons of "traditional" Japanese art and literature have over time incorporated various bird species who are in fact exogenous to the archipelago. Not only Japan's pictorial landscape, but its actual treescape, too, has accommodated some of the same creatures, who, even when they are not regarded as "pests," by definition have come to seem less "exotic."

NOTES

1. Translations of *Man'yōshū* include Donald Keene, ed., *The Manyoshu* (New York: Columbia University Press, 1965); J. L. Pierson, *Selection of Japanese Poems Taken*

from the Manyōsū (Leiden: Brill, 1966). An online version may be found at http://etext.lib.virginia.edu/japanese/manyoshu/index.html. For Sei Shōnagon's section on birds, see Ivan Morris, trans., *The Pillow Book of Sei Shōnagon* (New York: Columbia University Press, 1991), 67–69.

2. Edward S. Morse, *Japanese Homes and Their Surroundings* (New York: Dover, 1961), 227.

3. The classic study of *tengu* is M. W. de Visser, "The Tengu," *Transactions of the Asiatic Society of Japan* 36, pt. 2 (1908): 27–32. A more recent, illustrated study is Pat Fister, "Tengu, the Mountain Goblin," in *Japanese Ghosts and Demons*, ed. Stephen Addiss (New York: George Braziller in association with the Spencer Museum of Art, University of Kansas, 1985), 103–12.

4. The author of this work is known variously as Rogiku or Rokōan. It issued in 1797 from the Kyoto publisher Yoshinoya Tamehachi. For an online version, see http://www.origami.gr.jp/Model/Senbazuru/index-e.html.

5. Ego Michiko, *Inkyo daimyō no Edo kurashi* (Tokyo: Yoshikawa Kōbunkan, 1999), 125.

6. Michael J. Cooper, ed., *This Island of Japon: João Rodrigues' Account of 16th-Century Japan* (Tokyo: Kodansha International, 1973), 59. Incidentally, Rodrigues found the cranes tasty.

7. Matsuda Michio, *Ōedo tori goyomi: Senryū de bādouochingu* (Tokyo: Kawade Shobō, 1999), 177.

8. Morimoto Masahiro, "Sengokuki no taka kenjō no kōzō to zōtei girei," *Rekishigaku kenkyū*, no. 662 (September 1994): 1–15.

9. On the presentation of hawks, see Brett L. Walker, *The Conquest of Ainu Lands: Ecology and Culture in Japanese Expansion, 1590-1800* (Berkeley: University of California Press, 2001), 100–109.

10. On bird symbolism, see Merrily Baird, *Symbols of Japan: Thematic Motifs in Art and Design* (New York: Rizzoli, 2001), 101–21.

11. Suzuki Tōzō, *Nihon shokunin jiten* (Tokyo: Tōkyōdō Shuppan, 1985), 204. Suzuki writes that snares and nets were common, but all sources used in the present study mention birdlime.

12. Francis Hall, *Japan through American Eyes*, ed. F. G. Notehelfer (Princeton: Princeton University Press, 1992), 156.

13. Suzuki, *Nihon shokunin jiten*, 207.

14. Minami Hiroshi, "Aigan dōbutsu," in *Edogaku jiten*, ed. Nishimura Matsunosuke et al. (Tokyo: Kobundō, 1984), 398–99.

15. Sparrows were believed to represent loyalty and honor, which also made them a popular motif in family crests.

16. The story is related in Lafcadio Hearn, *Japanese Fairy Tales* (New York: Boni and Liveright, 1918), 77–79. Another of the many variants of the narrative may be found in A. B. Mitford, *Tales of Old Japan* (London: Macmillan, 1903), 173–74. In Mitford's version, it is the wife of the old man who cuts out the bird's tongue.

17. Hall, *Japan through American Eyes*, 386.

18. Kitamura Nobuo, *Kiyū shōran*, ed. Kondō Keizō, supplementary vols. 7–10 of *Nihon zuihitsu taisei*, ed. Nihon Zuihitsu Taisei Henshūbu (Tokyo: Yoshikawa Kōbunkan, 1979), 10: 272.

19. Arthur Adams, *The Travels of a Naturalist in Japan and Manchuria* (London:

Hurst and Blackett, 1870), 278.

20. See plate 22 in Dorothy Blair, *A History of Glass in Japan* (New York: Kodansha International in association with the Corning Museum of Glass, 1973), 30.

21. Terajima Ryōan, *Wakan sansai zue*, ed. Shimada Isao, Takeshima Atsuo, and Higuchi Motomi, 18 vols. (Tokyo: Heibonsha, 1985–1991), 6: 237.

22. Kojiruien Kankōkai, ed., *Kojiruien*, 51 vols. (Tokyo: Yoshikawa Kōbunkan, 1999), Dōbutsu: 537.

23. Asakura Haruhiko, ed., *Jinrin kinmō zui*, Tōyō bunko, no. 519 (Tokyo: Heibonsha, 1960), 154. In France, a small barrel organ called a *serinette* was developed during the eighteenth century in order to teach caged birds to sing. Japanese bird shops may have possessed something similar.

24. Kojiruien Kankōkai, *Kojiruien*, Dōbutsu: 537.

25. Kitamura, *Kiyū shōran*, 273; Kojiruien Kankōkai, *Kojiruien*, Dōbutsu: 537.

26. Kojiruien Kankōkai, *Kojiruien*, Dōbutsu: 538.

27. Ōtomo Kazuo, "Shōgun no takagari to Edo no toridoiya," *Shiryōkan kenkyū kiyō* 28 (March 1997): 112.

28. Nishimura et al., *Edogaku jiten*, 673.

29. F. R. Effert, ed., *The Court Journey to the Shōgun of Japan: From a Private Account by Jan Cock Blomhoff* (Leiden: Hotei, 2000), 102.

30. Asakura Musei, *Misemono kenkyū* (Tokyo: Chikuma Shobō, 2000), 347; Yosaburo Takekoshi, *The Economic Aspects of the History of the Civilization of Japan*, 3 vols. (London: Allen and Unwin, 1930), 2: 462.

31. Hall, *Japan through American Eyes*, 68–69.

32. Rutherford Alcock, *The Capital of the Tycoon: A Narrative of a Three Years' Residence in Japan*, 2 vols. (London: Longman, 1863), 1: 310–11.

33. Hall, *Japan through American Eyes*, 68–69.

34. Herman J. Moeshart, ed., *Journaal van Jonkheer Dirk de Graeff van Polsbroek, 1857-1870: Belevenissen van een Nederlands diplomaat in het negentiende eeuwse Japan* (Maastricht: Van Gorcum, 1987), 38. Polsbroek became vice-consul in 1859 and consul general in 1863.

35. Literacy increased steadily over the course of the Edo period. Ronald Dore has estimated that some 40 percent of the male population had attained the ability to read by the mid-nineteenth century. See R. P. Dore, *Education in Tokugawa Japan* (Berkeley: University of California Press, 1965; reprint, Ann Arbor: Center for Japanese Studies, The University of Michigan, 1992), 254.

36. Tsukamoto Manabu, *Edo jidaijin to dōbutsu* (Tokyo: Nihon Editā Sukūru Shuppanbu, 1995), 48.

37. Representative titles on avian voice development and song critique are *Yōōben* (How to raise nightingales; 1818) and *Yorozu gei maniawase* (Comparing all the arts; 1764), respectively. See Minami, "Aigan dōbutsu," 398–99.

38. Foreign goods could also enter Japan through the Ryukyu archipelago via Satsuma domain, or from the north via Matsumae domain on Hokkaido. There was also an official but insignificant trade with Korea through the island domain of Tsushima.

39. Hayashi Kō, *Tsūkō ichiran*, 8 vols. (Tokyo: Kokusho Kankōkai, 1912–1913), 4: 483. The Portuguese also imported a tiger and an elephant, but for some unknown reason the tiger stayed in Nagasaki.

40. Hayashi, *Tsūkō ichiran*, 2: 189–90, 211; 4: 488. The Dutch also brought an additional three birds, the name of which is transcribed in Japanese as *haruse*, but I have been unable to identify the species.

41. James R. McClymont, *Essays on Early Ornithology and Kindred Subjects* (London: Quaritch, 1920), 21–22; J. C. Mollema, ed., *De eerste shipvaart der Hollanders naar Oost-Indië* (The Hague: Martinus Nijhoff, 1936), 88–89, 298. The bird ultimately landed in the possession of the German emperor Rudolf II (1552–1612).

42. Christopher Schweitzer, *Voyages to the East Indies* (London: Cassell, 1929), 190. Schweitzer also claimed that the cassowary will eat "red-hot coals, tobacco-pipes, iron and leaden bullets; but doth not Digest any of 'em: It hath no Tongue, but makes a Noise as Shrill as that of a little Gosling." See ibid, 188.

43. Engelbert Kaempfer, *The History of Japan Together with a Description of the Kingdom of Siam, 1690-1692*, trans. J. G. Scheuchzer, 3 vols. (Surrey, U.K.: Curzon, 1993), 2: 278. Or see Beatrice M. Bodart-Bailey, ed., *Kaempfer's Japan: Tokugawa Culture Observed* (Honolulu: University of Hawaii Press, 1999), 240.

44. E-mail communication from Dr. R. Dekker, Leiden.

45. "Oranda Deshima no zu," by Watanabe Yūseki (1637–1839), in the collection of the Nagasaki Prefectural Art Museum. Reproduced in Paul van der Velde and Rudolf Bachofner, eds., *The Deshima Diaries: Marginalia, 1700-1740* (Tokyo: Japan-Netherlands Institute, 1992), frontispiece.

46. Terajima, *Wakan sansai zue*, 6: 321.

47. Van der Velde and Bachofner, *Deshima Diaries*, 456.

48. Netherlands Factorij Japan archive (hereafter abbreviated NFJ), doc. no. 238. The entry is for 1 November 1825. In addition to NJF, the principal manuscript collections used in this study are the Dutch East India Company General Archive (hereafter abbreviated VOC) and the Hoge Regering van Batavia Archive (hereafter abbreviated HRB). All three are housed at the Nationaal Archief in The Hague.

49. Pieter van Dam, *Beschryvinge van de Oostindische Compagnie* (The Hague: R. P. G., 1976), 407. See also Margot E. van Opstall, "Kamele op de landweg: Dieren als geschenk voor de shogun," in *In het spoor van de Liefde: Japans-Nederlands ontmoetingen sinds 1600* (Amsterdam: Bataafsche Leeuw, 1986), 71.

50. Terajima, *Wakan sansai zue*, 6: 320.

51. Jan van Riebeeck, *Journal*, 3 vols. (Cape Town: A. A. Balkema, 1952–1958), 2: 79, 412.

52. A. C. J. Vermeulen et al., eds., *The Deshima Dagregisters: Their Original Tables of Contents*, 11 vols. to date (Leiden: Institute for the History of European Expansion, 1986–), 9: 46. The birds were given instead to Suetsugu Heizō, the "regent" of Nagasaki, and to the shogunal steward Takaki Sakuemon (9: 48).

53. J. van Goor, ed., *Generale missiven van gouverneurs-generaal en raden aan Heren XVII der Verenigde Oostindische Compagnie*, 9 vols. to date (The Hague: R. P. G., 1960–), 9: 350.

54. The information in this table derives from NFJ, doc. no. 912.

55. The term in Dutch is *Rijstvogel* (rice-bird). It could also indicate a speckled munia, but the sparrow is more common. Both of these birds are found in Indonesia.

56. The term in Old Dutch appears, along with variant spellings, as *Thierry Bengale*. It is not certain what bird exactly is referred to, but today the term "Bengalese

finch" in English is used for the white-rumped munia.

57. *Glattig* is the term in Old Dutch. A 1914 lexicon, J. H. van Dale's *Van Dale's groot woordenboek der Nederlandsche taal* (Leiden: M. Nijhoff en A. W. Sijthof) notes the Indonesian designation *Glatik*, and equates the species with *Amadina oryzivora*. The latter term is no longer used in the scientific community, but *Amadina* remains a family name for some finches.

58. These birds are found in West Fiji.

59. NFJ, doc. no. 926. The position of Nagasaki *daikan* was hereditary, and the name Takaki Sakuemon was used by its holder in each generation.

60. NFJ, doc. no. 928.

61. NFJ, doc. no. 934.

62. NFJ, doc. no. 846.

63. NFJ, doc. no. 913.

64. See, for example, NFJ, doc. no. 912.

65. See Martha Chaiklin, *Cultural Commerce and Dutch Commercial Culture: The Influence of European Material Culture on Japan, 1700-1850* (Leiden: Research School CNWS, 2003), ch. 4, for a detailed description of the process.

66. VOC, doc. no. 13512. Cassowaries were specifically requested a total of nine times—in 1719, 1758, 1772, 1778, 1780, 1781, 1784, 1785, and 1788.

67. Van der Velde and Bachofner, *Deshima Diaries*, 249.

68. Ibid., 250.

69. The author is variously known as Joannes Jonstonus in Latin and as John Jonston in English.

70. VOC, doc. nos. 13515–13526. A revealing anecdote about the lack of seaworthiness in ostriches appears in Rob Nixon, *Dream Birds* (New York: Picador, 2000), 86. In 1912, bringing back ostrich stock from Barbary for the purpose of improving feather quality, in what was known as the Trans-Saharan Ostrich Expedition, one member noted: "with the rolling of the ship, the ostriches would get turned upside down inside their boxes and start kicking and struggling, and if not released might die. This meant that the members of the party got very little rest, for at any hour of the day or night, the warning kicking and struggling might be heard. This would necessitate one of the party going down to the hold, knocking the box apart, getting the bird the right way up, and nailing the box together again."

71. An explicit reference may be found in Captain [Vassili] Golovnin, *Memoirs of a Captivity in Japan, 1811-1813*, 3 vols. (Oxford: Oxford University Press, 1973), 3: 185.

72. Vermeulen et al., *Deshima Dagregisters*, 2: 119.

73. VOC, doc. no. 13570.

74. Vermeulen et al., *Deshima Dagregisters*, 8: 118 (23 February 1773).

75. Terajima, *Wakan sansai zue*, 6: 230, 233–34, 261–62, 285–86, 290. The "Nanjing pigeon" could have been one of several Southeast Asian pigeons or doves.

76. The original is at Keiō University library. A large portion of it has been reproduced in Isono Naohide and Uchida Yasuo, *Hakurai chōjū zushi* (Tokyo: Yasaka Shobō, 1992). The Dutch had colonies such as Suriname in South America, so it is not surprising that long-lived birds such as parrots would make their way to Indonesia.

77. It should be noted that the VOC collapsed at the end of the eighteenth

century. Nevertheless, Dutch trade continued after the fall of the VOC under more or less the same rules.

78. Richard Cocks, *The Diary of Richard Cocks: Cape-Merchant in the English Factory in Japan, 1615-1623,* ed. Edward Maunde Thompson, 2 vols. (London: Hakluyt Society, 1883), 1: 290. Cocks wrote, in his characteristically erratic spelling, as follows: "Tonmon Same sent to have a parrat wh'ch was in our shipp, which was thought goot to buy of the carpenter & geve hyme. Also I sent a munky to takkamon dono. Bothe wh'ch presents were taken in good parte. And Mr Wedmer, master mate, gave me a parakia & the chiruigin gave me the munkey I gave Taccamon dono." The English also had a dovecote on their factory in Hirado.

79. Kaempfer, *History of Japan,* 2: 214–15.

80. Carl Peter Thunberg, *Travels to Europe, Africa, and Asia Performed between the Years 1770-1779,* 3 vols. (London: W. Richardson, n. d.), 3: 28–29.

81. Vermeulen et al., *Deshima Dagregisters,* 9: 230.

82. Ibid., 10: 123. Another price list, in Japanese, exists in the collection of an interpreter family, but I have not yet been able to examine it to determine its purpose.

83. See, for example, NJF, doc. no. 231, which mentions a dead lory and Java sparrow being returned on 11 September 1818, as well as another expired lory on 16 October of the same year. NJF, doc. no. 232, reports the return of two dead green lories and a white cockatoo on 21 August 1819. See also C. T. van Assendelft de Coningh, *Mijn verblijf in Japan* (Amsterdam: Gebroeders Kraay, 1856), 35.

84. Vermeulen et al., *Deshima Dagregisters,* 10: 29 (31 August 1781), 115 (7 September 1786). Again in 1788, the Nagasaki magistrate requested canaries who had not been preordered (9: 167, 172).

85. Ibid., 8: 152.

86. Van der Velde and Bachofner, *Deshima Diaries,* 461.

87. HRB, doc. nos. 150–52.

88. Hayashi, *Tsūkō ichiran,* 4: 269.

89. HRB, doc. no. 141.

90. Kaempfer, *History of Japan,* 2: 214 (or Bodart-Bailey, *Kaempfer's Japan,* 209).

91. Vermeulen et al., *Deshima Dagregisters,* 9: 200.

92. The Dutch referred to the official as *Vogel-commissaris.* See Assendelft de Conigh, *Mijn Verbliijf in Japan,* 34.

93. J. F. van Overmeer Fisscher, *Bijdrage tot de kennis van het Japansche Rijk* (Amsterdam: J. Muller, 1833), 216.

94. Vermeulen et al., *Deshima Dagregisters,* 11: 143.

95. Many accounts can be found of such shipside dealings. In 1790, for example, Amasa Delano tells of Western Javanese coming to his ship in canoes to sell parrots and other birds. See his *Voyages and Travels* (Upper Saddle River, N. J.: Gregg, 1970), 37. A. W. Habersham, in *My Last Cruise* (Philadelphia: Lippencott, 1878), reports a similar encounter at an unidentified location while en route to Batavia in the 1850s (62). Around the same time, the travel writer Bayard Taylor depicts parrots and Java sparrows being offered in this way in the Sunda Straits. See his *India, China, and Japan* (New York: Putnam, 1882), 510.

96. Ihara Saikaku, *This Scheming World,* trans. Masanori Takatsuka and

David C. Stubbs (Rutland, Vt.: Tuttle, 1965), 107–8.

97. Vermeulen et al., *Deshima Dagregisters*, 2: 119.

98. Shiba Kōkan, *Kōkan saiyū nikki*, ed. Haga Tōru and Ōta Rieko (Tokyo: Heibonsha, 1986), 113. The parrot was probably of the cockatoo variety.

99. Hall, *Japan through American Eyes*, 422; Edward S. Morse, *Japan Day by Day*, 2 vols. (Atlanta: Cherokee, 1990), 2: 229–33.

100. Asakura, *Misemono kenkyū*, 347.

101. Kitamura, *Kiyū shoran*, 4: 233. See also Asakura, *Misemono kenkyū*, 341–43.

102. Asakura, *Misemono kenkyū*, 344–46.

103. Akisato Ritō, *Settsu meisho zue*. The work is also discussed in Asakura, *Misemono kenkyū*, 358. These teahouse-menageries sometimes displayed other birds and animals as well.

104. Laurence Oliphant, *Narrative of the Earl of Elgin's Mission to China and Japan*, 2 vols. (New York: Kelly, 1969), 2: 214–15.

105. Kaempfer, *History of Japan*, 3: 6–7 (or Bodart-Bailey, *Kaempfer's Japan*, 313).

106. Hiroko Johnson, "Western Influence on Japanese Art: Akita Ranga" (Ph.D. diss., University of Southern California, 1994), 109.

107. Kojiruien Kankōkai, *Kojiruien*, Dōbutsu: 929. The author, publisher, and date of *Shichō hitsuyōki* are unknown.

108. The work in question, *Kara kōmō tochōshū* (A collection of Chinese and Dutch imported birds) appeared in 1802.

109. Sonia Roberts, *Bird-Keeping and Birdcages: A History* (New York: Drake, 1973), 67–74.

110. Paintings in *Tōransen mochiwatari chōjū no zu* show that two Goura pigeons were brought by the Dutch in 1787 and 1832, but the term *blauwe duif* appears in documents more frequently than this and may also have referred to other species.

111. Francis L. Hawks, *Narrative of the Expedition of an American Squadron to the China Seas and Japan: Performed in the Years 1852, 1853, and 1854, under the Command of Commodore M. C. Perry, United States Navy, by Order of the Government of the United States* (New York: Appleton, 1856), 152.

112. Adams, *Travels of a Naturalist in Japan and Manchuria*, 300.

113. Ibid., 33–34.

114. Ego, *Inkyo daimyō no Edo kurashi*, 41. Under the requirements of the alternate attendance (*sankin kōtai*) system, domain lords spent half their time in the shogun's capital at Edo, and the rest in their home provinces.

115. C. Pemberton Hodgson, *A Residence at Nagasaki and Hakodate in 1859-1860* (London: Bentley, 1861), 119.

116. See Numata Jirō, *Western Learning*, trans. Rudolf Bachofner (Tokyo: Netherlands-Japan Institute, 1992).

117. Erwin Stresemann, *Ornithology from Aristotle to the Present*, trans. Hans J. Epstein and Cathleen Epstein, ed. G. William Cottrell (Cambridge, Mass.: Harvard University Press, 1975), 3–23.

118. Ibid., 27.

119. Paul Lawrence Farber, "The Development of Taxidermy and the History of Ornithology," *Isis* 68 (1977): 550.

120. Paul Lawrence Farber, *The Emergence of Ornithology as a Scientific Discipline, 1760-1850* (Dordrecht, Holland: D. Reidel, 1982), 26.

121. McClymont, *Essays on Early Ornithology and Kindred Subjects*, 31.

122. Ibid., 17, 23.

123. Toshinobu Yasunaga, *Ando Shoeki: Social and Ecological Philosopher in Eighteenth-Century Japan* (New York: Weatherhill, 1992).

124. Ibid., 119-140. Another translation has been published by Jeffrey Hunter as *The Animal Court: A Political Fable from Old Japan* (New York: Weatherhill, 1992).

125. NFJ, doc. no. 936.

126. Thunberg, *Travels to Europe, Africa, and Asia*, 3: 221.

127. See Takao Yamaguchi, "Von Siebold and Japanese Botany," *Calanus* 1 (1977): 13.

128. Given the size of ostriches, the Dutch were probably attempting to export young birds. It is possible that the acquisition of eggs represented an effort to hatch them. The incubation period for an ostrich is about six weeks. By contrast, some eggs were sent back to Europe for baking and eating.

129. Christopher Fryke, *A Relation of a Voyage Made to the East Indies* (London: Cassell, 1929), 27; François Valentyn, *Description of the Cape of Good Hope*, ed. E. H. Raidt, 2 vols. (Cape Town: Van Riebeeck Society, 1973), 2: 121.

130. David Elliston Allen, *The Naturalist in Britain: A Social History* (Princeton: Princeton University Press, 1976), 29–30.

131. Arthur E. Fowle, *Flat Glass* (Toledo, Ohio: Libbey-Owens Sheet Glass Company, 1924), 31–32.

132. Habersham, *My Last Cruise*, 236–37.

133. NFJ, doc. no. 235 (9 April 1822).

134. See Alfred W. Crosby, *Ecological Imperialism: The Biological Expansion of Europe, 900-1900* (Cambridge: Cambridge University Press, 1986). In general, Crosby focuses on the relationship between the Old and New Worlds rather than between Asia and Europe.

135. Wild Bird Society of Japan, *A Field Guide to the Birds of Japan* (Tokyo: Wild Bird Society of Japan, 1982), 306–7.

136. Terajima, *Wakan sansai zue*, 6: 298, 248.

137. Charlie van Kieboom, a man of mixed Dutch-Japanese parentage convicted by the British of spying for the Japanese, recalled that as a child around the year 1910, he would catch these birds in the mountains only to let them go when they and their offspring ate too much. See Harold S. Williams, *Shades of the Past: Indiscreet Tales of Japan* (Rutland, Vt.: Tuttle, 1959), 274–75.

138. Terajima, *Wakan sansai zue*, 6: 274.

From *Wakan sansai zue*. Courtesy of the C. V. Starr East Asian Library, Columbia University.

CHAPTER FIVE

Commercial Growth and Environmental Change in Early-Modern Japan: Hachinohe's Wild-Boar Famine of 1749

Brett L. Walker

The only aspect of this bizarre famine that historians really know for sure is that chroniclers of the day remembered it as the "wild-boar famine" (*inoshishi kegachi*) of 1749. From what can be pieced together from the few available sources, thousands of peasants from Hachinohe died when an intensification of slash-and-burn farming, fueled by economic growth during the Tokugawa period (1600–1868), combined with terrestrial and climatological environmental changes and converged on this small northeastern domain. This convergence disrupted local agricultural cycles, caused food shortages, and, ultimately, pitted the human population against wild boar in a life-or-death struggle for survival.

Like other domains, Hachinohe had faced worsening economic conditions throughout the eighteenth century, and so it took advantage of the commercialization of the economy by sponsoring cash-crop farming in the form of soybean cultivation to meet the growing financial demands of doling out retainer stipends and paying the other high costs of life in the Tokugawa polity. However, as peasants cleared new swaths of land for soybean cultivation, they in turn sparked changes in the land that led to an explosion of the wild-boar population. Wild boar thrived in the newly deforested terrain, a terrain that, with its ample brush and many tuberous plants, supplied them with shelter and food. Peasants constantly struggled against wild boar, deer, and monkeys in the Tokugawa period, but in Hachinohe conditions were made desperate by micro- and macroclimatological changes that nearly wiped out crops in 1749. When peasants sought to harvest what remained of their crops, or to supplement their diet with familiar wild plants, they competed with the booming wild-boar population for badly needed calories. Boar, too, scavenged for what remained of crops and rooted up wild plants. Eventually, conditions deteriorated to the point that catastrophe ensued: the domain became engulfed by deadly famine, and, later, aggressive wild boar actually "invaded" the streets of the Hachinohe castle town, terrifying townspeople. Despite this invasion, in Hachinohe townspeople and members of the samurai class remained relatively insulated from the repercussions of the food shortage, whereas about 10 percent of the peasant population died from famine-related causes.

The wild-boar famine, although limited to a small northeastern domain, was indicative of broader economic and political changes in eighteenth-century Japan. With the birth of the Tokugawa shogunate, domains that had previously been semiautonomous states became tightly linked to the new hegemonic capital in Edo (present-day Tokyo) through a variety of cleverly orchestrated political devices. Under the Tokugawa, Japan underwent substantial political centralization, and this centering process sparked commercial consolidation. Large cities sprouted as a result of the forced removal of samurai from farms to domain castle-towns, forming an urban system centered at Edo. Once in the cities, explains Herman Ooms, domain lords "faced the task of extracting tribute from the villages without direct use of coercive force."[1] This they did exceedingly well. However, alongside the rice tribute, the concentration of samurai and other townspeople in cities led in turn to the birth of consumer centers that further reshaped agricultural life. By the late seventeenth century, influential urban markets had emerged, and a new consumer class of urban commoners (*chōnin*) prospered from increasing commercialization throughout the country.[2] It was these same townspeople who, as seen in chapter 4, flocked to pet shops to purchase colorful exotic birds, many species of which had been imported by the Dutch or, later on, domestically bred by Japanese fanciers.

The pull of the cities altered the economies of more distant domains in a variety of ways. Most notably, as emerging markets, cities placed new pressure on the countryside to supply foodstuffs and cash crops for a growing urban population, whether to fill the bellies of city-based samurai or to deck out the well-clad dandies of the commercial and pleasure districts of Osaka and Edo. Sometimes in order to seize market share, but more often than not under economic pressure from lords who sought to promote industry inside their domains, farmers from outlying regions like Hachinohe modified their agricultural practice to take advantage of urban markets.[3] In the case of Hachinohe, soybean became the dominant cash crop, and was shipped by sea to Edo. This modification in agricultural practice resonated well beyond the type of crops grown, however, influencing the distribution and behavior of plant and animal species in the surrounding forests and deforested lands. In this context, changing agricultural practice in Hachinohe sparked the rapid emergence of an overabundance of hoofed herbivores, what Elinor Melville calls an "ungulate irruption." In her provocative study of the colonization of Mexico, Melville argues that the result of an explosion of the sheep population was the emergence of a "conquest landscape," which was characterized by massive soil erosion and crop damage inflicted by the ravenous and heavy-hoofed animals, and that these environmental changes ultimately undermined native agriculture.[4] The present chapter builds upon Alexander Bay's suggestion in chapter 3 that Hideyoshi's late sixteenth-century conquest of the lords of Kita Ōu constituted the colonization (and not the unification) of Japan's far northeast. It argues that in Hachinohe a similar conquest landscape emerged, one that spawned an irruption of, as Alfred Crosby notes, "possibly the 'weediest' of all large ungulates," the pig, or, in this case, the wild boar. The explosion of the boar population may be directly linked to economic changes that characterized the Tokugawa period as a whole.[5]

Besides illustrating the birth of a conquest landscape in Hachinohe, the wild-boar famine also exposes eighteenth-century Japan's fragmented distribution system, lack of central-government planning for emergencies, and reliance, at least in some domains, on export-based economies and monocrop agriculture. Hachinohe peasants, basically left to their own devices, responded to famine by requesting governmental assistance to hunt wild boar, and by conducting or participating in rituals designed to appease the various deities responsible for their own wellbeing. Though aid from both government and gods fell short of local needs, Hachinohe's responses to the wild-boar famine highlight various aspects of life among the eighteenth-century peasants of Japan's far northeast, including subsistence habits, concerns about the weather, food supplies, human-animal competition for calories, and agrarian transformation.

The first section of the present chapter looks at the expansion of upland farming in Hachinohe, explaining the environmental implications of swidden and other types of slash-and-burn agriculture that resulted from the dismantling of Hachinohe's medieval frontier culture and its integration into the early-modern order. Upland farming on the hillsides of Hachinohe encroached on customary boar habitat as farmers developed new plots for both subsistence and cash crops, even as fallow plots left behind became ideal habitat for the wild-boar population. A second section of the chapter reconstructs the climatological history of the northeastern section of the Japanese archipelago, documenting how weather trends of the day, particularly the Neo-Boreal (or Little Ice Ages, 1450–1850), caused crop failures and thus contributed to deadly famines. It was the weather, as much as any other factor, that pitted the human population against wild boar. The third section of the essay investigates state and nonstate responses to crop failure and the explosion in the wild-boar population by drawing on some comparative material, predominantly from early-modern England. Finally, a fourth section looks briefly at the larger relationship between early-modern Japanese humans and their wild-boar neighbors.

To date, the historiography of Japan's early-modern period portrays the peasantry as engaging in class-based struggles against an oppressive Tokugawa system, rationally regulating their households through crude forms of family planning such as infanticide, rising up to protest the unfair distribution of wealth and power in their villages, and participating in the political radicalism of the nineteenth-century imperial restoration.[6] In contrast, the present inquiry calls attention to an obvious yet understudied environmental dimension of rural life in the Tokugawa period: namely, the constant struggles against the weather, the soil, and other animal species that shaped everyday existence in the countryside. Historians point out that, along with political, social, and economic forces, dearth and famine caused by natural disasters (exemplified especially by the great Tenmei and Tenpō famines of the late eighteenth and early nineteenth centuries) also ignited forms of social disruption and organized response in agrarian communities that resonated well beyond the confines of village borders.[7] In the case of the wild-boar famine, however, it was not inanimate natural forces that ignited upheaval in Hachinohe: rather, it was forces from the world of nonhuman animals.

SOYBEAN CULTURE

With the rise of consumer centers such as Edo and Osaka, more than ever the countryside was tapped to supply the foods of everyday life. In the late seventeenth and early eighteenth centuries, farmland surrounding Edo and

Osaka took a turn toward nonfood cash crops, leading domain governments and savvy merchants to mobilize more distant lands in the northeast to fill the gap in foodstuffs.[8] The move to cash-crop farming was appealing because it translated into increased wealth at a time when domains badly needed funds, and cash-crop farming, along with by-employment initiatives, was often actively encouraged and sponsored by local governments.[9] In Aizu domain, for example, north of Edo, the local government oversaw an expansion of the sericulture industry in order to enrich that domain, which led to raw silk being sold to weavers in Kyoto and, later, to urban wholesalers setting up branch shops in Aizu.[10]

As recent historiography demonstrates, this commercial growth—or what some have termed protoindustrialization—transformed domain economies in important ways.[11] In a geohistorical analysis, Kären Wigen traces how protoindustrial growth repositioned the Ina valley in central Japan from a fairly self-sufficient regional economy to an "axis between Ise Bay and central Shinano." By the nineteenth century, the region had become the home of a robust "carrying trade," a site for the development of a pack-horse "through-trade," and, ultimately, a nexus for the consolidation of "putting-out complexes," or networks of cottage industries, which exported goods such as tiles, paper, and lacquerware. The Ina valley also played a role in finishing products. Local peasants turned raw hemp into hemp thread, cocoons into silk cloth, and soybean into products such as soy sauce.[12] Similar processes transformed Honshu's far northeast. In the case of Hachinohe, once horse farming was abandoned, soybean became the chief domain-managed export product, along with a limited amount of salt and iron. Unlike the diversity seen at the Ina valley, however, the protoindustrial pattern in Hachinohe was one of overspecialization in soybean (without a corresponding role as product finisher), a condition that would prove disastrous in a region that already relied too heavily on slash-and-burn farming.

Located in the center of Mutsu-no-kuni's Sannohe district in present-day Aomori prefecture, Hachinohe became a separate domain in the ninth month of 1664, when the second lord of Morioka domain, Nanbu Shigenao, died without an heir. As in other early-modern successional disputes, the shogunate intervened, doing so in the twelfth month of the same year. It partitioned the 100,000-*koku* Morioka domain (Japanese domains were measured by estimated rice yield, and 1 *koku* equaled 5.1 bushels in 1801), assigning the younger brother, Nanbu Shigenobu, 80,000 *koku* to continue the Morioka line whereas the other brother, Naofusa, received the remaining 20,000 *koku*. The 20,000-*koku* parcel became Hachinohe domain. In 1665, the Hachinohe castle town was designated administrative hub of a total of eighty-three villages stretching across three districts. By the eighteenth century, all cadastral surveys had been completed in Hachinohe, and the political and financial consolidation of this small northeastern domain was finished under the third and fourth lords.[13]

Despite its small size, Hachinohe emerged as a shipping power as early as 1667, when Nanbu Naofusa, no doubt wanting to promote local industry, paid his respects to Hachinohe ships in Edo that had just reached their destination by navigating around the Bōsō peninsula, a fairly novel feat at that date. Up until this time, ships had traveled along the Pacific coast of the main island of Honshu, where their cargo had been transferred to riverboats and transported up the Tone River and then down the Edo River to the shogunal capital. Nishimura Makoto, a noted local historian of Hachinohe, has stressed that Hachinohe vessels helped pioneer the direct marine route to Edo years earlier than similar merchant vessels from the larger Akita and Tsugaru domains.[14]

Nishimura submits that such shipping networks integrated Hachinohe into the changing commercial landscape of early-modern Japan. With the development of cities full of exploitative samurai and eager consumers, farmland in the alluvial Kantō plain surrounding Edo was converted to land for nonfood cash-crop production, and farmers began planting mulberry trees for the rapidly expanding sericulture industry. In areas surrounding Osaka, by contrast, cotton and indigo crops flourished. To increase production, fertilizers were imported from more distant areas, such as Kyushu, Shikoku, Setouchi, and Yamage, and even from the borderlands of Ezo, or present-day Hokkaido.[15] The increase in cash-crop farming eventually worked its way up the archipelago until many farms of the Kantō, and even beyond, had been geared for sericulture. Prior to this move to mulberry production, these Kantō farmlands had supplied soybean for popular foodstuffs such as miso, tofu, soy sauce, and *nattō* (fermented soybean). As part of a general improvement in Japan's standard of living in the Tokugawa years, such products came to constitute much of the everyday culinary regime of Japanese urbanites.[16] By the early eighteenth century, merchant vessels in search of new sources of soybean, and of fish mulch for fertilizer, began calling on Hachinohe ports. By 1746, merchant ships had become so common that the domain government established a port authority to oversee the export of soybean and fish-mulch fertilizer.[17]

Nishimura explains that as a result of powerful market forces emanating from large cities, the Hachinohe port came to resemble a "soybean harbor," and self-sustaining farm life in Hachinohe began to erode. Nishimura hints at the booming soybean export with some scattered tax figures. He points to one tally of 800 *ryō* for one year in export taxes from 1700. He then uses later tallies from Hachinohe domain that specify that tax rates for exported soybean were 7 *ryō* per 100 *koku*. If tax rates remained even remotely consistent, Nishimura insists, it would mean that somewhere around 11,000 *koku* of export crops were shipped from the Hachinohe port in 1700, about 10,000 *koku* of the total being soybean.[18]

Hachinohe's integration into the commercial economy did not revolutionize agricultural practice in a domain that had always relied on upland farming to produce millet (*awa*) and barnyard grass (*hie*) to feed people. However, integration did intensify upland swidden to make way for more plots for soybean to be exported, leading to the creation of a kind of third-world economy in the northeast. As in modern Bengal, critical food was exported even as the region was rocked by deadly famine. In Hachinohe, wetland rice cultivation, the mainstay of the Tokugawa agronomy, had always been limited. Simply, the weather was too cold for it and most of the farmland sat on a coarse volcanic plateau.[19] In this respect it was much like its larger neighbor, Morioka domain, where, as Susan Hanley and Kozo Yamamura observe, the "climate is as unsuited to rice cultivation as is the terrain."[20] Instead, upland farming (*hatasaku*) served as the lifeline of local peasants, in particular soybean, a high-protein crop popular throughout much of East Asia.[21] Unlike wetland agriculture, where fields can be used over and over again, both fallowing and crop rotation remained critical to maintaining productive yields in upland agriculture. Fallowing fields for several years was necessary because it allowed the soil to regain its fertility; failing to fallow could mean an eventual collapse in crop yields. Some postulate, for example, that the decline of the classic Mayan civilization of the tenth century was sparked when farmers shortened fallowing periods in order to supply grain to feed an expanding population. The theory continues that this change translated into depleted soil and, ultimately, crop failure, undermining the Mayan primary source of food.[22] In short, under conditions such as these, when cultivators exhausted upland plots, they abandoned them in favor of richer soil, leaving in their wake fallow lands that made excellent wild-boar habitat.

Soybean cultivation created prime habitat for wild boar, but it created less-desirable habitat for people. Nishimura, following a Marxist line, argues that the focus on soybean farming undermined peasant autonomy. He contends that because soybean was an export crop, it provided limited sustenance for the Hachinohe peasants in their agricultural rhythms. Furthermore, peasant populations readily consumed upland grains, whereas the stalks fed farm animals such as horses and oxen. The manure from these animals, then, could be used as fertilizer for the next crop. In other words, explains Nishimura, these simple crops fit nicely into the seasonal cycle of independent farm life in Hachinohe. Compared with barnyard grass, however, soybean, because it was shipped out of the domain, and then was processed and cooked before being eaten, did not make a good source of immediate sustenance for people, nor did it provide stalks to feed fertilizer-producing animals.[23]

Nishimura's line of thinking, however compelling, has its problems. On the one hand, soybean, while alive, serves as a nitrogen fixer in the soil. As a nodulating legume, the soybean plant forms a nitrogen-fixing symbiosis in the soil.[24] At the same time, the stalks themselves can make fine fertilizer, even without being fed to livestock. Regardless, following his survey, Nishimura concludes that the move to soybean farming weakened the agricultural self-sufficiency of the Hachinohe economy.[25] Although he paints an overly idyllic picture of peasant life prior to the advent of the Tokugawa shogunate, as a local historian, Nishimura offers a ground-zero account of how the commercialization of the early-modern economy reshaped, sometimes for the worse, the landscape in Japan's far northeast.

The demand for soybean exports in Hachinohe that led to an expansion of the already widespread practice of slash-and-burn farming also helped spark the wild-boar famine. In cultivating barnyard grass, millet, or soybean, slash-and-burn farming (*yakibatake* or *yakihata*) was central to crop rotation. Then, after a plot had been used for a couple of years, the tiller abandoned it in favor of richer soil, repeating the process. In the fallow fields, starchy tuberous plants such as bracken (*warabi*), wild yams (*yamaimo*), and arrowroot (*kuzu*) thrived. Instead of forests, then, the early stages of a conquest landscape emerged, and a thick second-growth brush came to characterize Hachinohe's hillsides. It was this landscape that provided a rich breeding ground for wild boar: they thrived on the starchy root plants, which they easily dug up with their sharp canine tusks, and found ample cover for raising their young.[26]

Japanese people, too, consumed these wild plants in times of dearth, and it is over this resource, one must presume, that wild boar and the human population competed for scarce food. Shiba Gorō (1859–1945), a samurai on the losing side of the Meiji Restoration of 1868, and whose family had been forcibly relocated from Aizu to Tanabu, near Hachinohe, recalled that tubers and bracken root were essential for survival on the Pacific-coast side of the northeast. Even with these wild vegetables, noted Shiba, "it was all we could do not to perish from cold or hunger." Shiba explained that in the winter "we gathered the plants that grew wild in the surrounding mountains and fields," and tried to consume locally grown soybean. Illustrating how troublesome it was to convert raw soybean to food, Shiba wrote that his father "thought he would try making tofu and went to great trouble to crush the boiled soy beans, but he finally had to give up." When this method failed, Shiba recollected, "we could dig out the roots of bracken from under the snow. These we pounded and washed repeatedly in a vat of water until the starch sank to the bottom. We then mixed the starch with rice bran, added salt, and made dumplings, which we threaded on a skewer and toasted over the fire."[27]

Not just Hachinohe, but other domains, too, found themselves trapped by the transforming export-based economy. Luke Roberts argues that the growth of markets in Osaka actually heightened the impact of famine within Tosa domain on the island of Shikoku. In 1734, for example, Tosa shipped over 20,000 *koku* of rice to Osaka wholesalers "in order to satisfy its creditors," despite the fact that it was suffering through a devastating famine. He reveals how ultimately Tosa had become dependent on the vibrancy of the Osaka market, increasing the chances of food shortages and the absence of relief in times of famine. Roberts highlights, moreover, the environmental implications of Tosa's export-based economy, or what could be described as the emergence of a conquest or protoindustrial landscape in that domain, pointing to the massive deforestation that occurred as a result of lumber exports. Exporting timber quickly emerged as a mainstay of Tosa finances, despite the fact that deforestation led to increasingly bald hillsides, the destruction of some waterways, and widespread soil erosion.[28] In Hachinohe, as will be discussed, different environmental problems related to the rise of an export-based economy can be seen as early as the mid-eighteenth century.

WEATHERING CHANGE

As Hachinohe's chronicles reveal, if any one problem, other than terrain, plagued the farmers of that domain, it was the weather. Two chronicles, in particular, illustrate the climatological conditions that led to a failure of the millet and barnyard-grass crops, and most likely the soybean crops as well. *Eiroku nikki* (Eiroku diary), for example, paints a compelling picture of pervasive unseasonable weather and the hardships caused by crop failure. In 1749, explains the chronicle, only a third of the usual snow fell, providing a poor snowpack and hence limited runoff, but it took an unusually long time for the snow to melt because of the extremely cold spring temperatures. Weather in the second month of the lunar calendar was fair, but in the third month, temperatures again plummeted and the wind and rain picked up. It took forty-seven to forty-eight days just for the seeds to sprout. From at least the fifth month onward, moreover, cold temperatures and high winds continued; it was so cold that farmers were forced to wear warm padded clothing (*wataire*) in the fields. Throughout the sixth month, the temperatures remained cold, and the final days of that month witnessed strong winds. The cold wind severely punished the immature upland crops, contributing to the extremely bad harvest (*daikyōsaku*).[29]

Common to times of crop failure, landowning farmers and seasonal laborers witnessed an increase in rice prices, and so, "in the seventh month," continues *Eiroku nikki*, "it was inevitable [that farmers] abandon their fields and [look for] loans, as well as dig for bracken root [*warabi no ne*]" to feed themselves. Other wild plants also served to sustain the threatened population. In the ninth month, for example, a kind of wild strawberry (*fubonshi*) ripened, and many people sought out the fruit to pick and eat. As the famine worsened progressively, more disturbing reports emerge from the chronicles. Some children were reportedly drowned by their parents in rivers because of the lack of food, while others could be heard yelling and crying in the streets. In Fukazawa and Shinden-dōri, conditions became particularly bad, and the bodies of people who had died of starvation piled in mountains.[30] Chroniclers admit that certain portents had cautioned of troubled times ahead. In the fifth month, for example, farmers had observed a red star, which remained until the seventh month, when an even more bizarre portent appeared. Farmers spotted a black-and-white crow making a nest from willow limbs; it gave birth to several young, one of which was pure white. In the memory of the chroniclers, such portents told of worse times to come as the ever-important harvest season drew near.[31]

The chronicle *Tenmei utateyana* (Tenmei fish trap) provides another brief, but nonetheless revealing, account of the weather conditions of 1749. Its author, Ueno Iemon, was fourteen years old in that year. At the time, he recalled, great winds uprooted massive trees, and farmers were forced to plant crops a second time because high winds ripped seedlings from the ground. The summer months were exceptionally cold, and seasonal weeders left the fields without finishing their tasks; one imagines that lingering weeds may have helped strangle already weakened crops. Only on a rare occasion did the skies ever clear, Ueno explained. From the eighth month onward, moreover, it rained constantly, and farmers were only able to produce about 40 percent of the normal amount of millet and barnyard grass. Ueno also told of problems concerning wild boar. Starting in 1746, boar raided crops in Hamaura-dōri, Shimoyamane, Tashiro, Kakunohama, and Toyabe. In these areas, explained Ueno, many vagrants (*hinin*) gravitated to the towns as a result of food shortages.[32]

The climatological fluctuations that influenced Japan's weather patterns from the seventeenth through the nineteenth centuries have attracted scholarly attention. Kikuchi Isao points out that most eighteenth-century famines that ravaged the northeast were sparked by extremely cold temperatures, high winds, and above normal rainfall. This harsh microclimate was concentrated on the Pacific-coast side of northern Honshu. These sustained cold rains and high eastwardly winds, which originate in the Okhotsk Sea, are known as the *yamase*. The *yamase* is characterized by high amounts of precipitation and cool temperatures, even in the late summer and early fall, which cause grain to fail to mature and ripen properly. Kikuchi explains that the *yamase* is specific to the region around Hachinohe; even neighboring domains presently part of Akita and Yamagata prefectures, for example, remained sheltered from the *yamase* by the Ōu mountain range.[33]

Beyond the realm of microclimates, however, the haunting descriptions of harsh winds and irregular cold temperatures at intermittent times suggest that Japan also experienced the global Neo-Boreal, or Little Ice Ages, between the early seventeenth and mid-nineteenth centuries. The

Neo-Boreal was an "on-again, off-again period of cold and climatic misery" that punished parts of North America, Europe, and East Asia. "Mountain glaciers advanced in all parts of the world," writes William Stevens. "In Europe, cold summers sometimes brought crop failures, and famine sometimes ruled Britain and the continent. Almost every European country lost entire harvests from time to time, and a lack of food touched off waves of migration out of eastern Europe. Some who stayed were reduced to eating pine bark, dogs, and cats. Some sold their children into slavery or even ate them, too."[34] Theories on what sparked the Neo-Boreal range from speculation that an influx of fresh water from melting glaciers in northern waters disrupted critical ocean currents to postulation that decreasing incidents of sunspot activity caused variations in ground-level solar intensity on earth, lowering terrestrial temperatures. However, no definitive explanation exists.[35]

In North America, archaeologists have joined historians in exploring the influence of the Little Ice Ages on prehistoric and historic human populations. The eighteenth- and nineteenth-century navigators of the Hudson's Bay Company, for example, kept detailed and accurate meteorological records, which in many cases are more thorough than records from the early twentieth century. These reports suggest that Manitoba, in particular, witnessed harsh climatic conditions during two periods, 1730–1740 and 1790–1820, dates that nearly correspond to the wild-boar famine. Archaeological evidence suggests that Little Ice Ages hit Native American populations during the same decades. Some prehistoric Native American groups experienced widespread depopulation, possibly a result of unseasonable weather shortening the corn-growing season, while others were forced to adapt to changing conditions by abandoning increasingly unproductive fields, and their agrarian existence, in favor of a seminomadic, wild-game hunting way of life.[36]

As illustrated by Chart 1, three Little Ice Ages, along with two interim Intervallic Ice Ages (essentially cold lulls between the major stages of the Little Ice Ages), struck the northeastern section of the Japanese archipelago.[37]

Chart 1: Little Ice Ages of Early-Modern Japan

Little Ice Age	1610–1650	Intervallic Ice Age	1650–1690
Little Ice Age	1690–1740	Intervallic Ice Age	1740–1780
Little Ice Age	1780–1880		

The two chronicles surveyed above—*Eiroku nikki* and *Tenmei utateyana*—support the notion that Japan experienced Little Ice Ages in the eighteenth century, and that they contributed to crop failures and extreme hardships in many agrarian communities. The wild-boar famine of 1749 fell in the second Intervallic Ice Age, but still at a time of dramatic changes in the weather. One can speculate that an Intervallic Ice Age, when combined with the explosion of the wild-boar population, sparked crop failures that were nearly as acute as in the full-blown Little Ice Age of 1690–1740 or later. In Hachinohe these abnormally low temperatures combined with terrestrial environmental changes to aggravate crop failures in 1749 to the point of famine. However, this is not to say that the cold and rainy weather harmed all plants and animals. Like the wetter and cooler conditions that marked the end of a prolonged drought in North America and that sparked a slow recovery of bison numbers on the Great Plains in the fourteenth century, a process that transformed Native American life, the Neo-Boreal might too have contributed to the increase of wild-boar and deer numbers in northeastern Japan.[38]

THE WILD-BOAR FAMINE OF 1749

As early as the 1730s, signs of an impending crisis were widespread in the Hachinohe area.[39] In the sixth month of 1737, the village headman of Kanjō requested firearms from the judicial magistracy for the purpose of killing wild boar who were running out of control in the Hachinohe-mawari district.[40] Six administrative districts (*tōri*) had been established in 1671: Hachinohe-mawari (eighteen villages from Sannohe and one village from Kunohe), Naganawashiro-dōri (twelve villages from Sannohe), Nakui-dōri (eleven villages from Sannohe), Karumai-dōri (nineteen villages from Kunohe), Kuji-dōri (eighteen villages from Kunohe), and Shiwa (four villages from Shiwa).[41] In the case of Kanjō, the judicial magistracy appears to have acquired the requested firearms, probably from domain authorities, although their mode of distribution and effectiveness against the boar remain unknown.[42] Nor were firearms the only means for reducing the wild-boar population in Hachinohe. Special breeds of hunting dog (possibly including the Kishū breed to be discussed in chapter 6) were also used. In 1746, the domain government promoted the breeding of such dogs to protect villages and crops.[43] However, the policy had little impact: as of the eighth month of the same year, crop damage from deer and wild boar was still reported to be endemic.[44] With few options left, the peasants of Hachinohe turned to ritual practice in order to ward off the swelling onslaught of wild boar. In the first month of 1749, on the very eve of the wild-boar famine, they offered prayers (*kigan*) at local shrines for healthy crops and an end to the menace of unruly ungulates.[45]

In concert with rituals, the peasants of Hachinohe turned toward more punitive measures, including massive hunting campaigns led by professional hunters. During one campaign, which lasted from the end of 1748 to the beginning of 1749, hunters tracked wild boar near villages in Hachinohe-mawari, and 804 boar were killed.[46] From that point forward, they hunted boar throughout the year, but predominantly in the winter. Winter probably proved the most productive time because it was in this season that boar began to build nests for farrowing the following spring. In the third month of 1749, moreover, peasants took their campaign to a new level, hoping to eliminate the thick brush where wild boar hid and gave birth to their young. In what resembles a scorched-earth campaign, peasants looked for wild-boar nests and habitat (*sumika*), and formal requests were made to burn these areas.[47]

All these efforts failed to stem the tide of the pending ungulate irruption. Years later, Ueno Iemon wrote that later investigations of temple registers (*shūmon aratame chō*) revealed that about 1,500 people had been displaced by the famine but subsequently returned to Hachinohe, whereas the death toll was about 3,000. He recalled that local temples and wealthy townspeople (*fuka*) had given handouts to those dislocated by the famine, and that later a memorial to the unknown victims (*muenzuka*) was erected in Hachinohe.[48] In the tenth month of 1751, one such memorial was erected to appease the divine spirits of the dead, disperse evil beasts, and beseech the gods for bountiful crops. It still stands in the city of Hachinohe, and reads:

> [Raised in] the tenth month of 1751, [this monument] respectfully honors the divine spirits of the departed, [and asks for] the dispersal of evil beasts and [the growth of] bountiful harvests of the five grains.[49]

In chronicles, most of the victims of the famine were described as *hinin*. *Hinin* apparently means in this context something like "vagrant," but in some regions indicated a legal status of outcaste (literally, a "nonhuman"). Interestingly, mainstream Japanese often identified medieval and early-modern "nonhuman" groups through their relationship with other animals. Such forms of discrimination against tanners and meat processors, one presumes, originated in part with the Buddhist *ongaeshi* tales explored in chapter 1. For those *hinin* in need, relief stations (*koyagake* or *kijingoya*) were erected to provide food, shelter, and some income for victims in locations such as Shinden-dōri.[50] Children over ten years old were given food aid for an estimated ten days, with the relief operation providing each person up to .18 liters or .384 pints of rice per day.[51] That same year, wealthy townspeople and peasants set up a shelter at the Taisen'in temple to distribute grain to people under pressure from the famine.[52] This type of nonstate famine relief shares some interesting similarities with its counterpart in early-modern England. John Walter asserts that, despite the fact that seventeenth-century England is often hailed as a full-fledged market society that quelled famine through national market networks and governmental initiatives such as the 1586 Book of Orders, most relief actually occurred in the form of "benevolence and charity" by members of the local gentry and clergy.[53]

In what is another similarity between early-modern Japan and England, Walter argues that reciprocity was expected of wealthier members of the community, and that this reciprocity sometimes took the form of aid in times of dearth. Even when governmental initiatives and national markets provided the bulk of famine relief, local charity from gentry and church still remained prevalent. Moreover, this aid was construed in highly moralistic ways: often members of the gentry sought to better their historical legacy after death or were motivated by Christian notions of charity. Walter writes that recent scholarship "on the relief of the poor in early modern England confirms that many communities continued to see traditional forms of neighborly reciprocities as an important source of aid for their own poor." Famine-sensitive areas drew on earlier forms of community relations, articulated with the lofty vocabulary of "benevolence and charity." Whereas in medieval England access to food and basic subsistence had once been the "right" of the peasantry, part of what some describe as a moral economy, in early-modern society it could be manipulated as an act of charity.[54]

The same might be said of early-modern Japan, though with some important distinctions. The fact that local monastic institutions and wealthy members of the community generated most aid for famine relief implies a continuing importance of traditional community relations, despite the widespread commercial growth and political centralization of the Tokugawa period. Few dispute the idea, articulated best by Thomas Smith, that as a result of market growth, Japan underwent a period of commercialization that gradually changed community-based relations among landowners and laborers to a more businesslike contract.[55] Yet, the response to the outbreak of famine in Hachinohe suggests that below the surface of commercialization and contracts lay a moral economy binding peasants and the state, as well as nonstate interests, which manifested itself in times of crisis.[56] The wealthy and monastic institutions oversaw relief in times of famine, often independent of domain orders. In Hachinohe, in other words, the burden of distributing aid fell on the local community.

Peasants also appealed to the various deities that controlled the weather and broader agricultural cycles. It was mentioned above that in 1749 prayers had been conducted in hopes of bringing in a better harvest and ridding Hachinohe of wild boar. Kikuchi observes that rituals and prayers, sponsored by both domain governments and wealthy households, were frequent in times of harvest failure, irregular weather, and famine. In particular he has found that during the better-documented great Tenmei famine of the 1780s, peasants participated in *hiyorigoi*, a ritual soliciting good weather, and *gokoku jōju*, or rituals to assure the ripening of the five grains.[57] As mentioned earlier, similar rituals were conducted during the wild-boar famine: peasants beseeched the gods for bountiful harvests and asked local deities to rid their world of wild boar.

Despite these efforts, of the 32,000 people who lived in Hachinohe (these numbers are from 1744), roughly 3,000 died in the wild-boar famine.[58] So high a mortality rate for a localized famine raises important questions about realm-wide strategies for famine relief in times of crisis. In early-modern Europe, several factors helped to stem the impact of famines. Most notably, crop diversification on a national level and the development of national market networks assisted in bringing badly needed foodstuffs to areas struck by harvest failures. Scholars suggest that in late seventeenth-century England a "mix of grains most suited to local soil-types and climate would have the beneficial effect of increasing the total output of grain." In theory, creating cross-regional markets meant that "local shortages and surpluses could be ironed out through a market network extending beyond the region and integrating several climatic zones." The ability to absorb local trouble spots into broader national commercial and food-distribution networks emerged as one of the hallmarks of early-modern England.[59]

By contrast, the highly fractionalized character of the Tokugawa polity made this type of "market network extending beyond the region" problematic. Conrad Totman suggests of Tokugawa agriculture that "because the cropping was so finely tuned, the margin of error was slender and modest irregularities in weather could produce a disproportionate fluctuation in crop yields, which quickly translated into scarcities." Subsequently, crop specialization led to an exacerbation of food scarcities when regions switched from food crops to cash crops, and they became "more dependent on food from other localities." It meant that when crops failed in a specific region, such as Hachinohe, which focused the majority of its agricultural attention on soybean, alternative crops were less likely to meet the needs of an increasingly hungry population. The nature of the Tokugawa system meant that supplies from other domains or the shogunate were slow in coming, as local lords "restricted exports to other regions lest reserves fail at home."[60] The response to the wild-boar famine in Hachinohe suggests that it could be every domain for itself when it came to famines in eighteenth-century Japan.

JAPAN AND THE EURASIAN WILD BOAR

Given early-modern Japanese reliance on upland grain farming, it should not be surprising that wild boar wreaked such havoc on the farmers of Hachinohe.[61] Wild boar, or even feral pigs, can have a devastating impact on people and the natural environment. Offering a case in point, Alfred Crosby argues that domesticated pigs were a central part of the sixteenth-century conquest of Central America. He writes only half in jest that somebody watching the "Caribbean islands from outer space during the years from 1492 to 1550 or so might have surmised that the object of the game going on there was to replace the people with pigs" and other imported ungulates such as sheep. Suggesting an ungulate irruption, Crosby explains that these animals "burgeoned so rapidly" that they probably had "much to do with the extinction of certain plants, animals, and even Indians themselves, whose gardens they encroached upon."[62] In some regions, because of their rapid adaptation to the warm Caribbean environment, feral pigs led the way in the conquest. Some Spanish historians even attribute greater importance to pigs in the conquest of Mexico than horses.[63] Simply put, these feral pigs (who resembled their fleet-footed and sometimes aggressive ancestors, the wild boar) ate native peoples and other animals out of house and home.

The feral pig who unleashed such devastation in America is a direct descendent of the Eurasian wild boar (Lin.: *Sus scrofa*), a highly sociable and clever animal who still inhabits much of Europe, Asia, and now many parts of North America after the species' introduction. James Serpell, a scholar of human-animal relations, explains that despite the popular image of pigs as filthy animals who prefer wallowing in the mud to anything else, wild boar are actually agile animals who inhabit woodlands and open forests. A wild-boar herd, called a sounder, is a matriarchal group that often consists of six or more related females and their offspring. Adult male boar are normally solitary. During the day or at dusk, these omnivores actively forage for a variety of foods, including fungi, ferns, leaves, roots, tubers, fruit, and nuts, as well as insects, carrion, ground-nesting birds, and small animals such as mice and frogs. They root up these morsels with powerful bony snouts and sharp canine tusks. The breeding season for wild boar peaks in December, gestation lasts about sixteen weeks, and farrowing occurs the next spring. Anywhere from three to fifteen young can be born in one litter; as they mature the females join the sounder, whereas the adult males become more solitary.[64]

In Japan, wild boar historically inhabited much of the Pacific-coast side of the archipelago (the warmer side of the Japanese islands with less snowfall), including Hachinohe and other sites in the northeast. Today, however, their habitat is largely restricted to southern Kyushu and Shikoku island, the Kii peninsula, and the southern half of the Chūgoku, Chūbu, and Kantō regions of Honshu. The virtual disappearance of wild boar from the northeast still perplexes zoologists; some, such as Chiba Tokuji, speculate that hog cholera (or classical swine fever) epizootics in the twentieth century wiped out wild boar in northern Honshu.[65] The early Japanese name for the wild boar was *i*, which was later combined with the character *shishi*, meaning flesh; hence the vernacular name *inoshishi*. Wild boar were also sometimes called *kusainaki*, a term that vaguely refers to the medicinal properties of its brain, and these ungulates became part of the early Japanese pharmacopoeia. Zooarchaeological data suggests that boar have been hunted in Japan since at least the Heian period (794–1185); early bronze bells depict hunting dogs chasing wild boar.[66]

In medieval and early-modern Japan, wild-boar hunting became even more popular with the spectacle of the grand hunt, or *makigari*, of the samurai. *Makigari* were orchestrated hunts in which samurai could flaunt their martial skills by slaughtering deer and wild boar whom they encircled in the mountains. Powerful samurai sponsored massive *makigari*, such as the celebrated hunt on the Okuno plain, where participants boasted of killing "six hundred wild boar, one thousand deer, thirty-seven bear, and three hundred squirrels."[67] Boar could be particularly challenging game to even the keenest marksman because, at least according to legend, they brushed up against trees, coating their hides with pine resin (*matsuyani*), and thus hardening an already tough skin. When a wild boar had been successfully shot, hunters often pulled out a hair from the back of its neck (*ikarige*) as a customary offering to local mountain deities.[68] Similar wild-boar hunts were prevalent in the Rajasthani court of India, where they symbolized the bounty of the land. Likewise, Victorian English fancied pig sticking, or stabbing wild boar with spears from horseback, to be the "very prince of sport."[69]

Japanese peasants were fond of wild-boar meat. Many believed that the flesh, because of its high fat content, had medicinal properties. Some held that wild-boar meat was effective in particular against epilepsy, certain skin ailments, and problems with the bowels. Boar liver, like bear gallbladder, was also prized in the Japanese pharmacopeia.[70] Tsukamoto Manabu, in his pioneering work *Edo jidaijin to dōbutsu* (Edo-period people and animals), has explored various aspects of human-animal relations during the Tokugawa period. Debunking many myths about the eating habits of early-modern Japanese, he points out that wild-boar meat was not the only form of porcine flesh consumed: there was also animal husbandry in Japan in the form of domesticated pigs, *inoko* and *buta*. Tsukamoto presents pages of compelling evidence to show that Japanese, since ancient times, have raised domesticated pigs.[71] Japanese observers such as Ikeda Kanzan, Nakamura Tekisai (1629–1702), and Tachibana Nankei wrote of domesticated pigs in Japanese towns and the countryside. Tachibana, for example, among his myriad observations of early-modern Japanese life, described domesticated pigs (*buta*) in Hiroshima.[72] Further supporting Tsukamoto's assertion, *Wakan sansai zue* (Illustrated Japanese-Chinese encyclopedia), a 1713 work already introduced in chapter 4, contains the following entry for wild boar (*inoshishi*):

> This species of animal, the wild boar, inhabits mountain recesses [*miyama*]. Its appearance is like that of a [domesticated] hog, but its belly is smaller, its legs are longer, and its hair is brown, or sometimes brown with a yellowish tint.... Its tusks [*kiba*] stick out of its mouth like those of an elephant [*zō*]. The amount of meat on some

> wild boar can come to 200–300 *kin* [about 120–180 kilograms]. It fights skillfully with tigers. Moreover, it is said that the wild boar brushes up against pine resin [*matsuyani*], which attracts sand and small stones and then hardens over the body like lacquer, repelling arrows. Most wild boar also cause damage to agricultural crops. It also eats snakes [and other small animals]. Hunters reflect that when hunting wild boar, you should never shoot the lead animal as it will run wildly and cause injury to someone.... For people suffering from skin ailments, the five viscera [*gozō*; i.e., liver, lungs, heart, kidney, and spleen] are said to be beneficial. Its meat is red like that of a horse, and is superior to that of a domesticated pig [*buta*]....[73]

Even cookbooks from the early eighteenth century describe recipes for dishes that contemporary Japanese might recognize as *butajiru*, or pork soup. In 1848, the farmer Ōkura Nagatsune (1766–1860) described pork as a fairly ordinary food in Japan.[74] In cities such as Edo, people could easily walk to butcher shops where, according to one European observer, they might buy "rabbits, hares, wild boar and deer without number."[75] And zooarchaeological evidence from present-day Shinjuku ward in Tokyo suggests that they did. Excavated sites have unearthed virtual dumping grounds of animal bones, including deer and wild boar.[76]

Samurai also relied on domesticated pigs to feed their prized fighting dogs (*mōken*) and hunting dogs (*kari inu*), and to feed dogs who were used in falconry (*takagari*), or later slaughtered to feed the prized hawks. Hosokawa family chronicles tell of domestic pigs being raised in Kokura domain. In 1630, for example, out of a litter of nine piglets, five were singled out to be used as hawk feed. Pointing to such examples, Tsukamoto argues that the image of the Japanese farmer peacefully harvesting the five noble grains (a hallmark of Confucian civility) without slaughtering animals (a telltale sign of barbarism) was created by early-modern literati.[77] Similar issues involving the invented traditions and boundaries of Japan's consumption habits and food cultures will be addressed in chapter 9, with regard to whaling and the consumption of whale meat . The points raised by Tsukamoto are critical because many historians continue to maintain that most Japanese had little to do with meat or the slaughtering of animals, leaving those untidy tasks exclusively to social outcastes.

Yet despite the efforts of hungry Japanese and their hawks, wild boar continued to flourish and pose problems for Japanese farmers. The situation was probably aggravated by shogun Tokugawa Tsunayoshi (1646–1709) and his "clemency for living creatures" (*shōrui awaremi*) orders of 1687, which restricted hunting throughout Japan, albeit with mixed results.[78] On the island domain of Tsushima, for example, farmers and samurai officials, already faced with difficult agricultural conditions, defied these orders and initiated, under the auspices of Suyama Don'ō, one of the most extensive ungulate-elimination programs in Japanese history. First, farmers on Tsushima constructed wooden fences around orchards and crops to keep wild boar out. When the resourceful animals found ways to dig up crops, or to eat fruit just prior to the harvest, they resorted to harsher measures. In what officials called the "order to track down wild boar and deer," beginning in 1700 and lasting for a period of about nine years, the domain launched a massive extermination campaign that culminated with the slaughter of an astonishing number of wild boar. In this campaign, the island domain of Tsushima was first divided into six sections, and fences were erected to contain the boar within these sections. Then, in succession, the wild boar were eliminated from each area.[79] It proved a time-consuming and expensive project, but officials hailed it as a success, as it virtually erased wild boar from Tsushima.[80] Elsewhere, less extreme measures were taken to combat wild boar. To protect crops from ungulate damage, deep pit-traps were dug. Sometimes the floors of such traps were lined with sharpened bamboo poles to impale the unsuspecting animal when it fell. The term *shishimichi*, or the "path of the boar," entered the vernacular as a metaphor for following such a road to misfortune. *Shishigaki*, or boar-repelling earthen walls, were also erected around fields to keep out wild ungulates. Some peasants burned material to create an offensive odor to repulse the animals, whereas others designed elaborate "scarecrows" to frighten them off. Finally, other agricultural communities resorted to building *shishigoya*, or wild-boar guardhouses, where humans could protect the fields during the critical harvest season.[81]

H. C. St. John, a captain in the Royal Navy who surveyed the coasts of Japan in the late-Tokugawa and early-Meiji years, noted problems that farmers had with wild boar. He wrote of the Kii area that "[w]ild boar and deer abound. At night they descend into the valleys, and not withstanding the fields are fenced in, and traps, rattles, and watchers are there also, they do a great deal of damage amongst the rice and sweet-potato crops. Wild boar are particularly destructive, trampling down even more than they eat. Pits are used, but with little success." He later added that Japanese "find it quite impossible to keep these animals from their fields. They fire off guns, keep rattles going, and sing and call out all night long from these watch huts which they put up all over their cultivation. Still, boar appear to get used to anything, or slip in during some unlucky moment the tired watchman falls asleep or goes and has a chat with the next nocturnal neighbor."[82] For Japanese farmers, as these descriptions attest, crop destruction caused by wild boar was a twenty-four-hour threat that required constant attention. In short, peasants were waging a war against ungulates, and competing for food sources that were tied to both their and the boar's survival.

It is worth noting briefly that a similar campaign continues to be waged by upland communities against wild boar, monkeys, deer, and other "pests" to this day, a campaign exacerbated by a combination of rural depopulation in the 1960s and back-to-the-soil movements throughout Japan. In a highly detailed study, Sutō Isao illustrates how many mountain villages, facing massive economic losses from crop damage caused by wild boar, continue to take punitive measures to keep the latter's numbers down. Wire snares, professional hunters, poison, various scarecrows, fences, and noise-making devices are employed to keep deer and wild boar out of crops. Those boar who are killed often end up butchered, their gallbladder sold in local pharmacies, whereas the meat makes its way to butcher shops or sometimes community feasts. Buddhist and Shinto rituals regarding the killing of these animals are observed. Sutō explains that many communities, along with professional hunters and trappers, make offerings to boar and related deities at small shrines scattered throughout upland areas.[83] Similarly, John Knight documents how recent deforestation in upland areas has caused widespread encroachment and crop damage by monkeys (*sarugai*), a situation that remains endemic in parts of Japan.[84] In Hachinohe, in the years around the wild-boar famine, along with wild boar and deer, monkeys, too, were killed.

In 1749, farmers working with domain authorities used devices similar to those described by Sutō to exterminate wild boar in Hachinohe. That year, hunters killed 200 boar in Hachinohe-mawari, while 246 were killed in nearby Kuji-dōri.[85] In the first month of the following year, the domain government ordered Nakasato Hachirōemon, a local hunter and evidently a member of the samurai class, to rid the countryside of wild boar. One month later, official hunting parties, staffed with expert hunters (*ryōshi*), reported having slaughtered 175 wild boar and injured 47.[86] But the campaign to exterminate the wild boar only grew more fierce after it was learned that upward of 650 *koku* of crops had been damaged in Karumai-dōri. It was claimed, for example, in the third month of 1751, that within the districts of five magistrates in Hachinohe an astonishing 2,923 boar were killed. Similarly, it was reported to the Hachinohe domain elder (*karō*) in the second month of 1755 that 240 wild boar and 2 monkeys were killed; in the first month of 1773, that 1,484 deer and wild boar were killed; and in the third month of 1780, that 1,831 deer and wild boar were killed, all throughout Hachinohe domain.[87] It is difficult to determine the overall results of these hunting campaigns on the boar and deer populations. As late as 1761—admittedly before the latter two hunts—wild boar remained numerous enough that they are said to have "invaded the castle town," chasing harried peasants and townspeople through the streets.[88]

Obtaining the firearms needed to rid the countryside of wild boar meant filing a request at the local magistrate's office. In 1750, Nakasato Hachirōemon filed such a request with the magistracy to keep some of the firearms and knives used in his domain-sponsored hunts. The following year, the magistrate of Hachinohe-mawari forwarded a request for sixteen guns for the purpose of hunting wild boar. Kikuchi writes that professional hunters and peasants tapped the military cache of Hachinohe castle in their war against rampant boar.[89] These government-sponsored hunts occurred despite the earlier efforts of shogun Tsunayoshi to restrict these efforts. Indeed, restrictions aimed at limiting wild-boar hunting throughout Japan no doubt contributed to the explosion of boar numbers in Hachinohe, just as nineteenth-century restrictions again deer hunting in Pennsylvania and New Mexico led to an explosion of deer populations in those states.[90] Yet, despite the orders of the Dog Shogun (as some remember Tsunayoshi), those seeking to rid their crops of wild boar or other agricultural pests easily obtained firearms. Tsukamoto lists firearms among the agricultural "tools" of the peasantry.[91] The borrowing of firearms was also practiced in Hachinohe. In 1765, for example, Tashiromura Sanjūrō requested a musket from the local magistrate to be used by professional hunters.[92] Thus, domains strictly regulated firearms, but professional hunters could gain access to these weapons to wage combat against ungulates and other wild animals.

CONCLUSION: CRITICAL LANDSCAPES

Like the "great cat massacre" explored by Robert Darnton, an episode in

French history that exposed the latent social tensions in a print shop decades before the French Revolution, the wild-boar famine reveals environmental tensions caused by protoindustrialization over a century before Japan's emergence as a major industrial power.[93] Moreover, just as Darnton's exploration shed light on issues of animal symbolism, witchcraft and ritual, and class conflict in France, the wild-boar famine offers a window onto early-modern Japanese attitudes toward nonhuman animals, hunting practices and ungulate control in the countryside, ritual forms of relief during natural disasters, and state and nonstate strategies for dealing with the threat of dearth and famine. Finally, just as protoindustrialization reconfigured and repositioned social and political relations within peasant communities throughout Japan, so too did it impact the natural environment in ways that directly threatened the ability of peasants to eke out a livelihood in the far northeast.

Historians point out that in Japan the political centering process of the early-modern period led to the rise of a commercialized economy, and that the rise of this new economy positioned some domains on the periphery as the exporters of products desired by the urban center. In Hachinohe, the focus on soybean as the dominant export crop led to the birth of monocrop agriculture, and, subsequently, Hachinohe became ever more vulnerable to potential harvest failure. However, as this chapter suggests, it also led to environmental changes that sparked an explosion in wild-boar numbers. Importantly, the wild-boar famine illustrates that protoindustrialization, and not just post-Meiji industrialization based on Western models, altered the environment. On the protoindustrial landscape, an ecological war between humans and boar was being waged in Hachinohe. It was a war fought day to day by Japanese peasants, and one that exposed the vulnerabilities of peasant life in the Tokugawa polity.

Modern Japanese studies in the West has seen an increasing amount of research on the environmental degradation caused by the economic "miracles" of the Meiji and postwar years, often focusing on the political and social reactions to the environmental crisis. Fred Notehelfer's pioneering article on the Ashio copper mine stands nearly alone in the field of Meiji studies, while somewhat more scholarship, albeit precious little of it by historians, exists on the postwar period.[94] In early-modern Japanese studies, however, despite the pervasive interest in the Tokugawa economic experience and its social consequences, only Conrad Totman, among scholars in the West, has asked serious questions about the environmental legacy of the seventeenth and eighteenth centuries.[95] Consequently, the modern industrial landscape is better known than the one it replaced, as is Japan's modern historical experience in general. Early-modernists, however, offer only scattered glimpses of the conquest or protoindustrial landscape in their work, despite the fact that it was this landscape that most directly influenced the lives of Japanese in the countryside. An environmental analysis of conditions in eighteenth-century Hachinohe reveals more than simply the social and economic implications of the transforming Japanese economy. It also exposes the ecological upheaval that accompanied such economic transformation, as well as the impact of this upheaval on the human world. In other words, the wild-boar famine reminds historians that human experience is always shaped by the environment.

NOTES

An earlier version of this essay appeared in the *Journal of Asian Studies*, to whose publisher, the Association for Asian Studies, the author expresses his gratitude. He would like also to thank the participants in the following conferences and workshops for their helpful comments on various drafts of the essay: Peasants in Comparative and Interdisciplinary Perspective: Landscapes of Identity, Nature, and Power (University of Illinois at Urbana-Champaign, 1999); Yale University ISPS Interdisciplinary Faculty Discussion Seminar on the Environment (Yale University, 1999); Modern Japan History Workshop (Columbia University, 1999); NEH Faculty Humanities Seminar (Montana State University at Bozeman, 2000). In particular, the author appreciates the thoughtful suggestions of Gordon Brittan, Carol Gluck, Andrew Gordon, Hara Yuka, Robert Hellyer, David Howell, Gregory Pflugfelder, Robert Rydell, Henry Smith, Ronald Toby, Conrad Totman, Tsuchiya Tatsuhide, Anne Walthall, Kären Wigen, and the careful readers for the *Journal of Asian Studies*.

1. Herman Ooms, *Tokugawa Village Practice: Class, Status, Power, Law* (Berkeley: University of California Press, 1996), 89.

2. John Whitney Hall and Marius B. Jansen, eds., *Studies in the Institutional History of Early Modern Japan* (Princeton: Princeton University Press, 1968), 169–88; Hayashi Reiko, "Provisioning Edo in the Early Eighteenth Century: The Pricing Policies of the Shogunate and the Crisis of 1733," in *Edo and Paris: Urban Life and the State in the Early Modern Era*, ed. James L. McClain, John M. Merriman, and Ugawa Kaoru (Ithaca, N.Y.: Cornell University Press, 1994), 211–33; James L. McClain, *Kanazawa: A Seventeenth-Century Japanese Castle Town* (New Haven: Yale University Press, 1982), 46–56, 101–12, 132–39; James L. McClain, "Space, Power, Wealth, and Status in Seventeenth-Century Osaka," in *Osaka: The Merchants' Capital of Early Modern Japan*, ed. James L. McClain and Wakita Osamu (Ithaca, N.Y.: Cornell University Press, 1999), 44–79; Nishiyama Matsunosuke, *Edo Culture: Daily Life and Diversions in Urban Japan, 1600-1868*, trans. Gerald Groemer (Honolulu: University of Hawaii

Press, 1997), 144–78; Noël Nouët, *The Shogun's City: A History of Tokyo* (Sandgate, U.K.: Norbury, 1990), 137–40; Yoshida Nobuyuki, ed., *Nihon no kinsei*, vol. 9, *Toshi no jidai* (Tokyo: Chūō Kōronsha, 1992).

3. Nakamura Satoru, "The Development of Rural Industry," in *Tokugawa Japan: The Social and Economic Antecedents of Modern Japan*, ed. Chie Nakane and Shinzaburō Ōishi (Tokyo: University of Tokyo Press, 1990), 81–96; Thomas C. Smith, *The Agrarian Origins of Modern Japan* (New York: Atheneum, 1959; reprint, Stanford: Stanford University Press, 1966).

4. Mike Davis, *Ecology of Fear: Los Angeles and the Imagination of Disaster* (New York: Metropolitan, 1997), 215; Elinor G. K. Melville, *A Plague of Sheep: Environmental Consequences of the Conquest of Mexico* (Cambridge: Cambridge University Press, 1997), 6–7, 47–59; Leader N. Williams, *Reindeer in South Georgia: The Ecology of an Introduced Population* (Cambridge: Cambridge University Press, 1998), 20.

5. Alfred Crosby, *Ecological Imperialism: The Biological Expansion of Europe, 900-1900* (Cambridge: Cambridge University Press, 1986), 173.

6. See Herbert Bix, *Peasant Protest in Japan, 1590-1884* (New Haven: Yale University Press, 1986); Thomas C. Smith, *Nakahara: Family Farming and Population in a Japanese Village, 1717-1830* (Stanford: Stanford University Press, 1977), 14, 59–85; Conrad Totman, "Tokugawa Peasants: Win, Lose, or Draw?" *Monumenta Nipponica* 41 (1986): 457–76; Stephen Vlastos, *Peasant Protests and Uprisings in Tokugawa Japan* (Berkeley: University of California Press, 1986), 1–5, 114–53; Stephen Vlastos, "Yonaoshi in Aizu," in *Conflict in Modern Japanese History: The Neglected Tradition* (Princeton: Princeton University Press, 1982), 164–76; Anne Walthall, *The Weak Body of a Useless Woman: Matsuo Taseko and the Meiji Restoration* (Chicago: University of Chicago Press, 1998), 100–260; James W. White, *Ikki: Social Conflict and Political Protest in Early Modern Japan* (Ithaca, N.Y.: Cornell University Press, 1995), 70–77, 204, 248, 296–312.

7. Harold Bolitho, "The Tempō Crisis," in *The Cambridge History of Japan*, vol. 5, *The Nineteenth Century*, ed. Marius B. Jansen (Cambridge: Cambridge University Press, 1989), 116–24; Mori Yasuhiko, "Kikin to ikki," in *Edo jidai no kikin*, ed. Kodama Kōta et al. (Tokyo: Yūzankaku Shuppan, 1982), 52–62; Nakajima Yōichirō, *Kikin Nihonshi* (Tokyo: Yūzankaku Shuppan, 1996).

8. William B. Hauser, *Economic Institutional Change in Tokugawa Japan: Ōsaka and the Kinai Cotton Trade* (Cambridge: Cambridge University Press, 1974).

9. Mark Ravina, *Land and Lordship in Early Modern Japan* (Stanford: Stanford University Press, 1999), 103–13, 141–47, 161–76.

10. Vlastos, *Peasant Protests and Uprisings in Tokugawa Japan*, 93–94.

11. David L. Howell, *Capitalism From Within: Economy, Society, and the State in a Japanese Fishery* (Berkeley: University of California Press, 1995), 1–23; Edward E. Pratt, *Japan's Proto-Industrial Elite: The Economic Foundations of the Gōnō* (Cambridge, Mass.: Harvard University Press, 1999); Saitō Osamu, *Puroto kōgyō no jidai: Seiō to Nihon no hikakushi* (Tokyo: Hyōronsha, 1985); Ronald P. Toby, "Both a Borrower and a Lender Be: From Village Moneylender to Rural Banker in the Tenpō Era," *Monumenta Nipponica* 46 (1988): 483–512; Walthall, *Weak Body of a Useless Woman*, 38–99; Kären Wigen, *The Making of a Japanese Periphery, 1750-1920* (Berkeley: University of California Press, 1995), 1–98.

12. Wigen, *Making of a Japanese Periphery*, 33, 59, 65, 79.

13. Kimura Motoi, Fujino Tamotsu, and Murakami Tadashi, eds., *Hanshi daijiten*, 8 vols. (Tokyo: Yūzankaku Shuppan, 1988–1990), 1: 81–82.

14. Nishimura Makoto, *Hachinohe no rekishi: Kodai shakai kara sangyō toshi made* (Hachinohe: Ikichi Shoin, 1977), 58.

15. See Howell, *Capitalism From Within.*

16. Susan B. Hanley, *Everyday Things in Premodern Japan: The Hidden Legacy of Material Culture* (Berkeley: University of California Press, 1997), 66–68, 77–94.

17. Nishimura, *Hachinohe no rekishi*, 67–68.

18. Ibid., 68. See also Edo Jidai Hitozukuri Fudoki Hensanshitsu, ed., *Edo jidai hitozukuri fudoki: Furusato no hito to chie*, vol. 2, *Aomori* (Tokyo: Nōsangyoson Bunka Kyōkai, 1994), 325–26.

19. On the environmental impact of colonialism and the creation of third-world economies, see Clive Ponting, *A Green History of the World: The Environment and the Collapse of Great Civilizations* (New York: Penguin, 1993). On the landscape of Hachinohe, see Iida Momo, *Inoshishi, teppō, Andō Shōeki: "Hyakushō gokuraku" Edo jidai saikō*, Ningen sensho, no. 192 (Tokyo: Ningen Sensho, 1996), 12.

20. Susan B. Hanley and Kozo Yamamura, *Economic and Demographic Change in Preindustrial Japan, 1600-1868* (Princeton: Princeton University Press, 1977), 126.

21. A. G. Norman, ed., *The Soybean: Genetics, Breeding, Physiology, Nutrition, Management* (New York: Academic, 1963).

22. Lane Simonian, *Defending the Land of the Jaguar: A History of Conservation in Mexico* (Austin: University of Texas Press, 1995), 21.

23. Nishimura, *Hachinohe no rekishi*, 70. See also William Wayne Farris, *Population, Disease, and Land in Early Japan, 645-900* (Cambridge, Mass.: Harvard University Press, 1985), 94–117; Iida, *Inoshishi, teppō, Andō Shōeki*, 22–23.

24. J. K. Ladha, ed., *Biological Nitrogen Fixation for Sustainable Agriculture* (Dordrecht, Holland: Kluwer, 1992), 120.

25. Nishimura, *Hachinohe no rekishi*, 70.

26. Edo Jidai Hitozukuri Fudoki Hensanshitsu, *Edo jidai hitozukuri fudoki*, 326; Hachinohe Shishi Hensan Iinkai, ed., *Hachinohe shishi: Shiryō hen*, 7 vols. (Hachinohe: Hachinohe-shi, 1970–1979), 1: 170–71; Iida, *Inoshishi, teppō, Andō Shōeki*, 13, 24–25; Nishimura, *Hachinohe no rekishi*, 71. See also Conrad Totman, *The Green Archipelago* (Berkeley: University of California Press, 1989; reprint, Athens: Ohio University Press, 1998), 35, 95.

27. Ishimitsu Mahito, ed., *Remembering Aizu: The Testament of Shiba Gorō*, trans. Teruko Craig (Honolulu: University of Hawaii Press, 1999), 87–88, 93–94.

28. Luke S. Roberts, *Mercantilism in a Japanese Domain: The Merchant Origins of Economic Nationalism in 18th-Century Tosa* (Cambridge: Cambridge University Press, 1998), 63–64, 74–79.

29. Aomori-ken Bunkazai Hogo Kyōkai, ed., *Michinoku sōsho* (Aomori: Aomori-ken Bunkazai Hogo Kyōkai, 1957), 175–76.

30. Ibid.

31. Ibid. See also Shinpen Aomori-ken Sōsho Kankōkai, ed., *Shinpen Aomori-ken sōsho*, 11 vols. (Tokyo: Rekishi Toshosha, 1968), 3: 13–14.

32. Aomori-ken Bunkazai Hogo Kyōkai, *Michinoku sōsho*, 175–76.

33. Kikuchi Isao, *Kikin to shakaishi* (Tokyo: Azekura Shobō, 1994), 23.

34. William K. Stevens, *The Change in the Weather: People, Weather, and the*

Science of Climate (New York: Delacorte, 1999), 45. See also Brian Fagan, *The Little Ice Age: The Prelude to Global Warming, 1300-1850* (New York: Basic, 2001).

35. Brian Fagan, *Floods, Famines, and Emperors: El Niño and the Fate of Civilizations* (New York: Basic, 1999), 187–88; Jean M. Grove, *The Little Ice Age* (London: Routledge, 1988).

36. Tim Ball, "As Cold As Ever I Knew It: Joseph Colen, February 22nd, 1802: The Changing Climate of Manitoba," *Transactions of the Historical and Scientific Society of Manitoba* 33 (1976–1977): 61–66; Celina Campbell and Ian D. Campbell, "The Little Ice Age and Neutral Faunal Assemblages," *Ontario Archaeology* 49 (1989): 12–33; William Green, "Examining Protohistoric Depopulation in the Upper Midwest," *Wisconsin Archaeologist* 74 (1993): 290–323.

37. Kikuchi, *Kikin to shakaishi*, 27–28.

38. Dan Flores, "Bison Ecology and Bison Diplomacy: The Southern Plains from 1800 to 1850," *Journal of American History* 78 (1991): 469.

39. Kikuchi Isao, *Kinsei no kikin* (Tokyo: Yoshikawa Kōbunkan, 1997), 121–23.

40. Hachinohe Shishi Hensan Iinkai, *Hachinohe shishi*, 5: 233.

41. Kimura et al., *Hanshi daijiten*, 1: 82.

42. Hachinohe Shishi Hensan Iinkai, *Hachinohe shishi*, 5: 233.

43. Kikuchi, *Kinsei no kikin*, 122; Tsukamoto Manabu, *Edo jidaijin to dōbutsu* (Tokyo: Nihon Editā Sukūru Shuppanbu, 1995), 166–74. See also Taniguchi Kengo, *Inu no Nihonshi: Ningen to tomo ni ayunda ichimannen no monogatari* (Tokyo: PHP Kenkyūjo, 2000).

44. Hachinohe Shishi Hensan Iinkai, *Hachinohe shishi*, 5: 370.

45. Ibid., 5: 418.

46. Ibid.

47. Ibid., 5: 419.

48. Shinpen Aomori-ken Sōsho Kankōkai, *Shinpen Aomori-ken sōsho*, 3: 13–14.

49. Kikuchi, *Kinsei no kikin*, 120.

50. Shinpen Aomori-ken Sōsho Kankōkai, *Shinpen Aomori-ken sōsho*, 3: 13–14.

51. Aomori-ken Bunkazai Hogo Kyōkai, *Michinoku sōsho*, 176.

52. Shōbuke Taneyasu, *Hachinohe han* (Aomori: Tōō Nippōsha, 1976), 239.

53. John Walter, "The Social Economy of Dearth in Early Modern England," in *Famine, Disease, and the Social Order in Early Modern Society*, ed. John Walter and Roger Schofield (Cambridge: Cambridge University Press, 1989), 106–28.

54. Ibid., 104, 128.

55. Smith, *Agrarian Origins of Modern Japan*, 140–56.

56. Irwin Scheiner, "Benevolent Lords and Honorable Peasants: Rebellion and Peasant Consciousness in Tokugawa Japan," in *Japanese Thought in the Tokugawa Period: 1600-1868*, ed. Tetsuo Najita and Irwin Scheiner (Chicago: University of Chicago Press, 1978), 39–62.

57. Kikuchi, *Kikin to shakaishi*, 29–31.

58. Edo Jidai Hitozukuri Fudoki Hensanshitsu, *Edo jidai hitozukuri fudoki*, 324.

59. John Walter and Roger Shofield, "Famine, Disease, and Crisis Mortality in Early Modern Society," in *Famine, Disease, and the Social Order in Early Modern Society*, 9–10.

60. Conrad Totman, *Early Modern Japan* (Berkeley: University of California Press, 1993), 242–45.

61. John Knight, "On the Extinction of the Japanese Wolf," *Asian Folklore Studies* 56 (1997): 140.

62. Alfred Crosby, *The Columbian Exchange: Biological and Cultural Consequences of 1492* (Westport, Conn.: Greenwood, 1972), 75.

63. Ibid., 77.

64. James Serpell, *In the Company of Animals: A Study of Human-Animal Relationships* (London: Blackwell, 1986; reprint, Cambridge: Cambridge University Press, 1996), 5–6. See also John O. Whitaker, ed., *National Audubon Society Field Guide to North American Mammals* (New York: Knopf, 1980), 639–42.

65. Chiba Tokuji, *Shuryō denshō* (Tokyo: Hōsei Daigaku Shuppankyoku, 1975), 105–7. See also the same author's *Ōkami wa naze kieta ka* (Tokyo: Shinjinbutsu Ōraisha, 1995), 195–98.

66. Okada Akio, *Dōbutsu: Nihonshi shohyakka* (Tokyo: Kondō Shuppansha, 1979), 94. See also Naora Nobuo, *Shuryō* (Tokyo: Hōsei Daigaku Shuppankyoku, 1968), 131–34.

67. Kitagawa Hiroshi, trans., *The Tale of the Soga Brothers* (Shiga, Japan: University of Shiga, Faculty of Economics, 1981), 36.

68. Okada, *Dōbutsu*, 95.

69. Ann Grodzins Gold and Bhojuram Gujar, "Wild Pigs and Kings: Remembered Landscapes in Rajasthan," *American Anthropologist* 99 (1997): 70–84. See also Harriet Ritvo, *The Animal Estate: The English and Other Creatures in the Victorian Age* (Cambridge, Mass.: Harvard University Press, 1987), 268–69.

70. Okada, *Dōbutsu*, 95.

71. Tsukamoto, *Edo jidaijin to dōbutsu*, 135–39.

72. Tachibana Nankei, *Tōzai yūki*, ed. Munemasa Isō (Tokyo: Tōyō Bunko, 1974), 90–91.

73. Terajima Ryōan, *Wakan sansai zue*, vol. 28 in *Nihon shomin seikatsu shiryō shūsei*, ed. Miyamoto Tsuneichi, Haraguchi Torao, and Tanigawa Ken'ichi, 32 vols. (Tokyo: San'ichi Shobō, 1968–1984), 533.

74. Tsukamoto, *Edo jidaijin to dōbutsu*, 135–39.

75. Michael Cooper, ed., *They Came to Japan: An Anthology of European Reports on Japan, 1543-1640* (Berkeley: University of California Press, 1965; reprint, Ann Arbor: Center for Japanese Studies, The University of Michigan, 1995), 284–85.

76. Kaneko Hiromasa, "Edo no dōbutsushitsu shokuryō: Edo no machi kara shutsudo shita dōbutsu itai," in *Edo no shokubunka*, ed. Edo Iseki Kenkyūkai (Tokyo: Yoshikawa Kōbunkan, 1992), plate no. 4, 220–42.

77. Tsukamoto, *Edo jidaijin to dōbutsu*, 139–49.

78. Beatrice Bodart-Bailey, "The Laws of Compassion," *Monumenta Nipponica* 40 (1985): 163–89; Harold Bolitho, "The Dog Shogun," in *Self and Biography: Essays on the Individual and Society in Asia*, ed. Gungwu Wang (Sydney: Sydney University Press for the Australian Academy of the Humanities, 1975), 123–39; Donald Shively, "Tokugawa Tsunayoshi, the Genroku Shogun," in *Personality in Japanese History*, ed. Albert M. Craig and Donald H. Shively (Berkeley: University of California Press, 1970; reprint, Ann Arbor: Center for Japanese Studies, The University of Michigan, 1995), 85–126. See also Tsukamoto Manabu, *Tokugawa Tsunayoshi* (Tokyo: Yoshikawa

Kōbunkan, 1998), 124–63.

79. Suyama Don'ō, "Inoshishi oitsume oboegaki," in *Nihon shomin seikatsu shiryō shūsei*, 10: 339–46.

80. Tanaka Takeo, *Taigai kankei to bunka kōryū* (Kyoto: Shibunkaku Shuppan, 1982), 242–44.

81. Okada, *Dōbutsu*, 94–95.

82. H. C. St. John, *Notes and Sketches from the Wild Coasts of Nipon: With Chapters on Cruising after Pirates in Chinese Waters* (Edinburgh: Douglas, 1880), 133, 168.

83. Sutō Isao, *Yama no hyōteki: Inoshishi to yamabito no seikatsushi* (Tokyo: Miraisha, 1991).

84. John Knight, "Monkeys on the Move: The Natural Symbolism of People-Macaque Conflict in Japan," *Journal of Asian Studies* 58 (1999): 622–47; John Knight, "The Soil as Teacher: Natural Farming in a Mountain Village," in *Japanese Images of Nature: Cultural Perspectives*, ed. Pamela J. Asquith and Arne Kalland (Richmond, U.K.: Curzon, 1997), 247–48.

85. Hachinohe Shishi Hensan Iinkai, *Hachinohe shishi*, 5: 440.

86. Ibid., 5: 445–46.

87. Kikuchi, *Kinsei no kikin*, 123.

88. Hachinohe Shishi Hensan Iinkai, *Hachinohe shishi*, 1: 171.

89. Kikuchi, *Kinsei no kikin*, 123–24.

90. Louis Warren, *The Hunter's Game: Poachers and Conservationists in Twentieth-Century America* (New Haven: Yale University Press, 1997), 48–70, 106–25.

91. Tsukamoto Manabu, *Shōrui o meguru seiji: Genroku no fōkuroa*, Heibonsha raiburari, no. 18 (Tokyo: Heibonsha, 1993), 9–95.

92. Kikuchi, *Kinsei no kikin*, 124.

93. Robert Darnton, *The Great Cat Massacre and Other Episodes in French Cultural History* (New York: Vintage, 1984), 75–104.

94. F. G. Notehelfer, "Japan's First Pollution Incident," *Journal of Japanese Studies* 1 (1975): 351–83. See also W. Puck Brecher, *An Investigation of Japan's Relationship to Nature and Environment* (Lewiston, N.Y.: Mellen, 2000); Jeffrey Broadbent, *Environmental Politics in Japan: Networks of Power and Protest* (Cambridge: Cambridge University Press, 1998); Norie Huddle and Michael Reich, with Nahum Stiskin, *Island of Dreams: Environmental Crisis in Japan* (New York: Autumn, 1975); Arne Kalland and Brian Moeran, *Japanese Whaling: End of an Era?* Scandinavian Institute of Asian Studies Monograph Series, no. 61 (London: Curzon, 1992); John Knight, "The Forest Grant Movement in Japan," in *Environmental Movements in Asia*, ed. Arne Kalland and Gerard Persoon (Richmond, U.K.: Curzon, 1998), 110–30; Margaret A. McKean, *Environmental Protest and Citizen Politics in Japan* (Berkeley: University of California Press, 1981); Akio Mishima, *Bitter Sea: The Human Cost of Minamata Disease* (Tokyo: Kosei, 1977); Frank K. Upham, *Law and Social Change in Postwar Japan* (Cambridge, Mass.: Harvard University Press, 1989).

95. *The Origins of Japan's Modern Forests: The Case of Akita*, Asian Studies at Hawaii, no. 31 (Honolulu: Center for Asian and Pacific Studies, University of Hawaii, 1985); Totman, *Green Archipelago*. See also Arne Kalland, *Fishing Villages in Tokugawa Japan* (Honolulu: University of Hawaii Press, 1995).

From *Wakan sansai zue*. Courtesy of the C. V. Starr East Asian Library, Columbia University.

CHAPTER SIX

Can the Subaltern Bark? Imperialism, Civilization, and Canine Cultures in Nineteenth-Century Japan

Aaron Skabelund

INTRODUCTION: THE COLONIAL DOG

Over the past several decades, historians have begun to explore the role of nonhuman animals in imperialism, either consciously in campaigns of military conquest and colonial rule or through the often-unintended consequences of "ecological imperialism."[1] Largely ignored, and perhaps even more important, was the metaphorical manipulation of beasts in imperializing and colonizing projects.[2] This chapter examines one of the less appreciated historical links between imperialism and animals, which took the shape of a dynamic that I term the "colonial dog." In the broadest sense, this dynamic describes a configuration of relationships between colonizers and colonized, between dogs who accompanied the human colonizer from the metropole and canines who already lived in colonized and colonizable regions, and among different cultural modes of human interaction with dogs. More specifically, by the colonial dog is meant here a particular set of dogkeeping practices and specific dog breeds that emerged first and foremost in Britain, but by the nineteenth century became entrenched also in continental Europe and North America, thereafter spreading across the globe together with imperial expansion.

To be sure, the term is anachronistic. Although both colonizers and colonized viewed specific dogs and dogkeeping practices as representative of imperial power, rarely did they see them as worthy of explicit note or analysis. The colonial dog was not a marked category, but instead was tacitly taken for granted as the standard canine, especially by colonizers. People talked far more often and explicitly about the characteristics of the "native dog" and the local human communities who interacted with it. The term "native dog," too, is problematic, with its baggage of colonial arrogance and anthropological conceit, but I deliberately use it instead of "indigenous" or "local" dog precisely because it is less anachronistic. It coexisted and was synonymous with other derogatory labels for the dogs of the periphery, such as "pariah" and "kaffir," which likewise were used to designate—and denigrate—humans, and whose historical connections with the colonial apparatus are obvious indeed.[3] In short, the otherness and explicit inferiority of the native, whether human or canine, was a central trope of colonial discourses, whereas the cultural peculiarities of the colonizers went for the most part unremarked.

Of all animals, why dogs? Part of the reason, as zoologist James Serpell has written, is that no animals, with the possible exception of apes, come as close to humans in affective and symbolic terms, and, by the same token, make a stronger claim to be treated as human. Thanks to their longstanding and intimate ecological connection with humans, dogs occupy a distinctive and liminal space between human culture and the rest of the animal world. Their tendency to roam between domestication and wildness positions them ambiguously between culture and nature, within and beyond human control. As creatures of metaphor, dogs oscillate between high-status animals and low-status people.[4] They are said simultaneously to possess admirable traits, such as loyalty, that make them akin to humans, and despicable attributes, such as filth, that render them unalterably unlike humans—or in the minds of some, like "other" humans.

The rhetorical pairing of the colonial dog with the native dog is central to this chapter's analysis. Both Westerners and the people whom they encountered in their colonies viewed the two sets of dogs as distinct, and subjected them to both explicit and implicit comparisons. Individuals on both sides of the colonial divide portrayed the colonial dog as possessing attributes worthy of the imperial power. Typically, they claimed that it was civilized, thoroughly domesticated but powerful, and they esteemed it as purebred. On the other hand, colonizers and many of the colonized described the native dog as primitive, aggressive but cowardly, and of mixed or wild breed. Within this ideological framework, governments throughout the colonial world initiated campaigns to eliminate canines—whether they were street, feral (that is, once-tame canines who had reverted to the wild), and wild dogs, or wolves, jackals, and coyotes—often under the immediate pretext of combating rabies or saving livestock. Such campaigns targeted native dogs rather than colonial dogs and have ensured the numerical and cultural supremacy of the latter breeds to this day.

To paraphrase Kathleen Kete, when people spoke of dogs, as inhabitants of empire often did, they spoke about their times, and of themselves and others.[5] Both in actual and in symbolic terms, dogkeeping and colonialism are closely linked. Asymmetrical power relationships of master and subject provide the logic for the interaction of dogkeeper and the pet, just as they connect the colonizer and colonized. The chief concern of the colonial master, like that of the dogkeeper, is that his subjects, as unpredictable as they might be, will prove loyal and useful. Conversely, his primary fear is that these dependable inferiors might turn upon him. It is precisely for this reason that the specter of rabies was and is so frightening: the trusted canine companion lethally biting its own master invokes fears of a particularly ominous kind. Herein may also lie the reason why colonizers so reviled street, wild, and feral dogs, since it was all too easy to regard them as domesticated dogs who had become degenerate and, while still relying on humans for sustenance through scavenging, had ungratefully turned their backs upon their wise and well-wishing benefactors. They were therefore to be trusted neither by "civilized" people nor by the better canine classes. Perhaps the unstable power relations inherent in both dogkeeping and colonialism provide one explanation, at least among animal metaphors, why dogs recur so pervasively as a salient trope in colonial rhetoric. Indeed, my invocation of Gayatri Chakravorty Spivak's famous query in the title of this chapter is meant to highlight the parallels between colonial and canine discourses.[6]

The dynamics of the colonial dog may be found in many, albeit not necessarily all, colonial projects during the age of New Imperialism, that is to say, the nineteenth and early twentieth centuries. It should be kept in mind, however, that in some colonial contexts different nonhuman-animal metaphors may well have figured larger. Each empire and colony possesses its own history and local peculiarities, and it is necessary to be culturally specific when speaking about imperialism—or, to be more accurate, imperialisms. Nevertheless, the model proposed here may contain something applicable nearly everywhere, if only in that Westerners took similar notions of the value of certain dog breeds and ways of dogkeeping wherever they went.

Although this essay alludes to other imperial situations, it focuses specifically upon the historical example of Japan. To be sure, Japan never became fully colonized, and so to speak of the "colonial dog" in this context may be inaccurate in the strictest sense. The term remains useful, nonetheless, because, by the late nineteenth century, Euro-American imperial and colonial dominion extended nearly everywhere throughout the world—including Japan, in the form of political ideologies and notions of Western progress, among other things—and opinions about dogkeeping and dog breeding were part of its cultural hegemony. Even though Westerners did not fully succeed in making Japan a colony, the nation's territorial sovereignty was nonetheless violated under the treaty-port system that took shape in the 1850s and would survive nearly till century's end. Foreigners never directly dictated policy within Japan, yet Europeans and Americans—as businessmen, government advisors, and privileged residents in the treaty ports—exerted tremendous political, social, and cultural influence on the country. The primary goal of the Meiji government's foreign and domestic policies for a half-century, and the principal reason that it hired foreign advisors, was to escape semicolonial status and regain full sovereignty by persuading the Western powers to revise the unequal diplomatic treaties that they had imposed. To achieve this end, Japanese leaders of the Meiji period (1868–1912) embarked upon a policy of Westernization under the twin slogans of "civilization and enlightenment" (*bunmei kaika*) and "rich country, strong military" (*fukoku kyōhei*).

Japan also differs from some other areas that experienced colonialism and imperialism because at the same time that its autonomy was compromised, it quickly began to encroach upon the sovereignty of its weaker Asian neighbors and, ultimately, became itself an imperial power with colonies of its own. The process was fast and mimetic. Within a few decades of the country's loss of full sovereignty in the early 1850s, the Meiji government began to emulate Western powers by threatening surrounding states using military, diplomatic, and economic means. Japanese leaders were motivated by an economic appetite for raw materials and markets and by a strategic ambition to bolster the nation's security against further encroachment by Western powers, yet paradoxically, they were driven also by nationalist desires for parity with those same Western empires. As the pairing of the official slogans of "civilization and enlightenment" and "rich country, strong military" suggests, a colonial empire, won through military might and economic self-sufficiency, was the ultimate proof of civilization in the nineteenth-century imperial world. The rapid and exceptional transformation of Japan from an object to a subject of imperialism also led to an equally remarkable metamorphosis of its native dogs.

CANINE IMPERIALISM: A DOG-EAT-DOG WORLD

In her influential studies of English attitudes towards animals in the nineteenth century, historian Harriet Ritvo has explored the complex interconnections of dog symbolism, dog breeding, and Victorian nationalism. While suggestive, her analysis of the English relationship with dogs and, for that matter, with all domestic animals is limited to the British Isles, and pays scant attention to England's vast global empire.[7] Just as English Victorians brought the animals of empire home for display in zoos and as hunting trophies, they similarly took to the imperium their enthusiasm for pets and particularly for the keeping of purebred dogs. Likewise, continental European powers and the United States transplanted these practices to their respective colonies. As a result, by the late nineteenth century, an imaginary canine geography had come into being, mirroring the imperial map of the human world. Because the culture of dogkeeping and enthusiasm for dog breeding flourished across the same span of time that Western colonialism covered the planet, there was no part of the world that escaped the imposition of this canine cartography.

Two organizational principles structured the imaginary geography. One was the identification of certain dog breeds with particular nation-states, as Ritvo has insightfully discussed in the case of the English Bulldog. The other was a hierarchy that valued breeds who originated in colonial metropoles far more than canines associated with those regions that were objects of imperialist ambition. Such institutions as the English Kennel Club and the American Kennel Club played an important role in codifying these principles through their practices of breed listing. An apt illustration may be found in the "Dog Map of the World," a 48-by-76-centimeter diagram published in London in 1933, which highlights the snug relationship between dogs, nation-states, and empires.[8] On its surface, the map simply shows breeds recognized by the American Kennel Club (AKC), but in a larger sense it illustrates the nationalization of dogs and their positioning within imperial power structures. At the center lies a map of the world, a two-dimensional representation of the globe's surface. Precise political boundaries are delineated only for the European continent, the United

States, and Canada. The borders of countries in the Middle East and parts of Asia are shown, but haphazardly. For Africa, South America, and various other regions, political borders are nonexistent. Numbers placed within the borders of each country correspond with particular dog breeds who are shown in two rows of squares that form a border around the map.

The majority of breeds recognized by the English Kennel Club and the AKC were from Britain, followed by several Western European countries and the United States. Such a distribution adheres to the conceit expressed by an English commentator in 1854 that there was "no civilized land where the canine race is more the companion of man than in Great Britain or any nation which has so many valuable varieties of it."[9] Indeed, of the approximately seventy breeds recognized by the AKC, thirty-eight hailed from the British Isles; another dozen or so originated in Germany, France, and the Low Countries; and three represented the United States. A strong association between canine breeds and nation-states had emerged by the late nineteenth century. The "nationality" of many breeds is evident simply from their names: English Fox Hound and English Setter, as well as German Shepherd, German Pointer, Yankee Terrier, and French Poodle. But nowhere was this connection stronger than in Britain, where the Bulldog came above all other varieties of dog to embody Britishness and empire. Once a dog associated with the working classes and used for the sport of bull baiting, the breed was elevated by Britain's middle classes during the nineteenth century into a symbol of British national and imperial might. As early as the eighteenth century, Scottish philosopher David Hume (1711–1776) claimed that the dog's courage made it peculiarly English, and nineteenth-century breed manuals consistently declared that it was England's national dog.[10]

In addition to becoming nationalized, dogs were placed within an imperial hierarchy that esteemed Western breeds more than those of colonial areas. This was in part the result of the emergence of dog fancying as an organized social enterprise first in Britain, and then in continental Europe and the United States. Dog enthusiasts, not surprisingly, devoted primary attention to dog breeds who had been created and existed within the borders of their own nation-states. The first British dog shows in the mid-nineteenth century in fact lumped together dogs from outside the West in a "Foreign Dog" category without consideration for breed or function.[11] The same bias was apparent in the breed-recognition system of Western kennel clubs, of which the 1933 "Dog Map of the World" provides a visual representation. The most striking difference was quantitative, in that few dogs were recognized as purebred outside the colonial metropoles. The AKC, for example, recognized none in Africa or Latin America except for the Mexican Chihuahua, and only a handful in the Middle East and Asia.

There were also at least two qualitative differences between Western dogs and those whom the map identified with peripheral regions. First, dogs associated with many colonial areas (or with postcolonial states in Latin America and Australia) were not domesticated breeds at all, but wild canines. Featured on the 1933 "Dog Map of the World," for example, were the Wild Dog of East Africa, the Cape Jackal, the South American Wolf, and the Australian Dingo. The absence of a representative domesticated dog in these areas reflected a perception that the geographical regions in question, as well as their peoples, remained uncivilized and savage. In only one case was an undomesticated canine placed within the boundaries of a "civilized" nation-state: the Timber Wolf, which on the map roams the northern edge of the border between the United States and Canada. The animal's positioning reflected its own shrinking geographic range in North America, since it had once populated much of the continent before being driven to the brink of extinction. It functioned here not as a symbol of the American or Canadian nation-states, but rather of a continent and its Native American peoples who had been subdued by civilization.

Second, the few recognized dog breeds associated with colonial areas were generally of two predictable types. One type was the lapdog. These small canines, also known as "toy dogs," included the Chinese Pekingese and the Japanese Spaniel. Westerners in both the metropole and the colonies described lapdogs as effeminate and exotic, and it is probably not a coincidence that these particular breeds were chosen to represent regions that were also viewed in the same terms. It seems that the characteristic gendering of Orientalism applied even to the world of dogs. Also linked with the colonies, albeit hypermasculinized rather than feminized, were several large dog breeds whose identity became strongly associated with hunting and military service. The Afghan Hound and the Rhodesian Ridgehound (Ridgeback), for example, were adopted by the British for military use and for safari hunting throughout their vast colonial empire. They served as the canine parallel of the Gurkha people of Nepal, whose ethnic identity became inseparable from military service after the English designated them to serve as soldiers in British colonial armies.

The breed associated with Japan on the 1933 "Dog Map of the World," and by Westerners more generally with that country, namely, the Japanese Spaniel, or *chin*, had a long and complicated history of representation. Japanese had bred this import from China for centuries, so that by the middle of the Tokugawa period (1600–1868) the *chin* had become a lapdog primarily for well-to-do women of the samurai and merchant classes, who raised it indoors alongside the cat. In fact, Japanese did not consider the *chin* to be a dog; rather, as the British Japanologist Basil Hall Chamberlain (1850–1935) observed, they spoke of "'dogs and pugs' (*inu ya chin*) as if the latter formed a distinct species."[12] Nevertheless, many Westerners, including Chamberlain, identified the *chin* as the representative canine of Japan.

The Tokugawa shogunate contributed to this view. It presented four *chin* along with rice, dried fish, and other gifts to Commodore Matthew C. Perry (1794–1858) when he arrived in his infamous "black ships" in 1853 to demand that the country establish political and diplomatic ties with Western powers. Perry, in turn, sent two of the spaniels, dubbed Miako (or Miyako, in today's prevailing orthography) and Shimoda, via Admiral Stirling of the British Navy, to Queen Victoria.[13] Whether or not Victoria ever received the animals is unclear. There is no record of her doing so, and because the dogs were of the "most delicate build," they might easily have perished during the course of an ocean voyage. The sailors named the other two gift dogs Master Sam Spooner and Madame Yeddo (an alternate spelling for the shogunal capital of Edo). The inspiration for the former is unclear, but the pairing of a male Western name and a female Japanese one suggests that Orientalist stereotypes may have been at play. Both of these dogs died at sea en route to the United States.[14] The commodore also sent two other pugs, named Yid-do (again, for Edo) and Jap, whom he had acquired by other means, to his daughter. Apparently only one of these dogs survived the journey. In 1860, an entourage of ambassadors from the shogunate visited the United States and called on Perry's widow at the home of her son-in-law, August Belmont, in New York City. It is said that when the group entered the house, the dog instantly and affectionately greeted its countrymen, a sight that moved Jane Perry to tears.[15]

Despite inauspicious beginnings, by the 1860s Japanese spaniels had become the rage of Europe and America. Such celebrated artists as Édouard Manet (1832–1883) and Pierre-Auguste Renoir (1841–1919) even featured them in their paintings.[16] The enthusiasm for the *chin* was part of a broader

Euro-American craze for things seen as quintessentially Japanese, which became known as *japonisme*. Many Western artists and artisans admired the work and imitated the techniques of their Japanese counterparts, viewing the island country as an exotic, enchanted land. An Orientalist fascination with the Japanese Spaniel, as well as its Chinese cousin, the Pekingese, continued in the West well into the twentieth century. These delicate, often enfeebled, and overly bred dogs stood as representatives of two Asian countries that were often regarded in a similar manner as weak, effeminate, and decadent.

Conversely, Westerners embarked along with their English Bulldogs, German Shepherds, and other colonial dogs as they participated in projects of empire building and colonial rule. Once in foreign lands, Westerners were often accompanied in public by large, often purebred, but always powerful, dogs. In areas where they feared attack by natives or by wild animals, as in Africa, they might take along two canines, one a large "attack" dog and the other a smaller "barking" dog.[17] In *Beasts and Man in India* (1891), John Lockwood Kipling (1837–1911), Rudyard's father and the curator of the Lahore Museum, observed that the "dog and the horse accompany [the British colonial] everywhere, for it is part of our insular vanity to declare that no other dogs and horses are half so good as ours. Packs of foxhounds are regularly imported; the subaltern, colonial officials, the private soldier, and the civilian bring bull-dogs, mastiffs, and terriers of every degree. Spaniels, retrievers, and greyhounds accompany sportsmen; the great Danes are occasionally seen, while ladies bring such pets as Maltese, Skyes, and Dandie Dinmonts, and dachshunds."[18]

In India and throughout the imperial world, Westerners valued these dogs for hunting, as guards, or simply as companions. Toby, a Scottish Terrier, likely fulfilled all three functions for his master, Sir Rutherford Alcock (1809–1897), the first British consul general to Japan. Unfortunately, the partnership came to a tragic end in September 1860, when on a return trip from Mt. Fuji, the dog was accidentally scalded to death during a visit to the hot springs of nearby Atami. Alcock mourned the passing of his "constant and faithful companion," and lamented that "[o]ne must have led the isolated life of a Foreign Minister in Japan, to realise the blank which the loss even of an attached dog creates."[19] As in the metropole, Europeans and Americans in colonial regions cherished dogs for their loyalty and their usefulness, but also for their physical prowess, or in other words, their capacity for violence.

Although the flourishing of pet culture from the eighteenth century onward certainly contributed to many Westerners taking dogs with them abroad during the age of New Imperialism, it was not the first time that canines had contributed to European expansion. During the exploration and conquest of the Americas in the sixteenth century, the Spanish, Portuguese, and English regularly trained large dogs, mainly mastiffs and greyhounds, to track, attack, and guard in their colonial endeavors. In the rough terrain of the New World, dogs became prized weapons, often considered more valuable than horses. Once victorious militarily, the Spanish were said to have pitted dogs against Native Americans accused of sedition and sexual crimes in public spectacles designed to intimidate the wider human population.[20] Although English commentators criticized such alleged excesses of Spanish rule, their countrymen resorted to similar techniques once they discovered the usefulness of dogs in their own colonies during the seventeenth and eighteenth centuries. Because the English, like the Spanish, considered Native Americans to be "brutish savages, which by reason of their godless ignorance, and blasphemous idolatry, are worse than . . . beasts," they had few qualms about treating them in the same category as nonhuman prey.[21] As historian Mark A. Mastromarino has written, Anglo-American colonists may have not used dogs for mere entertainment, but once they came to "believe that the only good Indian was a dead Indian, the adoption of such inhumane measures as hunting Indians with mastiffs and other dogs became inevitable."[22]

In sixteenth- and seventeenth-century Japan, the more circumscribed presence of Spanish and Portuguese explorers, missionaries, and traders gave rise to a purely symbolic deployment of dogs. Here, too, large, powerful dogs accompanied European explorers, but militarily there was far greater parity on the Japanese archipelago than in the Americas. Although the inhabitants of the islands trailed Europeans in military technology, they quickly acquired and mastered the expertise they lacked, such as the manufacture of firearms. Within a century of contact, the country's leaders, conscious of the European appetite for conquest and wary of the subversive potential of Christianity, forced all but a small group of Dutch merchants out of the archipelago. In this historical context, Europeans had no opportunity to put their dogs to military use, and perhaps because of these restricted circumstances, dogs became a more malleable metaphor than in the New

World. In general, the metaphorical use of dogs and other animals in colonial settings seems to have been more pronounced, or at least qualitatively different, when there was less inequality in political and economic power between the disparate cultures.

As in the Americas, certain dog breeds in sixteenth- and seventeenth-century Japan became strongly associated with Europeans. They appear frequently alongside Iberians in screens and other forms of Japanese artwork named for its subject matter, the figure of the Southern Barbarian (*Nanbanjin*). Japanese warlords, in turn, laid almost immediate claim to the physical strength, speed, and exotic nature of these newly arrived creatures in order to bolster their own status and political power.[23] They acquired the dogs as gifts or by purchase, and created compounds to breed and train dogs for fighting and hunting. Even after banishing from Japan all Europeans except for the Dutch, the Tokugawa shogunate and some regional rulers or daimyo continued to import dogs through the Dutch East Asia Company until at least the early eighteenth century (they imported exotic birds as well; see chapter 4).[24] The dog compounds and breeding facilities probably disappeared long before the shogunate did, and by the time Perry arrived in 1853, any trace of the few Iberian breeds had likely been absorbed into the wider dog population.

When Westerners and their dogs returned to Japan in the mid-nineteenth century, similar patterns reemerged. This time, the United States and European countries possessed a clear military advantage and extracted unequal treaties that granted them significant political and economic privileges in Japan. Still, Japan, unlike much of the world, was able to avoid outright colonization and, after the change of regimes from Tokugawa to Meiji in 1868, Japanese leaders embarked on a series of unprecedented political, economic, and social reforms that allowed the nation to become a world power in a generation. In this volatile geopolitical environment, dogs became entrapped in a discourse about the nature of Japan and what it ought to become, as the next section will explore in greater detail.

As elsewhere, Western diplomats, soldiers, missionaries, businessmen, and other visitors brought their dogs to Japan. And like their sixteenth- and seventeenth-century predecessors, the local Japanese population imagined a strong connection between foreign dogs and their masters. Echoing earlier Southern Barbarian artwork, the mid-nineteenth-century prints known as "Yokohama pictures" (*Yokohama-e*) captured the strange manners and dress of the foreign community, many of whom lived in the newly established treaty port. Artists of the day commonly portrayed Western soldiers, officials, merchants, and their families with canine companions. In an 1860 print, for example, Andō Hiroshige II (1826–1869) depicted what appears to be a large Borzoi-like greyhound alongside a fierce-looking and well-armed English soldier.[25] In the background, numerous dead ducks, presumably the kill of the soldier and his dog, hang from a broad rack.

Dogs appeared most frequently in the prints of Hashimoto Gyokuransai (also known as Utagawa Sadahide; 1807–ca. 1873). They are especially conspicuous in *Yokohama kaikō kenbunshi* (Report of things seen and heard in the open port of Yokohama; 1862), a widely read illustrated account of treaty-port life. Here and elsewhere, Hashimoto, through his images as well as accompanying text, prominently portrayed Westerners with Western-bred dogs, sometimes as they interacted in the treaty ports, but, in a few instances, as he imagined them in their home countries. The canines are invariably large, physically imposing dogs. The immense size of the dogs, who appear usually to be either pointers or huge spaniels, together with the fact that they diligently accompany their owners wherever they go, lends the human masters an unmistakable air of authority. Several Hashimoto prints, as well as works by other artists, show well-built dogs following their masters through the streets, or domestic scenes of foreign children playing with dogs, or entire families with their pets.[26] One suggestive print shows a carriage ridden by an American. A massive dog trots faithfully at its side. In the background looms the silhouette of a large black ship, possibly an allusion to Perry's vessels of nearly a decade earlier.[27] Together, the dog, the foreigner, and the ship subtly convey the military might and economic power of the West.

Hashimoto and other creators of "Yokohama pictures" were not the only ones who drew a visual association between Western imperialists and their dogs. In other representations of humans and dogs, national differences were overlaid with gender and class distinctions. The French illustrator and topical cartoonist, Georges Bigot (1860–1927), who lived in Japan from 1883 to 1899, frequently pictured Westerners accompanied by dogs in his drawings for both foreign and domestic audiences. In contrast, he rarely depicted Japanese people with dogs. Furthermore, Bigot's cartoons evince a distinct gendering of dogs, insofar as Western men appear with larger, hunting dogs, while illustrations of Western women and families usually feature smaller pets.[28]

In other images, differences of economic status were superimposed on national and cultural distinctions. *Seiyō dōchū hizakurige* (A Western shank's mare; 1870–1876), by the journalist and author Kanagaki Robun (1829–1894) and two collaborators, is a case in point. This book humorously described the turmoil resulting from the introduction of Western cultural forms in the early years of the Meiji period. Many of its illustrations depict dog bodies that bear a telling resemblance to the bodies of their owners. Hunched Japanese nonelites are positioned next to unkempt street dogs or small, round puppies, while tall-standing Westernized elites are accompanied by lanky, well-groomed Western canines.[29] Only one Japanese figure is shown with a lean Western hound. He is a well-to-do, dignified, bearded "gentleman" clad in a Western coat and top hat, and he holds a walking stick in one hand and the dog's leash in the other. He stands tallest among three male figures, positioned right to left on a two-page spread, who embody Japanese progression toward "civilization." The man on the right, labeled an "unenlightened person," represents a paragon of traditional Japan. He is a defiant-looking two-sworded samurai. His hair is bound in a topknot and he is dressed in a *haori* jacket and in *hakama*, a robe-like garment, wearing *zōri*, thonged sandals, on his feet. In his hand, he clutches a folded fan, and a sword hangs at each side of his waist. Next to him, in the center of the picture, appears an eclectically dressed young man, designated a "half-enlightened person." His clothing is Japanese, like that of the samurai, but his other apparel and implements are distinctly Western. He wears European footwear and a black, short-brimmed cap that reveals a closely shorn hairstyle. In his left hand he dangles a Western-style umbrella, while holding out a pocket watch in his right. The two less "enlightened" men face toward the "gentleman" on the left, as if to imply that he is the future of a "civilizing" Japan.[30] The presence of the Western dog validates his supposedly sophisticated status, and he is apparently the only one of the three worthy of owning such a canine. This impression is further enhanced by the fact that the hound assumes a confrontational stance toward the bizarrely dressed man at the center.

"Yokohama pictures" and other visual images revealed dog breeds and a way of dogkeeping never before seen on the archipelago. Other than lapdogs and dogs whom hunters in mountainous areas kept, the vast majority of dogs in mid-nineteenth-century Japan were semiferal canines who formed packs and claimed particular urban neighborhoods and villages as their territory. These dogs might best be called street dogs, because they lived in the roadways and on the outskirts of populated areas, and had limited attachment to people. Unlike canines who accompanied Westerners to Japan, they did not belong to anyone in particular, although some people in a neighborhood might take a liking to a certain dog and treat it kindly. Tsukamoto Manabu, a historian of Tokugawa Japan, has suggested that street dogs maintained a symbiotic relationship with their human neighbors. Humans provided dogs with food scraps, and because canines thought of the neighborhood or village as their territory, they functioned as guardians of the community, patrolling the area and warning their human neighbors of unfamiliar and suspicious intruders.[31]

Several Western visitors to Japan in the nineteenth century noted the surprise of Japanese when they saw foreign dogs. Laurence Oliphant (1829–1888), private secretary to Lord Elgin and chronicler of Elgin's mission to Japan in 1858, described how, during his first visit to Shimoda, Japanese seemed to take more interest in the canine foreigners than in the human ones:

> They manifested but little curiosity at us as we strolled about the streets, but I was amused to observe a crowd collected round about a dog belonging to one of our party, of the Shantung terrier breed, and which, though a purely Chinese dog, is scarcely to be distinguished from a Skye terrier. This long-haired specimen of the canine race created immense excitement and interest, both among Japanese dogs and men, as he trotted complacently along the streets of Shimoda.[32]

Approximately a decade later, a certain Mr. C. Barrow, clerk at J. C. Fraser and Company in Yokohama, set out to visit Miyanoshita, a village on the Izu peninsula. As his colleague J. P. Mollison recalled nearly forty years later in the *Japan Gazette*, at the time this trek on foot was a "very venturesome thing for one man alone." Indeed, Barrow likely made the trip in 1868 while civil war still gripped the country and when violence against foreigners remained commonplace. Barrow reached his destination without incident, and gave much of the credit to his only companion, a large black retriever called Jack. According to Barrow, Jack "was a constant source of wonder and delight to the villagers of all ages, who had of course never seen a dog of the kind before. He proved to be a sort of passport of their goodwill, because of his good temper, obedience and docility, in spite of his huge size."[33]

Japanese were no doubt fascinated to see dogs who were physically different than those whom they had previouly encountered. Other than the lapdog, most dogs in Japan resembled one another, and were not far removed from the wolf in general physical appearance. Although dogs on the archipelago differed somewhat in size and color, they did not exhibit the marked variety of form and hair length of European breeds, which prompted even Charles Darwin (1809–1882) to wonder how all domesticated dogs could have sprung from the same species.[34] Dogs indigenous to Japan were characterized phenotypically by broad triangular-shaped heads, large round muzzles, small pricked-up ears, and curled and upright tails. Apart from the *chin* and certain hunting dogs, Tokugawa Japanese rarely bred for particular traits, and additions to the canine gene pool had been limited for several centuries. For all the above reasons, it is not surprising that a glimpse of a foreign dog in nineteenth-century Japan carried considerable visual impact.

Next to appearance, Japanese seemed most surprised by the demeanor of foreign dogs. Native street dogs greeted with hostility strangers who "invaded" their neighborhoods, and they could not be easily controlled even by resident humans. Foreign dogs, by contrast, seemed to move singly with their masters from one place to another without barking or growling at strangers, and to answer more readily to their owners' commands. Foreigners, as well as Japanese, regularly commented about these behavioral differences. Oliphant distinguished between the "complacent" manner of the dog in his party, and the "immense excitement and interest [of] Japanese dogs and men." The wonder of villagers at the "good temper, obedience and docility" of Barrow's dog Jack implied a similar if more implicit contrast. Drastically different dog deportment accentuated the obvious physical disparities between native and foreign dogs.

Local inhabitants were probably also surprised by the customs of Western dogkeepers. Although the raising of dogs by individuals was not unknown in Japan, it was not something that most people practiced or were even familiar with. The fascination registered in Sadahide's numerous prints of dogs following around foreigners and frolicking with their children in their homes was one of novelty bred from unfamiliarity. The closest phenomenon in Japan was the keeping of lapdogs and hunting dogs, but it was limited in scale and was pursued deep within the interior of wealthy households, or else off in the mountains beyond the gaze of most. Owners of lapdogs or hunting dogs did not regard them as family pets or "man's best friend," as dogkeepers of the Western middle classes had begun to do by the nineteenth century. A few Japanese may have "adopted" dogs (or been adopted by dogs) from the neighborhood pack, but their bonds were less formal, intimate, and enduring than was the case in contemporary Western petkeeping. Other than the *chin*, an "adopted" dog would have never been brought into one's home. Edward S. Morse (1838–1925), an American zoologist who taught at Tokyo University from 1877 to 1879, observed that Japanese did not "pay attention to a dog," and did not indulge in petting.[35] Neither, apparently, was the concept of taking dogs for a walk known in Japan before Westerners arrived.

As in the sixteenth century, it did not take long for wealthy Japanese of the nineteenth century to acquire a taste for foreign dogs and the practices associated with them. The result was a mapping of imperial canine geography onto local class hierarchies, a pattern that occurred also in other colonial contexts. Ownership of a colonial dog became a means for affluent and upwardly mobile Japanese to prove their sophistication and status. It was one example of the widespread adoption of Western cultural forms during the early part of the Meiji era, one requiring not only an outlay of cash but a continuing set of daily practices. Acquiring a Western breed was an option for only the most well-to-do or well connected. Throughout the Meiji period, newspapers reported outrageous prices paid by the rich to import a particular breed, or the presenting of Western dogs to the emperor and other government officials. Purebred hunting dogs, such as English Setters and German Pointers, were the most expensive and the most sought after in late nineteenth-century Japan. A mid-Meiji photograph of the long-retired shogun, Tokugawa Yoshinobu (1837–1913), with a supply of ammunition about his midsection and a shotgun slung over his shoulder, and posing with his pointer, illustrates this new preoccupation among the wealthy.[36]

The supposedly sophisticated nature of Western canines was enhanced as early as the 1860s when a new word of English origin, *kame*, was coined for a dog of foreign breed. To the great amusement of anglophone Westerners, Japanese apparently created the expression when they heard foreigners calling to their dogs to "come here." The American zoologist Morse was one of many bemused observers who commented on the phenomenon. "[Y]ou ask for the name of dog and the answer will be

'Kumhere.' Many think that is the Japanese name for dog, whereas the name has been adapted from the English and American who, in calling a dog, say, 'Come here!' 'Come here!'—and the Japanese in these parts have supposed that the word represents the English name for dog, which in Japanese is *inu*."[37]

If Japanese in the middle of the nineteenth century associated Western dogs with foreigners in the treaty ports, by the end of that century the association had expanded to include the indigenous upper classes. By the 1880s, a foreign dog was practically an essential complement to one's top hat or frilly dress, as exemplified by the center panel of an 1889 triptych by the print artist Inoue Tankei (or Inoue Yasuji; 1864–1889) showing a well-to-do Japanese family enjoying a spring day in Tokyo's Asakusa Park with some sort of small hound.[38] Similar associations appear in a lithograph titled "Kiken bijin" (Elite beauty; 1888). The print shows a woman posing with what appears to be a spitz puppy arrayed in matching Western clothing.[39] The woman's blue dress, with white, gold, and red trim, is coordinated with a frilly collar of gold and red fabric that surrounds the dog's neck. The portrayal hearkens back to depictions of elite Tokugawa women with their lapdogs. At the same time, the artist is clearly familiar with contemporary dogkeeping practices in Europe, where elite society journals prescribed the proper clothing changes for a lapdog over the course of a day.[40] The lithograph quintessentially evokes the so-called Rokumeikan era of the 1880s, when the drive for Westernization reached its height and Tokyo's privileged gathered at the posh Deer-Cry Pavilion (Rokumeikan) to host foreign dignitaries and partake in ballroom dancing. Unlike the contemporaneous fascination with Western dogs, the enthusiasm for ballroom dancing did not last. It quickly went out of fashion after conservative politicians shrilly criticized a Rokumeikan masquerade ball, attended by high government officials including Prime Minister Itō Hirobumi (1841–1909) and his "Dancing Cabinet," as a silly, demeaning attempt to win the approval of foreigners.

The more subtle practice of keeping a Western dog drew less criticism, but did not escape it entirely. In a letter to the editor published in the daily *Yomiuri* newspaper in 1880, for example, a reader signing himself Tokibō related an episode that he claimed reminiscent of the extravagant treatment of dogs during the rule of the fifth Tokugawa shogun Tsunayoshi (1646–1709). Tsunayoshi had enacted, as seen in chapter 5, a series of unpopular animal-protection measures that earned him the nickname Dog

Shogun after his death.[41] Tokibō wrote of a recent incident in which the *kame* of a wealthy household had allegedly barked fiercely at a man delivering goods. The visitor fended off the dog with a stick, only to be reprimanded by a household servant for treating the dog poorly. Referring to the dog in the most respectful language, the servant declared that the deliveryman ought even to be thankful that the dog had considered biting his dirty leg.[42] Elements of class criticism are clearly evident in Tokibō's letter, and his mention of Tsunayoshi adds a political dimension to the censure.

In a similar manner, there seemed to be an implicit condemnation of the wealthy sport of hunting with dogs in an 1888 open letter from Shiga Shigetaka (1863–1927) to Prime Minister Kuroda Kiyotaka (1840–1900). Shiga wrote: "[A]lthough you are a man of affairs, we simply ask that when you go hunting with your dogs on official holidays or after work, you should get off at Hasuda or Koga stations and take a look at the wretched condition of the local inhabitants.... Only when the people of all the provinces of a nation are rich can the nation as a whole be rich; only when the nation is rich can its army be strong."[43] For an agrarian nationalist like Shiga, Western hunting dogs represented a citified and extravagant foreign affectation, much as ballroom dancing might have done. Despite such criticisms as Tokibō's and Shiga's, the rich and powerful did not give up their taste for Western breeds, however. A 1901 article in the *Yomiuri* noted that some fifty different non-Japanese breeds dwelt in Tokyo (constituting an estimated total of around 6,000 animals), and that native dogs were disappearing.[44]

CIVILIZATION AND RACIALIZED NATIONALISM

In Japan and elsewhere, many indigenous elites as well as foreigners regarded Western dog breeds as icons of enlightenment and domestication. By the same token, they disparaged native dogs as barbaric and savage. Nevertheless, explicit words of praise for the colonial dog were relatively rare. Just as discourses about whiteness or masculinity were submerged in most colonial contexts, the unstated, admirable qualities of the colonial dog usually provided an implicit foil for criticism of the native dog—and by extension, the native human. This pattern was manifest, in different inflections, throughout the imperial world. Westerners and many members of local upper classes explicitly and implicitly compared the two groups of dogs using the languages of civilization and scientific racism. Even as they were speaking about dogs, they projected their preoccupations and prejudices about "other" humans through their very act of representing.

The concept of civilization—the notion that certain human societies, primarily European ones, were more culturally advanced on a linear grid of development than other, "barbarian," societies—came to dominate Western thinking during the eighteenth and nineteenth centuries. Discourses of civilization pervaded the second wave of imperialism and colonialism, and were imposed onto the canine world. The colonial dog and its native foil became reference points for demonstrating the supposed civility of the Western colonizer and savagery of the colonized. Observers contended that Western breeds were calm, peaceful, and brave animals, whereas native dogs were easily agitated, aggressive, but cowardly. They regarded the colonial dog as a loyal and trusted companion when compared to the native dog, which was said to be devious and to dislike "civilized" foreigners. In this way, colonial dogs were portrayed as culturally, if not intellectually, enlightened, and native dogs as backward and old-fashioned.

Westerners and the Japanese who emulated them characterized Western breeds as the archetypes of resolute yet restrained domesticity, and portrayed native dogs as an embodiment of belligerent and craven wildness. Recall Barrow's comments about the "huge size" yet "good temper, obedience, and docility" of his dog Jack, and Oliphant's observations of the foreign dog strolling "complacently" through the milling streets of Shimoda in contrast to the "immense excitement [of] Japanese dogs and men." By conflating local humans and canines, Oliphant subtly suggested that the two groups shared a similar tendency toward excitability.

The British diplomat Alcock's comparison between native street dogs and certain Japanese men was not nearly so subtle. Alcock disparaged street dogs as the "only real nuisance of Japanese cities, in addition to the two-sworded Samourai [*sic*]."[45] Alcock may have not realized how apt his comparison was. Like street dogs, many members of the warrior class in the late Tokugawa period were *rōnin*, or roaming masterless samurai. *Rōnin* existed for a variety of reasons—among others, the death or ouster of a lord and difficult economic conditions sometimes drove warriors to seek their fortune elsewhere—but increasingly in the mid-nineteenth century, many were samurai who had forsaken their masters to support the imperial cause and drive out foreign "barbarians." Alcock was no stranger to the threat posed by *rōnin*. In 1861, he narrowly escaped death in a nighttime attack by samurai assassins who killed two of his countrymen and wounded his assistant, Oliphant.[46] The actions of a stray dog—its breed is unclear—who had earlier befriended Oliphant, and had alerted him that night to the attack by barking furiously, apparently did little to atone for the offenses of his canine colleagues in the eyes of foreigners.

Before the decade was over, "two-sworded ruffians" had attacked another one of Alcock's colleagues stationed in the city, Sir Harry Parkes (1825–1885), British minister plenipotentiary to Japan from 1865 to 1883. The incident occurred as Parkes was returning home with his dog from a meeting with the Japanese foreign minister on 28 September 1869. "Providentially," Parkes recalled, the would-be assassin "missed both me and my dear old Shah."[47] Although Parkes seems to have felt a close bond with his canine companion, presumably a Western breed, its Oriental name, Shah, is suggestive. Perhaps many Westerners involved in imperial projects had similar appellations for their dogs, reflecting the worldwide scope of their empires and the day-to-day exoticism that it involved.[48] The use of Oriental names also highlights the liminal position and metaphorical pliability of dogs, who could be regarded as privileged enough to be a part of the colonial in-group, but simultaneously despised and degraded enough to be named as colonized "others."

Nearly every foreigner, it seems, had something negative to say about the native dogs she or he encountered in Japan. Lady Kate Lawson, a member of the Japan Society and of the Red Cross Society of Japan, may have considered herself a friend of the Japanese, but she was no fan of their dogs. With a typical British pride, she wrote in the early twentieth century that the "Japanese dog is not the friend and companion of his master as is the English."[49] Lawson's compatriot, Isabella Bird (1831–1904), a travel writer who journeyed through northern Japan in 1878, similarly complained that the "primitive Japanese dog—a cream-coloured wolfish-looking animal, the size of a collie, very noisy and aggressive, but as cowardly as bullies are—was in great force in Fujihara, and the barking, growling, and quarreling of these useless curs continued at intervals until daylight; and when they are not quarreling, they were howling."[50] In the eyes of many Westerners, native dogs manifested uncontrollable belligerence but in the end were craven, while their own dogs were docile and domesticated but powerful when called upon to fulfill the commands of their masters.

Some Westerners asserted that such belligerence was an inborn or inbred characteristic of both dogs and humans in Asia. This was precisely the claim of Robert Fortune (1813–1880), an English horticulturalist who visited Japan and China during the 1850s. In his travelogue *Yedo and Peking: A Narrative of a Journey to the Capitals of Japan and China* (1863), Fortune made the following observation about canines in the former city:

> The dogs here [Edo] were the only animals which showed their enmity to us, and this they did in a manner not to be mistaken. They rushed out ... and barked at us in the most furious manner; but they are cowardly withal, and generally keep at a prudent distance.
>
> These dogs appear to be of the same breed as the common Chinese dog, and both have probably sprung from the same stock. It is curious that they should have the same antipathy to foreigners as their masters. For however civil and even kind the natives of Japan and China appear to be, yet there is no doubt that nine-tenths of them hate and despise us. Apparently such feelings are born with them, and they really cannot help themselves. That we are allowed to live and travel and trade in these countries is only because one class makes money out of us, and another and larger one is afraid of our power. I fear we must come to the conclusion, however unwillingly, that these are the motives which keep Orientals on their good behavior, and force them to tolerate us amongst them. The poor dogs have the same feelings implanted in their nature, but they have not the same hypocrisy, and therefore their hate is visible.[51]

Fortune recognized perceptively how empires operate, and acknowledged that most local people resented the presence of Western officials and merchants. He admitted to the inequalities of colonial practice, but he quickly dismissed, or rationalized, the disparities by explicitly comparing Japanese and Chinese people with less-than-human dogs. If Asian dogs and humans shared the same inborn "nature," Fortune intimated, then Western economic and political supremacy was justifiable.

Although local Japanese did not express such extreme aversion toward native dogs, they recognized differences in behavior between colonial and native canines, and similarly employed the idiom of civilization to describe them. "The Story of Enlightened and Unenlightened Dogs" (Kaika to fukaika no inu no hanashi), probably published originally in a pamphlet titled *Bunmei kaika* (Civilization and enlightenment; 1874), provides a striking example.[52] As is obvious from the title, the story relied on the same civilizationist rhetoric that many Westerners used to talk about canines. The tale, of course, is not about dogs at all, but is a parable deployed by the powerful to persuade the populace to embrace the government's policy of Westernization through "civilization and enlightenment."

The story's canine cast of characters consists of two rival packs of native street dogs living in adjacent neighborhoods. One day, the leader of one pack meets with the boss of the other gang. He expresses his concern that, even though the world is changing around them through the influence of civilization and enlightenment, "we dogs are not adapting." "We dogs are still old-fashioned," remarks the canine critic, "still marking our territory by a single hedge or sewer ditch" and "feuding with the dogs on the next block." By contrast, Western dogs are supposedly enlightened because they eschew such "stingy things as fighting over a lousy block or half-block of territory," and instead "follow four and five feet behind their master's horse or buggy." "They rarely fight amongst themselves," continues the leader of the first pack, "and if one of our kind barks at them, they simply make a face as if to say, 'I don't have time for your foolishness' and continue on their way." He then proposes that Japanese street dogs stop doing "such unenlightened things as barking at people dressed in Western attire, and instead, like Western dogs, obtain the rights of freedom and independence that allow [them] to go anywhere without worrying about whose territory it is."

The leader of the second pack, unconvinced, rejects the suggestion. Apparently, as restaurants move their establishments from traditional neighborhoods to more up-and-coming quarters, the "enlightened" dogs who inhabit the latter have access to more leftovers than they can possibly eat, while their "unenlightened" counterparts, including those of the second pack, become increasingly miserable. The hungry canines' gloom, the tale moralizes, is a "result of their refusal to listen to the ideas of civilization and enlightenment." According to the literary scholar Ishii Kendō, the story was one of the more effective narratives produced by the cultural proponents of Westernization."[53] Perhaps it derived its persuasive power from depictions of everyday life with which people could readily relate. Because of their daily contact with such dogs, audiences were able to recognize the behaviors described as relevant to, rather than distant and distinct from, their own experience.

To justify their imperial and colonizing ventures around the world, Westerners drew not only on the ideas of civilization but also on Occidental science. The theories of Charles Darwin that gained popularity during the second half of the nineteenth century greatly influenced Western colonial and imperial policies. Although in some instances Darwinian theory, as articulated in the pioneering *On the Origin of Species by Means of Natural Selection* (1859), challenged religious and other conceits that aligned native peoples with nonhuman animals, Darwinian science was by no means free from cultural and human biases. Indeed, elements of what later would become known as Social Darwinism were imbedded in the mature work of Darwin himself. Darwin saw, for example, the emergence of morality in humans as little more than an evolution of animal social instincts. At one point in *The Descent of Man* (1871), the evolutionary philosopher compared human "savages" with dogs, in that both "imagine that natural objects and agencies are animated by spiritual or living essences." Furthermore, Darwin contended that dogs had intellectual and moral faculties rivaling those of "savage" inhabitants of Tierra del Fuego. Whereas Fuegians allegedly demonstrated no feelings of religious devotion to a higher being, a dog exhibited a "love for his master, associated with complete submission, some fear, and perhaps other feelings." Some believe, Darwin continued, "that a dog looks on his master as on a god."[54] Is this not the embodiment of the ideal colonial dog, whose devotion surpasses that of the "savage" native?

Assumptions of racial and cultural superiority made explicit in Social Darwinism intensified the dichotomies of domestic and wild, civilized and savage, and equated them with colonizer and colonized. In turn, these notions were projected onto animals themselves. Westerners used the language of science and racism to claim the superiority of Western breeds over native ones, and of pureblooded creatures over those of mixed blood. This was especially true of dogs, those prized pets who live in greater proximity and intimacy with people than any other nonhuman animal. Some Victorian Bulldog enthusiasts, for example, maintained that the most serious threat to the breed was "infusion of foreign blood."[55] Others argued that if the Bulldog became detached from English soil it would inevitably degenerate. Concerns about degeneration echoed prevailing scientific theories about the deleterious affects of tropical, disease-ridden climates, as well as Social Darwinist anxieties about miscegenation with inferior groups. One defender of the Bulldog's "British blood" even reasoned, in circular fashion, that foreign blood "must be inferior because it is foreign."[56]

If fear existed that the colonial dog might degenerate when exposed to the climes and wiles of the colonial tropics, it was a foregone conclusion in the minds of some Western canine experts and enthusiasts that degeneration was the explanation for the abhorrent state of indigenous canines. Such was the view of Robert Leighton (1859–1934), the author of a 1907 work titled *The New Book of the Dog*. Native or "pariah dogs," which are "found in almost all oriental towns prowling about their own particular encampment, and in measure protecting the greater encampments of their human friends," wrote Leighton, are " domestic dogs which have degenerated into semi-wildness, yet which remain as by inherited habit, in association with mankind." Unlike Western dogs, he claimed, no native dogs composed a distinctive breed; instead they were "all mongrels." "By the process of indiscriminate interbreeding and influence of environment, they acquire [a] local character," Leighton cautioned, but they ought not, in his opinion, be regarded as a legitimate breed.[57] As with the ideas of civilization, the language of scientific racism pervaded the canine world.

Japan's contact with imperialism in the nineteenth century coincided with an age of rampant Darwinism and Social Darwinism across the imperial landscape. Morse, the American zoologist, commented on dogs frequently, and is perhaps not coincidentally also the individual credited by some historians with having introduced Darwinian thought to Japan. In his writings on Japan for Western audiences, Morse proved himself to be one of the most sympathetic observers of local society. Nevertheless, like nearly every other Westerner, he had few kind words for the dogs of the country.

In their rhetoric, Morse and other Westerners often used elements of scientific and racial discourse to characterize native dogs and to contrast them with the colonial dog. In Japan and elsewhere, Westerners portrayed native dogs as wolflike in behavior, appearance, and in breed. Sometimes they described street dogs as "mongrels," with a "good deal of European admixture," which was probably increasingly true as time passed.[58] More often, though, they commented that native dogs looked and acted more like wolves (or sometimes foxes) than the domesticated dog breeds with whom they were familiar. "[M]ost of the dogs one sees in Japan," Morse recorded in his journal, later published as *Japan Day by Day* (1917), "are of a wolf variety; they do not bark but howl."[59] Similarly, George Hilaire Bousquet (1845–1937), a French legal advisor to the Meiji government, reported that, while traveling in Japan in 1874, his group repeatedly had to protect its own dogs from wolfish native dogs. "These creatures with their heavy forms, enormous size, long wild hair, elongated snouts, small deep-set eyes and prominent fangs, are because of their hunter instincts far closer to wolves than the peaceful setter ... who just came to hide between my legs. Our caravan was obliged several times since the beginning of our trip to defend our setters by throwing stones at these aggressors."[60] Here we find one of the few admissions on the part of Westerners that native breeds might actually be stronger than the colonial dog.

Physically and in some ways even behaviorally, native dogs did indeed resemble wolves. Even today, some taxonomists point to the wolfish appearance and behavior of Japanese dog breeds and, conversely, the doglike appearances of the extinct wolves of Japan. Japanese dogkeeping practices, and the resulting blurry ecological boundary between street dogs, wild dogs, feral dogs, and wolves, actually made crossbreeding a possibility.[61] At the same time, Westerners and their aversion to "wolfish-looking" native dogs must be understood in the context of Euro-American scientific and cultural prejudices. Many Westerners saw wolves and other wild canines as enemies of civilization who had to be forcefully eliminated. They often deployed dogs—either practically or metaphorically— as partners in their extermination campaigns, and so found the gray zone between *Canis familiaris* and *Canis lupus,* between tameness and wildness, between trusted companions and wily adversaries, deeply unsettling.

Westerners regarded wolflike local dogs either as never having been completely domesticated or as having degenerated from a domesticated state. They alleged that the wild nature of native dogs was the result of interbreeding with presumably lower species, such as the wolf or the fox. Morse characteristically drew upon Darwin's work on degeneration when he described canines on the northern island of Hokkaido:

> If it is possible to get a cross between a dog and a fox there is certainly fox blood in these creatures. Every village has a pack of dogs, and at night they are very noisy, making sounds like cats, but more infernal; they howl and squeal, but never bark. Darwin had observed in his work on domesticated animals that when dogs relapse from their cultivated state to a semi-savage one, they lose the bark and take on the howl again. Wild creatures to which they are related never bark, but howl.[62]

In this way, Westerners contrasted the degenerate and devolved state of native dogs with the thoroughly evolved colonial dog, who, they boasted, was purebred. Such expressions reflected recurring colonialist obsessions about the mixing of races. As one English commentator remarked, "No one would plant weeds in a flower garden, [so] why have mongrels as pets?"[63]

Heaping further pejoratives upon the backs of Japan's dogs, Westerners invoked the late nineteenth-century language of hygienic science to describe them as diseased or particularly susceptible to disease. In contrast with a country and a people whom they generally praised for cleanliness, foreign observers viewed the street dogs who inhabited Japan as disorderly and downright filthy. A typical example may be found in an 1888 editorial in the English-language *Japan Weekly Mail*, which commented on the mixed blood and sullied condition of native dogs. The newspaper, probably drawing on erroneous scientific theories circulating in Europe at the time, reported that the development of rabies was less severe in native breeds than in full-blooded foreign dogs because of the former's "mongrel" nature.[64] Still, the paper warned, the wretched state of native dogs posed a grave threat to the health of the foreign community. It alleged that in Japan and China, hydrophobia occurred with greater frequency in foreign settlements than elsewhere in the country. "The development of the disease is not so formidable in the native as it is in foreign-bred animals, the reason being that the latter are more full-blooded. Yet there is room to believe that many of the wretched, mangey curs which slink about the streets of Honmura [in Yokohama] and elsewhere in a half-comatose condition, are suffering from a mild form of hydrophobia, which they may transmit by biting or other infection to their stronger congeners of alien strain, which in turn may bite their masters. There are some pariahs daily on view whose case, in pity to themselves, demands the merciful employment of club or poison."[65] In Meiji Japan as elsewhere, the quality of this mercy would reveal itself in antirabies and other extermination campaigns.

CLASS CONTROLS AND THE CAMPAIGN AGAINST RABIES

From the 1870s onward, the Meiji regime used the pretext of rabies to translate crescendoing cultural expressions of distaste for native dogs and wolves into government policy. As articulated by the *Japan Weekly Mail*, it was ill-bred native "curs" who were seen as the biggest threat by the government and its foreign advisors, both official and self-appointed. And so it was that, despite not being the sole bearers of a feared disease, native canines bore the brunt of a half-century-long campaign to cleanse Japan of hydrophobia and to civilize its streets. Foreign dogs largely escaped the campaign because of their identification with Westerners and the native upper classes. By the late 1880s, Matsumori Taneyasu (1825–1892), a natural historian in Yamagata prefecture, noted that while the "seed" of foreign dogs was spreading rapidly, "Japanese dogs have been deliberately killed from time to time since the Meiji Restoration."[66]

Extensive killing of canines began, in part, at the behest of the Meiji government's official advisors, and was motivated by ideas of civilization and racialized science as much as it was by epidemiological concerns. One figure who contributed importantly to the formulation of this policy was the American D. W. Jones (1851–?). One of many foreign employees hired by the government to assist Japan in its efforts to modernize, Jones resided in the country from 1873 to 1879. During his last four years there, he was entrusted with extensive authority to oversee the creation of a sheep and dairy-cattle operation at the Shimōsa ranch in Chiba prefecture, and to train a generation of animal-husbandry specialists from across the nation. Like many other foreigners, Jones had little regard for native dogs, and when they began to attack sheep on the ranch, he was in a position to do something about it. Immediately after assuming his duties, he requested that Chiba prefecture begin to exterminate dogs within a broad area around Shimōsa. In a letter enlisting support from district and village officials, he reported many incidents of wild dogs killing sheep and ponies, and recalled the recent and widely reported death of an eight-year-old girl bitten by street dogs in Tokyo. Jones did not mention rabies specifically, but there was probably little need to do so. Just two years earlier, an outbreak in nearby Tokyo had left nine people dead.

Jones employed the familiar rhetoric of civilization and science in condemning native dogs. While conceding that in Japan there were "some good dogs who have the ability to protect the property of their master and ward off burglars," he claimed that such dogs were "quite rare, and most dogs in Japan are offensive, despicable, and evil. These dogs were originally called the wolf-dogs of the eastern barbarians; they are of a savage nature, and are not the kind of dogs that a civilized people like the Japanese ought to keep."[67] Jones sought to vilify dogs in Chiba, and throughout Japan, by connecting them historically with the "eastern barbarians," the ethnically distinct, horseriding Emishi people discussed in chapters 1 and 3, who had lived in northeastern reaches of the archipelago and long resisted the control of the Yamato state. By doing so, Jones adopted, ironically, the same idiom of "barbarism" that xenophobic samurai had only recently employed to characterize Westerners like himself, and that Yamato elites a millennium earlier had employed against the nonagrarian peoples of the far northeast. Apparently, Jones's request was effective. The prefecture immediately implemented a program that rewarded people for eliminating canines commensurate with the proximity of the animal to the ranch, except those "accompanying foreigners." [68] Over the next decade, the government eradicated over 1,200 canines annually in the area. In a double irony, Jones's work for the government was cut short when he was seriously wounded in an attack by what Alcock had called the other "nuisance" of Japan—sword-wielding ruffians.[69]

The events in Chiba were part of a campaign to eliminate canines throughout the country. In the 1870s, the extermination of the archipelago's *Canidae* populations extended from the newly incorporated Ryukyu islands in the south to the northern island of Hokkaido. By the turn of the century, the Meiji government, anxious about rabies and influenced by the ideology of civilization and science, had driven Japanese wolves to extinction, decimated the wild-dog population, and eliminated many of the street dogs who had roamed populated areas and their outskirts.

To be sure, the elimination of native dogs and wolves did not begin with foreigners or take place solely under the sway of adopted Western ideology. Rabies had afflicted the archipelago's canine populations long before, and some very serious outbreaks had occurred during the eighteenth century. Hiraiwa Yonekichi (1898–1986), a zoologist who in the early twentieth century wrote extensively about wolves and dogs, speculated that already in the Tokugawa period such outbreaks set in motion a gradual erosion in the respect for wolves that had traditionally existed in Japan's agricultural communities. Before the onslaught of rabies, he argued, farmers had esteemed these wild canines with a sort of spiritual reverence, viewing them as benevolent partners who contained crop-raiding herbivores such as the wild boar discussed in chapter 5. Thereafter, early-modern villagers began to fear wolves as disease-crazed predators, and organized hunts to eliminate them from surrounding mountains. Rabies had a similar if less severe effect on human-dog relations during the Tokugawa period. Antirabies measures were limited to the killing of diseased dogs, but in certain hard-hit villages the keeping of dogs was banned entirely and each household was expected to kill one healthy dog in hopes of slowing the spread of the disease.[70]

Even so, the widespread slaughter of dogs by the Meiji government that began in the 1870s marked a significant departure from earlier Tokugawa practices. Regional and municipal governments made specific legal changes that broadened their ability to eliminate dogs. They authorized anyone to kill a diseased dog, rather than delegating the task to police alone. Many governments followed Chiba prefecture's lead and began to round up dogs who were not sick by offering bounties for the pelt of any canine caught wandering the streets or countryside. For the entrepreneur, this could be a lucrative business. Working together, two or three people could easily dispose of one to two hundred dogs daily and take home a handsome profit.[71] During these same years, Tokyo prefecture issued the country's first edict regulating domesticated dogs. The measures defined the duties of dog owners, requiring them to put on their dogs a collar and tag (*chikukenhyō*) with the proprietor's name and address. The statute also mandated that owners must kill their dogs if they became hydrophobic, and specified that if any dog, diseased or not, bit or hurt a person, it was to be put down.[72] Measures like this one were often supported by rules that authorized the extermination of any unlicensed dog. The new laws encouraged people either to civilize dogs by turning them into pets through Western-style dogkeeping practices, or to dispose of them altogether.

Government regulations and the effort to eliminate roaming dogs specifically targeted indigenous breeds. Native breeds, or dogs of mixed breed, were precisely the canines who were likely to wander the streets or live on the edge of cities or villages. Contrary to the expectations of authorities, the new ordinances prompted few changes in human-dog interaction in urban neighborhoods and villages, where the relationship between the two had traditionally been a communal one. Even if a particular individual had a liking for a dog and showed it special affinity, he or she was unlikely to take on responsibility for collaring and tagging the dog as mandated by the new regulations. And if a dog was not tagged, it could legally be destroyed.[73]

Little opposition greeted the new regulations and roundups of dogs. The specter of rabies, whether real or imagined, persuaded most people to abide by the rules without complaining. Because there was not a large constituency of dog owners, at least in the early Meiji period, the government did not need to worry about offending their sensibilities. Some people objected to the new canine policies, but they did so less out of concern for dogs than out of a desire to grind a different axe. For example, the following 1877 letter to a newspaper editor from an individual named Akasaka vented considerable spleen at foreign privilege and upper-class arrogance, while concern for native dogs appeared incidental:

> When a Japanese dog is spotted without a tag, people yell "Get it! Kill it!" and treat it as if it were the enemy, but why do they turn a blind eye in the case of Western dogs? Is it that they treat them with reserve because the dogs, too, have come here from foreign lands? Recently one witnesses many [Western] dogs biting and barking at passersby, but in the eyes of their owners even these evil dogs appear to be gentle creatures. Shouldn't people understand that no matter how expensive a dog may be, if it harms people, it ought to be speedily killed? Even dog fanatics ought to comprehend that humans are more important than dogs.[74]

Foreign breeds were often protected merely by virtue of being foreign. Such dogs were usually owned by Westerners or well-to-do Japanese who could afford these sorts of canines and were more apt to collar, tag, and prevent them from wandering the streets. Even if an owner neglected to do these things, the very physical appearance of foreign dogs sometimes saved them because authorities and dogcatchers did not want to risk being responsible for killing the pet of someone influential, whether a protected foreigner or a prominent Japanese. It was complaints from precisely such owners about dogs being immediately exterminated, along with objections to the killing of dogs in public, that prompted a revision of Tokyo's domestic-dog ordinance in 1881. The central government ordered the creation of dog pounds where canines would be impounded for a week rather than being killed at once. It also cautioned the police to be especially careful in how they handled the dogs of foreigners. The other notable revision was a change from a per-head reward for canines to a daily salary for those who rounded up dogs. This modification, and the initial impoundment of dogs, made the work less lucrative. For a time, the changes mollified foreigners' complaints. At the turn of the century, however, after treaty revision allowed foreigners to live outside the treaty ports, problems arose once more, and so police began to round up dogs only late at night or early in the morning.[75]

The prospect of treaty revision, and especially the possibility of foreigners and Japanese living in the same neighborhoods, created anxieties within both groups. Again, these worries were projected onto dogs. During the 1870s, many Japanese were more immediately concerned with the possibility of foreigners traveling freely within the country (*naichi ryokō*) than they were with mixed residence (*naichi zakkyo*), the latter of which required formal revision of the unequal treaties, and would be realized only in 1899. Interestingly, some early Meiji intellectuals, including the educator and government official Nishi Amane (1829–1897), voiced more unease about traveling canines than they did about their human companions. In a speech delivered in November 1874 to the Meirokusha, a society of leading Meiji advocates of "civilization and enlightenment," Nishi proposed a gradual relaxation of laws restricting the travel of foreigners to prepare Japanese for this interaction. He acknowledged, however, that foreigners would likely inflict at least seven kinds of "injuries" (*gai*) if they were allowed to move unrestrained throughout the country. Fifth among these wrongs, Nishi declared, was that Japanese "will be troubled by the dogs that accompany them."[76] Fukuzawa Yukichi (1835–1901), generally considered the most important "enlightened" thinker of the early Meiji period, disagreed with Nishi on the broader issue of travel by foreign persons, arguing that it was premature to permit it. However, he did not take the threat of their dogs too seriously. His response to Nishi's canine concerns in the society's publication, *Meiroku zasshi*, seemed almost flippant: "We naturally need not be concerned with regulations to prevent foreigners from being accompanied by dogs. Whether they are accompanied by dogs or tigers is optional."[77]

As before, many foreigners continued to be concerned about what they might encounter on Japan's thoroughfares and byways. Throughout the last decades of the nineteenth century, Europeans and Americans repeatedly complained about the inability of the Japanese government to eliminate street dogs and the threat of rabies. However real or unreal the epidemiological concerns behind them, such anxious expressions functioned more often than not as coded language about treaty revision and the imminent loss of foreigner's privileged and protected status in Japan. Like Alcock's comparison of street dogs to masterless samurai, Western apprehensions about "wild and uncared for ... brutes of all description [who] wander about the streets with impunity," as the *Japan Weekly Mail* put it in 1897, were related to their worries about lower-class Japanese whom they might meet on the roads and byways after treaty revision was enacted.[78] Colonial and native dogs served as eminently malleable metaphors to express such fears.

The satiric cartoons of the French expatriate Bigot are particularly evocative of these worries. Bigot was highly critical of the Meiji government and opposed to treaty revision because it would eliminate the advantaged position of foreigners, and perhaps endanger his own ability to publish his characteristically derisive cartoons. Though he sold his drawings to a variety of publications, Bigot was best known for his magazine *Toba-e* (Toba pictures), launched in 1887, which was named for a twelfth-century Kyoto abbot said to have created ink handscrolls depicting birds and other creatures engaging in humorous activities.[79] Bigot, in contrast, featured nonhuman animals fairly infrequently in his work. When he did, rarely did beasts stand in for people, except in a few of Bigot's more biting cartoons of Japanese as monkeys "aping" Westerners by attempting to waltz and wear Western clothing at such venues as the Rokumeikan. Dogs appeared probably more than any other animal, but almost never did they stand in for individual human subjects. Instead, they mirrored more generally the behavior or culture of Japanese and Westerners as Bigot saw them.

One illustrated story titled "Heaving a Foreigner over a Cliff for Fun" featured a Western and a native dog and underscored Bigot's worries about treaty revision. It advocated the "suppression," if not "elimination," of lower-class rowdies whom Bigot believed to be threatening to Westerners. The narrative, written in English, tells of a European embarking on a walk to a waterfall with a fellow foreigner and an upper-class Japanese friend, accompanied by a puppy of Western breed. As they walk, a native dog approaches the puppy and sniffs its rear end. The next frame depicts the three humans nearing a wayside stall where they notice three coolies drinking sake. Sitting alert next to the coolies, its head turned to the side as if to draw the attention of one of the coolies to the foreigners, sits the native dog. In the following frame, one of the coolies "wantonly" kicks the puppy who is "gamboling along in front of [its] master." When the foreigner protests, the three drunken coolies turn on him and proceed to toss him over the edge of a cliff. His two friends, mysteriously, have wandered off and are oblivious to his plight. Fortunately, a branch breaks the man's fall. After scaling back to the top of the ravine, he finds a policeman and files a complaint against the miscreants. The officer, however, only "reprimand[s] them in a fatherly way," telling them that it is "wrong to throw foreigners over cliffs." The story concludes with the following sardonic observation: "And this policemen was a member of that force which [some people] would have us understand is efficient and sufficient to protect foreign life and interests in Japan after

Treaty Revision becomes an accomplished fact."[80]

Increasingly, in the late nineteenth century, the desire of Westerners to rid the streets of unruly dogs collided with a growing interest in issues of animal welfare. From the late eighteenth century, a growing social concern for the proper treatment of nonhuman animals had emerged in England and, to a lesser degree, elsewhere in Europe and America, the manifestations of which rippled outward toward Japan almost a century later. Initially, these concerns were expressed in a particularly self-serving manner. Since at least the 1870s, Westerners had often protested against their own dogs being mistakenly picked up as strays and eliminated. By the 1880s, though, foreigners began to express less self-interested objections to the government's dog-control measures, and to articulate them in terms of animal protection. A minority of foreigners, such as Morse, held Japanese treatment of nonhuman animals to be superior to that of the "civilized" West. In this "pagan country," wrote Morse, "animals are always so kindly treated that you have to step out of the way or over hens, dogs, cats, and pigeons, and even the black crows."[81] Japanese people, he specifically noted, never threw stones at dogs. A growing number of Westerners, however, were less approving of Japanese animal ethics. This sentiment was voiced in a *Japan Weekly Mail* editorial of 1884, penned by an unnamed foreign newspaper reporter. The editorial expressed indignation that, except for "those of the very highest culture, [the] maltreatment of animals is quite as common in the better ranks of society as in the lowest." The writer called on Japan to make changes that would bring "credit upon her name," but conceded that it was not hopeful that anything could be done to alter the situation soon.[82]

Nevertheless, concerns about animal welfare rarely extended beyond the expatriate community. Because these sentiments were largely limited to a few foreigners, and even fewer Japanese (particularly those who had lived abroad), they were not able to gain broad cultural traction. It was not until 1902 that an animal-welfare organization was established in Japan, and that organization, the Society for the Prevention of Abuse to Animals (Dōbutsu gyakutai bōshikai), was founded largely at the behest of the government, which was concerned about protecting horses for military use. Six years later, the Society expanded its attention to include the canine and feline populations. In 1914, volunteers formed the Japan Humane Society (Nihon jindōkai), the first truly private animal-welfare organization, albeit one with strong Western connections in terms both of membership and of philosophy. It would not be until the emergence of a professional middle class in the 1920s, and especially the maturing of that class in the 1960s and 1970s, that concerns about animal welfare gained a wider acceptance, as well as a measure of political influence.

As evidenced by the authorities' campaigns to eliminate dogs, government efforts at canine control had the effect of regulating the human political and social order. Street dogs were seen as unruly and disorderly, like certain classes of people, who often lived in the same poor neighborhoods as the canine constituency whom the government pronounced threatening. Perhaps this is one reason that Meiji political cartoonists frequently depicted supporters of the People's Rights Movement, which challenged the ruling oligarchy in the 1870s and 1880s, as native street dogs. Another reason for cartoonists' use of the native dog was, as historian Peter Duus points out, for punning effect: the phonetic readings of the characters for dog (*ken*) and rights (*ken*) are identical.[83] In a manner reminiscent of antirabies campaigns in nineteenth-century England, the Japanese government targeted dogs belonging specifically to the lower socioeconomic strata of the human population. The relationship of social class to canine control was most evident in the nationwide implementation of dog taxes in the late 1890s, which were designed to encourage people who could not afford the tax to turn their dogs in to the pound for extermination.

Perhaps the policy was a success. An article in the daily *Yomiuri* several years later implied as much. The piece, signed by a certain Matsuo, was one of a series of short commentaries composed by several different reporters that ran on the newspaper's front page. Each article was in its entirety just one paragraph long and followed by an English translation—practically the only English that appeared in the paper. In this particular piece, Matsuo wrote: "The dogs which used to bark at people walking through back streets two or three years ago keep quiet nowadays. Nor do they bark at ladies in foreign costume or cyclists. That civilization is making steady progress in Japan may be noticed by the most cursory observer."[84] Why did Matsuo choose this dual-language column as an appropriate venue for his discourse on dogs? Perhaps it was an attempt to give notice to the world that Japan had, like Western countries, at last attained the highest standards of civilization, even to the last dog. At the same time, one cannot help but wonder if canines really had become civilized, or whether there were no barks merely because the dogs concerned had been eradicated.

THE STRONGEST DOG ON THE BLOCK

By the turn of the century, Japan had in many respects drawn nearly even with the Great Powers in geopolitical terms. In 1894, the Meiji government fulfilled its forty-year-old goal of revising the unequal treaties, a move that eliminated the extraterritorial privileges of foreigners, but also forced the Japanese government to allow them to live outside of the treaty ports, a prospect once the source of considerable anxiety among Japanese and foreigners alike. In the following year, the country demonstrated its military might to the world at large by defeating the Qing empire in the Sino-Japanese War, as the result of which it acquired its first overseas colony, Taiwan. Tellingly, Japanese authorities continued their campaign to eliminate street and wild dogs in the newly won island territory.[85] Thus, by the end of the nineteenth century, Japan had completed its transformation from an independent but not completely sovereign object of imperialism into an emerging colonial empire. Nevertheless, for reasons of racial and cultural prejudice, Japan was denied equal membership in the imperialist club, and therefore remained insecure about the fragility of its position. In addition to Taiwan, Japanese negotiators had succeeded in compelling Chinese leaders to cede them the Liaodong peninsula on the mainland, but in just over a week, Germany, Russia, and France demanded that the Japanese government renounce its claims to that territory, which, ironically, would enter Russian hands in less than three years' time. Still, the end of the century represented a defining moment in Japan's rise as a colonial power, even if it did not drastically alter the imperial map of the world.

Tectonic rumblings in imperial geopolitics triggered similar groans in the world of dogs. An event that occurred toward the end of the century foreshadowed developments that would grow more conspicuous several decades later. The occasion was a dispute triggered by the creation of a statue of Saigō Takamori (1828–1877) and his dog in late 1898 to commemorate the thirtieth anniversary of the Meiji Restoration. Saigō had been one of the principal leaders of the Restoration that brought the current oligarchic regime to power, but nine years later he launched an unsuccessful rebellion against the government, in which he perished. Authorities' unveiling of the statue, and its physical positioning with Saigō facing the imperial palace rather than his home province of Satsuma, the stronghold of rebel forces in the 1877 uprising, signaled graphically the regime's attempt to reorient and rehabilitate Saigō's political standing from that of a rebel against the Meiji state to a hero of the Restoration.[86] To this day, the statue remains a prominent landmark at the edge of Ueno Park in Tokyo.

Ironically, the small, seemingly insignificant, dog standing next to Saigō created almost as great a stir as the authorities' political repositioning of Saigō. Much public excitement and commentary greeted the unveiling of the statue. Planners, including the art patron Kuki Ryūichi (1852–1931) and art critic Okakura Tenshin (1862–1913), selected the team of Takamura Kōun (1852–1934) and Gotō Sadayuki (1849–1902), sculptors who had been chosen to depict in bronze such political favorites as Kusunoki Masashige, a fourteenth-century warrior known for his devotion to the emperor, atop his horse in front of the imperial palace. Newspapers discussed the fact that Takamura represented Saigō in casual robe-like *hitoe,* hunting rabbits with his dog, rather than in a military outfit on the battlefield, a guise for which Saigō was much better known. Portraying Saigō in military garb might have left viewers wondering which uniform he was wearing: the one he had donned as a leader of the Meiji Restoration or the one that he later assumed as an enemy of the Meiji state. The dog drew a degree of attention disproportionate to its size. As was the case with other members of the Meiji elites, Saigō enjoyed hunting with dogs, many of which were canines of Western origin. He was said to have been particularly fond of a dog named Tora (Tiger), a big, fierce, floppy-eared Western canine. In order to depict Saigō's dog accurately, Gotō studied Western dogs in Yokohama and visited Satsuma to view Tora's posterity. He even completed a mock-up of a large Western dog with floppy ears, but in the end scrapped it and formed the figure that stands beside Saigō to this day. Art historians think that Satsuma partisans and Kuki may have persuaded Gotō to create Saigō's dog in the image of the local Satsuma breed.[87] The finished product, which appeared to be a dog of indistinct or mixed origin, seemed not to satisfy anyone. The statue of the dog was criticized because it was not big enough to be like the dog that Saigō was thought to have kept. The strongest criticisms, though, were aimed at the small dog's prominent ears. Not only were they perked up unlike a Western dog's, but they went too far in the other direction, because they were "pricked up like a rabbit's." As an article in the daily *Hōchi* noted, the pointy ears of the bronze dog made it look like a *chin* lapdog of Chinese origin, or at least as if it contained *chin* blood.[88]

The timing is telling. It is striking that this controversy over the ears of a seemingly innocuous dog sculpture followed closely in the wake of Japan's recent geopolitical successes and setbacks: its victory in the Sino-Japanese War, its acquisition of Taiwan, and the retrocession of the Liaodong peninsula. Undoubtedly, concerns over the dog's appearance stemmed from a heightened sense of national pride, coupled with anxiety, which was in turn projected in a canine direction. The discomfort that some people felt with Gotō's portrayal of the dog as being of mixed breed echoed worries about the most controversial provision of treaty revision due to be implemented in the following year, which allowed for the geographic intermingling of the races in neighborhoods outside of the treaty ports. Furthermore, the perception of Chinese blood, even of a canine variety, as a stain on the dignity of a newly canonized national hero bore ugly traces of a popular chauvinism that the Sino-Japanese War had recently stirred into a frenzy, and that would survive well into the following century. At any rate, the incident marked one of the earliest articulations, however tentative and short-lived, of an expression of pride in native dog breeds and a reaction against interbreeding, or at least against the artistic representation of crossbreeding between native dogs and those of foreign origin.

As with the animal-welfare movement, a full expression of this sentiment, the creation and elevation of the so-called Japanese dog (*Nihon inu*) did not emerge until a bourgeois middle class arose in the 1920s.[89] In part, this may have been because it was not until such a constituency developed that the ownership of dogs, and in this case, the keeping of native dogs, became widespread enough for a reconsideration and revaluation of these much-maligned canines to take place. Before the late 1920s, dog-care and breed manuals had in fact barely mentioned native dogs. Urbanization may have played a role in their reevaluation as well. The isolation from the countryside that is characteristic of urban modernity led, not only in Japan but elsewhere, to a desire to reconnect with the natural world, albeit in a domesticated form—or as Kathleen Kete has put it, to install a "beast in the boudoir."[90] Finally, political changes were certainly an important factor. Actively encouraged by the government, the public embrace of native dogs grew and reached its height during the imperial fascism of the 1930s.

It was then that native dogs, long despised as disorderly, savage, and wolflike, were rediscovered and revalorized. A group of private dog enthusiasts, the Society for the Preservation of the Japanese Dog (Nihon inu hozon kai), together with the Ministry of Education, transformed the native dog into the "Japanese dog," an icon of purity, loyalty, and bravery, superior to both Western dogs and the native dogs of Japan's colonies. At the request of the Society, the Ministry in the 1930s designated seven breeds on the archipelago as "Japanese" natural treasures worthy of state interest and regulation. During the same decade, the Ministry used native dogs extensively in school textbooks and public sculptures as a means of encouraging youngsters and adults alike to emulate the qualities supposedly embodied by these canines. The most impactful of the stories was the still-famous tale of Chūken Hachikō (1923–1935), or "Loyal Dog" Hachikō, a canine who was said to have faithfully awaited the return of his dead master for years outside of Tokyo's Shibuya Station. Many other stories aimed at young audiences, both in government and popular publications, celebrated the exploits of "Japanese" military dogs. Most often, these tales featured "German" shepherds, the breed most widely deployed by the imperial army. Other narratives, however, touted the battlefield exploits of "Japanese" dogs, all the more remarkably so because these dogs were probably never successfully employed by the Japanese military. Once denigrated by Westerners and Japanese alike, native dogs had truly been transformed. Perhaps a subaltern dog can bark, but only if it becomes a colonial dog.

CONCLUSION: THE NATIVE DOG

This chapter has traced the path of the colonial dog as a means of shedding light on the dynamics of colonial humanity and global imperialism from the mid-nineteenth to the early twentieth century. Its history reveals a complicated configuration of relationships among humans, dogs, imperial structures, and the languages of nationalism, civilization, and scientific racism that humans have used to describe them. Although the bulk of data marshaled here derives from the specific experience of Japan, it is clear that similar patterns emerged in other imperial contexts. Part of the reason for such historical commonalities is that Western imperialists took shared notions of the worth of particular dog breeds and modes of dogkeeping wherever they ventured. Throughout Asia, Africa, and the Americas, Westerners repeatedly idealized dog breeds from the metropole, while denigrating the native canines of the colonial periphery. A few non-Japanese examples will help to underscore this claim.

In striking and interrelated ways, the history of the colonial dog in

Korea paralleled that of its geographic neighbor, Japan. Here, too, Westerners who visited the country in the late nineteenth century demonized native dogs using the rhetoric of civilization and racialized science, thereby veiling their underlying criticisms of Korea and Koreans. One senior American advisor to the Korean government in the 1880s, for example, characterized the country's typical canine as "a hanger-on of civilization rather than a part of it," a statement that could equally well have described his sentiments about the nation as a whole.[91] As she did in Japan, the British travel writer Isabella Bird complained about native dogs in Korea. Contrasting them with the dogs of her homeland and using almost exactly the same words that her compatriot Lady Kate Lawson would use a few years later to describe dogs in Japan, Bird wrote in 1897 that dogs in Korea were "neither friend nor companion of man."[92] Bird, in fact, thought dogs on the peninsula to be so savage and unruly that they were "ignorant of Korean and every spoken language." Perhaps this is why she expressed no typical British qualms about the Korean culinary custom of consuming canines, only matter-of-factly noting, "When young he is killed and eaten in spring."[93]

As in Japan, though, this was not the last yelp of native dogs. Dogs in Korea underwent a transformation nearly as dramatic as their cousins across the straits, and it may have been, ironically, Japanese imperialism that was in large part responsible for Korea's postcolonial revaluation of its canine heritage. During the 1930s, apart from the seven breeds that the Ministry of Education designated as "Japanese" national treasures, Japanese colonial authorities in Korea granted similar status to two peninsular dog breeds, the Poongsan and the Jindō. This bureaucratic canonization surely did not arise out of pure concern for the canines themselves or for the Korean populace, but like other facets of colonial modernity, such as industrialization and the spread of primary education, served the purposes of the imperial power. It was part of a larger strategy on the part of Japanese leaders to naturalize colonial rule on the peninsula by using everyday social customs and environmental objects to assimilate and obliterate Korea as a nation-state. After Koreans regained independence and the peninsula was divided politically, each of the two states that claimed to be the true representative of the Korean people chose one of the breeds as its own. The North Korean regime picked the Poongsan breed. And in the south, the government of President Park Chung Hee (1917–1979) declared the Jindō to be national treasure number fifty-three during the rabid nationalism of the early 1960s. The dog was especially worthy of selection, its fans claimed, because it had long been a fierce defender of the Korean nation. It was said that on the day before the armada of Japanese warlord Toyotomi Hideyoshi (1537–1598) invaded Korea in the late sixteenth century, thousands of Jindō dogs faced the sea and barked viciously in the direction of the Japanese islands.[94]

There would be no such transformation of native dogs in postcolonial India, albeit there was far less chance that they would be eaten. For religious and cultural reasons, canines had long been despised in South Asia, so that local populations found it especially difficult to understand the British colonial's typical fondness for dogs. The subcontinental distaste for canines might have given the British less reason to belittle native dogs who were already the "outcastes" of South Asian fauna, but they tended to do so anyway, contrasting them to colonial dogs using predictable religious, civilizationist, and scientific rhetoric. The writings of the Kiplings—John Lockwood and his more famous son Rudyard (1865–1936)—highlight these proclivities. The elder Kipling, for example, utilized the familiar language of civilization to contrapose colonial and native dogs. The "Indian pariah," or "pie dog," he wrote, "reveals more of the currish side of canine character than English dogs and dog lovers are aware of. He uncovers more of his teeth when he snarls—and he often snarls—than the civilised dog; he slinks off with inverted tail at the mere hint of a blow or a caress, and his shrill bark echoes the long note of the great dog-father, the wolf, and the poor cousin the jackal. In a fight he does not abandon himself to the delight of battle with the stern joy of the English dog, but calculates odds and backs down with an ignoble care for his skin. In short, he is a *lendi* [shit], a cur, a coward."[95]

Rudyard echoed his father's observations in a number of his stories. In one piece, "Garm—A Hostage" (1925), Kipling recalled taking care of Garm, an English Bullterrier, for a fellow British officer on the subcontinent. At first, the autobiographical narrator thinks the task to be troublesome, in addition to which his own dog, a smaller terrier, resents the other canine's presence. However, after the bullterrier single-handedly saves the small terrier from an attack by a pack of nearly a dozen native dogs, both master and pet come to respect the newcomer. The fight scene dramatizes Kipling's perception of "yellow pariah-dogs"—described as "half-wild, starving beasts"—and "English dogs" as mortal enemies. According to Kipling, it is only through cunning, by overwhelming numbers, or with a rabid bite that the "measley" pariah dog can prevail over a colonial dog, and on this occasion several of the former die trying in vain.[96]

Still, insisted Kipling the father, there was hope for Indian dogs. The longtime resident of India believed that "British influence" was stimulating "a slow but indubitable revolution now taking place in favour of the dog." The "Hindu; and the Muhammadan,—the most conservative of races," he wrote, "may cherish his ancient grudge [against canines], but both are learning that the dog of good caste is a useful companion and friend." Kipling *père* went so far as to claim that an "indigenous canine aristocracy" had by now emerged. He declared several native breeds to be of "good caste," even as he repeatedly attributed to them various faults. In order to account for the redeeming characteristics, Kipling quoted the rhetorical question of another Englishman who wondered, "Are they indigenous, or is it possible that their stock can have been derived from us?"[97]

Any hope for Indian dogs and humans, the elder Kipling seemed to imply, was dependent on, or as least derived from, the British. An unidentified "modern philosophical writer," he reported, "says the British Empire in India is but 'a romantic episode' destined to pass away and leave no recognisable trace." Not so, countered Kipling. Not only were the colonized adopting the British "science [of] care and lore of dogs," he maintained, but the "English dog has come to stand as a highcaste animal of respectable birth." Kipling assured his readers that "[n]ative ladies see that European animals are unlike the unclean creatures of the street, and are anxious to adopt them." The Spaniel, Bulldog, and other English breeds were "thought most highly of," Kipling claimed, and English names were becoming "naturalised and Persianised after the liquid Oriental manner." Thus Spot, for example, had on the subcontinent reportedly degenerated into Eespot. One favorite Anglo-Indian dog name, though, ripe with irony, retained its original English form: "Bully."[98]

As a result of this influence, the senior Kipling concluded, the British legacy was destined to survive in India forever. "[T]hough we may pass away and be forgotten," he predicted, "the dogs we loved will remain as permanent colonists." Staying on in India, though, was evidently not without its pitfalls for the colonial canines. Mixing with lesser, native breeds, and dwelling in the unfamiliar environment of India, Kipling asserted, would inevitably lead to degeneration, both physical and moral. "[I]t appears to be a fact that the creole dog, born in India of imported parents, develops some of the characteristics of the indigenous animal. His head, especially his nose, grows longer and narrower, he loses substance in the neck, chest, and loins; he stands on higher legs and wags a longer tail than his British-born parents. The climate exerts a deteriorating influence on his moral qualities, and he loses some of the courage, temper, and fine spirits which are the birthright of a good dog in the West."[99]

In southern and central Africa as well, dogs figured large in nineteenth- and early twentieth-century colonial discourses. Emblematic of European anxieties about the mixing of the human races on the continent was the pervasive use there of such racialized idioms as "mongrel," "bastard," and "kaffir." European discussion about dogs in Africa tended to foreground concerns about breed more than civilization, and the obsession with purity of blood seems to have grown as European colonial powers increasingly found their political grasp and moral authority on the continent threatened in the twentieth century. South African officials, for example, recommended in 1948—the same year that the apartheid government of the National Party came to power—that game laws license purebred dogs at one pound per head and that "mongrel" dogs be taxed at a higher rate, "particularly unsterilized bitches." The proposal thus echoed white African fears of being overwhelmed numerically and sexually by black Africans. As the anthropologist Robert J. Gordon has noted, many whites believed that "mongrel bitches owned by Africans tended to breed indiscriminately like their owners."[100]

Interaction with Native Americans on the part of nineteenth-century American settlers registered similar inflections, even if historians have not traditionally acknowledged this context as one of empire. Not only had the Spanish and English of colonial times used dogs to hunt down Indians, but their post-Revolutionary progeny deployed them, too, albeit chiefly in metaphorical ways, as they pushed the borders of the new nation westward. American writers of the nineteenth century conventionally described the native canines of the frontier as creatures vastly inferior—like their human companions—to Old World pure breeds, believing that they were "even a 'notch below' the mongrels of Europe."[101] The inferiority of native dogs, some commentators professed, was the result of a close affinity to wolves. By contrast, it was asserted, no such biological link connected wolves with pedigreed dogs. In an 1803 essay, Benjamin Smith Barton (1766–1815), a renowned natural historian and early theorist of race, explained that the common lineage of Indian dogs and wolves was the reason that the former "will never attack or pursue a wolf, which common dogs readily do." Native American dogs, alleged Barton, "have less fidelity and will steal from masters."[102] Thus, native dogs, like wolves, became imbued rhetorically with traits stereotypically ascribed during the period to Native American humans: namely, cunning and double-crossing treachery.

The common element that binds together these various colonial contexts—and the dynamic of the colonial dog—was the power apparatus of imperialism itself. Over the course of the nineteenth century, as never before, Western colonizers spread their political authority, economic appetites, and ideologies of religion, civilization, race, and science across the globe. Wherever they went, they were accompanied by the colonial dog, whom they used to reinforce their authority, both practically and, more significantly, on a symbolic level. In this manner, colonizers created an imaginary canine cartography that was structured by, and in turn helped to structure, the dynamics of colonial humanity and the harsh realities of imperialism. Perhaps by listening for the bark of the subaltern dog, historians may learn to attune their ears more closely to other silences that shaped the colonial world.

NOTES

Earlier versions of this chapter were presented at the Western Conference of the Association of Asian Studies, the Columbia University Seminar on Modern Japan, and the "Animals / History / Japan" symposium. The author would like to thank the participants at those venues for their comments; the editors for their guidance and suggestions; and the staffs of the American Kennel Club, the C. V. Starr East Asian, Butler, and Lehman libraries at Columbia University, and the Yokohama Archives of History.

1. See, for example, Alfred W. Crosby, *Ecological Imperialism: The Biological Expansion of Europe, 900-1900* (Cambridge: Cambridge University Press, 1986); Mark A. Mastromarino, "Teaching Old Dogs New Tricks: The English Mastiff and the Anglo-American Experience," *Historian* 49 (1986): 10–25; Elinor G. K. Melville, *A Plague of Sheep: Environmental Consequences of the Conquest of Mexico* (Cambridge: Cambridge University Press, 1994); John Grier Varner and Jeannette Johnson Varner, *Dogs of the Conquest* (Norman: University of Oklahoma Press, 1983); Eric R. Wolf, *Europe and the People without History* (Berkeley: University of California Press, 1982).

2. Work on this topic has only begun to emerge. See, for example, Robert J. Gordon, "Fido: Dog Tales of Colonialism in Namibia," in *African Environments: Past and Present,* ed. JoAnne McGregor and William Beinart (Oxford: Curry, 2003), 240–54; Nancy J. Jacobs, "The Great Bophuthatswana Donkey Massacre: Discourse

on the Ass and the Politics of Class and Grass," *American Historical Review* 106 (2001): 485–507; Jacob Tropp, "Dogs, Poison, and the Meaning of Colonial Intervention in the Transkei, South Africa," *Journal of African History* 43 (2002): 451–72. Thanks to Marcia Wright and Gregory Mann for bringing these articles of their fellow Africanists to my attention, and to Robert J. Gordon for sharing with me his then unpublished article.

3. "Pariah," originally used to label members of a very extensive low caste in southern India, quickly became a term of aspersion for any person or animal of a degraded or despised class. Apart from its original usage, it was most often deployed toward dogs, not only on the Indian subcontinent but throughout the colonial world, including Japan, and in other areas regarded as "backward," such as eastern Europe. Similarly, Westerners employed "kaffir," a derogatory term for black Africans, to mark other animal and plant objects, especially dogs, throughout that continent.

4. James Serpell, "From Paragon to Pariah: Some Reflections on Human Attitudes towards Dogs," in *The Domestic Dog: Its Evolution, Behaviour, and Interactions with People* (Cambridge: Cambridge University Press, 1995), 245–56.

5. Kathleen Kete, *The Beast in the Boudoir: Petkeeping in Nineteenth-Century Paris* (Berkeley: University of California Press, 1994), 2.

6. Gayatri Chakravorty Spivak, "Can the Subaltern Speak?" in *Marxism and the Interpretation of Culture*, ed. Cary Nelson and Lawrence Grossberg (Urbana: University of Illinois Press, 1998), 271–313.

7. See the following path-breaking works by Harriet Ritvo: *The Animal Estate: The English and Other Creatures in the Victorian Age* (Cambridge, Mass.: Harvard University Press, 1987); *The Platypus and the Mermaid, and Other Figments of the Classifying Imagination* (Cambridge, Mass.: Harvard University Press, 1997); "Pride and Pedigree: The Evolution of the Victorian Dog Fancy," *Victorian Studies* 29 (Winter 1986): 227–53.

8. Joseph Patterson Sims, "A Dog Map of the World: The Countries of Origin of Some Seventy Breeds of Domesticated Dogs—Half of Them Evolved in the British Isles!" (London: London Illustrated News, 1933). Although I will refer to it as the English Kennel Club, the official name of this pioneering organization is simply and tellingly The Kennel Club.

9. Keith Thomas, *Man and the Natural World: Changing Attitudes in England, 1500-1800* (Oxford: Oxford University Press, 1983), 108.

10. Ibid., 108; Ritvo, "Pride and Pedigree," 50–51.

11. Mary E. Thurston, *The Lost History of the Canine Race: Our 15,000-Year Love Affair with Dogs* (Kansas City: Andrews and McMeel, 1996), 109.

12. Basil Hill Chamberlain, *Japanese Things; Being Notes on Various Subjects Connected with Japan, For the Use of Travelers and Others* (1890; reprint, Tokyo: Tuttle, 1971), 401.

13. V. W. Collier, *Dogs of China and Japan, in Nature and Art* (London: Heinemann, 1921), 177–78. For depictions of two of the dogs given to Perry, see Matthew Calbraith Perry, *The Japan Expedition, 1852-1854: The Personal Journal of Commodore Matthew C. Perry*, ed. Roger Pineau (Washington: Smithsonian Institution Press, 1968), figs. 156n, 156o. Mi[y]ako and Shimoda are both place names, the former referring to the imperial capital, today's Kyoto, and the latter to a small port that was designated as the location of the first U.S. consulate in Japan as a result of Perry's

diplomatic negotiations with shogunal representatives.

14. Henry P. Davis, ed., *The New Dog Encyclopedia,* (Harrisburg, Pa.: Stackpole, 1970), 670–77. The origins of Master Sam Spooner's name may have to do with a certain D. C. Spooner, a partner of Russell and Company and vice consul in Macaó, who put his "magnificent Chinese estate ... at the squadron's disposal for headquarters" while Perry was waiting to sail for the Ryukyu islands and then Japan. See Perry, *Japan Expedition,* 56. It is interesting to note that Perry's grandson, August Belmont Jr., served as president of the American Kennel Club from 1888 to 1916.

15. Masao Miyoshi, *As We Saw Them: The First Japanese Embassy to the United States* (New York: Kodansha, 1994), 52. Thanks to Ian Miller for leading me to this incident.

16. Robert Rosenblum, *The Dog in Art from Rococo to Post-Modernism* (New York: Abrams, 1988), 52–56.

17. Gordon, "Fido," 241.

18. John Lockwood Kipling, *Beast and Man in India: A Popular Sketch of Indian Animals in Their Relations with the People* (London: MacMillan, 1891), 307. Kipling uses "subaltern" in its original sense (and thus quite differently from Gayatri Spivak) to refer to a commissioned British military officer below the rank of captain.

19. Rutherford Alcock, *The Capital of the Tycoon: A Narrative of a Three Years' Residence in Japan,* 2 vols. (London: Longman, 1863), 1: 434–35; Meiji Bunka Kenkyūkai, *Meiji bunka zenshū bekkan: Meiji jibutsu kigen* (Tokyo: Nihon Hyōronsha, 1984), 1451. As Barbara Kolk, a librarian at the American Kennel Club, repeatedly reminded me, one must be careful not to equate present-day breeds with dogs who were called by the same name before breeds became standardized in the late nineteenth century. Alcock's Scottish Terrier was probably much larger (perhaps by as much as twenty centimeters) and more muscular than today's dogs. An early nineteenth-century Scottish Terrier had an excellent scenting ability and was considered to be a superb hunter of foxes and badgers. Breeding has led to a smaller pet dog not particularly known for its tracking abilities, but the Scottish Terrier has evidently lost neither its feisty nature nor its high-pitched bark. See John T. Marvin, *The Book of All Terriers* (New York: Howell Book House, 1976), 27–31.

20. Varner and Varner, *Dogs of the Conquest,* 193; Marion Schwartz, *A History of Dogs in the Early Americas* (New Haven: Yale University Press, 1997), 161–64.

21. Thomas, *Man and the Natural World,* 42.

22. Mastromarino, "Teaching Old Dogs New Tricks," 25.

23. Tsukamoto Manabu, *Shōrui o meguru seiji: Genroku no fōkuroa,* Heibonsha raiburari, no. 18 (Tokyo: Heibonsha, 1993), 184–203.

24. Paul van der Velde and Rudolf Bachofner, eds., *The Deshima Diaries: Marginalia, 1700-1740* (Tokyo: Japan-Netherlands Institute, 1992), 280.

25. Hugh Cortazzi, *Victorians in Japan: In and Around the Treaty Ports* (London: Althone, 1987), 174, fig. 1.

26. For examples, see Gountei Sadahide, *Yokohama kaikō kenbunshi* (Tokyo: Meicho Kankōkai, 1967), 88–89, 96–97, 128–31, 168–71, 185–86, 193, 220–21; Kanagawa Kenritsu Rekishi Hakubutsukan, *Yokohama ukiyoe to sora tobu* (Yokohama: Kanagawa Kenritsu Rekishi Hakubutsukan, 1987), 44, 49, 52, 55, 59, 75, 97, 114.

27. Okada Akio, *Inu to neko* (Tokyo: Mainichi Shinbunsha, 1980), 119. Yet another Sadahide print depicts a Westerner attempting to take a photograph of

American ships in the harbor as three large Western dogs stare into the lens, wriggle between his legs, and chew on the camera stand. See Gountei, *Yokohama*, 112.

28. Shimizu Isao, ed., *Meiji mangakan* (Tokyo: Kōdansha, 1979), 89, 94, 105.

29. Kanagaki Robun, Ochiai Yoshiiku, and Kan Fusao, *Seiyō dōchū hizakurige* (Tokyo: Bankyūkaku, 1870), vol. 1, hanrei, 5v–6r, 19r; vol. 7, hanrei, 16v–17r; vol. 15, hanrei, 25v–26r. I thank John Mertz for suggesting these images.

30. Ibid., vol. 12, hanrei, 2v–3r.

31. Tsukamoto Manabu, *Edo jidaijin to dōbutsu* (Tokyo: Nihon Editā Sukūru Shuppan, 1995), 235.

32. Laurence Oliphant, *Elgin's Mission to China and Japan* (1859; reprint, Hong Kong: Oxford University Press, 1970), 89–90.

33. Cortazzi, *Victorians in Japan*, 215; Daily Press, *The Chronicle and Directory for China, Japan, and the Philippines, for the Year 1869* (Hong Kong: Daily Press, 1869), 58.

34. Charles Darwin, *The Origin of Species by Means of Natural Selection; The Descent of Man and Selection in Relation to Sex*, Great Books of the Western World, no. 49 (Chicago: Encyclopedia Britannica, 1955), 347.

35. Edward S. Morse, *Japan Day by Day, 1877, 1878-79, 1882-83*, 2 vols. (Boston: Houghton Mifflin, 1917), 1: 388.

36. "Tokushū: Tokugawa Yoshinobu," *Taiyō*, no. 449 (April 1998): cover page.

37. Morse, *Japan Day by Day*, 1: 246.

38. Mary Crawford Fraser, *A Diplomat's Wife in Japan: Sketches at the Turn of the Century*, ed. Hugh Cortazzi (New York: Weatherhill, 1982), 112, fig. 1.

39. Ogi Shinzō and Maeda Ai, eds., *Meiji Taishō zushi*, 17 vols. (Tokyo: Chikuma Shobō, 1978), 1: 250. The artist is unknown.

40. Kete, *Beast in the Boudoir*, 84–87; John K. Walton, "Mad Dogs and Englishmen: The Conflict over Rabies in Late Victorian England," *Journal of Social History* 13 (1979): 222.

41. Harold Bolitho, "The Dog Shogun," in *Self and Biography: Essays on the Individual and Society in Asia*, ed. Gungwu Wang (Sydney: Sydney University Press for the Australian Academy of the Humanities, 1975), 123–39.

42. Tokibō, "Yosebumi," *Yomiuri shinbun*, 18 May 1880, 4.

43. Maruyama Masao, "The Ideology and Dynamics of Japanese Fascism," in *Thought and Behavior in Modern Japanese Politics*, trans. and ed. Ivan Morris (London: Oxford University Press, 1963), 41.

44. "Tokyo shinai ni kasanaru kaiinu to kaineko," *Yomiuri shinbun*, 27 October 1901, 4.

45. Alcock, *Capital of the Tycoon*, 1: 200. Of masterless samurai, that other threat of the streets, Alcock recorded: "I met in the 'tokaido' [highway] many officers in groups and others alone, armed with their two swords (about as dangerous and deadly weapons as men can well possess), and evidently intoxicated. They were drunk in various degrees, but all—the best of them—were in a state utterly unfit to be at large in a great thoroughfare, or trusted with weapons by which they might in an instant inflict wounds or grievous injury.... [T]hey are not only insolent, and as a general rule offensive in their gestures and speech when they meet foreigners, but are very prone to put themselves directly in the path, and either dispute passage

with an air of menace, or sometimes even attempt to strike either horse or rider." Ibid., 127.

46. Cortazzi, *Victorians in Japan*, 102–4.

47. Frederick Victor Dickens, *The Life of Sir Harry Parkes II* (1894; reprint, Wilmington, Del.: Scholarly Resources, 1973), 149. This attack should not be confused with a more famous ambush that occurred the previous year on 23 March as Parkes proceeded to his first interview with the Meiji emperor. In that assault, Parkes had come even closer to death. The incident led to an imperial edict prohibiting attacks on foreigners. The whereabouts of Shah during the earlier attack are unclear.

48. In a similar vein, E. N. Lambert, a young assistant at the Yokohama branch of the Hongkong and Shanghai Banking Corporation and resident of the city's foreign enclave of Yamate in the early twentieth century, named one of his dogs Togo, either in honor or in disdain of Admiral Tōgō Heihachirō (1848–1934), who by defeating Russia's Baltic fleet in the Sea of Japan became the hero of the Russo-Japanese War of 1904–1905. E. N. Lamberts photo album, no. 11 (Ac1-211c), photo no. 38, Yokohama Archives of History, Yokohama, Japan.

49. Lady Kate Lawson, *Highways and Homes of Japan* (London: Adelphi Terrace, 1920), 212.

50. Isabella L. Bird, *Unbeaten Tracks in Japan* (London: Murray, 1911), 86. Fujihara is near Nikkō in Tochigi prefecture. Bird also recorded: "As animals are not used for milk, draught, or food, and there are no pasture lands, both the country and the farm-yards have a singular silence and an inanimate look; a mean-looking dog and few fowls being the only representatives of domestic animal life. I long for the lowing of cattle and the bleating of sheep." Ibid., 99.

51. Robert Fortune, *Yedo and Peking: A Narrative of a Journey to the Capitals of Japan and China* (London: Murray, 1863), 96–97.

52. "Kaika no inu to fukaika no inu no hanashi," in *Bunmei kaika zenshū*, ed. Yoshino Sakuzō (Tokyo: Nihon Hyōronsha, 1929), 33–34.

53. Ibid., 2.

54. Darwin, *Descent of Man*, 303.

55. Ritvo, "Pride and Pedigree," 251.

56. Ibid.

57. Robert Leighton, *The New Book of the Dog: A Comprehensive Natural History of British Dogs and Their Foreign Relatives, with Chapters on Law, Breeding, Kennel Management, and Veterinary Treatment* (London: Cassell, 1907), 524–25.

58. Ernest Mason Satow and A. G. S. Hawes, *A Handbook for Travellers in Central and Northern Japan* (Yokohama: Kelly, 1881), 40.

59. Morse, *Japan Day by Day*, 1: 388. An encounter with a "savage, wolfish-looking dog" appears elsewhere in Morse's journal (1: 103). Morse's description of that dog as "bark[ing] viciously" and then "retreating and howling" partially contradicts his claim above that most native dogs "do not bark but howl."

60. George Hilaire Bousquet, *Le Japon de nos jours* (Paris: Hachette, 1877), 209.

61. See Brett L. Walker, *The Lost Wolves of Japan* (Seattle: University of Washington Press, 2005).

62. Morse, *Japan Day by Day*, 2: 18.

63. George Taylor, *Man's Friend, the Dog* (New York: Stokes, 1891), 7.

64. In England during the 1880s, several highly regarded scientists blamed an increase in rabies on inbreeding and the resultant excitability of pedigreed dogs. See Walton, "Mad Dogs and Englishmen," 227.

65. *Japan Weekly Mail*, 8 March 1883, 132.

66. Taniguchi Kengo, *Inu no Nihonshi: Ningen to tomo ni ayunda ichimannen no monogatari* (Tokyo: PHP Kenkyūjo, 2000), 191–92.

67. Kunaichō, ed., *Shimōsa goryū bokujōshi* (Tokyo: Kunaichō, 1974), 90–91.

68. Tsukamoto, *Edo jidaijin to dōbutsu*, 164.

69. Ibid., 67.

70. Ibid., 162–63.

71. Imagawa Isao, *Inu no gendaishi* (Tokyo: Gendai Shokan, 1996), 86.

72. Ibid., 85.

73. "Chikukenhyō no nai inu ya kyōken wa bokusatsu," *Tōkyō koshinbun*, 1 July 1880, in *Meiji nyūsu jiten*, ed. Edamatsu Shigeyuki, Sugiura Tadashi, and Yagi Kyōsuke, 9 vols. (Tokyo: Mainichi Komyunikēshonzu, 1983–1986), 2: 42.

74. Akasaka, "Yosebumi," *Yomiuri shinbun*, 10 August 1877, 4.

75. Imagawa, *Inu no gendaishi*, 87–90.

76. Nishi Amane, "Travel by Foreigners within the Country (Naichi Ryokō)," in *Meiroku Zasshi: Journal of the Japanese Enlightenment*, trans. William Reynolds Braisted (Cambridge, Mass.: Harvard University Press, 1976), 287–93.

77. Fukuzawa Yukichi, "Refuting Nishi's Discussion on Travel by Foreigners in the Country," in *Meiroku Zasshi*, 319–24.

78. *Japan Weekly Mail*, 7 August 1897, 141.

79. Julia Meech-Pekarik, *The World of the Meiji Print: Impressions of a New Civilization* (New York: Weatherhill, 1987), 187.

80. S. Bigot, *Le Japon en 1897* (Tokyo: publisher unknown, 1897), unpaginated, Paul C. Blum Collection, Yokohama Archives of History, Yokohama, Japan. Another cartoon in the same volume imagines the "charming country of Japan" after the amended treaties have been implemented. It depicts foreigners and their dogs strolling down an avenue in head-to-toe (or -tail) armor. The new apparel, reads the French caption, is "now being used by foreign residents and tourists in Japan" to protect themselves, presumably from Japanese people and street dogs.

81. Morse, *Japan Day by Day*, 1: 264. See also 1: 193–94.

82. "The Treatment of Animals," *Japan Weekly Mail*, 13 September 1884, 258–60.

83. Peter Duus, "Presidential Address: Weapons of the Weak, Weapons of the Strong—The Development of the Japanese Political Cartoon," *Journal of Asian Studies* 60 (2001): 993.

84. Matsuo, "Sono hi sono hi," *Yomiuri shinbun*, 30 May 1903, 1.

85. After taking control of Korea in 1905, Japanese colonial authorities initiated similar campaigns in that territorial possession as well. See Abe Yoshio, "On the Corean and Japanese Wolves," *Journal of Science of the Hiroshima University* 1 (1930): ser. B, div. 1, Zoology, 33–38.

86. Takashi Fujitani, *Splendid Monarchy: Power and Pageantry in Modern Japan* (Berkeley: University of California Press, 1998), 91–92.

87. Yoshida Chizuko, "Saigō-san no aiken," *Ueno* no. 417 (January 1994): 16–17; Emi Chizuko, "Kindai kokumin kokka no naka no Ueno Saigō Takamori dōzō:

Sono kensetsu katei to kinō o megutte" (Master's thesis, Tokyo Geijutsu Daigaku, 2001), 27–32.

88. "Nanshū dōzō no aiken ga mondai," *Yūbin hōchi shinbun*, 18 August 1899, in *Meiji nyūsu jiten*, 6: 221.

89. As we have seen, some Japanese remarked as early as the 1870s and 1880s that native breeds were disappearing, but seemingly little concern was expressed about this trend. A 1901 newspaper article, as noted earlier, reported that because the number of pure-blooded Japanese dogs was gradually decreasing and the number of mixed-breed dogs was growing rapidly, it was very difficult to find a pure Japanese dog in the city. The tone of the article was dispassionate, however, and although it began by addressing Japanese dogs, it concluded with a lengthy discussion of what Western breeds were used for hunting in Japan. Despite the title, which spoke of "kept felines" as well as canines, cats do not appear. See "Tōkyō shinai ni kasanaru kaiinu to kaineko."

90. Kete, *Beast in the Boudoir*. See also Thomas, *Man and the Natural World*.

91. Percival Lowell, *Chosön: The Land of the Morning Calm; A Sketch of Korea* (Boston: Ticknor, 1886), 234.

92. Isabella L. Bird, *Korea and Her Neighbors: A Narrative of Travel, with an Account of the Recent Vicissitudes and Present Position of the Country* (Rutland, Vt.: Tuttle, 1986), 45.

93. Bird, *Korea and Her Neighbors*, 45.

94. Han'guk Minjok Munhwa Yongu Won, ed., *Han'guk minjok munhwa tae paekkwa sajon*, 27 vols. (Kyonggi-do Sondgnam-si, South Korea: Academy of Korean Studies, 1991), 21: 247–48.

95. Kipling, *Beast and Man in India*, 296.

96. Rudyard Kipling, "Garm—A Hostage," in *Collected Dog Stories* (Garden City, N.Y.: Doubleday, 1934), 19–44.

97. Kipling, *Beast and Man in India*, 304–6.

98. Ibid, 306–9.

99. Ibid., 309.

100. Gordon, "Fido," 247–49.

101. Thurston, *Lost History of the Canine Race*, 160.

102. Ibid.

From *Wakan sansai zue*. Courtesy of the C. V. Starr East Asian Library, Columbia University.

CHAPTER SEVEN

Orientomology: The Insect Literature of Lafcadio Hearn (1850–1904)

David B. Lurie

> His work is so superior in both quality and quantity that when speaking of our country's insect literature [*konchū bungaku*] one cannot avoid Yakumo.
>
> —Konishi Masayasu[1]

Nowhere is the complex interaction between the categories of alien and familiar more apparent than in the writings of Lafcadio Hearn, a nearly stateless journalist and novelist who, in a decade and a half spanning the end of the nineteenth and the beginning of the twentieth centuries, found a home in Japan and became its premier interpreter to readers in the North Atlantic states.[2] Through extensive translation into Japanese, moreover, this cultural traveler made a curious roundtrip, coming to play much the same role of interpreting "Japan" to Japanese audiences. Although the power and verve of Hearn's best writing remains untarnished, the quaint Orientalism of much of his work would seem to doom him to the status of a quirky minor figure, a footnote to the literary histories of the United States and Japan. And yet, to dismiss him thusly—or rather, to leave him to the ministrations of a coterie of dedicated aficionados—would be a mistake. Despite its limitations, Hearn's work contains suggestive meditations on the relation between other and self, the nature of Eurocentric modernity and the fate within it of the non-European "native," and the inseparability of a remembered past from the remembering present.

Hearn's numerous essays on insects provide one of the most productive entry points into the central themes of his work. This chapter investigates the nature and structure of his portrayals of bugs, who form an important part of, as Brett Walker terms it, Japan's "nonhuman majority." For many, including Hearn, insects may be said to constitute the nonhuman other par excellence. In the mysterious, multitudinous, and bizarre world of insect form and behavior, Hearn found the perfect symbolic vehicle for communicating the ambivalent mixture of horror and delight, of fear and desire, that marked his own tumultuous experience in Japan and elsewhere.

LAFCADIO HEARN / KOIZUMI YAKUMO

As one of this chapter's claims for Hearn's insect writings is that they implicitly link natural history with autobiography, it may be useful to begin with a review of his strikingly peripatetic life.[3] He was born Patricio Lafcadio Tessima Carlos Hearn on the Aegean island of Levkas in 1850, the second son of Charles Bush Hearn (1818–1866), a surgeon in the British army, and a Greek woman named Rosa Antonia Cassimati (1823–1882). The couple had married in 1849 over the objections of both their families. Charles, a neglectful, absentee parent, had the marriage annulled in 1856; Rosa returned to Greece and remarried, but eventually became mentally ill and was confined to an asylum from 1872 until her death ten years later. Hearn, then known as Patrick, an anglicized version of his given name, was brought up in Dublin by a stern great-aunt. His only education was at a brutal French Catholic boarding school near Rouen and an equally strict academy in the north of England, where he lost the sight in his left eye due to a schoolyard injury.

In 1869, at the age of nineteen, Hearn emigrated to the United States, where, between spells of abject poverty and homelessness, he gradually built a reputation as a newspaper reporter and book reviewer in Cincinnati and, from 1877, in New Orleans. He first made a name for himself with a series of lurid stories about a sensational murder case, and much of his reporting was concerned with the sordid underside of urban life. Hearn frequently wrote about African-American culture and folklore, and in Cincinnati in 1874 he went through a marriage ceremony with Althea Foley, a former slave who had served as a cook in his boarding house. Because of antimiscegenation laws, their marriage had no legal standing, and their relationship had ended by the time of his move to New Orleans three years later.

In 1882, Hearn published his first book, a translation of some French short stories by Théophile Gautier (1811–1872), titled *One of Cleopatra's Nights*. Over the following half-decade he penned a collection of folktales from various cultures (*Stray Leaves from Strange Literature*; 1884) and an adaptation of six East Asian stories called *Some Chinese Ghosts* (1887). Also during the 1880s, Hearn compiled a collection of Creole proverbs and a Creole cookbook, evidence of his considerable interest in the hybrid culture of New Orleans. A trip to an island in the Gulf of Mexico inspired his first novel, *Chita: A Memory of Last Island* (1889), which was a tremendous popular success.

In 1887, Hearn left New Orleans for New York, a place he despised and shortly fled for the Caribbean island of Martinique. Several trips there, one an extended stay of nineteen months, resulted in a series of essays in *Harper's Monthly*. He eventually collected these in *Two Years in the French West Indies*, and wrote a second novel, *Youma: The Story of a West-Indian Slave*; both were published in 1890. In the spring of the same year, at thirty-nine years of age, Hearn traveled by train to Vancouver and then boarded a ship to Japan on an assignment to write for *Harper's*. At this stage in his life, he was already a widely published, well-known, and highly successful writer. One imagines that had the *Abyssinia* sunk en route, Hearn would still be known as a minor figure in late nineteenth-century American letters and reportage.[4]

Such was not the case, however, and in April 1890, Hearn arrived in Yokohama. Less than two months later, he acted on long-standing resentments and severed his ties with *Harper's*, a characteristically dramatic move that left him with little means of supporting himself until he befriended Basil Hall Chamberlain (1850–1935), a pioneering scholar of Japanese language and culture, then at the end of his tenure as the first Professor of Japanese and Philology at the Imperial University in Tokyo. Chamberlain arranged employment for Hearn as an English teacher at the Middle and Normal schools in Matsue, a small city near the celebrated Izumo shrine on the Japan Sea coast about 230 kilometers west of Kyoto. Much of Hearn's first book on his new country of residence, *Glimpses of Unfamiliar Japan* (1894), is devoted to his experiences in this provincial outpost.

In January 1891, Hearn married Koizumi Setsu (1868–1932), a recently divorced woman from an impoverished family of former samurai retainers to the Matsue domain. In the following years he taught in Kumamoto, a city on the southern island of Kyushu (1891–1894), briefly held a position as editorial writer at the English-language *Kobe Chronicle* (1894–1895), and eventually became Professor of English Language and Literature at Tokyo Imperial University (1896–1903). In 1896, just before leaving Kobe, Hearn became a naturalized Japanese citizen, taking the name Koizumi Yakumo. Throughout these years, he was a regular contributor to the *Atlantic Monthly*, and by the time of his death in 1904, his American publishers had brought out eleven books on Japan under his name.[5]

Undoubtedly, the central theme of Hearn's life consists in the series of dramatic transformations that he underwent. His national identity was never clear. He was stigmatized for his Greek origins as a child, and spent most of his life in the United States, but held British citizenship until his Japanese naturalization. Perhaps even more remarkable than the list of places where he lived was the lack of continuity in his relations with other people. With a few notable exceptions, Hearn's friendships tended to be short-lived. There were many instances in which he abruptly terminated relationships, the best known of which was his break, around 1896, with Basil Hall Chamberlain, the reasons for which remain unclear.[6]

However, the most striking transformation of Hearn's life, at least for our purposes, was the one that made him Koizumi Yakumo. He had in fact changed his name once before, after arriving in the United States, when he began to use Lafcadio instead of his given name, Patrick. But the complication of his identity that accompanied this second shift in nomenclature was far more dramatic. Readers and critics ever since have been fascinated by his late-in-life naturalization, not least because it allows Hearn to stand as a representative figure of the Westerner becoming infatuated with Japanese culture—or, indeed, with any culture other than his or her own—and "going native."

And yet, a glance at Hearn's writings published after naturalization reveals that in them he maintains the rhetorical perspective of an outsider, the quasi-scholarly Orientalist pose of the Western expert on Japanese culture. The following sentences from the essay on "Dragon-flies" in *A Japanese Miscellany* (1901) are typical of any number of similar passages:

> The people who could find delight, century after century, in watching the ways of insects, and in making such verses about them, must have comprehended, better than we, the simple pleasure of existence. They could not, indeed, describe the magic of nature as our great Western poets have done; but they could feel the beauty of the world without its sorrow, and rejoice in that beauty, much after the manner of inquisitive and happy children.[7]

Viewed from the vantage point of the early twenty-first century, this kind of Orientalist posture is irritatingly familiar. But, although Hearn was undeniably of his time in his conceptualization of the non-Western other, his self-positioning in his published writings is not as simple as this passage makes it seem. As will be discussed below, Hearn repeatedly toyed with the possibility of a non-Western self—of a shift in authorial identity that would parallel the shift in national identity marked by his becoming Koizumi Yakumo in 1896. Indeed, this chapter argues that the insect, as literary subject and natural object, provided a crucial medium for the metamorphoses in identity that make the writing "I" of Hearn (or Yakumo) more complex than is initially apparent.

The linguistic circumstances of Hearn's Japan writings are also complex. Despite his habit of littering his writings with untranslated Japanese terms and referring to recently acquired Japanese books or overheard Japanese conversations, Hearn never learned the language thoroughly.[8] He managed to pick up a smattering of spoken Japanese, but he could read and write only the simple *kana* syllabaries. He and his wife communicated in a pidgin-style mixture of English and Japanese that friends referred to as "Hearn talk" (*Herun-san kotoba*). Whether deliberately or inadvertently, Hearn's texts themselves sometimes approximate a similarly interlingual quality, with their frequent inclusion of Japanese words (sometimes undefined), their occasional complaints about the untranslatability of words or utterances, or their thankfully rare attempts at literal translation.[9] Another aspect of this peculiarly Hearnian interlingualism is that his works were translated into Japanese very quickly, and that many authors and readers in Japan have tended to treat them as Japanese texts written by Koizumi Yakumo, rather than as translations of English texts written by Lafcadio Hearn.

Despite their interlingual tendencies, all of Hearn's works on Japan were in fact written in English. When Hearn retold folktales and ghost stories, he was recasting material that he had accessed through an interpreter or through what his wife was able to communicate to him. Many of his essays, especially those on insects, contain translations of poems relating to the topic under discussion, most frequently in the short seventeen-syllable *hokku* (haiku) form. These poems, and much of the information that these texts provide, were culled by his students and associates from Japanese literary collections and traditional encyclopedias. Specifically, in order to assemble information and literary material for his insect writings, Hearn depended heavily on Ōtani Masanobu (1875–1933), a former Matsue student who was a disciple of the renowned poet Masaoka Shiki (1867–1902), and Minari Shigenobu (1874–1962), a relative of Hearn's wife Setsu who was a researcher at the Historiographical Institute of Tokyo Imperial University.[10]

Taking into account the largely uncredited contributions of these and other assistants results in a vision of Hearn/Yakumo as a corporate author, directing a team of researchers and "informants" and recasting their work in his distinctive prose style. As is the case with ethnographic writing, the voices of these informants have a complex relationship to that of the person claiming responsibility for the text. In the many instances of translations incorporated into essays, or traditional stories recast in accounts of folklore, the voice of Hearn, the scholar and translator (for that is what he often poses as), derives its authority from the knowledge about Japan and the Japanese that it claims, but also from the voice of the other that it represents.

This inclusion of so much translated and reported material in a framework that obscures the conditions under which the actual author obtained it can be interpreted as dishonest and deceptive, but this chapter refrains from making such judgments. The nature of the research underlying Hearn's Japan writings is of interest here primarily as it relates to the frequent ambiguity in his location of himself in the texts. As will be clear below, there are moments when Hearn's authorial self seems on the verge of becoming, not a European observer, but a non-European other—not entirely unlike the canines of the previous chapter, who were able to roam, according to context, between categories of cultural insider and outsider. Hearn's writings approach, but never fully or consistently claim, a writing voice with status equivalent to the citizenship of Koizumi Yakumo, one that endows them with a very different kind of authority than that of a Western scholar-translator. In this connection, and especially considering Hearn's obsession with reincarnation and the influence of previous lives on the self, the insect plays a privileged role as a mediating figure, a metaphorical and literal means of moving the self from one world to the next, or from one nationality to another.

INSECTS IN A JAPANESE GARDEN

The twelve books that Hearn wrote on Japan contain eleven shorter works devoted entirely to insects.[11] After the appearance of *Glimpses of Unfamiliar*

Japan in 1894, he published one book a year until his death in 1904. Each of the four collections published between 1898 and 1901 features one piece of insect literature.[12] The earliest and best known of these is Hearn's much-anthologized discussion of "Insect-Musicians," which appeared in 1898. In it, he provides a fascinating history of the popularity of singing insects, dwelling in considerable detail on the thriving eighteenth- and nineteenth-century business of catching and raising them, a form of animal commerce that thrived alongside the bird trade already examined in chapter 4. The piece incorporates an illustrated catalogue of different species, with translations of poems about them (unlike Hearn's other insect studies, most of these poems are in the thirty-one-syllable *tanka* form rather than the seventeen-syllable *hokku*). The subsequent 1899 essay on "Silkworms" examines the appearance of said creatures and the techniques used for raising them, then shifts into a discussion of the author's ideas about comfort, suffering, and spiritual evolution. Hearn deployed his characteristic combination of historical and cultural survey, together with a collection of short poems, again in 1900 and 1901, training his gaze in turn on "Sémi," or cicadas, and on "Dragon-flies."[13]

The last two collections published during Hearn's lifetime register a dramatic increase in the amount of attention paid to insects. *Kottō* (1902) contains three works explicitly devoted to these creatures: "Story of a Fly," a narrative of a maid reincarnated in insect form; "Fireflies," another detailed insect study; and "Kusa-Hibari," a short but touching meditation on Hearn's relationship with a tiny singing cricket called the "grass-lark."[14] Hearn's last collection, the 1904 *Kwaidan*, features another insect tale, "The Dream of Akinosuké," about a man who spends years living in an ant colony in the space of a few minutes' dream. Furthermore, it devotes an entire section to three "Insect Studies." They include a long essay in which "Butterflies" receive the same treatment previously given to cicadas, dragonflies, and fireflies; a brief but strange meditation on "Mosquitoes"; and a Spencerian discussion of the society of "Ants" and the future evolution of human ethics.[15]

Although these insect works are concentrated in Hearn's later books, there are ample signs of his obsession with bugs in his earlier writings. Indeed, as will be discussed below, one of the keys to Hearn's insect literature is the well-known 1892 essay "In A Japanese Garden," one of his first publications on Japan. Elements of his complex affinity for insects, Japan, and, especially, Japan's insects are also hinted at in the conclusion to that tour de force of his early Japanese reportage, "My First Day in the Orient," where Hearn writes:

> I lie down to sleep, and I dream. I see Chinese texts—multitudinous, weird, mysterious—fleeing by me, all in one direction; ideographs white and dark, upon sign-boards, upon paper screens, upon backs of sandaled men. They seem to live, these ideographs, with conscious life; they are moving their parts, moving with a movement as of insects, monstrously, like *phasmidae*."[16]

Drawn, as Roland Barthes was in his *Empire of Signs*, to alien texts at once meaningful and opaque, Hearn dwelt extensively on the appeal of a writing system he never mastered.[17] But more importantly for the present inquiry, the above passage reveals an ambivalent mixture of attraction and repulsion towards insects: "multitudinous, weird, mysterious," moving "monstrously," with "conscious life." As will become clear in the discussion of spirit and reincarnation below, this notion of "conscious life" is central to what might be called Hearn's spiritual entomology.

Much of Lafcadio Hearn's work is closely allied with horror writing—in terms of style and subject matter he shares many similarities with such American masters as Edgar Allan Poe (1809–1849) and H. P. Lovecraft (1890–1937)—and his insect literature certainly includes elements of fear and loathing. These sinister aspects are not incidental, and we will return to their significance later on. But one of the striking traits of Hearn's interest in insects is the fondness and admiration with which he describes them. These characteristics are evident in the two primary concepts that animate his depiction of insects: microcosm and metamorphosis. An examination of microcosm will provide a starting point for this discussion. Later, we will turn to the even more complex and evocative topic of metamorphosis.

To treat insects as microcosmic is to take them as enacting on a smaller scale the workings of larger creatures and their realms of being—Japan's other nonhuman animals, human societies, natural systems more broadly, and so on. In the case of Hearn's writings on insects, such a microcosm may be found in one of his earliest essays on Japan, "In a Japanese Garden," which appeared in the *Atlantic Monthly* in 1892 and was included in the first collection published after his arrival, *Glimpses of Unfamiliar Japan* (1894). While describing the various parts of his garden, Hearn proceeds through three principal narrative modes: personal reflection, Japanological study, and the retelling of traditional folklore.[18] Indeed, as the preceding overview suggests, the eleven later works that are explicitly about insects may be loosely divided into these three modes as well.

Hearn begins "In a Japanese Garden" by describing the structure and environs of his third residence in Matsue, then devotes several pages to gardens in general, including a fascinating discourse on stones.[19] At this point he pauses to inform the reader that the "soul of the [Japanese] race comprehends Nature infinitely better than we do, *at least in her visible forms*" (emphasis added).[20] By suggesting that Western science has an advantage in its knowledge of the invisible—a reference to chemistry as well as to microscopy—this concluding qualification hints obliquely at a faith in the achievements of science that is not evident in many later insect essays.

Both the power and the limitations of scientific knowledge are central themes for Hearn, who was torn between Spencerian visions of a universal science of evolution and romantic notions of spiritual transcendence. Indeed, a key aspect of the appeal of insects for him is that they seem to present a means of dispelling this ambivalence. In his 1901 essay on dragonflies, Hearn similarly distinguishes between visible and invisible aspects of the natural world, but with very different intentions. He muses:

> If they [Japanese poets] could have seen the dragon-fly as we can see it—if they could have looked at that elfish head with its jewelled ocelli, its marvellous compound eyes, its astonishing mouth, under the microscope,—how much more extraordinary would the creature have seemed to them! ... And yet, though wise enough to have lost that fresh naive pleasure in natural observation which colors the work of these quaint poets, we are not so very much wiser than they in regard to the real wonder of the insect. We are able only to estimate more accurately the immensity of our ignorance concerning it. Can we ever hope for a Natural History with colored plates that will show us how the world appears to the faceted eyes of a dragon-fly?[21]

In this passage, Hearn overturns his earlier dichotomy between the visible and the invisible, and moves from suggesting that Western science affords a deeper insight into the forms of nature to insisting on an ultimate "unknowability" of nature that transcends all cultural oppositions. It is no accident that the shift turns on the possibility of seeing things from the insect's point of view. As shall be discussed below, Hearn is obsessed with precisely such movements from the human to the insectoid.

To return to "In a Japanese Garden," Hearn's general discussion of gardens ends with the claim that the Japanese variety does not attempt to create an "ideal landscape," but rather to "copy faithfully the attractions of a veritable landscape, and to convey the real impression that a real landscape communicates." The importance of the garden lies in a mimetic relationship to nature, but in a mimesis that is peculiarly literary. "It is therefore at once a picture and a poem; perhaps even more a poem than a picture," he explains. But this is not the only characteristic of garden representation. Another aspect that makes Japanese gardens so appealing to Hearn is their miniature, microcosmic quality. Among the features of Hearn's ideal garden are "miniature hills," while his "favorite" section is one where the "centre is occupied by a pondlet—a miniature lake ... containing a tiny island, with tiny mountains and dwarf peach-trees and pines and azaleas."[22] These diminutive items have specific associations in Hearn's work, as indicated by the following passage from "My First Day in the Orient," which is representative of any number of similar effusions:

> Elfish everything seems; for everything as well as everybody is small, and queer, and mysterious: the little houses under their blue roofs, the little shop-fronts hung with blue, and the smiling little people in their blue costumes.[23]

For Hearn, the microcosmic appeal of the garden is inseparable from the miniature nature of the entire nation of Japan.

Having concluded its discussion of gardens in general, "In a Japanese Garden" moves through a series of descriptions of the living things that occupy the specific garden of Hearn's home in Matsue. In an exhaustive catalogue that ranges from shrubs, trees, and flowers to frogs, fish, insects, birds, and other nonhuman animals, Hearn provides an overture for much of his future writing on Japan. Almost all of his insect writings, and many of his other assorted studies and folktale retellings, appear in miniature in this discourse on his garden.

Moreover, with its elegiac insistence on the later disappearance of that which he has described, this passage from the conclusion of the essay could easily serve as a preface to Hearn's collected works on Japan:

> Yet all this—the old katchiū-yashiki and its gardens—will doubtless have vanished forever before many years. Already a multitude of gardens, more spacious and more beautiful than mine,

> have been converted into rice-fields or bamboo-groves; and the quaint Izumo city, touched at last by some long-projected railway line—perhaps even within the present decade—will swell, and change, and grow common-place, and demand these grounds for the building of factories and mills. Not from here alone, but from all the land the ancient peace and the ancient charm seem doomed to pass away.[24]

There are two points in Hearn's conclusion to the garden essay that call for special attention. The first is the positioning of the speaker, who is deictically present only in the "mine" of the second sentence: "a multitude of gardens, more spacious and more beautiful than mine." That "mine" recalls the "I" that is subsumed in the "we" of the passage on "the soul of the race" quoted before, an "I" that is implied by the language and style of the entire essay. It is the European self that Hearn returned to throughout his published writings, even after becoming Koizumi Yakumo.

And yet the situation of this implied European self is not so simple. In the essay, Hearn is, after all, situating himself as the proprietor of the endangered space of Japanese premodernity that is "his" garden. There is a touch of exaggeration here, as the garden in question, rented to him for a few months by the Negishi family, is not really his property. More to the point, though, Hearn's claim of ownership may be seen as situating him implicitly on the *Japanese* side of the split between European self (represented by the encroaching railway and other icons of modernity) and Asian other (represented by the preservation of nature in the traditional garden). Such a move is also apparent in the following passage, which verges on an explicit acknowledgment of the tensions inherent in Hearn's self-depiction:

> Each day, after returning from my college duties, and exchanging my teacher's uniform for the infinitely more comfortable Japanese robe, I find more than compensation for the weariness of five class-hours in the simple pleasure of squatting on the shaded veranda overlooking the gardens.[25]

Both the change in clothing and the posture ("squatting") of the narrator suggest a shift from the European identity of normal-school English instructor to the Japanese identity of garden proprietor and aficionado. As has been already mentioned, it is not unusual for a Hearn essay to toy with situating the authorial self as an Orientalized other. Perhaps these poses serve a purpose similar to Orientalist pronouncements about the "soul of the race," as they resolve, if only temporarily, the divided self of Hearn/Yakumo into one or the other.

To return to the conclusion of "In a Japanese Garden," there may be a shade of bad faith in Hearn's refusal to acknowledge his complicity in the changes he decries, for without the modernizing imperatives of late nineteenth-century Japan, there would have been no place for a teacher of English in Matsue. The very disappearance that Hearn mourns is the prerequisite for his own appearance on the scene. Indeed, one could even argue that it is this disappearance that enables him to discover, retroactively, the existence of premodern Japan itself. However, it would be unfair to criticize this hypocrisy too harshly. It is true that Hearn owed his presence to precisely that which he denounced most vocally, and his descriptions of Japan and the Japanese people often maintain the essentialized otherness of which the aforementioned pronouns are symptomatic. Nevertheless, there are also moments in which Hearn attempts to use that otherness critically. The Orientalism of passages like the following should not blind us to their complexity and ambivalence:

> Surely we have something to learn from the people in whose mind the simple chant of a cricket can awaken whole fairy-swarms of tender and delicate fancies. We may boast of being their masters in the mechanical, their teachers of the artificial in all its varieties of ugliness; but in the knowledge of the natural, in the feeling of the joy and beauty of the earth, they exceed us like the Greeks of old. Yet perhaps it will be only when our blind aggressive industrialism has wasted and sterilized their paradise—substituting everywhere for beauty the utilitarian, the conventional, the vulgar, the utterly hideous,—that we shall begin with remorseful amazement to comprehend the charm of that which we destroyed.[26]

Although the essay from which the preceding quote is taken, "Insect-Musicians," appeared in the 1898 collection *Exotic and Retrospectives*, it has clear rhetorical parallels with Hearn's previously quoted conclusion to the earlier "In a Japanese Garden," including the use of the term "charm," a key word for the author. "Not from here alone," Hearn wrote, "but from all the land the ancient peace and the ancient charm seem doomed to pass away."[27]

The preceding discussion has underlined the importance of the garden essay as an overture for Hearn's insect writings, but the mournfully prophetic tone of its concluding passage brings us to a second key point: the garden essay stands as emblematic of Hearn's writings on Japan in that it constitutes a discourse of the vanishing, to use Marilyn Ivy's evocative terminology. Ivy writes of "recurrent yet elusive forms of absence that haunt the historical present of that place called Japan." This haunting, ghostly alternation between presence and absence animates Hearn's work as much as it does the texts and subjects that Ivy examines. In Hearn's ghost stories, as in those of *Tōno monogatari* (Tales of Tōno; 1910), by the folklorist Yanagita Kunio (1875–1962; see chapter 2), the supplementary logic of nostalgia produces what Ivy calls "narratives of revenant knowledge."[28] A similar spectral discourse is at work in the contradictory account of Hearn's discovered and disappearing garden inhabitants, producing meaning at the same time that meaning is lost.

For Hearn, the issue is not just an alternation between the presence and absence of the premodern. There is also a different presence, a phantom of the modern, one that frequently reveals itself as an apparition within his paeans to premodern charm, much as the European self emerges within his sentences. Perhaps the best example of this lurking modern lies in Hearn's technological figuration of the natural, purely premodern realm of the insects. A cicada is said to sound like the "noise of a sewing-machine in full operation," the chirping of a cricket is compared to the "tiniest electric bells," and a mosquito's bite is likened to an "electric burn." A firefly's light is a "tiny dynamo" that could be used "as a phototelegraph." One essay gives a long catalogue of insect appendages that includes "tongues that are drills," "living scissors and saws and boring-pumps and brace-bits," and "exquisite elfish weapons which no human skill can copy, even in the finest watch-spring steel."[29] Given the passion with which Hearn denounced the developed Western nations as "masters in the mechanical," the ambivalence and equivocation of his discourse on the premodern can clearly be seen in these returns of the technological repressed.

The last aspect of "In a Japanese Garden" that invites exploration is the way in which these complex interrelations between self and other, European and Japanese, modern and premodern, are lodged within a web of insect references, both explicitly and implicitly. In this respect as well, the essay is an overture of impressive scope. Many of the insects appearing in it—butterflies, singing insects, dragonflies—subsequently became the subjects of full-length studies. But perhaps the most significant insects in the essay may be found in two folkloric narratives that introduce the concept of reincarnation in insect form, an idea that became one of Hearn's central intellectual preoccupations. The first is the story of a maid who kills herself after coming under suspicion for theft, and is reincarnated as a fly: "her spirit passed into the body of a strange little insect, whose head faintly resembled that of a ghost with long disheveled hair." The second is the tale of a twelfth-century warrior named Sanemori who was killed in a ricefield and "became a rice-devouring insect, which is still respectfully called ... Sanemori-San."[30] For Hearn, the ghostly and the insectoid have a tendency to switch places, to metamorphose into each other, and connections between the two appear repeatedly throughout his writings.[31]

For the purposes of this chapter, the most significant aspect of Hearn's early foray "In A Japanese Garden" is that, by including these two narratives of reincarnated insect ghosts amid ruminations on the loveliness of the vanishing non-European past, it combines the most important themes of Hearn's subsequent writing on Japan. The insect, it turns out, is not merely a symbolic repository of the aesthetic or natural values of the Orient. It is also a destination, a state into which humans can, and do, transform. As examination of his later insect works will reveal, through their association with reincarnation, insects link Hearn's concern with the disappearing world of premodern Japan and his obsession with personal, cultural, natural—and even physical—forms of memory.

REINCARNATION, GHOSTS, AND METAMORPHOSES

The insect literature that Hearn began to publish several years after "In a Japanese Garden" teems with references to insect reincarnation. Indeed, one account is devoted entirely to just such a tale: "The Story of a Fly," from the 1902 collection *Kottō*. In it, the ghost of a maid returns in the form of a large fly who pesters her master and mistress until they decide to pay for a memorial service for her. Thereupon it dies, and is buried in a cemetery with a grave marker. Other insect-reincarnation narratives include stories of fireflies who are ghosts of twelfth-century warriors, members of the Genji and Heike clans, and of two sisters, one reborn as a grasshopper and the other as a cricket.[32] Numerous other texts make similar connections between insects, souls, and the dead. Hearn discusses the "Ghost dragon-fly" and a grasshopper called the "horse of the dead" (*hotoke uma*) in his essay on "Dragon-flies," as well as in a short piece called "Buddhist Names of Plants and Animals."[33] In addition to constantly treating insects as creatures *with* souls, Hearn cites cases of souls themselves manifested in the form of insects: where masses of fireflies appear before a battle in which souls are separated from the bodies of the fallen, where butterflies are ghostly manifestations of dead souls, and where the soul of a sleeping man appears in the form of an enormous butterfly.[34]

But Hearn also devoted more essayistic writing to a sustained consideration of the specific issue of insect reincarnation, especially while discussing cicadas, beliefs in goblins, and mosquitoes. The link between insect metamorphosis and human reincarnation is made explicit in the following passage from "Sémi," the essay on cicadas that appeared in the 1900 *Shadowings*.

> As the metamorphosis of the butterfly supplied to old Greek thought an emblem of the soul's ascension, so the natural history of the cicada has furnished Buddhism with similitudes and parables for the teaching of doctrine.
>
> Man sheds his body only as the sémi sheds its skin. But each reincarnation obscures the memory of the previous one: we remember our former existence no more than the sémi remembers the shell from which it has emerged.[35]

This paraphrase of Buddhist doctrine is contradicted elsewhere in Hearn's work, for he seems to have been reluctant to believe that past existences are completely inaccessible. In "Kusa-Hibari," a 1902 elegy to a pet cricket, Hearn writes: "Of course he did not learn the song. It is a song of organic memory—deep, dim memory of other quintillions of lives, when the ghost of him shrilled at night from the dewy grasses of the hills." In the essay on fireflies, Hearn even goes so far as to propose that matter itself has access to its previous lives: "I cannot rid myself of the notion that Matter, in some blind infallible way, *remembers*" (emphasis in original).[36]

These notions of organic or even physical memory stem from Hearn's attempts to synthesize his understanding of the Buddhist doctrines of reincarnation and the nature of the self with the psychological theories of his idol, Herbert Spencer (1820–1903), to whom he awarded such accolades as, "the greatest philosopher that has yet appeared in this world."[37] References to the eminent Victorian thinker abound in Hearn's writings, as do opaque discussions of the "scientific" foundations for ideas about reincarnation. Perhaps the following passage from an essay heavily reliant on

Spencer's *Principles of Psychology* (1855) will serve to clarify the notion of organic memory deployed in connection with the pet cricket's song:

> Instinct, in the language of modern psychology, means "organized memory," and memory itself is "incipient instinct,"—the sum of impressions to be inherited by the next succeeding individual in the chain of life. Thus science recognizes inherited memory: not in the ghostly signification of a remembering of the details of former lives, but as a minute addition to psychological life accompanied by minute changes in the structure of the inherited nervous system.[38]

Hearn's preoccupation with reincarnation and insistence that past lives must be accessible in some form contributed to his interest in these elements of Spencer's psychology, but his desperate love for a vanishing premodernity also made it imperative that he award memory a privileged position in his thought.

This line of thinking on organic memory, which, Hearn implies, is a species of reincarnation, is particularly tied up with insects, and with the phenomenon of humans becoming insects through rebirth or otherwise. In the bathetic conclusion to "Kusa-Hibari," Hearn suggests a parallel between himself and the singing cricket whose death, through starvation with grisly consequence, that essay mourns. "Yet, after all," he writes, "to devour one's own legs for hunger is not the worst that can happen to a being cursed with the gift of song. There are human crickets who must eat their own hearts in order to sing."[39] Here the notion of a "human cricket" is advanced more as rhetorical flourish than as actual transformation, but the figure of human becoming insect is treated as real in another work from *Kottō*, the same collection in which "Kusa-Hibari" appears.

Indeed, though it is ostensibly not even about insects at all, that short piece, entitled "Gaki," is the central Hearn essay for any consideration of these relations between insect and self. Hearn begins by describing an epiphany he experienced while sitting on a beach in Suruga, on the Pacific coast near Mount Fuji. Contemplating dragonflies, crickets, cicadas, and crabs, he is convinced anew of the truth of reincarnation, and these thoughts lead him to musings on the potential for rebirth as a *gaki*, or "goblin":

> So it depends on ourselves whether we are to become insects or goblins hereafter; and in the Buddhist system the difference between insects and goblins is not so well defined as might be supposed. The belief in a mysterious relation between ghosts and insects, or rather between spirits and insects, is a very ancient belief

> in the East, where it assumes innumerable forms,—some unspeakably horrible, others full of weird beauty.[40]

Hearn proceeds to run through some examples of insect beliefs, and then devotes a great deal of space to cataloguing different types of *gaki* and suggesting correspondences between them and various types of insect. He cites, for example, *gaki* who eat "wigs," "street filth," and the "refuse of funeral-pyres and the clay of graves," and states that "moths, flies, beetles, … and other unpleasant creatures seem thus to be indicated."

But the similarities between insects and the supernatural *gaki* go beyond such behavioral parallels. Metamorphosis itself, Hearn argues, is the peculiar aspect of insects that makes them available for folk-beliefs and speculative correspondences:

> In our visible world there are no other creatures so wonderful and so mysterious; and the true history of certain insects actually realizes the dreams of mythology. To the minds of primitive men, the mere facts of insect-metamorphosis must have seemed uncanny.[41]

The important point here lies in the way this passage makes clear what was only suggested in the cicada essay's discussion of metamorphosis and reincarnation: it is the "true history" of insect life that makes bugs so symbolically powerful. The parallels Hearn dwells upon here form a metaphoric hinge between natural and cultural history; it is not a coincidence that "primitive men" are mentioned in the passage, for the essay has become an exercise in speculative anthropology.

The "Gaki" essay concludes with a series of fantasies about the type of insect body into which Hearn would prefer to be reincarnated. He eventually decides:

> In fact I have not been able to convince myself that it is really an inestimable privilege to be reborn a human being. And if the thinking of this thought, and the act of writing it down, must inevitably affect my next rebirth, then let me hope that the state to which I am destined will not be worse than that of a cicada or a dragonfly;—climbing the cryptomerias to clash my tiny cymbals in the sun—or haunting, with soundless flicker of amethyst and gold, some holy silence of lotus pools.[42]

This lovely conclusion to an essay that has also dwelt upon the frightening or repulsive aspects of insect life—recall Hearn's earlier references to "unspeakably horrible" forms and "unpleasant creatures"—consciously subverts the notion of rebirth in *gaki* form as punishment for misdeeds in a previous life. It is worth noting that both of the insects mentioned as appealing destinations of reincarnation were subjects of full-length studies in previous Hearn works (cicadas in the 1900 *Shadowings* and dragonflies in the 1901 *A Japanese Miscellany*). Even more importantly, the settings of the imagined activities of Hearn-become-insect are classic loci of his pure Japanese premodernity: a stand of cryptomeria, or Japanese cedars, and silent "lotus pools."

The links between Hearn's imagining himself as an insect and his fondness for this kind of "Oriental" setting become even clearer in one of the last works published in his lifetime: the essay on mosquitoes that forms one of the three "Insect Studies" appended to the ghost stories of *Kwaidan* (1904). Hearn begins by lamenting the infestation of mosquitoes in his Tokyo neighborhood. It turns out that they come from the standing water in containers at the graves of a nearby cemetery:

> Well, it is in these tanks and flower-vessels that mine enemies are born: they rise by millions from the water of the dead;—and, according to Buddhist doctrine, some of them may be reincarnations of those very dead, condemned by the error of former lives to the condition of *Jiki-ketsu-gaki,* or blood-drinking pretas.... Anyhow the malevolence of the *Culex fasciatus* would justify the suspicion that some wicked human soul had been compressed into that wailing speck of a body....[43]

Citing the Western extermination technique of pouring a kerosene film onto the surface of the stagnant water in which the mosquito larvae live, the essay lingers humorously on the difficulties presented by the large number of receptacles in cemeteries, and then deftly equates mosquitoes with the "charm" of premodernity:

> To free the city of mosquitoes it would be necessary to demolish the ancient graveyards;—and that would signify the ruin of the Buddhist temples attached to them;—and that would mean the disparition of so many charming gardens, with their lotus-ponds and Sanscrit-lettered monuments and humpy bridges and holy groves and weirdly-smiling Buddhas! So the extermination of *Culex fasciatus* would involve the destruction of the poetry of the ancestral cult,—surely too great a price to pay![44]

Using language reminiscent of that employed in earlier essays like "My First Day in the Orient" and "In a Japanese Garden," the passage lauds the beauty of graveyards and gardens and, significantly, raises the possibility of their being "demolish[ed]," of their "disparition"—that is, of their vanishing. Once again, the garden filled with insects appears as a microcosmic figuration of the appeal of a purely non-Western Japan whose appearance and disappearance are inextricably linked.

Having reaffirmed the connection between insects and the poetic Japanese past, Hearn fits himself into the picture. First, he suggests that he may be linked to Japan through a previous life, claiming that whenever he hears a temple bell, he "become[s] aware of a striving and a fluttering in the abyssal part of my ghost,—a sensation as of memories struggling to reach the light beyond the obscurations of a million million deaths and births."[45] As discussed above, this emphasis on memory is symptomatic of Hearn's insect imaginary, as is this obsolete usage of "ghost" as "spirit" or "soul." "Ghost" is a crucial term for Hearn, who seems to have been bewitched by the tension between its early, general sense of "spirit/soul" and the more limited modern meaning of a dead soul's manifestation in the world of the living. In the following passage from a brief sketch titled "Hōrai," also from *Kwaidan*, the link that this word provides between the living and the dead, the present self and the past other, is apparent.

> This atmosphere ... is enormously old.... It is not made of air at all, but of ghost,—the substance of quintillions and quintillions of generations of souls blended into one immense translucency,—souls of people who thought in ways never resembling our ways. Whatever mortal man inhales that atmosphere, he takes into his blood the thrilling of these spirits, and they change the senses within him.[46]

The "Hōrai" of this sketch is a legendary Chinese wonderland, characteristically associated with the vanishing paradise of Japan, a place with an "atmosphere" of "ghost" that is very much the same place as the "charming" cemetery landscape detailed in the preceding quote and the site of the singing and flitting cicada and dragonfly of the "Gaki" essay.[47]

The aspect of the "Mosquitoes" essay that deserves emphasis, however, is Hearn's focus on himself and his own reincarnation, which becomes more explicit in a concluding, facetious turn to the future:

> And, considering the possibility of being doomed to the state of a *Jiki-ketsu-gaki*, I want to have my chance of being reborn in some bamboo flower-cup, or *mizutamé*, whence I might issue softly, singing my thin and pungent song, to bite some people that I know.[48]

What is most interesting in this transformative conclusion is what has been going on beneath the surface: by implicitly suggesting that he is the reincarnation of some past Japanese and explicitly imagining himself as a future mosquito, Hearn has doubly located himself within the Orientalized pure premodernity of the cemetery. Two transformations lurk beneath the metamorphosis of the mosquitoes before they "rise" or "issue" from the water: the dramatic changes undergone by a modernizing and Westernizing Japan, and the actual transformation that Hearn himself experienced a decade before this essay was published, namely, his metamorphosis into Koizumi Yakumo.

Although Hearn never explicitly completes this autobiographical circle in his published works on insects, it is difficult not to see the complex relocation of the narrator's self in this essay as an intensified version of the play with a potentially Japanese self that is evident elsewhere in his writings. In his work, the insect serves as a medium for shifting the self, for allowing movement from a Western to a Japanese identity. That which is most radically inhuman Hearn uses to connect what he saw as radically different forms of humanity. In the same way, the insect mediates between the absolute modern of nineteenth-century technology, of "blind aggressive industrialism," and the pure natural beauty of an idyllic, vanishing past. It is of course the mosquito's bite, accompanied though it may be by song, that is "sharp as an electric burn."[49]

EPILOGUE: HEARN'S GHOST

Hearn/Yakumo lurks in odd corners of modern Japanese culture. His life and work influenced intellectuals as divergent in their interests as the folklorist Yanagita Kunio and the philosopher Nishida Kitarō (1870–1945).[50] Symptomatic of this enduring significance is his appearance in the nationalistic 1938 essay "Nihon e no kaiki" (Return to Japan) by the poet Hagiwara Sakutarō (1886–1942). Early in the essay, Hagiwara writes of the Japanese that

> ... if in the future they were to make Western civilization their own, and become capable of competing with the various power-

> ful countries of the white men in all manner of military capability and industrial production, they would immediately awaken from the deluded worship of the West, and return to their own race-consciousness [*minzokuteki jikaku*]—this was the prediction, thirty years ago, of Hearn, that is, Koizumi Yakumo [*Hān no Koizumi Yakumo*]. And it is the case that this poet's prediction has gradually been realized in the Japan of Shōwa.[51]

In both the equivocal use of his two names and the citation of him as a "poet" (*shijin*)—a reference to heightened aesthetic sensibilities rather than to specific generic production—this passage locates Hearn in an awakening that takes place *between* Japan and the West, a returning that is at once spatial, temporal, and spiritual. As he becomes first Koizumi Yakumo and then simply a poet, he is, in a sense, successfully reincarnated as a Japanese nationalist, some twenty years after his death.

One of the most meaningful of Hearn's returns takes place in "Den'en no yūutsu" (Gloom in the country), a 1919 novella by Satō Haruo (1892–1964) that itself stands as one of the finest pieces of modern insect literature. This work, which documents the mental deterioration of a Tokyo writer in a countryside teeming with bugs, is punctuated with hallucinatory reveries about insects. In one of the most extensive of these reveries, the protagonist pauses to recall sympathetically Hearn's desire to be reborn as a bug: "'Merely to be born human is not necessarily good fortune,' said a certain poet of the grass-lark. 'It might be good to become such an insect when next I am reborn.'"[52] Located a few lines after a quotation from the renowned early-modern poet Matsuo Bashō (1644–1694), this elliptical reference reincarnates Hearn as a potentially Japanese author even more effectively than the line from Hagiwara's essay. Moreover, as in Hearn's own writings, that relocation is effected through the medium of insect rebirth. It is no accident that Satō's novella itself is concerned with the spectral disappearances and transformations of modernity and their fragmenting effect on the self of the narrator. Appearing as it does at a climactic moment of that story, as in so many other places, the ghost of Hearn continues to haunt Japan.

NOTES

1. Konishi Masayasu, *Mushi no bunkashi* (1977; paperback reprint with revisions, Tokyo: Asahi Shinbunsha, 1992), 229.

2. For their comments on previous incarnations of this essay, I thank Paul Anderer, Zachary Lesser, Yukio Lippit, and Sophie Volpp. I am grateful also to Karen

Olsson for suggesting the neologism that became the title.

3. Luckily for students of Hearn's life and writing, there are two useful new reference works devoted to him: Robert L. Gale, *A Lafcadio Hearn Companion* (Westport, Conn.: Greenwood, 2002), a collection of summaries and capsule biographies, and Hirakawa Sukehiro, ed., *Koizumi Yakumo jiten* (Tokyo: Kōbunsha, 2000), which is a superb resource despite its inexplicable lack of an index of English names and titles. The inherent interest of Hearn's life story, no less than that of his writings, has inspired a remarkably large number of biographies. In addition to the Gale and Hirakawa references, I have consulted in particular Jonathan Cott, *Wandering Ghost: The Odyssey of Lafcadio Hearn* (New York: Knopf, 1991), and Paul Murray, *A Fantastic Journey: The Life and Literature of Lafcadio Hearn* (Folkestone, U.K.: Japan Library, 1993).

4. Several of Hearn's pre-Japan books are still available in paperback reprints, and information about his work appears in general discussions of late nineteenth-century American letters. Hearn is often identified as a local colorist, especially in connection with his work on New Orleans. With its extensive quotations from his writings, Jonathan Cott's *Wandering Ghost* provides a helpful introductory cross-section of this early work, which may be surveyed in more detail through Edward Larocque Tinker's early biography, *Lafcadio Hearn's American Days* (New York: Dodd, Mead, 1924) and the first four volumes of *The Writings of Lafcadio Hearn* (16 vols. [Boston: Houghton Mifflin, 1922]). Robert Gale's *Companion* provides more detailed references to other sources for Hearn's Cincinnati and New Orleans journalism.

5. The year after Hearn's death saw the posthumous publication of a twelfth book, a collection of essays and stories titled *The Romance of the Milky Way* (Boston: Houghton Mifflin, 1905). With the exception of the last book to emerge in his lifetime, the 1904 *Japan: An Attempt at Interpretation*, in which Hearn tried his hand at a comprehensive analysis of Japanese history and culture that was heavily influenced by Herbert Spencer, all of his books on Japan were collections of personal essays, sketches, retellings of folklore, and quasi-academic studies, some previously published and some appearing for the first time in book form. The titles of these ten collections provide an excellent sense of the quaint Orientalism of much of their content: *Glimpses of Unfamiliar Japan* (1894), *Out of the East: Reveries and Studies in New Japan* (1895), *Kokoro: Hints and Echoes of Japanese Inner Life* (1896), *Gleanings in Buddha-Fields: Studies of Hand and Soul in the Far East* (1897), *Exotics and Retrospectives* (1898), *In Ghostly Japan* (1899), *Shadowings* (1900), *A Japanese Miscellany* (1901), *Kottō: Being Japanese Curios, with Sundry Cobwebs* (1902), *Kwaidan: Stories and Studies of Strange Things* (1904). It stands as testimony to their enduring appeal that most of these works are still available in paperback reprint editions; they are also collected in volumes 5 through 12 of *The Writings of Lafcadio Hearn*. Hearn's works on Japan can be sampled in several anthologies, including *Writings from Japan*, ed. Francis King (Harmondsworth, U.K.: Penguin, 1984), *Lafcadio Hearn: Japan's Great Interpreter*, ed. Louis Allen and Jean Wilson (Folkestone, U.K.: Japan Library, 1992), and *Lafcadio Hearn's Japan: An Anthology of His Writings on the Country and Its People*, ed. Donald Richie (Tokyo: Tuttle, 1997).

6. On the relationship between Hearn and Chamberlain, see Yuzo Ota, *Basil Hall Chamberlain: Portrait of a Japanologist* (Richmond, U.K.: Japan Library, 1998), 127–201. Its consideration of their friendship and its dissolution, which includes a great

deal of material on debates about Hearn's character and intellectual ability, reveals the intensity with which readers and critics still respond to his personality a century after his death.

7. "Dragon-flies," in *A Japanese Miscellany: Strange Stories, Folklore Gleanings, Studies Here and There* (1901; paperback reprint, New York: ICG Muse, 2001), 97.

8. Given that Hearn was already forty when he arrived in Japan, and that he spent the remaining decade and a half of his life working intensely to support himself and his family as a writer and a teacher of English, his failure to become fluent or literate in Japanese is perhaps not as surprising as it first might seem.

9. One such literal translation is, "'I-your-servant mochi-for this-world-in no-use-have. Saké-alone this-life-in if-there-be, nothing-beside-desirable-is.'" See "From Hōki to Oki," in *Glimpses of Unfamiliar Japan,* 2 vols. (1894; paperback reprint, 2 vols. in 1, Tokyo: Tuttle, 1976), 560. Although Hearn continued to include Japanese linguistic elements freely in his writings, this quote, which appeared in his first Japan book, is particularly egregious.

10. Konishi, *Mushi no bunkashi,* 231. Short biographies of the two men may be found in Hirakawa, *Koizumi Yakumo jiten,* 92–93, 614–16.

11. The present chapter is concerned primarily with these eleven works, and with other substantial discussions of insects in Hearn's published writings on Japan. I do not pretend to have exhausted Hearn's oeuvre, which in addition to its size is fraught with bibliographic problems stemming from his immense pre-Japan journalistic output (much of which remains unanthologized), his voluminous correspondence, and the many posthumous publications of written versions of his Tokyo Imperial University lectures. It is clear that Hearn's interest in insects predated his sojourn in Japan. There are newspaper editorials that anticipate one of his last insect works, the essay on "Ants" in the 1904 collection *Kwaidan*: "Insect Politics" (1878), "Insect Civilization" (1881; in *The New Radiance and Other Scientific Sketches,* ed. Ichiro Nishizaki [Tokyo: Hokuseidō, 1939], 56–58), and "News About Ants" (1882; in *Occidental Gleanings,* 2 vols., ed. Albert Mordell [New York: Dodd, Mead, 1925], 2: 48–52). There is also an 1876 essay on "Butterfly Fantasies" in *An American Miscellany,* ed. Albert Morrell (New York: Dodd, Mead, 1924), 190–93. As for material contemporary with the published Japan writings treated in this chapter, there are Tokyo Imperial University lectures on "Some Poems about Insects" (in *Interpretations of Literature,* 2 vols., ed. John Erskine [New York: Dodd, Mead, 1917], 2: 238–71) and "Some French Poems on Insects" (in *Life and Literature,* ed. John Erskine [New York: Dodd, Mead, 1917], 266–83), as well as a separately published volume containing another lecture on *Insects and Greek Poetry* (New York: Rudge, 1926). Hearn's love of insects has not gone unnoticed by anthologists. The posthumous *Japanese Lyrics* (Boston: Houghton Mifflin, 1915) contains a section on "Insect Poems" (1–9); one of Hearn's researcher/informants, Ōtani Masanobu, brought out a bilingual collection of insect works, *Koizumi Yakumo: Mushi no bungaku/Insect Literature* (Tokyo: Hokuseidō, 1921); and an expanded collection of new Japanese translations of Hearn's insect writings has been published more recently (Nagazawa Sumio, trans., *Chō no gensō* [Tokyo: Chikuchi Shokan, 1988]). The present chapter's epigraph is taken from entomologist Konishi Masayasu's marvelous discussion of the cultural history of insects, which contains a brief, informative section devoted to Hearn's insect writings (*Mushi no bunkashi,* 229–32), drawing in turn on an earlier essay, "Koizumi Yakumo to mushi," *Rekishi to*

jinbutsu 5, no. 2 (February 1975): 24–26. Another helpful discussion of Hearn's interest in insects ("Mushi") may be found in Hirakawa, *Koizumi Yakumo jiten*, 630. The author of that entry also has a more extensive essay devoted mainly to *Kwaidan*'s "Insect Studies": Ushimura Kei, "Mushi mezuru Hān," *Hikaku bungaku kenkyū* 47 (1985): 156–64.

12. Nothing was published in 1903, but in the following year, the last of his life, Hearn's publishers brought out two works: his final collection, *Kwaidan*, and his long analysis, *Japan: An Attempt at Interpretation*.

13. "Insect-Musicians," in *Exotics and Retrospectives* (1898; paperback reprint, Tokyo: Tuttle, 1971), 39–80; "Silkworms," in *In Ghostly Japan* (1899; paperback reprint, Tokyo: Tuttle, 1971), 59–70; "Sémi," in *Shadowings* (1900; paperback reprint, Tokyo: Tuttle, 1971), 69–102; "Dragon-flies," in *A Japanese Miscellany*, 63–102.

14. "Story of a Fly," in *Kottō: Being Japanese Curios, with Sundry Cobwebs* (New York: MacMillan, 1902), 55–62; "Fireflies," in *Kottō*, 135–70; "Kusa-Hibari," in *Kottō*, 235–42.

15. "The Dream of Akinosuké," in *Kwaidan: Stories and Studies of Strange Things* (1904; paperback reprint, Tokyo: Tuttle, 1971), 143–56; "Butterflies," in *Kwaidan*, 179–204; "Mosquitoes," in *Kwaidan*, 205–12; "Ants," in *Kwaidan*, 213–40.

16. "My First Day in the Orient," in *Glimpses of Unfamiliar Japan*, 28. *Phasmidae* are walkingsticks: large, primarily tropical insects camouflaged by their resemblance to twigs.

17. Hearn wrote that "these ideographs have a speaking symmetry which no design without a meaning could possess" (ibid., 3–4). This and other meditations on the graphic elements of the newly experienced Japanese cityscape fill "My First Day in the Orient," which is, among other things, an account of the impact of writing on the illiterate foreign visitor. The chapter immediately following it in *Glimpses of Unfamiliar Japan* is "The Writing of Kōbōdaishi," a breathless retelling of fantastic feats of inscription by Kūkai (774–835), founder of the esoteric Shingon school of Japanese Buddhism as well as a renowned calligrapher (ibid., 29–33).

18. This useful tripartite division reflects internal differences in Hearn's work on Japan, but there are of course many cases of overlap and intersection among the three categories. Indeed, the curious way in which Hearn's and other Victorian writing on Japan is alternately charming and repugnant is due in large part to the ease with which these three modes combine and recombine with one another. Such shifts in mode are intimately connected to the complexities of Hearn's authorial identity.

19. The house, now the site of a museum commemorating Hearn's life and work, overlooks the moat of Matsue castle. It was the residence of the Negishi family, former retainers to the lords of Matsue domain. Young Negishi Iwai (1874–1933) was a student of Hearn, and his father rented the house to Hearn and his wife Setsu from June to November 1891.

20. "In a Japanese Garden," in *Glimpses of Unfamiliar Japan*, 346.

21. "Dragon-flies," 97–98 (ellipses in original).

22. "In a Japanese Garden," 349, 361.

23. "My First Day in the Orient," 2.

24. "In a Japanese Garden," 384. "Katchiū [*kachū*] yashiki" refers to the residential compound of a retainer to a domain lord, such as Hearn's landlords, the

Negishi family, had once been.

25. Ibid., 382.

26. "Insect-Musicians," in *Exotics and Retrospectives*, 80.

27. "In a Japanese Garden," 384.

28. Marilyn Ivy, *Discourses of the Vanishing: Modernity, Phantasm, Japan* (Chicago: University of Chicago Press, 1995), 21, 242.

29. "Sémi," in *Shadowings*, 52; "Kusa-Hibari," 236; "Mosquitoes," 207; "Fireflies," 138; "Gaki," in *Kottō*, 195.

30. "In a Japanese Garden," in *Glimpses of Unfamiliar Japan*, 363–64, 372–73. A note appended to the Sanemori account mentions a third story involving a doctor whose ghost becomes a cucumber-eating insect (ibid., 373).

31. In her highly sentimental account of life with her husband, Koizumi Setsu provides the following list of "Hearn's favorite things": "the west, evening glow, summer, the sea, swimming, plantains, cedars, deserted cemeteries, insects, ghost stories, the story of Tarō Urashima, and that of Hōrai." See her "Reminiscences," trans. Yoji Hasegawa, in *A Walk in Kumamoto: The Life and Times of Setsu Koizumi, Lafcadio Hearn's Japanese Wife*, written and edited by Yoji Hasegawa (Folkestone, U.K.: Global Oriental, 1997), 39. It is not a coincidence that in this list insects are lodged between graveyards and spectral narratives; in Hearn's own work as well, they constantly appear in stories of the dead and their hauntings.

32. "Fireflies," 140; "Insect-Musicians," 65–66.

33. "Dragon-flies," 70, 74; "Buddhist Names of Plants and Animals," in *A Japanese Miscellany*, 109–10.

34. "Fireflies," 154; "Butterflies," 184–85; "The Dream of Akinosuké," 154.

35. "Sémi," 98.

36. "Kusa-Hibari," 237; "Fireflies," 169.

37. "Ants," 237.

38."The Idea of Preëxistence," in *Kokoro: Hints and Echoes of Japanese Inner Life* (1896; paperback reprint, Tokyo: Tuttle, 1972), 230.

39. "Kusa-Hibari." As noted above, *kusa-hibari* literally means "grass-lark." Elizabeth Stevenson implicitly recognizes the autobiographical implications of the conclusion of this essay when she uses that evocative name as the title of a reissue of her Hearn biography: "When reading a major part of Hearn's literary production, it is not uncalled for to think of him as a 'Grass Lark'" (introduction to *The Grass Lark: A Study of Lafcadio Hearn* [New Brunswick, N. J.: Transaction, 1999; republication of work originally titled *Lafcadio Hearn* (New York: Macmillan, 1961)], xv).

40. "Gaki," 184. *Gaki* is the Japanese term for the Buddhist *preta* or hungry ghost; Hearn prefers to render the word as "goblin."

41. Ibid., 193.

42. Ibid., 198–99.

43. "Mosquitoes," 209 (ellipses in original).

44. Ibid., 210–11.

45. Ibid., 212.

46. "Hōrai," in *Kwaidan*, 176.

47. The link between "Hōrai" and Japan is clarified in the conclusion of the sketch, which laments that "Evil winds from the West are blowing over Hōrai; and the magical atmosphere, alas! is shrinking away before them" (ibid., 178).

48. "Mosquitoes," 212.

49. "Insect-Musicians," 80; "Mosquitoes," 207. It is worth recalling that in the concluding passage of "Insect-Musicians" referred to here, and quoted earlier at length, Hearn remarks of the Japanese that "in the knowledge of the natural ... they exceed us like the Greeks of old" ("Insect-Musicians," 80). Such positive references to the ancient Greeks abound in his work. They function as another implicit autobiographical link based on memory and, perhaps, reincarnation, for Hearn was intensely aware of his Greek heritage on his mother's side. In this connection as well, insects play a mediating role: "it should be interesting to the Japanese student to know that his own people accord with the old Greeks in their appreciation of insect music as one of the great charms of country life" (*Insects and Greek Poetry* [unpaginated]).

50. See Koizumi Bon, "Yanagita Kunio," in Hirakawa, *Koizumi Yakumo jiten*, 653–55; Michiko Yusa, "Nishida and Hearn," *Monumenta Nipponica* 51 (1996): 309–16.

51. Hagiwara Sakutarō, "Nihon e no kaiki," in *Hagiwara Sakutarō zenshū*, 5 vols., ed. Murō Saisei et al. (Tokyo: Shinchōsha, 1960), 4: 477. The Shōwa period lasted from 1926 to 1988.

52. Satō Haruo, "Den'en no yūutsu," in *Teihon Satō Haruo zenshū*, 38 vols. (Kyoto: Rinsen Shoten, 1998–2001), 3: 221. For an alternate English rendering of this passage in the context of a complete translation of the novella, see Francis B. Tenney, trans., *The Sick Rose: A Pastoral Elegy* (Honolulu: University of Hawaii Press, 1993), 40. The narrator's paraphrase of Hearn's pronouncement appears to have conflated the famous essay on the grass-lark ("Kusa-Hibari") with the passage on reincarnation from the end of the "Gaki" essay (quoted earlier); both essays appear in *Kottō*. Satō Haruo was a passionate devotee of Hearn's work, and even translated a selection of his American writings (*Koizumi Yakumo shoki bunshū: Sentō tōhanki hoka shihen* [Tokyo: Hakusuisha, 1934]).

From *Wakan sansai zue*. Courtesy of the C. V. Starr East Asian Library, Columbia University.

CHAPTER EIGHT

Didactic Nature: Exhibiting Nation and Empire at the Ueno Zoological Gardens

Ian Miller

On the afternoon of 20 March 1882, Japan's first modern zoo, the Ueno Zoological Gardens, located in Tokyo's Ueno Park, opened its gates to an eager crowd of some seven hundred people. Today, some one hundred and twenty years later, Japan is home to more zoos than any other country in the world save the United States, and over one third of the Japanese population visits a zoological garden or aquarium each year. This percentage is nearly matched in the United States, where more people visit zoos annually than attend all professional baseball, football, and basketball games combined.[1] In other words, the world's two largest capitalist economies are also home to the globe's greatest concentrations of zoological gardens, a situation that prompted writer and zoo curator Nippashi Kazuaki to rank Japan and the United States as the world's two "great zoo powers" (*dōbutsuen taikoku*).[2] Although his remark may have been somewhat tongue-in-cheek, Nippashi is correct in tying zoological gardens to political and cultural power. In a manner akin to the institutions in Europe and the United States on which it was modeled, the opening of the state-run Ueno Zoological Gardens marked a departure from prior practices of animal spectatorship in Japan.[3] The zoo, as a new form of didactic spectacle, seemed to marshal the animal kingdom in support of Japanese claims to membership in the international community of civilized humanity, a cultural and scientific distinction that carried significant political consequences in the nineteenth century.

The display of captive nonhuman animals as signs of strength, munificence, and distinction has a history that stretches far back into the human past.[4] The Aztecs maintained an extensive menagerie; Charlemagne kept collections of captive animals as emblems of his potency; and the circus played a crucial role in ancient Roman social and political life. As the first section of this chapter will discuss, Japan, too, has its own traditions of popular animal spectatorship, dating back several centuries. In nineteenth-century Japan, as in Europe and the United States, modern zoological gardens drew on these cultural antecedents, recalibrating and regulating them according to the new logic of modernity. Zoos such as Ueno were arenas for the exposition of imperial beneficence and national progress. They marked a nation's international place according to an increasingly homogenized set of criteria and channeled heterogeneous cultural practices into artificial landscapes that were in the process of being replicated, in various configurations, in capitals and cities around the globe. The present chapter traces the cultural emergence of Japan's first and most influential zoo—the Ueno Museum Attached Zoological Garden, as the institution was formally known until it became the Imperial Museum Zoological Garden in 1889—identifying some of the key ways in which the gardens produced knowledge and naturalized power during Japan's Meiji era (1868–1912).

Like all zoological gardens, the Meiji-period zoo ordered nature—through the bodies of captive animals—in the service of humanity. More precisely, the early Ueno Zoo provided a medium through which the imperialist and nationalist culture of modernity could be inscribed in the register of nature and then broadcast to mass audiences on an unprecedented scale. This feat was accomplished through a series of deceptively simple moves, communicating ideology and molding practice via structured human encounters with captive live animals.

As scholars of museum studies have long recognized, the meaning of an object is inflected by the context in which it is exhibited. The removal of fauna from its natural habitats to such highly urbanized environments as Ueno Park, the center of the modern Japanese state-run exhibitionary complex, alters the ways in which it is understood. Consequently, it is necessary to view the zoological garden as a cultural formation embedded in the wider political and social milieu rather than treat the institution or its collection as discrete entities. Understood in this way, the zoo comprises a collection of nonhuman animals ordered according to cultural and scientific taxonomies, whose construction and functions are shaped by a multitude of factors. Labels and guidebooks, lectures and safari stories, textbooks and the built environment all influenced the meaning of the zoogoing experience in Meiji Japan. These textual and architectural practices, in turn, were informed by the wider concerns of the day. Put succinctly, animals were collected, cataloged, and made to *mean* something in the Meiji-period zoo. Furthermore, those meanings were almost always addressed, whether directly or obliquely, to the intertwined subjects of imperial dominion and national identity.

The ties between the Ueno Zoo and the museum to which it was "attached" were more than incidental. Until 1924 the Ueno Zoo operated as a subsidiary component of the National Museum that was also located in Ueno Park. As part of the museum, the zoo was chartered as an institution of didactic enlightenment. At a certain level, both the zoo and the museum were built with an eye to enriching the minds of the nation's populace, to cultivating behaviors and opinions deemed valuable by the Meiji state and its supporters. The functions of the two institutions differed in some key ways, however. Whereas the museum, among other things, acted as guarantor of the nation's cultural provenance by rendering the diversity of the past into a national narrative, the zoological garden drafted animals and nature into the service of the Japanese nation-state and its claims to representing a national civilization. In performing these functions, both institutions addressed domestic and international audiences. Internally, they worked as didactic spectacles, communicating information and speaking to the distribution of social and cultural power in modern Japan. Externally, they served as venues for the exhibition of Japanese claims to cultural parity with the West and superiority within Asia, as the second section of the chapter will discuss.

As Kay Anderson points out in her work on the history of Australian zoological gardens, the zoo is a creation of modern western European culture that flourished in the context of European imperialism.[5] Human order reigns within the walls of the zoo as the primacy of human culture over animal nature is reasserted at every turn, and this order is presented as both benevolent and rational. One of the primary conceits of the zoological garden and European imperialism has always been that educated humans, much like colonial administrators, know how to care for animals better than animals or imperial subjects themselves. From the day the London Zoo opened its gates to the public in 1828, modern zoos have been recognized as venues for the demonstration of caring and compassion, as places where royalty, governments, members of the upper classes, and everyday patrons alike can put their generosity—toward the animals or toward their social inferiors—on display for all to see.

In zoological gardens around the world this ideological assertion of power has been supported by a common rhetoric. The institutional mission of zoos is almost always tied to notions of scientific progress, popular education, and healthful recreation; and, as the imperial age approached its zenith in the nineteenth century, new orthodoxies of "proper" animal treatment were emerging on a transnational scale. In this respect, zoos were (and still are) moral showcases, providing clearly recognizable venues for the display of national compassion towards the (seemingly) helpless, voiceless animals behind the bars. Even within the confines of zoos, the human dialogue with animals, as pointed out in the introduction of this volume, remains decidedly one-sided. The "humane" treatment of captive animals arbitrated judgments about national civilization and racial or ethnic evolution in an age when such attributions could mean the difference between liberty and repression, particularly in the case of countries threatened by imperialism. It should not be surprising, then, that the Ueno Zoo was not only Japan's first zoo, but the first zoological garden in Asia not constructed under a colonial regime.

Of course, during the Meiji era, as now, people did not consciously go to the zoo to "enact narratives of moral development" or "situate themselves on the empowered side of the human-animal dualism." They went to have fun. Tokyoites and out-of-towners alike went to Ueno to see animals who had been made famous in storybooks and news articles, to satisfy their curiosity about the workings of nature, to distract their children, and to enjoy the park's famous cherry blossoms. School children went because administrators scheduled highly anticipated field trips to the zoo, complete with instruction guides for teachers, a practice that began soon after the Ueno complex opened. The Ueno Zoo was a place to escape the strictures of everyday life and seek respite from the gloom of an increasingly denatured cityscape. Visitors went there to relax in an environment that seemed to transport nature right into the heart of the metropole.

It is this state of leisured recreation that makes zoos such effective conduits of ideology. Most often, zoogoers engage in sanctioned activities not because they must, but voluntarily and with pleasure. The zoological garden makes leisure activities productive, using its displays and captive animals to convert scientific knowledge and political concerns into lighthearted spectacles. These motives and operations are still very much in force today, and Tokyoites still flock to Ueno. Now, thirty years after reaching a world-historical high of over eight million patrons per year during the "panda boom" of the 1970s and 1980s, some three million people go to the Ueno Zoo each year. Currently, the zoo, an institution that was the epitome of novelty in the 1880s, is comfortably woven into the social fabric of Japan's capital and largest city. A popular cliché holds that all Tokyoites visit the zoo at least four times during their lifetimes: first when they are children, then as teenagers on a date with their sweethearts, next when they have children of their own, and finally as grandparents escorting their grandchildren.[6] The zoo, it appears, has been carefully woven into the fabric of modern Japanese life.

BEFORE THE ZOO: ANIMAL SPECTACLE IN EARLY-MODERN JAPAN

In a 1935 essay entitled "Dōbutsuen ron" (On the zoological garden), zoologist Kashiwaoka Tamio lamented the state of Japan's zoos, arguing that, when compared with those of such "first-class countries" (*ittōkoku*) as the United States and Germany, they appeared to have "barely progressed beyond the realm of the sideshow [*misemono*]."[7] A good zoo, he said, was an essential part of any world metropolis, and the Ueno Zoo lagged behind current international standards. In Kashiwaoka's opinion, Japanese zoological gardens lacked in research facilities, educational outreach programs, and collection activities. Meanwhile, such cities as London and New York housed institutions that represented more than simple animal spectacles; they were instead "instructional gardens" (*kyōzaien*) dedicated to preserving animals on the threshold of extinction and educating the wider public. If Japan's zoos, led by Ueno, failed to close this gap, Kashiwaoka feared, they risked embarrassing not only themselves, but Japan as a nation. More attention, he argued, had to be paid to the state of the nation's zoological gardens if Japan wished to count itself as a "civilized country" (*bunmeikoku*).[8]

Whether he meant to do so or not, Kashiwaoka made a historical argument when he compared Japanese zoos to "sideshows" (*misemono*). Sideshows have a history in Japan that probably stretches back at least as far as the Heian period (794–1185). During the early-modern Tokugawa era (1600–1868), they became an increasingly common sight around temples and marketplaces. Early-modern sideshows like the ones Kashiwaoka referred to were fundamentally commercial enterprises, and they provided the primary viewing ground for live exotic animals.[9] In such early-modern cities as Edo (today's Tokyo) and Osaka, dancing dog and monkey acts could be found next door to human "freaks," lifelike animated dolls, supposedly holy relics, and novel technologies imported from abroad. Cows with six legs were kept in small pens, porcupines were placed in metal cages and poked with rods to make their quills stand on end, and tiger hunts were reenacted with actual tigers or large dogs costumed to look like big cats. All the while, hawkers stood outside, calling customers to curtained entrances, where they paid a small fee to pass inside and see the proffered goods.

For Kashiwaoka, the sideshow symbolized the denigrated Tokugawa past, a feudal place that catered to the whims of unenlightened commoners, luring them in by appealing to their basest desires and spitting them out none the better (albeit somewhat poorer) for the experience. Japan's zoos, he argued, needed to enlighten the populace, and they were failing. "There are still many in this country," he wrote in evident ire, "who cannot tell a lion from a tiger from a leopard."[10] In Kashiwaoka's opinion, zoos were places where caged animals should be put to use as pedagogical instruments in the service of scientific advancement and national development, places that would teach the proper names and places for things to the public. His critical assessment of early-modern Japan's vibrant culture of animal spectatorship highlights the fact that, although Japanese had been looking at captive animals for centuries, the meanings solicited by those encounters changed significantly over time.

Early-modern sideshows may not have placed a premium on the generation of scientific consciousness or the development of a knowledgeable national citizenry, but the fact remains that the fundamental activity of both zoos and sideshows is the exhibition of animals caged for human purposes.[11] In this regard the zoo owes an obvious debt to early modernity. Early-modern Japanese had the opportunity to examine a diverse assortment of exotic specimens. According to Isono Naohide's estimates, over ninety varieties of exotic birds were imported into the Japanese islands during the early-modern period, including an ostrich, cassowaries, and numerous varieties of pheasant.[12]

Some of these creatures made their way into private collections. Others, however, were made available to the wider public, for a fee, of course. By the mid-nineteenth century, urbanites in the country's largest cities—Edo, Osaka, Kyoto, and Nagoya, at the very least—could view birds in decidedly more refined environments than the sideshow. Most notable were the so-called peacock teahouses (*kujaku jaya*) and flower-and-bird teahouses (*kachō jaya*), which chapter 4 has already introduced. Edo, in particular, was home to a lively teahouse culture. These enterprises, which had long been set up temporarily for festivals, developed into permanent structures over time, growing in number as the city's human population increased. Proliferation brought specialization, and some houses began using rare animals to rope in customers. One scholar has estimated that there were as many as twenty-nine thousand teahouses in Edo by 1800, of which, of course, only a small minority housed animals.[13]

Predictably, Edo's vibrant commercial districts of Asakusa and Ryōgoku were home to the most innovative businesses, which included deer teahouses (*shika jaya*) and exotic-beast teahouses (*chinjū jaya*) in addition to the more conventional and more numerous flower-and-bird variety. Exotic-beast teahouses exhibited foxes and monkeys, among other creatures.[14] Patrons paid a small fee to enter, then paid a premium on the refreshments that they purchased while they sat under trees and gazed at the kept animals. Many of the grounds incorporated small gardens alongside the cages.

Larger, more costly exotic megafauna—the big cats, bears, camels, and elephants that most people associate with zoos today—tended to appear in sideshows rather than in the more quaint teahouses. Sideshows were mobile, allowing their owners to move from place to place in pursuit of new audiences and greater profits. The list of rare or unusual mammals who arrived in Tokugawa Japan is shorter than that of the more common birds, but it is nonetheless impressive, belying any assertion that Japan was entirely sequestered from the outside world during the Tokugawa period. Spectacular captives such as leopards, tigers, camels, and Asian elephants arrived during the eighteenth and nineteenth centuries, making their way into private collections and sideshows. In sideshows, these animals became featured attractions, moving frequently in order to maintain the sense of novelty that lured patrons. The systems for advertising such events, which thrive on word of mouth and the ephemeral thrill of the unexpected, grew increasingly complex with time. By the middle of the nineteenth century, polychrome souvenir broadsheets circulated through urban areas advertising the latest arrivals and most shocking discoveries.[15]

As Tsukamoto Manabu notes, and as several chapters in this volume serve to underscore, the use of animals as emblems of power or markers of authority was fairly widespread during the Tokugawa period.[16] Samurai over the centuries used horses, hawks, and hunting dogs to express publicly their political authority. Live animals and animal products were incorporated into the official system of status discrimination in early-modern Japan, becoming signs of social distinction. Ownership of certain varieties of hawks, for example, was highly regulated. As Brett Walker has demonstrated, the taste for these markers of distinction drove early-modern trappers to pursue desirable species with unprecedented vigor, placing strains on Hokkaido's raptor population in the process. The use of these animals, primarily in hunting and falconry, carried heavy symbolic weight, providing an effective means for the expression of political power.[17] Much as in the case of the English foxhunt, when samurai traversed territories in pursuit of game, they could simultaneously survey their possessions and make themselves visible to their subjects.[18] For elites who did not, strictly speaking, need the calories gained from the kill, the hunt expressed power over life and death, humans and nonhuman animals, territory and time.

Such practices were not unusual during the early-modern era, but the public display of caged exotic animals as explicit markers of political power was decidedly less common. Collections of caged animals held by samurai were generally private and available only to select individuals. Although the number of such collections increased gradually during the late eighteenth and early nineteenth centuries, Tokugawa Japan was not home to anything comparable in scale to the royal menageries of early-modern Europe.[19] There were a very few instances in which exotic animal-captives were conspicuously put to public use as totems of political power, however. The best-known example is almost certainly that of the "Shogun's elephant," an Asian pachyderm kept by the eighth Tokugawa ruler, Tokugawa Yoshimune (1684–1751), who, as already noted in chapter 4, harbored a variety of exceptional zoological interests. The story of the elephant is remarkable in a number of ways, not least because the Tokugawa leaders did not maintain significant menageries. In a certain sense, therefore, the elephant was an anomaly. At the same time, the human uses to which the elephant was put clearly demonstrate the abundance of venues for the commodification and symbolic use of unusual and exotic fauna that existed in early-modern Japan.

In 1728, two Asian elephants of Vietnamese origin, one male and one female, were offloaded from a Chinese ship in the port of Nagasaki. The pair was destined for the city of Edo, seat of the Tokugawa shogunate. Unfortunately, the female died soon after arrival, but the male began the long walk to the capital the following year.[20] He did not make the trip alone. Somewhat reminiscent of the elaborately outfitted and regulated journeys made by domain lords as well as foreign legations to hold audience with the shogun in Edo, the elephant was accompanied by a well-equipped entourage that included no fewer than seventeen people at its smallest.[21] In major population centers such as Osaka, the size of the contingent grew considerably as the animal was paraded before gawking crowds who turned out to see the extraordinary beast.[22] The elephant's itinerary itself was laden with meaning. As the elephant paraded from Nagasaki to Edo, it reinforced the idea of Edo as the political center of the country. The extraordinary animal may have lingered in Kyoto, even making its way to the imperial court, but its final destination was Edo castle, not the palace of the emperor. Such was the geography of Tokugawa power.

As a possession of the shogun, the elephant was, not surprisingly, accorded special status and treated with a considerable amount of caution. The expense of its transport was transferred to domains along the route north, which were commanded to ready large amounts of fresh food in preparation for the beast's arrival and to renovate bridges in anticipation of its tremendous weight. Commoners along the road were directed to extinguish fires and remain quiet as the entourage passed. Dogs and cats were to be locked away, horses and oxen to be kept from calling out so as not to spook the behemoth. The shogun's elephant was even granted an imperial court rank as part of its inspection by the emperor in Kyoto, where the procession stopped for a short rest before continuing on to Edo. In all, the journey took about two and a half months, during which time the elephant passed not only through the southern metropolises of Osaka and Kyoto but through hundreds of smaller towns and villages along the way, providing a show—and a public display of the international, and even interspecial, reach of shogunal prestige—for tens of thousands of people.

Two days after the contingent arrived in Edo, Yoshimune viewed the elephant. A wide variety of shogunal retainers, including some of quite mean rank, were shown the animal, and word of the astonishing creature kept by the shogun quickly spread. Yoshimune ordered the animal housed in one of his residences and he displayed it on occasion. Clearly, the vision of such a mighty beast kept captive at the whim of the ruler constituted an impressive display of power. Elephant-patterned goods became all the rage in Edo, and stories about the animal circulated throughout the archipelago, appearing in numerous books and circulars. The kabuki actor Ichikawa Danjūrō II (1688–1758) even incorporated an elephant scene into one of his stage performances.[23]

By 1730, however, Yoshimune's interest in the elephant had apparently worn off, and the shogunate decided that it could no longer bear the cost of keeping it. The search for a suitable buyer produced no results, however, and the elephant continued to be housed in the ruler's residence near Edo Bay. Two years later, in 1732, keepers hit on a creative way of defraying the cost of keeping the animal: they began packaging its dung and selling it in Edo and Osaka as a cure for smallpox.[24] When, thirteen years after the elephant first arrived in Edo, Yoshimune finally decided that, smallpox cure or no, he no longer had use for the animal, it was announced that it would be passed on to a peasant named Gennosuke residing in the nearby village of Nakano. Gennosuke hoped to capitalize on the popularity of the smallpox remedy and quickly put the animal to work. His treatment of the elephant was apparently rather harsh, however, and the animal died a year later at twenty-one, an extremely young age for its species.[25]

The elephant's value by no means ended with its death. Upon receiving word of its demise, the shogunate ordered that the animal's hide be removed and delivered to Edo castle, after which it was sold to a glue maker in Nara, who resold it to someone in Kyoto for inclusion in one of the city's increasingly common *bussankai*, or exhibitions of natural products.[26] Animal products were regular features at such exhibitions, circulating through a variety of contexts where city crowds could examine them. All or part of an individual animal might end up on display or for sale at an exhibit of pharmacopoeia (*yakuhinkai*), a botanical display (*honzōkai*), or in a collection of natural-history specimens (*hakubutsukai*).[27] The elephant's skull, tusks, and the skin from its trunk were also preserved. They were eventually installed at a temple in Nakano, where they provided an enticement at temple unveilings (*kaichō*), luring patrons and their money into the sacred precincts on select occasions. The skull was put on regular public display sometime in the late nineteenth century. It remained a tourist attraction until Allied bombs destroyed the temple where it was housed in 1945.[28]

The story of Yoshimune's elephant draws attention to the diverse ways in which early-modern Japanese utilized animals, both alive and dead, within their symbolic and financial economies. The different contexts through which the young animal and its remains circulated shifted it in and out of what Arjun Appadurai might call the "commodity phase" of its social life—placing it in situations where its exchangeability for another object or currency became its most relevant feature.[29] Without considering the transactions of social capital—the prestige that accrued to the shogunate, for example—that proliferated around the animal at nearly all stages of its career, the elephant went through no fewer (and perhaps several more) than five such moments of commercial exchange: it was purchased by Chinese merchants, sold to the shogun, transferred to Gennosuke, passed to a glue maker, and put on display at a *bussankai*. The elephant's novelty and symbolic potency also spawned a range of ancillary products, engaging the animal in the elaborate systems of commodification that made early-modern Japan's urban environments some of the most dynamic on the planet.

This process of animal commodification and exchange accelerated and broadened across Japan's "long nineteenth century." Related dynamics were at work in the Meiji-period zoological garden. There, however, animal commodities were caught up in much more extensive international exchange networks that moved larger quantities of more diverse wildlife across greater distances at unprecedented speeds. By recontextualizing animals the zoo transformed the early-modern taste for animal spectacle into a productive use of leisure time, mobilizing the spectator's gaze in support of the Meiji state's modernizing efforts. Using the structured contrast between human spectators and animal captives typical of zoo culture, the state-employed managers of the Ueno Zoological Gardens sought to redefine Japan's place in both international and natural terms.

THE NATURE OF IMPERIALISM: SEPARATING HUMANS AND ANIMALS AT UENO ZOO

Across the nineteenth-century world, the significance of the (implicitly, nonhuman) animal—as both a means of production and symbol of human progress away from our presumably animal past—remained closely tied to notions of national strength and cultural progress. It is in this connection that the special significance of the Ueno Zoo, as Asia's first zoological garden not built under a colonial government, reveals itself. The most fundamental ordering principle of the modern zoo is the separation of "human" patrons from the "animals" on the other side of the bars. This was particularly true of nineteenth-century zoos, which featured the sort of stark, barred cages that many people today associate with prisons and animal cruelty.[30] In nineteenth-century Japan, maintaining this human-animal separation was a matter of no less than national concern. Western imperialism was approaching its full meridian at the time of the Meiji Restoration in 1868, and the country's political and intellectual leaders quickly became aware of the dangers attached to being labeled "brutish" or "wild." Indeed, notions of animality had mediated Japan's first canonical encounter with the imperialist West, namely, the arrival of the United States Navy's "black ships" and their commander, Commodore Matthew C. Perry (1794–1858), in Edo Bay in 1853. The official published account of the American expedition reveals the conceptual centrality of the human-animal divide to the imperialist enterprise, highlighting the ways in which theriomorphic rhetoric—the attribution of animal qualities to human beings—facilitated the division of the human world into "civilized" and "barbarian" (to use Perry's nomenclature) peoples.[31]

Perry's first sight of Japanese sumo wrestlers is the most telling example of this pattern. "Some twenty-five or thirty huge men, naked with the exception of a narrow girdle around the loins, were paraded before us. Never have I seen grouped together so many brawny men, giving a better idea of an equal number of stall-fed bulls than human beings."[32] The ambivalence that was built into Perry's understanding of animality acted as a sort of cultural gyroscope, providing a mechanism through which manifestations of Japanese vitality and strength, embodied in the "hardness" of the "naked giant" sumo wrestlers, which might have disturbed his assumptions of American superiority, could be converted into signs of animality and therefore barbarism. Perry was further granted the opportunity to touch and inspect one of the "massive" athletes. "I was requested to feel the hardness of his double bull neck. When he observed that I manifested much surprise, he exhibited his gratification by a self-satisfied grunt."[33] The stoic wrestler did not speak even in the heat of the bloody sumo demonstration that followed, expressing his competitive spirit by "constantly howling and screeching at the top of his lungs, making a noise similar to that of dogs in combat."[34] In this recounting, which was closely tied to the threat of violence and warfare, Japanese seem to oscillate between humanity and animality, never emerging as full-fledged civilized people. Conversely, Perry and his contingent stand as consummately humane exemplars of civilized behavior. The anxiety of a threatening encounter is thus converted into an affirmation of difference and superiority.

The paired attribution of sublimity and depravity is not unique to nineteenth-century American conceptions of the animal. As anthropologist Richard Tapper notes, such dualistic animal metaphors surface again and again in a variety of cultures, including Japan's.[35] Within these dualistic structures of thought, animals, or those painted as animalistic, are either elevated to the realm of godliness or relegated to the status of the denigrated "other." There is no muddy in-between, only alternation between these two extremes, one godly, the other beyond the pale. In 1853, the Japanese wrestlers' display of prowess appears to have both attracted and repelled Perry. His response was to portray the foreigners as almost superhuman, their size and strength pushing at the boundaries of what was humanly possible.

Confronted with the question of how to depict this display of potency in a people he considered inferior, Perry chose the metaphor of the bull, a typical mascot of virility and physical strength in the American cultural vernacular.[36] In this bodily sense, the wrestler is a creature to be both admired and feared. At the same time, it is clear that Perry's intent was not simply to praise when he described the "giants" in animalistic terms. Bulls and dogs, the two animals to whom Perry likens the wrestlers, function metaphorically as symbols of impropriety, danger, and inferiority, insofar as they require human discipline in order to be domesticated. In this subordinate aspect, the wrestlers are not highly trained athletes, but brutes who cannot live up to the etiquette of civilized interaction. They do not speak, as humans do, but rather grunt like beasts.

In what is certainly an unintended evocation of the zoo's function, Perry matter-of-factly described the wrestlers' performance as existing solely for the "edification and amusement" of the American delegation.[37] The rhetorical move is typical of imperialist travelogues and, indeed, imperialist ideology in general. When Perry placed himself in the position of the amused observer, he insulated himself from the object under observation, situating himself above and apart from the entertaining (animal) object. This same removed, contemplative stance is, as the following section of this chapter will discuss in further detail, the crux of the zoogoing experience. Zoological gardens, like natural-history museums and botanical gardens, provide an encounter with a natural world that is always already objectified, a situation that empowers the observer, placing him or her in the position of the knower rather than the known, the looker rather than the object under consideration.

The differentiation between humans and animals active in Perry's account was integral to a matrix of similar binaries, ones that emerged as the basic structure of modern culture in Japan and elsewhere. The Ueno Zoological Garden was built in accordance with these homologous oppositions, and they were reiterated daily within its walls. To name those most obviously at work inside the zoo, they included human/animal, culture/nature, civilized/barbarian, present/past, self/other, native/exotic, domesticated/wild, discourse/body, and rational/superstitious.[38] As the cultural critic Michel de Certeau has argued, such oppositions provided the foundation of modern consciousness, actively segregating regions of culture and legitimizing one side of each binary at the expense of the other. Through the manufacture of difference, these dualisms form a feedback loop with the uneven social relationships that structure modern societies, drawing on inequality even as they facilitate its reproduction and naturalization.

For de Certeau, the "group (or individual) is legitimized by what it excludes … and it discovers its faith in the confession that it extracts from a dominated being."[39] This "confession" takes the form of knowledge, systematic notions garnered from the effective transformation of the "other"—typically the animal in the case of the zoo, the sumo wrestler in Perry's instance—into an object to be studied or observed. Modern life constitutes itself through these acts of exclusion and extraction, and the nineteenth-century zoo sought to realize these distinctions in lived space. The early zoo was a mechanism that, at its root, worked to extract knowledge, both cultural and scientific, from the dominated bodies of the animals housed in its cages, drafting that knowledge into the service of a variety of concerns that had little to do with the actual nonhuman animals penned inside. The Meiji zoo converted "nature" and "animals" into signifiers of "culture" and "civilization." The taxonomic perfection of Ueno's highly ordered landscape, which implied the possibility of objective knowledge and cast patrons in the role of inquisitors seeking a confession, transposed the bewildering diversity of the natural world into a spectacular affirmation of Japanese humanity. This momentous conversion was enabled primarily by the instatement of the human-animal dualism that certifies orthodox conceptions of the modern human subject.

Human-animal dualism was deeply embedded in nineteenth-century Western thought. The idea reached its canonical form in René Descartes's

(1596–1650) *Discours de la méthode*, published in 1637, in which the author famously argued that animals were more akin to automata than to humans. Such a conception took it for granted—indeed, it was predicated on the insistence—that animals were devoid of creativity, feelings, and language. Conversely, human beings were not the fellows but rather the inverse of animals, standing proudly, and volubly, apart from the realm of beasts primarily through the creative act of speech.[40] In the context of Cartesian dualism, the "howling and screeching" of Perry's sumo wrestlers took on a more damning significance.

At first glance, the observations that Charles Darwin outlined in his *On the Origin of Species by Means of Natural Selection*, published in 1859, would seem to undermine such a stark Cartesian bifurcation.[41] After all, from an evolutionary perspective, all creatures are aligned along a common continuum, a conception that bears greater resonance with the Platonic-Christian idea of the Great Chain of Being, or even with the Buddhist notion of karmic interconnectedness emphasized in early Japanese animal tales (see chapters 1 and 2 of this volume), than it does with the French philosopher's strict dualism.[42] In evolutionary terms, humans and animals differ only in the course of their development. In actual practice, however, the blurring of the line between animals and humans that Darwin enabled served, ironically, to augment the efficacy of the sort of theriomorphic logic used by Commodore Perry, logic that was crucial to the practices of imperialism. When viewed through nineteenth-century eyes, natural selection could appear to describe the means by which human superiority had been established, displacing the source of separation between man and beast from an external deity to a process internal to all organisms.[43] In effect, Darwinism facilitated the inscription of human hierarchies into the register of nature. As Julia Thomas has ably demonstrated in her analysis of social Darwinist ideology in Japanese discourse, this mode of inscription operated as effectively in late nineteenth-century and twentieth-century Japan as it did in Europe and the United States.[44]

A 1902 special issue of the popular youth magazine *Shōnen sekai* (Boy's world), published in celebration of the twentieth anniversary of the Ueno Zoo's opening, illustrates some of the ways in which the institution may have put this theriomorphic logic into practice. As in many similar publications, the issue's front pages are devoted to paintings and photographs of the zoo's most popular or unusual animals. These included a fierce polar bear purchased from the famous German animal dealer Carl Hagenbeck (1844–1913), a pair of lions given to the Japanese emperor by the king of Ethiopia, a tiger received from a sultan, an American porcupine, a large Japanese bear, a rare breed of Mongolian wild horse acquired from China at the urging of senior statesman Itō Hirobumi (1841–1909), an Australian cassowary (the "fire-eating bird" of chapter 4), camels procured during the Sino-Japanese War (1894–1895), an Indian elephant, and, finally, an African hippopotamus, mouth gaping wide. Whereas in a typical issue of *Shōnen sekai*, the zoo photos might have shared space with other icons of masculine culture—sumo wrestlers, university athletes, military heroes, or impressive machines like trains and warships—this special number was devoted entirely to Ueno, and so its animal stars monopolize the bill. The painted cover depicts a virile male lion under a large banner reading ZOO in Japanese. The animal appears to be stepping through the bars of its cage, walking out to greet the reader.[45]

One of the longest articles takes the form of a tour, mapping out a route for readers to follow as they stroll, in fantasy or reality, through the gardens.[46] The narrative walk begins, logically enough, at the zoo gates, informing readers of the types of ticket available and how to purchase them. It then provides a truncated version of the zoo's extensive list of rules:

1. Ticket holders who are drunk and/or disorderly may be kept from entering the grounds or may be removed from the gardens.
2. Pets and other animals may not be brought into the gardens.
3. Visitors may not throw sticks or rocks into the cages or threaten animals with walking sticks, umbrellas, and the like.
4. Visitors may not feed the animals without permission.
5. Visitors may not leave designated pathways or pick flowers on the grounds.[47]

These rules, probably familiar to one degree or another to zoogoers around the world even today, were posted on a large placard that all visitors passed as they entered the grounds. They were also printed, in various versions, in official guidebooks sold at zoo kiosks.

The magazine, after providing this list of regulations, makes explicit one of the zoo's primary functions, namely, the alignment of Japanese public practice with Western norms. The rules for proper conduct were nearly identical to those in European and American zoos, and the model of behavior at

Ueno was often explicitly foreign. After urging proper conduct at all times, the author chides his young audience with a simple, if somewhat startling by today's standards, statement: "Westerners never break these rules." The implied follow-up, of course, is "so neither should you."[48] The magazine holds the imperialist West up as a normative exemplar against which Japanese subjects were to measure their own human behavior.

As they walked and looked, visitors became participants in an ideological project that sought to separate them from beastliness and barbarism, placing them—together with Westerners—on the empowered side of the dualisms identified by de Certeau and mobilized by Perry. The ideal zoo-going experience was to be one of civilized curiosity, a state made evident, in part, by the structured contrast with the wild animals on the other side of the bars. Those animals could be made to stand for more than an overgeneralized notion of nature. The specific content of a particular animal's story could be shaped through labels, guidebooks, postcards, display architecture, and the outside discourses that were inscribed in youth magazines, children's books, and textbooks, which regularly featured specifically identifiable animals from Ueno's collection.

This sort of disciplinary calculus could be put to work not only to align Japan with the West, but also in support of Japan's own imperial project. The imagined tour makes the latter function explicit when it none-too-subtly links Ueno's three captive camels, one of the zoo's most popular exhibits, with the Chinese nation. The camels, captured and put to use by the Imperial Japanese Army during the Sino-Japanese War before being shipped to Tokyo for display in the zoo, were housed in the popular "live-animal war trophy" (*senrihin dōbutsu*) section of the zoo, which was constructed in 1897 using 4,600 yen donated by the Meiji emperor.[49] "At first glance, the camel appears to be just a clumsy, quiet, somewhat stupid animal, but its actual disposition is quite bad," the author writes. "Foreign sources say that camels are actually depraved beasts. This is certainly true. If camels were people, they'd be just like the Chinese."[50]

A sketch next to the passage shows a vaguely anthropomorphized camel sinking its teeth into the back of a supine horse, a "noble" animal regularly associated with the Meiji emperor and the imperial army in the iconography of the period.[51] In this case, in fact, the horse probably *was* the former property of the imperial army. The camel enclosure was situated alongside a pen for former army horses (*gunba*) who had been awarded special medals for meritorious service to the Japanese nation in public ceremonies at the zoo. Labels in front of each of the cages included specific, often lengthy, biographies of each animal.[52] The magazine reproduced and circulated certain of these stories, and the entire special issue, like numerous competing youth magazines and story collections, speaks—as do the narratives of the colonial dog seen in chapter 6—to the project of empire, using animals to tell of foreign adventure and imperial conquest.

CIVILIZED BY NATURE: THE ZOOLOGICAL GARDEN AND MEIJI JAPAN'S EXHIBITIONARY COMPLEX

In the mid-nineteenth century, Japanese were simultaneously confronted with the spectacle of Western power and the power of Western spectacle. The construction of the Japanese zoo was one part of the complex response to this confrontation. As Japanese began traveling abroad, they encountered an Occidental culture obsessed with exhibitions and visual consumption.[53] Nineteenth-century Europe was home to one of the central transformations of the modern age, the translation of the world into a system of representations that claimed to be both objective and comprehensive. It was neither, of course; but the period unquestionably saw an immense proliferation of venues built for public display, places where citizens could go to indulge their taste for spectacle. Put simply, like the Tokugawa-period urbanites discussed earlier, nineteenth-century Europeans liked to look: look at fine art, look at archeological objects, look at the latest technology, look at botanical samples, look at exotic people, and look at themselves. They also enjoyed looking at nonhuman animals, both exotic and domesticated. Generally speaking, in terms of raw attendance, zoos in Europe were second only to the more transient national and international exhibitions, a pattern common to Meiji Japan as well.

The idea of putting unusual animals on display was hardly new to nineteenth-century Japanese; but as travelers to Europe and North America soon realized, the Western regime of examination differed substantially from the sorts of visual practices that were familiar at home. For one thing, Europe's governments and upper classes poured capital into public institutions dedicated to focusing the wandering eyes of their subjects. The same period witnessed the birth of the modern zoological garden, the museum, and the botanical garden, all public cultural institutions dedicated, rhetorically at least, to apolitical recreation, education, and the development of specialized knowledge. It quickly became evident to Japanese observers that this culture of didactic spectacle might be one of the keys to Western commercial productivity and national strength. The Ueno Zoo was constructed as part of Japan's answer to these spectacles of power and progress. The zoo was a key component of Tokyo's Ueno Park exhibitionary complex, perhaps the grandest showcase for the public display of the Japanese nation-state's claims to cultural parity with the imperialist West in the late nineteenth century.[54]

Art historian Tony Bennett has traced the emergence of a new mode of seeing in late eighteenth- to mid-nineteenth-century Europe, a period that saw a deluge of curious objects—and animals—flood into European capitals from exotic colonial locales. This visual revolution involved the relocation of tremendous quantities of cultural and scientific property from the realm of private ownership—typified by cabinets of curiosities but inclusive of sideshows and the like—into "public institutions administered by the state for the benefit of an extended general public."[55] Bennett has aptly labeled the institutional constellation that developed the "exhibitionary complex," a term that encompasses everything from museums to exhibitions to zoological and botanical gardens. The institutions involved were characterized by the movement of bodies and objects into "progressively more open and public arenas where, through the representations to which they were subjected, they formed vehicles for inscribing and broadcasting messages of power" throughout society. They developed at much the same time as the penitentiary, which sits at the center of Michel Foucault's well-known study of modern criminal punishment. Whereas the exhibitionary complex exposed objects to the public gaze, however, the modern regime of penal corrections, exemplified by the relentless disciplinary gaze at work inside Jeremy Bentham's (1748–1832) Panopticon, was increasingly hidden, concealing discipline behind the solid walls of the penitentiary. Inside its gates, the behavior of inmates was subject to constant scrutiny; inmates were always available for observation.[56]

The modern zoological garden shares elements of both Bennett's exhibitionary complex and Foucault's carceral archipelago. It sits uneasily between the two, a circumstance that may help to explain the peculiar feelings of sadness that frequently accompany visits to the zoo. The nineteenth-century zoological garden was a theater of disciplinary techniques in which discipline was often represented as play or pedagogy. In fact, as Watanabe

Morio points out, modern penitentiaries, to the extent that they are institutions devoted to enabling the unhindered gaze, share common origins with the zoo.[57] Both institutions owe a great deal to technologies developed in the grand menageries of Europe's royal houses. In these extensive gardens, typified by Schoenbrunn and Versailles, the seat of the sovereign was located at the hub of a representation of the natural world, encircled by animal enclosures that appeared to radiate outward from the royal center. In theory, at least, the captive animals held in the enclosures were to be visible to the eye of the sovereign at all times. While royalty dined or entertained, their centrality to the natural order was symbolically confirmed by the landscape in which they took their leisure. Foucault notes the same dynamic: "The Panopticon is a royal menagerie; the animal is replaced by man, individual distribution by specific grouping, and the king by the machinery of a furtive power."[58]

Something similar might be said of the modern zoological garden, which owes a debt to both the menagerie and the Panopticon. The zoological garden, one can argue, is a penitentiary in which the inmate is replaced by the animal. Criminal classifications become biological nomenclature. And the furtive power of the disciplinary gaze is that of the hungry eyes of spectators. In other words, the zoo is a modern menagerie in which the gaze of the spectator mimics the gaze of the sovereign; and these masquerading monarchs or child emperors can be every bit as petulant as the absolutist rulers that they impersonate. Zoo administrators in Japan and around the world are accustomed to complaints that certain animals—perhaps instinctually given to remaining concealed—are not fully visible at all times. The cost of admission, many zoogoers assume, buys one the right to see each animal at one's own leisure. We expect zoo animals, representatives of their species and of nature itself, to conform to our will and to our expectations.

Such a discussion raises the question of how we might best characterize the place of captive animals in terms of relations of production and consumption. In the zoo, as in circuses and sideshows, live animals embody both labor and commodity. And, like Karl Marx's stereotypically tyrannical shop master, viewers and administrators both demand their "money's worth" from the animals on display. We insist that animals "perform"—often literally—for us, even if that performance is something as basic as remaining visible. Concerned as Marx was with preindustrial and industrializing societies, places where animal labor is crucial to the wider economy, he himself provided one answer to this question. In a move typical of the sharp distinction between nonhuman animals and humans commonly made during the nineteenth century, Marx classified the former alongside primitive tools as instruments of labor, arguing that they had no will and should therefore be considered simple physical conductors of their master's will. "The animal is immediately identical with its life-activity. It does not distinguish itself from it. It is *its life-activity*. Man makes his life-activity itself the object of his will and of his consciousness."[59]

This argument is too simple. It minimizes the complex question of animal consciousness, or at the very least instinct, feeling, and sensation, in favor of a simplistic notion of animal-as-object. Such a stance is echoed in the early zoo, where animals were most often presented as simple objects or scientific specimens. Should we therefore discard Marxian categorizations altogether? Tim Ingold's work suggests that retaining them while renovating our understanding of human-animal relations may lead to some troubling, if significant, conclusions. Like Ingold, I dispute the facile assertion that animals are simple tools. Caged animals are no exception. The commonly held idea that creatures in pens are akin to lazy, pampered children misses the simple reality of the situation that confronts us when we see a caged animal: before us stand living beings who have been confined for human purposes. These living beings have been transformed into embodied labor, and, if we follow Ingold's suggestions, it can be argued that the creatures in question, as labor embodied, are more akin to human slaves than to simple tools.[60] Of course, there are significant differences between a human slave and a captive silverback gorilla; but in many ways the magnitude of those differences is only as great as the differentiation between human and nonhuman primates, a differentiation given more shape and texture within the exhibitionary space of the zoo than, say, in modern primatology.

Nineteenth-century zoos laid the animal world at the feet of their patrons, offering them a series of commanding views and affording them an opportunity to play, at least temporarily, at dominion. The zoo was—and still is—literally an object lesson in power, providing spectators with a highly contextualized taste of mastery, allowing them the momentary thrill of becoming the observer rather than the observed, the sovereign rather than the subaltern, the subject rather than the object of knowledge. In the process of looking, spectators were encouraged to interiorize the knowing gaze that was generated within the exhibitionary complex, in effect becoming self-knowing and therefore self-regulating. We monitor ourselves and others as we pass through the spaces of the zoo. Through its rhetoric, the exhibitionary complex encouraged spectators to "identify with power, to see it as, if not directly theirs, then indirectly so, a force regulated and channeled by society's ruling groups but for the good of all."[61] The zoological garden, like other components of the exhibitionary complex, fostered passive consent with the ideological projects it sponsored, and may well have generated active, voluntary support.

Nineteenth-century Japanese were hardly immune to the empowering thrill that accompanied encounters with caged beasts. Members of the elite, government-sponsored Iwakura mission, who visited the United States and Western Europe from 1871 to 1873, were themselves intrigued by the elaborate animal spectacles of modern Euro-American zoos, and they apparently delighted in the feelings induced by the vision of exotic animals held captive for their viewing pleasure. The official account of the mission's travels, compiled by Kume Kunitake (1839–1931), the prominent historian who was special assistant to Iwakura Tomomi (1825–1883), head of the mission, describes numerous visits to zoological gardens and other components of the exhibitionary complex. The company's visit to London's Regent's Park Zoo, opened to the public in 1828 and destined to become one of the models for the Ueno Zoo, is particularly telling:

> In the gardens, paths meandered among hills and woods and lakes. The greenness of the trees and shrubs was offset by the brightness of the gravel paths. The wooded hills were charming in appearance. At every step one paused; at every turn one raised one's head. There was not enough time to gaze at everything. In the midst of this landscape, enclosures had been created with various different structures, and in them were kept birds and animals which had been sought and trapped all over the world. There were placid beasts such as the elephant and the camel, and ferocious creatures such as bears, wolves, and jackals. The woods quaked at the roaring of the lions, tigers, and leopards; the air shivered at the screeching of eagles, hawks, and falcons.[62]

Kume's paean to the zoo continues with a lengthy listing of the exotic animals that the group encountered. The text reveals his excitement and his desire to provide a comprehensive inventory of the creatures observed during the visit, perhaps inspired by the claims to encyclopedic representation made by the zoo itself. In a pitch-perfect evocation of one of the slogans of the modern tourist industry, Kume gushed, "There were so many things to see that we were oblivious to the fact that night was falling."[63] They were completely captivated by spectacle.

The vision of Regent's Park conveyed in Kume's account is edenic. After describing bounding kangaroos and frolicking peacocks at peace in their enclosures, Kume noted: "Inside the tropical house, where the humidity of spring was maintained by steam heat, parrots squawked and monkeys played. The air was fragrant with the scent of flowers. Small, brightly colored birds twittered as they flitted about their cages." Kume's zoo is literally a machine-made garden. It is a place where humans express benevolent command over the entirety of nature, even over the seasons. When Kume recounted the vast numbers of tropical birds stored in the garden, he was struck not only by the beauty of the specimens but by the marvel of the technologies devoted to keeping them. "If they are not kept in conditions appropriate to their natures, then even if they do not die they will waste away and will not be worth seeing. By that alone can be seen the degree to which the care of animals has progressed as a science in this country."[64]

Clearly, the experience was more than one of simple innocent wonder—although wonder is certainly a crucial aspect of the subjectivity that the zoo seeks to elicit. Rather, Kume tied the pleasures of the zoo to concrete concerns. In the nineteenth century, zoological gardens were a recognized gauge of national strength. Zoos could express a nation's technological progress, its control over nature and natural resources, and its ability to shape populations into productive, self-supporting citizens. It was a measure of progress and prestige. Kume, like his Western counterparts, seemed to see this relationship as self-evident. He heaped praise on Regent's Park and England ("We saw nothing in Europe to compare with the richness of this zoo"), and he ranked Holland a close second. In the end, however, he judged the Dutch zoo to be slightly "inferior," because its landscape was lacking and the number of species represented did not match London's broad collection. The index of nature provided by the Dutch zoo was less authoritative. Less impressive zoos reflected poorly on the nations that housed them, and Kume repeatedly passed judgment on a country's ability to manage its natural resources based on the state of its zoological gardens.[65]

That these modern gardens shared something with Japan's sideshows and teahouses was evident to Kume and his companions. Nevertheless, the zoological gardens surpassed Japan's existing animal displays in terms of both scale and efficacy. One of the first discussions of a zoological garden, written just nine days after the members of the Iwakura mission arrived in San Francisco, their first stop, highlights the novel function of zoos' didactic displays, as well as the perceived benefits that accrued to the nation through such focused visual encounters:

> In the West there are botanical gardens and zoological gardens in every city. In Japan, too, there are gardens and parks where people can look at animals and birds, but the scale is not the same. These gardens may look somewhat similar to those in the West, but the original aim in setting them up is very different. In the West, they are intended to attract people's eyes and ears so they can actually see things for themselves and discriminate, in order to promote industry and to promulgate knowledge and learning. Such projects are expensive, but the cost is not a worry because eventually there is a great profit.[66]

Zoos, it was recognized, productively focused the gaze of their spectators, sharpening their powers of perception and thus their ability as workers. Botanical and zoological gardens "promote the material sciences and encourage the discovery of advances in agriculture, industry, and commerce. They serve, therefore, as a means to promote national wealth."[67] The pursuit of productivity was not decadent or luxurious; it was the motor of national growth and the guarantor of national independence in an imperial age.

Reasoning of this sort did not begin with the Iwakura mission; rather, it grew out of a longer and culturally broader nineteenth-century movement to subordinate eclectic practices of collection and consumption to greater national causes. Ordered presentation was believed to yield ordered perception and practice. The Western exhibitionary complex provided a new model of order on an entirely unprecedented scale. When Fukuzawa Yukichi (1834–1901), perhaps the most influential sponsor of "civilization and enlightenment" (*bunmei kaika*) ideology in Meiji Japan, traveled abroad as a member of one of the shogunate's earliest missions to the West, he made many of the same observations as did Kume. For Fukuzawa, the zoo, together with the museum and the exhibition, was distinct from its Japanese counterparts. Its presentations were comprehensive in nature and arranged to communicate useful knowledge effectively.

Fukuzawa coined the Japanese term for "zoological garden," *dōbutsuen,* in his widely read travel account *Seiyō jijō* (Conditions in the West;

1866).[68] Rather than use preexisting vocabulary, which might be taken to refer to Edo's teahouses and sideshows, Fukuzawa chose to coin a new word, one appropriate to the new institution. This neologism owed a clear debt to corresponding nomenclature in the West, where the idea of animation and voluntary motion is closely tied to understandings of the animal. The characters for *dōbutsu* (now the standard Japanese term for "animal") literally signify an "animated or moving thing," while *en*, meaning "garden, park, or farm," may also be found in the designation for modern parks, *kōen*, or "public gardens." The term *dōbutsu* would also find its way into other animal-related neologisms, notably "zoology" (*dōbutsugaku*), which rapidly became the term of choice in scientific discourse. In language as well as in practice, the zoo was separated from its Tokugawa predecessors.

The Ueno Zoo came into being as part of the Meiji state's efforts to institutionalize the new ways of seeing encountered in Europe. In the words of Sano Tsunetami (1822–1902), the most influential voice in early exhibition policy and the first person to use the word *dōbutsuen* in Meiji government documents (in a policy paper written in 1875), the purpose of Japan's exhibitionary complex was to "develop people's knowledge and technical skill through the education of the eye" (*ganmoku no oshie ni yorite hito no chikō gigei o kaishin seshimeru*). For Sano, the museum, not the exhibition or the zoological garden, was the ideal medium for these efforts to increase productivity (*shokusan kōgyō*) via the "power of the gaze" (*ganshi no chikara*). The zoo was not far away, but it played a supporting role. Sano envisaged a "grand, pristine, beautiful park surrounding the museum" that would contain botanical and zoological gardens. This imagined concentration of institutions, which influenced the form of the future Ueno Park complex, would not only provide healthy distraction, but would focus the eyes of patrons, helping them to see forward into new realms of learning and knowledge by fostering their powers of discrimination.[69]

Administration of the zoological gardens was placed under the control of the Home Ministry's Exhibition Bureau (Hakubutsukyoku), which was formed in preparation for Japan's participation in the Viennese International Exhibition of 1873. The Bureau was charged with constructing and operating the Ueno museum and zoological gardens in addition to managing national and international exhibitions. In 1881, the year before the museum complex in Ueno opened, the Bureau was moved from the Home Ministry to the newly created Ministry of Agriculture and Commerce, a decision that reflected a belief that exhibitionary practices influenced a nation's commercial prowess and its ability to manage natural resources. Management of the zoo was assigned to the Bureau's Natural History Section (Tensanka), one of the least prestigious sections within its bureaucracy because of its ties to animals and agriculture.[70] As was the case with Sano, Bureau officials tended to value text over bodies and art over nature. Such a bias meant that the zoo, while undeniably important, was often treated as something of a lower-class stepsibling of the more refined museum. Drawing on longstanding upper-class prejudices against popular entertainment and contact with most animals, many of the museum's elite managers derided the institution as little more than a circus or sideshow.

The above arrangement continued until 1924, when the zoological garden was transferred, together with Ueno Park itself, to the Parks Section of the Tokyo municipal government in celebration of the wedding of the crown prince, the future Shōwa emperor, Hirohito (1901–1989). When the Ueno museum and the zoological gardens, which officially represented the museum's "second attached hall" (*daini fuzokukan*), opened their gates in 1882, the Meiji emperor, Mutsuhito (1852–1912), became their first official patron. His debut there would not be the last appearance of an emperor on the grand stages provided by these civic institutions that came to bear the imperial name.[71] The general public may have temporarily assumed the sovereign gaze on their occasional visits to the zoo, but they were urged to believe that this play existed only at the pleasure of the emperor. The royal relationship with the zoo was cinched in 1886 when administration of the entire museum complex was transferred to the Imperial Household Ministry as a cultural bulwark against the coming uncertainty of constitutional government. If the museum and zoological garden ordered time and nature, they did so in the service of the imperial institution, not the Diet. The Ueno Museum Attached Zoological Garden was formally renamed the Imperial Museum Zoological Garden in 1889, the same year in which the constitution authorizing the new national legislature was promulgated.[72]

Unrefined though it may have been, the zoo was the museum's cash cow. It is hardly surprising that, given the popularity of early-modern sideshows, the zoo pulled in large attendance numbers. Tickets were sold separately for the museum and the zoo, which stood several hundred meters apart from each other within the grounds of Ueno Park. The more prestigious museum presided over the park, sitting at the elevated terminus of the longest sightlines available within its grounds; the zoological gardens were located in a shallow wooded valley on the park's western edge, chosen because it provided good access to water and did not interfere with the park's vistas. The cost of zoo entry was set at one *sen* (Tuesday through Saturday) and two *sen* (on Sundays) in 1882. The museum was considerably more expensive, costing three *sen* on weekdays, two *sen* on Saturdays, and five *sen* on Sundays.[73]

The gap between the two tickets, however, closed slightly as managers responded to two realities. First, contrary to the fears of officials, poorer patrons were generally not disorderly during their trips to the museum. Their behavior, it could be said, was by and large appropriate to the context. They acted as if they were at the nation's premier museum, not at one of the city's sideshows. Second, visitors were willing to pay as much to see exotic animals as they were to view the nation's historic treasures, a reality that must have dismayed museum administrators. By 1902, twenty years after the zoo first opened, the cost of entry was four *sen* for the zoological garden and five *sen* for the museum. From an early date children paid less than adults, school groups began paying reduced admission rates in 1887, and soldiers began receiving free entry in 1905 in recognition of their service in the Russo-Japanese War, which concluded in that year.[74]

The zoo drew more paying visitors than the museum from the beginning. In the first year alone, the disparity topped thirty thousand people, the museum attracting 174,444 patrons and the zoo bringing in 205,504. The gap doubled in the following year: 123,672 for the museum and 184,992 for the zoo. By 1885, the number had nearly doubled again, with the zoo boasting over one hundred thousand more spectators than its more staid sister institution (92,471 versus 195,587). In 1888, attendance broke 350,000, fueled by the display of the zoo's first elephants. Ten years later, spurred on by the zoo's new role as the display case for "live-animal war trophies" garnered during the Sino-Japanese War of 1894–1895, which included mules, big cats, horses, and dogs as well as the aforementioned camels, attendance approached one million for the first time. It was a barrier that finally toppled in 1907 with the arrival of the zoo's first giraffes.[75]

These gate receipts were crucial to the financial stability of the museum, which, while administered by the conservative Imperial Household Ministry, exploited the zoo's popularity while keeping capital reinvestment to a minimum. The museum's relative lack of commitment to the zoological garden and its failure to support natural-history exhibitions in general fueled efforts in the late 1880s to sever the zoo's connection with the museum by transferring the Natural History Section to the Ministry of Education, where some believed it would be put to better use. These proposals were quashed in 1889 by Kuki Ryūichi (1852–1931), ally of Okakura Tenshin (1862–1913), who became the general director of the museum in the same year. Kuki's institutional priorities were clear. "Much of the museum's revenue comes from the zoological garden. Annual income from all components of the museum ... stands at approximately 7,600 yen, and the zoological garden accounts for more than 4,000 of that, providing over half of the museum's revenues. The zoo is a tremendous help to our finances."[76] If the zoo was to be moved, Kuki argued, it could seriously injure the museum, and, in turn, weaken a set of institutions organized under the Imperial Household Ministry. The zoo stayed where it was.

TELLING TALES: THE CULTURAL BIOGRAPHY OF A YOUNG BEAR

In the early spring of 1891, a group of Ainu living in the mountains above the village of Sarufutsu in Sōya County (on Hokkaido Island) captured a pair of bear cubs, apparently in preparation for an upcoming Bear Festival, or *iyomante*.[77] Bear festivals remained a part of regular Ainu cultural practice in the late nineteenth century, and the collection of these two bears would most likely have been carried out by a group of men who had trapped live bear before. The first cub captured, a healthy animal with a thick coat of black fur, was placed in a pen outside of one of the hunters' homes and fed a standard diet in preparation for its ritual sacrifice at the festival, which was scheduled for autumn. Although the successful capture of the young bear was certainly a cause for Ainu celebration, its seizure was probably little different from other similar events within recent memory. The capture of the second cub, however, started a process that would come to involve, in the broadest terms, thousands of people, drawing attention from local officials, university professors, high-ranking bureaucrats, crowds of Tokyoites, and, in all likelihood, the Meiji emperor himself.

The second cub was pure white.[78] The animal's extraordinary coloring (or lack of coloring) marked it as a coveted rarity for Ainu and metropolitan Japanese alike. White animals were traditionally seen as auspicious omens in Japan and China, and the gift of such an animal to the sovereign carried heavy symbolic weight.[79] This value persisted well into the modern period, where the comparative rarity of albino specimens, combined with the older associations of white with purity, continued to mark them as exceptionally valuable. By the time the young albino bear reached the Ueno Zoo in the late summer of 1891, it had moved from the northern edge of a rapidly changing national periphery to the center of a nascent Japanese empire.

Word of the extraordinary cub's capture spread quickly and eventually came to the attention of a certain Beka, an Ainu who worked as watchman for a local Japanese landowner. Beka, in turn, passed the remarkable news along to his employer, Kobayashi Chūkichi. By the end of spring, Kobayashi and a group of at least six prominent Japanese from the area had made the climb up into the mountains, seen the cub, decided that they wanted it, and acquired it from its Ainu captors. Since the only primary documents recounting this encounter are written from a Japanese perspective, the details of the exchange remain uncertain. It is evident, however, that the transfer of ownership was not entirely consensual.

A four-page letter addressed to the head of the Imperial Household Ministry, Hijikata Hisamoto (1833–1918), and written by the local county governor, Hayashi Kenzō, on behalf of Kobayashi and his colleagues, announced their intention to donate the "extremely rare" bear to the imperial house in the name of "all of the residents of Sōya county." It goes on to explain how Kobayashi and company acquired the cub:

> Former natives (*kyūdojin*) living in the mountains above the village of Sarufutsu were keeping a pair of bear cubs—one white, one black—whom they had captured at the end of April of this year. These natives believed that the white cub was a sacred beast (*reijū*) and were raising it entirely differently from the black one. One of their wives waited on the animal day and night, providing the pure white bear with special food and seeing to its every need.

The Japanese visitors were impressed with the animal and inquired how much its keepers would take to part with it. It is hardly surprising that the Ainu response was not positive. Hayashi's account continues:

> We asked Beka, who works for Kobayashi Chūkichi, how much they would take for the animal. He said that it was not for sale, that it was revered as a deity by the locals, and that it had to be honored in the festival planned for the coming October. They were resolute in their refusal to part with the animal, saying that a

> sacred beast such as this one had not been seen in these mountains since times long past.[80]

In the end, the contingent from Sarufutsu managed to walk away with the bear, although exactly how they accomplished this feat in the face of apparent Ainu recalcitrance is unclear. The documents imply that Beka acted as a go-between, brokering a deal that included a sum of money and may have involved a certain amount of intimidation.

The transaction was both a material and a symbolic act. When the young bear changed hands it was wrenched out of one symbolic system and installed into another, continuing a process of investment and exchange that started with the original Ainu hunting party and that would persist until after the bear was dead.[81] For the Ainu, the animal was sacred, something wondrous to be cared for materially and spiritually, celebrated, and, in the ultimate acknowledgement of its sacred nature and importance to the community, sacrificed and reincorporated into the social body through the mechanism of the bear-festival feast.[82] Kobayashi and his partners made something else of the white cub, using it as a different kind of, though perhaps no less mystical, ritual object, one capable of drawing the attention of the nation's leaders and representing in the form of a living, breathing being a complex network of social and cultural relationships. As with the Ainu, the bear carried a heavy symbolic load for the Japanese group. When they crated it off to Tokyo, they shipped a living metonym, a stand-in, for the Ainu people. The Ainu themselves had imbued the remarkable animal with spiritual value, placing it at the center of a rite that, in Hayashi's opinion, encapsulated the essence of a rapidly disappearing Ainu culture.[83]

Hayashi's writing presents the bear festival in a detached voice, fashioning it into an object out of a timeless, uncivilized past, to be treated with little more than aloof interest. For Hayashi, at least when shaping his thoughts according to the conventions of official correspondence, the entire episode dramatized on a smaller scale the story of an archaic Ainu culture encountering, and being subsumed by, the civilized Japanese present.[84] The expropriation of the bear-god by the landowners—an act not welcome by the Ainu—was cloaked in the language of benevolent governance, phrased in a mishmash of Confucian truisms and "civilization and enlightenment" rhetoric typical of official discourse in regional Japan during the Meiji period. The story that Hayashi's correspondence told was one that reaffirmed the propriety of the imperial government's actions in Hokkaido and reproduced, in a pattern with obvious pre-Meiji precedents, the Ainu as a measure against which Japanese civility could be gauged.[85]

The more confused reality of day-to-day Ainu-Japanese relations in Meiji-period Hokkaido is nevertheless evident in the figure of Beka, who moved between the two cultural realms in a manner that was probably more typical, for members of both groups, than Hayashi implies. As Brett Walker pointed out, this sort of asymmetrical exchange system has a long history in Japanese relations with the Ainu, and animals have long played an important part in those relations. Kobayashi did not acknowledge this social and cultural interpenetration in his official correspondence, however. Instead, he cast the gift as one originating in a peripheral present that was rapidly fading into the past, a past that in turn confirmed the centrality of the present-day imperial metropole. The bear was made to embody an Ainu identity on the cusp of dissipation. It was a mascot of imperialist nostalgia.[86]

Various modes of capitalist exchange had been in place in Hokkaido since at least the early-modern period, and at one level the purchase of the bear was yet another example of this longer pattern. When the Sarufutsu landowners bought the bear, they were putting a price on a sacred object, abstracting its value into the realm of exchange. The abstraction disembedded the bear from the social context of northern Hokkaido, converting it, in a process similar to that discussed by historians such as Walker and David Howell, into an object that could move freely within Japan's increasingly elaborate system of commodity circulation.[87] As it entered into the commodity state, however, the bear also mediated the reinstatement of a set of inequitable relationships on the local level, passing power to the Japanese landholders along with its body. Further, when the bear moved into the custody of the Imperial Household Ministry, which administered the zoological garden, it brokered yet another asymmetrical exchange, offering the symbolic value generated by its scarcity and cultural significance, in turn, to the Meiji emperor. In three stages, then, the capture and exchange of a single young bear worked to cast Ainu religious practice as an archaic artifact and outdated antonym of "enlightened" Japanese cultural practice valuable for aesthetic reasons; to express the increasingly comprehensive power of the central government and its local representatives on the nation's geographical and cultural margins; and to knit those who inhabited the margins into a symbolic network devoted to the maintenance of the emperor as an embodiment of the Japanese national polity.

The bear's arrival at the Ueno Zoo marked its debut in the staged spectacle of Japan's first modern zoological garden, where during its short life it appeared as one member of an ensemble animal cast rather than as a star on the regional ritual stage. The late nineteenth-century zoological garden was an archive filled with similar stories, many of them buried behind labels describing little more than animals' species and points of origin. When the bear arrived at Ueno in the late summer of 1891, it entered a new system of cultural representation and material exchange, and its story was added to the dozens of similar narratives attached to each of the animals displayed in the garden's cages and enclosures.

The young bear was featured in one of the first series of postcards that the zoo produced. The 1902 image shows a white bear lying on the floor of an open cage, where it is watched over by a darker-coated companion of the same species. The second bear is sitting up, gripping the bars of the cage with both paws as it looks off the page, returning the spectator's gaze. The bars seem to be there to lean upon, not to restrain the animals. The dark bear appears to be smiling while its companion sleeps peacefully. These mass-produced postcards, created for a national and international audience, circulated images of zoo animals to unprecedented numbers of people across tremendous distances, and they did so in a manner that was recognizable in a myriad of social settings.

Much of this work was accomplished by the text that frames the image. The top of the page situates the image in space. The postcard is from the Zoological Gardens in Ueno Park, Tokyo. This, of course, makes it useful in the manner of all such postcards. "Wish you were here," with the emphasis on where, exactly, *here* is and how it differs from *there*. For a nineteenth-century Western audience, the expectation was that such information would be provided in terms recognizable to the card's purchaser and the ultimate receiver. For Japanese consumers, however, the printed English marks the zoo as an exotic locale within the country's largest metropolis. A visitor from the Japanese countryside, for example, might see an excursion to the Ueno Zoo as more than a trip to the big city. It could also mean an exciting, yet buffered, encounter with the international world, a walk through a liminal space that lingered between here and any number of exotic *theres*. This feeling was heightened by the exoticism of the zoo's architecture and the regular use of foreign animal trainers, particularly in the park's elephant shows, which featured South Asian men said to enjoy a mystical communion with the elephants, themselves human symbols of the exotic. A typical show ended with the animal characters waving Japanese flags held in their trunks while the crowd cheered and the trainer took a bow.[88]

The text under the image and in the upper right-hand corner situates the animals along a different set of axes. The English name makes the animal available to foreign (and in particular, European and American) visitors to the zoo, placing it in familiar categories and exhibiting the ability of Japanese managers to speak in recognizable terms. These are "Japanese Black Bears," and one of them is an albino. They are also *Ursus torquatus japonicus*, a Linnaean designation that is authorized by the universalism of science and that signals one of the greatest differences between Ueno and the sideshows of Edo. The zoological garden was envisaged, after all, as a site for the propagation and display of a scientific consciousness. It was meant both to develop Japanese subjects' familiarity with the up-to-date nomenclature of zoology and to put managers' control of that nomenclature on display in a form meaningful to a visitor of any national origin.

In the Latin idiom, animals were rendered as scientific specimens, part of a comprehensive and seemingly objective system of representation that crossed boundaries and erased differences in the name of progress and objective knowledge. As Mary Louise Pratt argues, this language was central to Europe's colonial expansion, providing a deceptively neutral idiom that worked to abstract the entirety of nature, including "savage" human beings, from local contexts and to bring it under the sway of scientific knowledge. Once an animal—or indeed any thing or being—could be known in these terms, it became an object that could be identified, classified, and expropriated.[89] Japanese imperialists learned this lesson quickly and well. During the 1930s and 1940s, Japanese botanists, zoologists, and anthropologists stood in the vanguard of the imperial effort, identifying objects, tagging them, and shipping them back to the metropole for study and exhibition.

Postcards such as this one also helped to generate an animal hierarchy within the zoological gardens. Only certain animals were chosen for elevation to the postcard pantheon. These animals were often given recognizable individual names, shaping them into personalized characters with whom zoogoers could maintain an individual relationship. Naming and inclusion in marketed material created value, designating certain animals as more significant than others—"cute" or "ferocious" mammals are named far more often than other animals, for instance—and creating enduring relationships that were beneficial to the zoo.[90] A child is much more likely to want to go back and see Kang Kang, to choose a well-known Chinese panda, than he or she is to see Panda Number One. And a zoo is much more likely to devote resources to an animal that brings in paying customers or attracts attention.

Such was certainly the case with the young albino bear, who was not only unusual in color but the property of the Meiji emperor. The zoo housed dozens of such imperial animals—gifts from foreign governments and from influential Japanese, for the most part—and each of them was treated with special care. Advisers to the emperor were notified when the animals became sick or died, a practice that continues to this day. The picture of the bear on the postcard is in fact deceiving: the animal in the picture is not sleeping but is actually dying. The bear arrived at the zoo sick, and its condition slowly deteriorated with time. Foam appeared at the edges of its mouth, it was lethargic, and it could not eat solid food. The animal did not die from neglect, however, but rather because nineteenth-century veterinary science had little to offer it.

The animal was given the best medical treatment available in Japan at the time, receiving far greater attention than many human subjects of the emperor. At least three university-trained professionals examined it, each finding something different wrong. Among these was Ishikawa Chiyomatsu (1861–1935), the head of the zoo at the time, who studied under the prominent German experimental biologist August Weismann (1834–1914). Ishikawa was one of the most important exponents of natural selection in Japan, publishing the widely read *Shinka shinron* (New theories on evolution) in 1891.[91] As head of the museum's Natural History Section, Ishikawa played a crucial role in the Ueno Zoo's early history, pushing museum administrators to update the zoo's collection and bring the institution into line with European standards. His outspoken activism was his downfall, however, and he was forced to resign in 1907 after a scandal surrounding the costly deaths of the first two giraffes to set foot in Japan.[92]

The problem was that few professionals, even those as prominent as Ishikawa, had a deep understanding of the physiology of exotic animals. The expert in whom museum administrators placed the greatest faith, a foreign professor hired to teach at the Agricultural College of Tokyo Imperial University, failed to identify the animal at all, believing that it was a "polar bear sickened by Tokyo's warm weather."[93] His first recommendation, which traveled all the way to the desk of the general director of the museum and through the office of the Minister of Agriculture and Commerce, claimed that the "polar bear" was being mistreated and that it needed to be kept in a cooler climate.[94] The professor's tone was critical, implying that Japan's imperial zoo was not up to the task of maintaining such unusual species. Ishikawa, as the person immediately responsible for the bear's care, responded somewhat tersely that the gentleman was misinformed, and that perhaps he should return to the zoo for another examination. When he returned, the professor discovered his mistake, adding that there was nothing he could do to help the animal other than to wash its mouth with cool water, which appeared to comfort the animal but did little to improve the underlying illness.[95]

The bear died in its cage at the Ueno Zoo on 31 October 1895. Its age could be estimated at somewhere around five years. As with its counterparts in other parts of the world, the prewar Ueno Zoo was a lethal place for animals, and truncated lives were the norm rather than the exception. As with Yoshimune's elephant, corporeal death did not put an end to the bear's symbolic life, however. Its carcass was quickly turned over to a taxidermist, a member of a profession that developed rapidly in Meiji Japan as increasing numbers of specialists and hobbyists began keeping collections of natural-history specimens. The taxidermist removed the bear's coat, still valued because of its unusual color and probably more appreciated because the animal had been a popular attraction at the zoological garden.

Though the bear's documentary trail appears to run cold with the removal of its skin, similarly unusual animals tended to follow one of three paths after they died at the zoo. As property of the imperial house, coats and specimens deemed desirable were often incorporated into the imperial collection, retreating from public view in a reversal of the exposure that marked the emergence of the exhibitionary complex in the first place. Moreover, after Hirohito reached maturity, certain specimens may have found their way into his laboratory. The Shōwa emperor's highly publicized interest in biological research was more than just an expression of symbolic authority. He maintained lengthy dialogues with prominent academics, supporting research and publishing papers of his own. As a whole or in parts, unusual specimens might also have found their way into university laboratories and dissection halls, feeding knowledge and material into a scientific establishment as anxious to encounter new specimens as were the children who poured into Ueno in search of Ali the Lion or Hanako the Elephant. And finally, particularly famous zoo characters were often transferred into the collections of science museums or one of the Animal Halls found in national and international exhibitions. There, they were rendered via taxidermy into caricatures of themselves, lifelike renderings of "natural animals" waiting for spectators, or historians, to come along and breath symbolic life back into them.[96]

NOTES

1. Kay Anderson, "Animals, Science, and Spectacle in the City," in *Animal Geographies: Place, Politics, and Identity in the Nature-Culture Borderlands*, ed. Jennifer Wolch and Jody Emel (New York: Verso, 1998), 28. It is worth noting that the first zoological garden in the United States, the Philadelphia Zoo, opened its gates in 1874, just eight years prior to the Ueno Zoological Gardens. On the history of zoological gardens in the United States, see Susan Hanson, *Animal Attractions: Nature on Display in American Zoos* (Princeton, N.J.: Princeton University Press, 2002).

2. Nippashi Kazuaki, "Nihon no dōbutsuen no rekishi," in *Dōbutsuen to iu media*, ed. Watanabe Morio (Tokyo: Seikyūsha Raiburarī, 2000), 152.

3. For a survey of the history of zoological gardens, see David Hancocks, *A Different Nature: The Paradoxical World of Zoos and Their Uncertain Future* (Berkeley: University of California Press, 2001). See also Eric Baratay and Elisabeth Hardouin-Fugier, *Zoo: A History of Zoological Gardens in the West*, trans. Oliver Welsh (London: Reaktion, 2002). R. J. Hoage and William A. Deiss, eds., *New Worlds, New Animals: From Menagerie to Zoological Park in the Nineteenth Century* (Baltimore: Johns Hopkins University Press, 1996) offers a good assortment of introductory essays. For a groundbreaking analysis of animals' role in Victorian culture, see Harriet Ritvo, *The Animal Estate: The English and Other Creatures in the Victorian Age* (Cambridge, Mass.: Harvard University Press, 1987). On Carl Hagenbeck's influential Hamburg Tiergarten, see Nigel Rothfels, *Savages and Beasts: The Birth of the Modern Zoo* (Baltimore: Johns Hopkins University Press, 2002). The cultural implications of modern animal spectatorship are explored in Bob Mullan and Garry Marvin, *Zoo Culture: The Book about Watching People Watch Animals* (Urbana: University of Illinois Press, 1987). A useful introduction to the history of the zoological garden in Japan may be found in Sasaki Tokio, *Dōbutsuen no rekishi: Nihon ni okeru dōbutsuen no seiritsu* (Tokyo: Nishida Shoten, 1975). The Ueno Zoo's in-house history also stands as an excellent piece of research: Onshi Ueno Dōbutsuen, ed., *Ueno dōbutsuen hyakunenshi: Tsūshi hen* (hereafter, *Tsūshi hen*; Tokyo: Daiichi Hōki Shuppan, 1982).

4. Humans are, of course, animals. Nevertheless, contrary to the conventions of this volume, I have chosen for heuristic reasons to distinguish in certain instances between human and nonhuman animals using the traditional "human"/"animal" binary. The elaboration of this historically constituted barrier is central to my arguments on the importance of the zoo as a tool of anticolonial resistance and imperial expansion.

5. Anderson, "Animals, Science, and Spectacle in the City."

6. See Watanabe Morio, "Media to shite no dōbutsuen," in *Dōbutsuen to iu media*, 46.

7. Kashiwaoka Tamio, "Dōbutsuen ron," *Tōkyō kōtō jūi gakkō kaishi* 5 (1935): 6.

8. Ibid., 8.

9. The most detailed account of animal displays in the early-modern period may be found in Wako Kenji, "Nihon ni okeru dōbutsuen no hattatsu katei ni kansuru kenkyū" (Ph.D. diss., Tokyo University, 1993).

10. Kashiwaoka, "Dōbutsuen ron," 9.

11. John Berger explores the implications of this insight in "Why Look at Animals?" in *About Looking* (New York: Vintage, 1980), 3–28.

12. Isono Naohide, "Umi o koete kita chōjūtachi," in *Mono no imēji: Honzō to hakubutsugaku e no shōtai*, ed. Yamada Keiji (Tokyo: Asahi Shinbunsha, 1994), 81.

13. Katō Hidetoshi, *Toshi to goraku* (Tokyo: Kashima Shuppankai, 1969), 11.

14. Wako, "Nihon ni okeru dōbutsuen no hattatsu katei ni kansuru kenkyū," 25.

15. Peter Kornicki, "Public Display and Changing Values: Early Meiji Exhibitions and Their Precursors," *Monumenta Nipponica* 49 (1994): 179.

16. Tsukamoto Manabu, *Edo jidaijin to dōbutsu* (Tokyo: Nihon Editā Sukūru Shuppan, 1995).

17. Brett Walker, *The Conquest of Ainu Lands: Ecology and Culture in Japanese Expansion, 1590-1800* (Berkeley: University of California Press, 2001), 102. For a related discussion, see Tsukamoto, *Edo jidaijin to dōbutsu*, 196–216.

18. On the English foxhunt, see Garry Marvin, "Unspeakability, Indelibility, and the Structures of Pursuit in the English Foxhunt," in *Representing Animals*, ed. Nigel Rothfels (Indianapolis: Indiana University Press, 2002), 139–58.

19. For European examples, see Hancocks, *A Different Nature*, 1–33.

20. It appears that keepers fed the animals sweets in order to keep them obedient, and that the diet may have led to the female's illness. The best basic summary of the elephants' story may be found in Takashima Haruo, *Dōbutsu torai monogatari* (Tokyo: Gakufū Shoin, 1955), 122–31. For a discussion of various sources that relate the elephants' history, see Kajima Takao, *Shiryō Nihon dōbutsushi* (Tokyo: Yasaka Shobō, 1977), 573. See also Ōba Osamu, "Kyōhō-ban 'zō' no subete," in *Mono no imēji*, 92–114.

21. On the diplomacy and spectacle of early-modern travel, see Ronald P. Toby, "Carnival of the Aliens: Korean Embassies in Edo-Period Art and Popular Culture," *Monumenta Nipponica* 41 (1986): 415–56; Constantine Vaporis, *Breaking Barriers: Travel and the State in Early Modern Japan* (Cambridge, Mass.: Harvard University Press, 1994).

22. An elephant had not been widely seen in Japan since 1602, when an Asian elephant was presented to Tokugawa Ieyasu (1542–1616). See Takashima, *Dōbutsu torai monogatari*, 123, 125.

23. Ibid., 127.

24. Kajishima, *Shiryō Nihon dōbutsushi*, 574.

25. Isono, "Umi o koete kita chōjūtachi," 72–75.

26. On the *bussankai* as a predecessor to Meiji exhibitions, see Kornicki, "Public Display and Changing Values," 171–84.

27. The content and intent of such displays were changeable. I have

enumerated the most-often used names in order to illustrate the myriad of venues that were available for the display of animals and animal products during the early-modern period, but the reality was that a *bussankai* might not differ significantly from a *yakuhinkai* or *hakubutsukai*. See Kornicki, "Public Display and Changing Values," 167–96. For a related and engaging discussion, see Angus Lockyer, "Japan at the Exhibition, 1867-1970" (Ph.D. diss., Stanford University, 2000).

28. Kashima, *Shiryō Nihon dōbutsushi*, 574.

29. Arjun Appadurai, *The Social Life of Things: Commodities in Cultural Perspective* (New York: Cambridge University Press, 1986), 13. On the ability of commodities to "come to life," see Walter Benjamin, "On Some Motifs in Baudelaire," in *Illuminations*, ed. Hannah Arendt, trans. Harry Zohn (New York: Schocken, 1968), 155–200; Wolfgang Haug, *Commodity Aesthetics, Ideology, and Culture* (New York: International General, 1987).

30. For a critical meditation on cages and captivity, see Randy Malamud, *Reading Zoos: Representations of Animals and Captivity* (New York: New York University Press, 1998), 105–78. It is worth noting here that, from the nonhuman animal's point of view, glass enclosures and the like are not necessarily superior to barred cages. Bars, in many cases, add a third dimension to the animal's freedom of movement, providing climbing apparatus in cages that might otherwise be bare. They also allow for the circulation of air, scents, and sounds.

31. Matthew C. Perry, *The Japan Expedition, 1852-1854: The Personal Journal of Commodore Matthew C. Perry*, ed. Roger Pineau (Washington: Smithsonian Institution Press, 1968), 159.

32. Ibid., 190.

33. Ibid.

34. Ibid., 192.

35. Richard Tapper, "Animality, Humanity, Morality, Society," in *What Is an Animal?* ed. Tim Ingold (New York: Routledge, 1988), 51.

36. On masculinity and the rodeo, see Frederick Errington, "The Rock Creek Rodeo: Excess and Constraint in Men's Lives," *American Ethnologist* 17 (1990): 628–45.

37. Perry, *Japan Expedition*, 193.

38. Kay Anderson's work explores the multiple implications of this mode of apprehension. See her "Animals, Science, and Spectacle in the City." Also see Susanne Kappeler, "Speciesism, Racism, Nationalism … or the Power of Scientific Subjectivity," in *Animals and Women: Feminist Theoretical Perspectives*, ed. Carol J. Adams and Josephine Donovan (Durham, N.C.: Duke University Press, 1995), 320–52.

39. Michel de Certeau, *The Writing of History*, trans. Tom Conley (New York: Columbia University Press, 1988), 5. It should be noted that this moment of separation, which de Certeau argues began with the division of time into past and present, roughly coincides with a similar break that sits at the center of much of Foucault's work. See Michel Foucault, *The Order of Things: An Archaeology of the Human Sciences* (New York: Pantheon, 1971).

40. René Descartes, *Discourse on Method and Meditations on First Philosophy*, trans. Donald A. Cress (Indianapolis: Hackett, 1980). See also Brian Reed, "Organisms and Minds: The Dialectics of the Animal-Human Interface in Biology," in *What Is an Animal?* 100-109.

41. Charles Darwin, *On the Origin of the Species by Natural Selection, or, The Preservation of Favoured Races in the Struggle for Life* (London: Murray, 1859).

42. On Darwinism as partially reconstituting the earlier notion of the Great Chain of Being, see Joyce Salisbury, *The Beast Within: Animals in the Middle Ages* (New York: Routledge, 1994), 178.

43. For a more detailed discussion of this process as it played out in Victorian England, see Ritvo, *Animal Estate*, 39–42.

44. Julia Adeney Thomas, *Reconfiguring Modernity: Concepts of Nature in Japanese Political Ideology* (Berkeley: University of California Press, 2001).

45. *Shōnen sekai* 8, no. 4 (April 1902).

46. "Ueno dōbutsuen," ibid., 107.

47. For a representative selection of rules for Ueno zoogoers across time, see Onshi Ueno Dōbutsuen, ed., *Ueno dōbutsuen hyakunenshi: Shiryō hen* (hereafter, *Shiryō hen*; Tokyo: Daiichi Hōki Shuppan, 1982), 93–100.

48. "Ueno dōbutsuen," 117.

49. Onshi Ueno Dōbutsuen, *Tsūshi hen*, 48–54.

50. "Ueno dōbutsuen," 116–17.

51. For more on the military use of animals and of horses in particular, see Takeichi Ginjirō, *Fukoku kyōba* (Tokyo: Kōdansha, 1999).

52. Onshi Ueno Dōbutsuen, *Tsūshi hen*, 150–57.

53. Timothy Mitchell, *Colonising Egypt* (Berkeley: University of California Press, 1988), 13. See also Martin Heidegger, "The Age of the World Picture," in *The Question Concerning Technology and Other Essays*, trans. and ed. William Lovitt (New York: Harper and Row, 1977), 115–54.

54. Takashi Fujitani touches upon Ueno Park's important place within the ritual topography of the Japanese nation-state in *Splendid Monarchy: Power and Pageantry in Modern Japan* (Berkeley: University of California Press, 1996), 81–82.

55. Tony Bennett, "The Exhibitionary Complex," in *Culture/Power/History: A Reader in Contemporary Social Theory*, ed. Nicholas B. Dirks, Geoff Eley, and Sherry B. Ortner (Princeton: Princeton University Press, 1994), 137.

56. Michel Foucault, *Discipline and Punish: The Birth of the Prison*, trans. Alan Sheridan, 2d ed. (New York: Vintage, 1995).

57. Watanabe, "Media to shite no dōbutsuen," 15–28. For a similar argument, see Mullan and Marvin, *Zoo Culture*, 89–115.

58. Foucault, *Discipline and Punish*, 203.

59. Karl Marx, "Economic and Philosophic Manuscripts of 1844," in *The Marx-Engels Reader*, ed. Robert Tucker, 2d ed. (New York: Norton, 1978), 75–79.

60. Tim Ingold, *Hunters, Pastoralists, and Ranchers* (New York: Cambridge University Press, 1980), 88.

61. Bennett, "Exhibitionary Complex," 130.

62. Kume Kunitake, *Iwakura Embassy, 1871-1873: A True Account of the Ambassador Extraordinary and Plenipotentiary's Journey of Observation through the United States of America and Europe*, ed. Graham Healey and Chushichi Tsuzuki, 5 vols. (Princeton: Princeton University Press, 2002), 2: 67.

63. Ibid., 2: 68.

64. Ibid.

65. Ibid.

66. Ibid., 1: 69.

67. Ibid.

68. Fukuzawa Yukichi, *Seiyō jijō* (Tokyo: Shokodō, 1870), 35.

69. Sano Tsunetami, "Ōkoku hakurankai hōkokusho," May 1875; reprinted in Onshi Ueno Dōbutsuen, *Shiryō hen*, 9–10. For a related and more in-depth discussion, see Lockyer, "Japan at the Exhibition," 79–123.

70. Onshi Ueno Dōbutsuen, *Tsūshi hen*, 34–36.

71. Zoo visits were but one part of the creation of the emperor's public persona, which was one of the primary political accomplishments of the Meiji period. For discussions of the larger process, see Fujitani, *Splendid Monarchy*; Carol Gluck, *Japan's Modern Myths: Ideology in the Late Meiji Period* (Princeton: Princeton University Press, 1985), esp. 73–101.

72. Hijikata Hisamoto, "Toshoryō hakubutsukan kara teikoku hakubutsukan e," 16 May 1889, in "Reikoku Meiji 22" ledger, Tokyo Zoological Society Archives; reprinted in Onshi Ueno Dōbutsuen, *Shiryō hen*, 18.

73. By way of comparison, the average cost of ten kilograms of white rice in Tokyo at the time was eighty-two *sen*. A bowl of noodles (*soba*) cost just under one *sen*. See Shūkan Asahi, ed., *Nedanshi nenpyō: Meiji Taishō Shōwa hen* (Tokyo: Asahi Shinbunsha, 1988), 114, 161.

74. Onshi Ueno Dōbutsuen, *Shiryō hen*, 73–79.

75. Ibid., 93–100.

76. Kuki Ryūichi, "Teian," March 1889; reprinted in ibid., 19.

77. On the politics of Ainu cultural representation, see Katarina Sjoberg, *The Return of the Ainu: Cultural Mobilization and the Practice of Ethnicity in Japan* (Langhorne, Pa.: Harwood, 1993).

78. Hayashi Kenzō et al. to Hijikata Hisamoto, 27 July 1891, in "Dōbutsuroku Meiji 24" ledger, Tokyo Zoological Society Archives. For an interesting consideration of the meanings of white in modern Japan, see John Dower, *War without Mercy: Race and Power in the Pacific War* (New York: Pantheon, 1986), 156–63, 205–15.

79. On the significance of white animals, see Tiziana Lippiello, *Auspicious Omens and Miracles in Ancient China: Han, Three Kingdoms, and Six Dynasties* (Sankt Augustin, Germany: Institut Monumenta Serica, 2001); Donald L. Phillippi, *Norito: A Translation of the Ancient Japanese Ritual Prayers* (Princeton: Princeton University Press, 1990), 18.

80. Hayashi et al. to Hijikata, 27 July 1891.

81. It is important to emphasize that this process did not begin with the arrival of the group from Sarufutsu. It began with the Ainu hunters, who were primed to find value in such an animal by their own set of learned and inherited principles.

82. On the history of animal sacrifice in Japan, see Nakamura Ikuo, *Saishi to kugi: Nihonjin no shizenkan/dōbutsukan* (Kyoto: Hōzōkan, 2001).

83. Hayashi et al. to Hijikata, 27 July 1891.

84. For a discussion of similar moves in modern anthropology, see James Clifford, *The Predicament of Culture: Twentieth-Century Ethnography, Literature, and Art* (Cambridge, Mass.: Harvard University Press, 1988).

85. For an in-depth examination of this longer history, see Walker, *Conquest of Ainu Lands.*

86. On the symbolic malleability of animals, see Steve Baker, *Picturing the Beast: Animals, Identity, and Representation* (Urbana: University of Illinois Press, 1993). Mary Louise Pratt touches on similar relationships in other, notably European and South American, contexts in *Imperial Eyes: Travel Writing and Transculturation* (New York: Routledge, 1992).

87. See David L. Howell, *Capitalism from Within: Economy, Society, and the State in a Japanese Fishery* (Berkeley: University of California Press, 1995); Walker, *Conquest of Ainu Lands*, esp. 73–127.

88. Tōkyō Teishitsu Hakubutsukan, *Ueno dōbutsuen annai* (Tokyo: Tōkyō Teishitsu Hakubutsukan, 1902), 2.

89. Pratt, *Imperial Eyes*, 38–68.

90. Mullan and Marvin, *Zoo Culture*, 8–12.

91. For Ishikawa's writings on natural selection, see Ishikawa Chiyomatsu Zenshū Kankōkai, ed., *Ishikawa Chiyomatsu zenshū*, 10 vols. (Tokyo: Kōbunsha, 1936).

92. Onshi Ueno Dōbutsuen, *Tsūshi hen*, 45–47.

93. Kuki Ryūichi, "Shirokuma chiryō no ken ni tsuite shuryōkyokuchō e kaitōan," in Onshi Ueno Dōbutsuen, *Shiryō hen*, 280.

94. Ibid.

95. Ishikawa Chiyomatsu to Kubota Kazuo, 9 March 1892, in "Dōbutsuroku Meiji 25" ledger, Tokyo Zoological Society Archives; reprinted in Onshi Ueno Dōbutsuen, *Shiryō hen*, 280. Janson to Ishikawa Chiyomatsu, 29 June 1892, in "Dōbutsuroku Meiji 25" ledger, Tokyo Zoological Society Archives; reprinted in Onshi Ueno Dōbutsuen, *Shiryō hen*, 281.

96. On taxidermy and realism in animal displays, see Jane Desmond, "Displaying Death, Animating Life: Changing Fictions of 'Liveness' from Taxidermy to Animatronics," in *Representing Animals*, 159–79. See also Donna Haraway's classic "Teddy Bear Patriarchy: Taxidermy in the Garden of Eden, New York City, 1908-1936," in *Culture/Power/History*, 49–95.

From *Wakan sansai zue*. Courtesy of the C. V. Starr East Asian Library, Columbia University.

CHAPTER NINE

The Ambivalence of Whaling: Conflicting Cultures in Identity Formation

Jessamyn R. Abel

For nearly two centuries, whaling has played a central role in the formation of Japanese international identities, shaping both domestic and foreign perceptions of the nation and its position in the global community. In particular, the whaling industry has had a changing relationship to notions of "lawfulness" and "civilization." At critical moments in Japanese history, this nexus of industry and discourse molded both Japanese and American images of Japan and its role in the world.[1] Two pivotal moments in this history occurred during the 1850s and in the 1980s. Both were colored by different kinds of imperialist confrontations with the United States, and both helped to fix notions of Japan's international identity as well as to determine the content of its "traditional" and "modern" cultures. At both junctures, new animal symbolisms emerged along with new tensions in the interplay between Japanese and American diplomatic policies.

In the mid-nineteenth century, American whalers stood at the forefront of U.S. relations with Japan, bringing home with them an impression of that country as a dangerous and mysterious land. Their experiences in Japan, or more typically in its nearby waters, helped build support for efforts by the U.S. government to demand that the Tokugawa shogunate establish diplomatic and trade relations with the West. In Japan itself, the development of the domestic whaling industry played a part in the efforts of mid-century reformers to reinvent their country as a Western-style nation-state and member of the Euro-American—or, to use the prevailing imperialist rhetoric of the day, "civilized"—international community.

Over the next century, changes in the whaling industry, as well as in the international community's perceptions of whaling in general, led once again to the creation of new Japanese identities. By the 1980s, the ongoing debate over whaling had produced images of Japan marked by stunning contrast. Where conservationists saw an international renegade, whaling advocates found a persecuted nation struggling to protect an industry inherent to its "traditional" culture. Reexamining these two moments in Japanese history from a whale's-eye perspective offers an opportunity to assess the ambiguities that are inherent in the creation of national identities, as well as to unravel one particular instance of what Eric Hobsbawm has referred to as the "invention of tradition."[2]

TYPHOONS AND TYCOONS: MELVILLE BRINGS JAPAN TO AMERICA

Beginning in the 1820s, European and American whaling ships expanded their search for whales into the northern Pacific near Japan, prompting the earliest recorded instances of American-Japanese contact.[3] Although the island nation had stood largely outside of American consciousness in the early nineteenth century, whalers drew new attention to Japan when they brought home an awareness of this "strange" land at journey's end. Their encounters, though limited by the deliberate policies of the Tokugawa shogunate, helped to mold an image of Japan in American popular culture as a remote and perilous archipelago that was, nevertheless, steadily drawing closer to the United States. This cultural bridging of the Pacific, which began with increasing ship traffic, accelerated with the settlement of California during the mid-nineteenth century.

An early, and in many ways representative, American portrayal of Japan may be found in *Moby Dick*, Herman Melville's (1819–1891) classic novel of 1851.[4] Melville had himself roamed the Pacific on the deck of a whaling ship in the early 1840s, although, like most of his seafaring comrades, he never actually set foot on Japanese shores. Significantly, however, his work mentions Japan and its people or their ships over twenty times.[5] In the novel, Japan functions as a recurring emblem of the dangerous, exotic, and seemingly lawless lands that whaling ships encountered in their ever-expanding hunt.

Symbolic of Japan's status as a land of peril and mystery was its identification as the place where the sailor's worst enemy, the most violent of tempests, was born. Melville closely associated Japanese waters with the death and destruction caused by the typhoon. He wrote, "[I]n these resplendent Japanese seas, the mariner encounters the direst of all storms, the typhoon. It will sometimes burst from out that cloudless sky, like an exploding bomb upon a dazed and sleepy town."[6] Earlier in the novel we learned that on one of the *Pequod*'s previous whaling excursions, a typhoon off the coast of Japan had sent three of the ship's masts overboard, and the peg-legged Ahab had himself been "dismasted off Japan" by Moby Dick.[7] During the ship's final voyage, the crew again find themselves battling a Japanese typhoon, strong enough to tear the ship's sails from its masts.[8]

Adding to the threat of Japan's typhoons was the sheer distance of the northwestern Pacific from whaling ports in the United States. According to Melville's narrator, Ishmael, Moby Dick had been spotted near Japan, and Captain Ahab planned to go that far, through "almost all the known Sperm Whale cruising grounds of the world" in his pursuit of the white leviathan.[9] Even for the globe-circling whaler, Japan stood as the farthest point from home an American could journey, almost otherworldly in its distance from "civilization."

At the same time, the crossing of the ocean by whalers and other ships steadily brought Japan closer to Americans. Paradoxically, Melville depicted the two countries at times as being connected, rather than separated, by the shared waters of the Pacific. "The same waves wash the moles of the new built Californian towns, but yesterday planted by the recentest race of men, and lave the faded but still gorgeous skirts of Asiatic lands, older than Abraham; while all between float milky-ways of coral isles, and low-lying, endless, unknown Archipelagoes, and impenetrable Japans."[10] Whalers helped make crossing the Pacific a regular occurrence, while the settlement and eventual statehood of California brought the United States directly to that ocean's shores. Simultaneous developments thus transformed the North Pacific from a chasm into a bridge, one that increasingly tied together American and Japanese national fortunes. The metaphorical shrinking of the Pacific, an act performed in part by whaling ships, brought Japan firmly into the American popular imagination at the same time that it embroiled Japan in expanding U.S. economic and political interests in Asia.

Even as regular Pacific crossings in the nineteenth century brought Japan closer to America, the overwhelming impression that the country continued to make on Melville's whalers was the legacy of the Tokugawa shogunate's policy of "isolation" from the West, a complex foreign-relations dynamic already discussed in chapter 4. In an effort to keep out what shogunal officials saw as the potentially harmful monotheistic doctrines of

Christianity, the Tokugawa shoguns had long restricted contact with Westerners, with the exception of a limited trade with the Dutch East India Company at Nagasaki. It enforced these "maritime prohibitions" (*kaikin*), first proclaimed in the late 1630s, well into the nineteenth century, even as the growing presence of Western ships in the seas around Japan began to intrude on this relative—and heretofore relatively successful—seclusion. The isolation policy, which sought to keep whalers, among others, away from Japan's shores, created an image of that country in the Western imagination as mysterious, closed, and separate from the larger community of law-governed nations. Melville repeatedly refers to Japan as "impenetrable" or "locked," borrowing a metaphor of aperture and closure that had circulated widely in the West since the 1727 publication of Engelbert Kaempfer's *History of Japan*.[11] Holding the keys to Japan out of reach, as it were, was Japan's political leadership, embodied above all in the person of the shogun, also known to early nineteenth-century Americans as the "Tycoon" (from the Japanese word for "great lord"), or else mistaken for Japan's emperor, who was a different figure altogether.

In *Moby Dick*, when Starbuck, the chief mate of the *Pequod*, contemplates the murder of his captain, he bolsters his courage with thoughts of Japan's geographic and political isolation. "The land is hundreds of leagues away, and locked Japan the nearest. I stand alone here upon an open sea, with two oceans and a whole continent between me and law."[12] For Starbuck, as for Western whaling and trade ships in general, the land of Japan was, practically speaking, no land at all. Japan's supposed lawlessness—which is to say, its rulership's deliberate withdrawal from European networks of diplomacy and trade in favor of East Asian ones—barred it, within the nineteenth-century Western imperialist mindset, from recognition as a "civilized" nation.

As whalers increasingly found themselves in need of supplies or refuge in the vicinity of the Japanese archipelago, however, pressures against Japanese isolation from the West increased. By 1851, even the novelist Melville found it appropriate to suggest that the time was nigh for the shogunate to open the country's doors to Westerners, and that it was up to whalers to carry out the task of prying Japan's closed door ajar. Making connections with the "opening" of other Pacific countries, Melville boasted that whalers had already been responsible for the survival and development of colonies in Australia and Polynesia.

> That great America on the other side of the sphere, Australia, was given to the enlightened world by the whaleman. After its first blunder-born discovery by a Dutchman, all other ships long shunned those shores as pestiferously barbarous; but the whale-ship touched there. The whale-ship is the true mother of that now mighty colony. Moreover, in the infancy of the first Australian settlement, the emigrants were several times saved from starvation by the benevolent biscuit of the whale-ship luckily dropping an anchor in their waters. The uncounted isles of all Polynesia confess the same truth, and do commercial homage to the whale-ship, that cleared the way for the missionary and the merchant, and in many cases carried the primitive missionaries to their first destinations.[13]

For Melville, only whaling ships possessed the requisite boldness to visit the barbarous shores of Australia and the Polynesian Islands, where their crews planted the seeds of "civilization" and prepared the soil where less adventurous missionaries and merchants could later spread its roots. The same course of events, Melville believed, would follow in Japan. "If that double-bolted land, Japan, is ever to become hospitable, it is the whale-ship alone to whom the credit will be due; for already she is on the threshold."[14] According to Melville's expectations, Japan would not remain a "locked" land for long. The growing presence of whaling ships in the North Pacific, he predicted, would permit whalers once again to perform an ambassadorial role and bring Japan into the "enlightened" Western world. And indeed, within two years of the publication of the novel, Melville's expectations would come true—albeit not, as he had predicted, from the decks of "whale-ships" but from powerful gunboats. In 1853, an American flotilla commanded by Commodore Matthew C. Perry (1794–1858) cruised menacingly into Edo Harbor with the express aim of "opening" Japan. "Credit" for this forcible unbolting may have been due to more than whaling ships alone, yet it is nonetheless true that Perry sailed in the wake of an entire generation of whalers.

Facilitating whaling and other maritime traffic in the North Pacific was in fact one of Perry's primary goals. American whaling ships generally stayed abroad for several years at a time, necessitating occasional stops for supplies or repairs. However, the Tokugawa shogunate's maritime prohibitions prevented whalers from making even such limited contact so long as they were in the vicinity of a Japan that remained "closed." Furthermore, European and American sailors shipwrecked on Japanese shores were not so much rescued as they were captured, and local officials treated them as outlaws, sometimes even ordering their execution. Americans who advocated an official diplomatic mission to Japan evoked such stories of maltreatment to bolster their case.[15] One of Perry's demands was thus a more humane treatment of castaways and permission for American ships to stop in Japanese ports for coal and provisions. Using humanitarian (if subtly threatening) rhetoric, the letter from President Millard Fillmore that Perry delivered to the shogun contained the following clause:

> Many of our ships pass every year from California to China, and great numbers of our people pursue the whale fishery near the shores of Japan. It sometimes happens in stormy weather that one of our ships is wrecked on Your Imperial Majesty's [*sic*] shores. In all such cases we ask and expect that our unfortunate people should be treated with kindness, and that their property should be protected till we can send a vessel and bring them away. We are very much in earnest in this.[16]

Fillmore requested further that American ships be allowed to stop in Japan for food, water, and other supplies. Thus, the capitalistic interest in promoting the expansion of the U.S. "whale fishery," as well as other economic endeavors, such as the establishment of a coaling station for a projected trans-Pacific steamship line, found a politically expedient and morally legitimating idiom in the rhetoric of humanitarianism. It bears noting, however, that in this nineteenth-century American context, "humane" referred to the proper treatment by humans of other humans, and not of other species.

FROM CASTAWAY TO CAPTAIN: MANJIRŌ BRINGS AMERICA TO JAPAN

Increased ship traffic in the Pacific meant not only that foreigners were occasionally marooned in Japan, but also that crews of foreign whaling ships occasionally rescued Japanese castaways. As Melville wrote in *Moby Dick*, whaling ships occasionally picked up "queer castaway creatures found tossing about the open sea on planks, bits of wreck, oars, whale-boats, canoes, blown-off Japanese junks, and what not."[17] Marooned mariners saved by European or American whalers were among the only Japanese people of the time to have firsthand experience with Westerners, other than those who dealt with Dutch traders at Nagasaki (see chapter 4). Because of the shogunate's strict policies against virtually all direct contact with Western countries, these castaways were often unable to return to their homeland or were treated with intense suspicion when they did. Tokugawa authorities generally regarded those rescued and returned by Western ships as contaminated through their contact with foreigners, and feared that they might spread Christianity's monotheistic doctrine. Far from valuing any knowledge that castaways might have gained from their experiences abroad, shogunal officials viewed them as potentially subversive. However, the example of Nakahama Manjirō (1827–1898)—also known as John Manjirō or John Mung—marked an important turning point in the attitudes of some officials toward such "queer castaway creatures" and toward contacts with the West more generally.

Fourteen-year-old fisherman Manjirō was shipwrecked along with four companions on a small, uninhabited Pacific island in 1841.[18] After several months of surviving primarily by eating albatross, the castaways were rescued by the crew of an American whaling ship. The vessel delivered them to Hawaii, but Manjirō, invited by the captain, William Whitfield, to accompany him back to his home in Fairhaven, Massachusetts, remained onboard, learning American whaling techniques along the way. For ten years he lived abroad, studying English and navigation, as well as how to make barrels for whale oil. Manjirō spent two years at sea on an American whaling ship and soon thereafter began his long journey home to Japan via California and Hawaii, where he rejoined two of his fellow Japanese castaways. The three were finally able to return to Japan a full decade after having set off on their ill-fated fishing trip. After initially landing in the Ryukyus, the trio was brought to the southern Japanese domain of Satsuma, which controlled Ryukyuan politics, for questioning. Satsuma's ruler, the reformist daimyo Shimazu Nariakira (1809–1858), hoped to strengthen his domain with the help of Western technology and questioned Manjirō at length about his experiences. After further interrogation by representatives of the Tokugawa shogunate, in particular to assure that the men had not converted to Christianity, the three were allowed to return to their homes in the domain of Tosa on Shikoku.

The treatment of Manjirō and his compatriots by the Satsuma lord hints that some leaders, particularly those from "outsider" (*tozama*) domains, which had historically opposed Tokugawa rule, saw the mastery of knowledge and technical skills from the West as a means to give them an upper hand against the shogunate in Edo. Frequent attempts by Europeans and

Americans to establish formal relations with Japan during the first half of the nineteenth century had further exacerbated growing tensions between powerful outsider domains such as Satsuma and Tosa and entrenched shogunal councilors. While the shogunate continued to insist on its policy of isolation from the West in the face of such outside pressures, local lords like Nariakira began to envision the potential benefits of relations with Western powers. The rulers of Satsuma and Tosa, both of which would become leading domains in the 1868 overthrow of the Tokugawa shogunate, treated Manjirō's knowledge of American language, culture, and technology as valuable capital for strengthening their own domain polities and economies. Tosa officials even took the unusual step of bestowing on the common-born Manjirō the rank of samurai and making him a teacher in an official school of the domain, where his students included such reformers as Sakamoto Ryōma (1836–1867) and Gotō Shōjirō (1838–1897), who would become important figures in the events surrounding the Meiji Restoration.[19]

When shogunal officials likewise recognized the value of Manjirō's expertise, they granted him an even higher samurai rank so that he could serve Edo during negotiations with Commodore Perry. It was at this time that Manjirō, who, as a commoner, had only a given name, was allowed to take a surname, for which he chose Nakahama, after the name of his Tosa hometown. In contrast to previous castaways, who were often simply turned away, punished, or otherwise discouraged from sharing any knowledge gained from their contact with Western mariners, Manjirō became a precious resource for nineteenth-century shogunal and domainal reformers seeking to reinvent Japan in the face of Western imperialism and its diplomatic as well as economic pressures. As an industry that brought large numbers of European and American ships to Japanese waters, whaling became one of many factors instigating the reinvention of Japan as an economically competitive and diplomatically cooperative nation.

By teaching his countrymen American navigational, surveying, and whaling techniques, Manjirō took part in the early stages of the creation of a large-scale commercial whaling industry in Japan. Whaling had formed a significant sector in the local economies of some coastal villages during the Tokugawa period, but the scale of the industry did not nearly approach that of Western whaling. In contrast to the far-flung migratory networks of whale fisheries exploited by Western ships, Japanese caught whales with nets and harpoons from shore-based rowboats, and even then only when the creatures came close enough to shore. During the seventeenth century, it is likely that only about sixty whales per year were taken in all of Japan.[20] Soon after the American and British discovery of the whaling grounds surrounding Japan, however, hundreds of whaling ships from the United States and Europe began to operate in nearby waters. In 1846, for example, close to three hundred whaling ships from the United States sailed into the vicinity of the Japanese archipelago. One ecological consequence of this influx of Western whalers was that their Japanese counterparts witnessed a drastic reduction in the number of whales swimming in Japan's coastal waters close enough to catch them using the existing net method. Their livelihood threatened, Japanese whalers sought to revolutionize their trade, looking to Americans, then the most productive—or rather, destructive—whalers, as a model.[21]

In 1861, Manjirō sent a proposal to the shogunate outlining the economic advantages of the American style of whaling over the Japanese, and suggested that learning and instituting "foreigners' methods of whaling as soon as possible" would contribute to the "prosperity of the country."[22] By justifying his suggestions to the shogunate in terms of the "prosperity of the country," Manjirō evoked a political rationale that, up to that point, had referred primarily to domain governance, but one that later became a key to the development of the modern Japanese nation-state.[23] The shogunate responded by making him captain of the vessel *Ichiban-maru*, and Manjirō led the first known Japanese attempt at American-style pelagic whaling, which involved the use of handheld bomb lances from rowboats lowered from a larger sailing vessel at sea. In 1862, he was sent to Hakodate, on the southern tip of Hokkaido, to teach this pelagic technique to local whalers.[24] Of course, Manjirō was not the only figure responsible for changing the whaling industry in the waning years of the Tokugawa shogunate. But the story of his return to Japan—both the unprecedented degree of trust that both domainal and shogunal officials placed in him, and their willingness to make use of his unique set of experiences abroad—well illustrates the drive to remodel Japan's whaling industry and with it many other aspects of Japanese society.

Manjirō's experiences after his return to Japan underline the changing nature of his homeland and its global position in the mid-nineteenth century. Although the Tokugawa shogunate still feared certain influences from Western societies, in particular the spread of Christianity, its councilors proved eager to take advantage of Manjirō's newly acquired knowledge as an expert in the English language and American whaling methods. As Melville concurrently suggested in *Moby Dick,* Japan was moving closer to the community of "civilized" Western nations, refashioning its identity from a "closed" country to one actively seeking out knowledge from abroad. True to Melville's speculation, it was indeed whalers who helped begin the process of integrating Japan into the "lawful" and "civilized" imperialist world.

In the West, whaling was big business, and ships circumnavigated the globe in pursuit of their prey. No obstacle, even an island country that preferred to fend off foreign influences, could stand in the way of the fortunes to be made in whaling and trade in East Asian waters. Europeans and Americans demanded access to Japanese ports and, in turn, forced an end to the Tokugawa shogunate's policy of isolation from the West. Even as whaling in the mid-nineteenth century helped to create an American perception of Japan as a remote and dangerous place, ripe for the whaler's civilizing hand, the utilization of Manjirō's knowledge and expertise symbolized the emergence of a new Japanese identity as a "civilized" and "enlightened" nation and member of the Euro-American international community, both as a participant in the global whaling industry and as a partner in diplomacy and trade.

WHALING REGULATIONS AND JAPANESE INTERNATIONALISM

The expansion of Japanese whaling that had begun with the first voyage of the *Ichiban-maru* would make Japan one of the leading whaling nations by the early twentieth century. Japanese whalers continued to pursue various foreign models for the technological advancement of their fishery, learning not only from the United States, but from European whaling powers as well. Indeed, although early reformers had actively sought Manjirō's teachings, most Japanese efforts at whaling by the American methods proved unsuccessful. Moreover, simultaneous with Japan's disillusionment over American-style pelagic whaling, the American whaling fleet began to lose its global dominance.

Beginning in the 1860s, a new technique developed by a Norwegian, Svend Foyn, revolutionized whaling around the world. Foyn's use of steam ships and grenade lances not only enabled whalers to catch more whales, but also changed the contents of their catch, as it allowed them to net faster creatures. In addition, new technologies increased profits by facilitating greater extraction of oil and more extensive use of the whale carcass.[25] As a result, the Norwegian method would have a more lasting impact on Japanese whaling than had the American techniques introduced by Manjirō. At the same time, the new whaling technologies that spread to nations around the world in the late nineteenth and early twentieth centuries enabled catches on such an unprecedented scale as to reduce desirable species of whale to dangerously low numbers. The threat to whale stocks prompted international efforts at regulating whaling, resulting in the formation of an entirely new kind of global regime in which Japan would play an active role, largely through its cooperation with other whaling nations and international organizations.

After the first Japanese attempt at whaling by the Norwegian method in 1896, the industry developed steadily throughout the early twentieth century.[26] However, the Pacific War had a devastating effect on Japan's whaling industry, since military officials requisitioned large ships for the war effort, leading to a resurgence of small-scale coastal whaling. By the end of the war, Japan had lost almost the entirety of its whaling fleet and more than half of its prewar whaling grounds. Because of acute food shortages in Japan immediately after the war, the Allied Occupation promptly authorized the resumption of international whaling by Japanese ships and actively promoted the consumption of whale meat. Under American auspices, Japan's whaling industry quickly recovered. Whale meat became an indispensable part of the Japanese diet, composing an astonishing forty-seven percent of the total animal protein consumed by Japanese people in 1947.[27]

As a player in the international economic arena of whaling, the Japanese government and whaling industry could not ignore the prevailing global trend towards regulation in the first half of the century, followed by a turn towards whale conservation in the second. As improved whaling methods stimulated the industry, dwindling stocks exposed the need for regulation. The Japanese Ministry of Agriculture and Commerce responded by issuing domestic "Whaling Control Regulations" (*Kujiraryō torishimari kisoku*) in 1909.[28] These guidelines formed a legal basis for the subsequent integration of international regulatory principles, which began to take shape in the 1920s.

As early as 1925, the League of Nations warned that whales would become extinct without multilateral regulation, and called for international cooperation in the management of whale resources on the part of nations with large whaling industries. In 1929, the Norwegian government, in tandem with the International Council for Exploration of the Seas, established the Bureau of International Whaling Statistics. Two years later, the International Whaling Convention was opened for signature under the auspices of the League of Nations.[29] The Japanese government did not formally adhere to any international whaling conventions until 1951, but it revised its whaling regulations in 1934, 1938, and 1949 in order to incorporate the principles of the international whaling conventions of 1931, 1937, and 1946, respectively. Though not proactive in the area of international whaling regulation, the Japanese government followed the decisions of international regulatory bodies even when Japan was not a member of those organizations. Herein lies one example of the diverse ways in which Japanese leaders sought continued participation in the broader international community even after Japan's infamous withdrawal from the League of Nations in 1933. In whaling, an element of internationalism persisted in Japan even at a time when the government had severed relations with various formal bodies of international law and cooperation.[30]

In the decades following the war, Japanese representatives became more active in the multilateral regulation of whaling. At the same time, however, the gradual sway of international sentiment toward whale conservation, and consequently away from Japanese economic interests, made cooperation increasingly difficult. The 1946 International Convention for the Regulation of Whaling, in order "to provide for the proper conservation of whale stocks and thus make possible the orderly development of the whaling industry," established the International Whaling Commission (IWC), a body that continues to regulate international whaling today.[31] Japan joined the IWC in 1951. Historians often refer to the IWC of the 1950s and 1960s as a "whalers' club," an organization focused more on the development of the whaling industry and protection of whale-oil prices than on the conservation of species.[32] Its character would change, however, by the late 1960s, when over-fishing threatened to annihilate certain species of whale, and environmental groups began to exert pressure on whalers worldwide by mobilizing public opinion against whaling. In response, the IWC implemented stricter regulations, geared more toward preserving species than supporting the price of whale oil. The industry confronted a growing, nearly global, consensus against whaling, creating a conflict between the goals of international regulators and the dwindling number of whaling nations.

By the 1970s, nonwhaling nations had come to dominate the IWC, and whaling became largely an ethical issue rather than an economic one. Looking back from the 1980s, one Japanese writer described the shift cynically—if not without a certain amount of insight—as follows:

> American anti-whaling and environmental conservation groups ... cried, "Whale stocks are nearing extinction," and "Whaling destroys the ocean's ecological system." These reasons for opposition have no scientific basis, so when circumstances took a turn for the worse, they changed their call to "Because whales have a high level of intelligence and are mammals, we must not kill them," and then "Killing whales is unethical," and "We shouldn't kill such cute whales."[33]

During the 1960s, high-profile research on whales proved that cetaceans possessed a high degree of intelligence (in human terms, of course), and major environmental organizations adopted the whale as a symbol of their global causes. Under the formidable pressure of such groups, the prevailing philosophy of regulation shifted from one of limiting catches in order to maintain the size of whale populations to one of saving whales as an ethical good in and of itself. So long as regulation consisted of limits on the size of annual catches, Japanese whalers could comply. But the view that killing whales was immoral—a view, ironically, embraced by the very nations whose whalers had spearheaded the forward march of "civilization" only a century earlier—left no acceptable space for the Japanese whaler's livelihood. Whatever the reasoning, the international tide had shifted against whaling, setting the stage for a collision with industry advocates. The United Nations Conference on the Human Environment, held in Stockholm in 1972, adopted a resolution calling for a ten-year moratorium on commercial whaling. At the end of that decade, the IWC declared a total ban on all commercial whaling, beginning with the 1985–1986 season. The decision brought about a crisis in Japanese cooperation with the international regulation of the whale fishery. Once more, whaling had become a flash point in Japan's relations with the United States, and Japan faced what may be described as a sort of "green" cultural imperialism—an imperialism that was different in its rhetoric, yet not dissimilar in its Euro-American biases, from the dog-eat-dog imperialism of the nineteenth century (see chapter 6).

The absoluteness of the IWC ban on whaling made Japanese compliance difficult. Neither whaling companies nor the Japanese government wished to end the practice of whaling entirely, and Japan formally registered an objection with the IWC. Under the rules of the commission, any member nation could exempt itself from a decision of the body, and hence the binding nature of the regulations, by filing such an objection. According to international law, Japanese whalers should have been able to continue whaling, albeit within the constraints of existing quotas. However, in response to the Japanese demurral, the United States threatened to cut Japanese rights to fish in American waters, which was a far more profitable activity than whaling, under a U.S. law allowing sanctions against any nation attempting to undermine a conservation program designed by an international fishing treaty. Eventually, Japanese and American negotiators reached an agreement under which Japan would avoid sanctions by ceasing commercial whaling within two years of the moratorium's commencement. Even then, however, Japanese managed to continue—and still continue—whaling on a small scale, using a loophole in the moratorium agreement that allows whaling for "research purposes." Iceland also continued whaling for research, shipping most of the meat to Japanese markets.

Over a century earlier, in the pages of *Moby Dick* as well as in American culture more broadly, whaling had drawn attention to a "locked Japan" and helped to mold its international identity as dangerous, lawless, and uncivilized. Echoing this image in the late twentieth century was a new sort of "outlaw" identity for Japan, one that emerged from Euro-American pressures to cease commercial whaling and Japan's in-name-only cooperation with international regulations. Japan was now a "renegade" and "barbaric" country not because it stubbornly resisted the approaches of Western whalers, but because it openly whaled and consumed whale meat, behaviors that had recently been defined as inhumane. This new image was the result of Japanese efforts to resist, as they had in the previous century, Euro-American pressures to change.

WHALES TO SAVE OR WHALES TO EAT?

During the 1980s, whaling developments related to the IWC played out against a backdrop of global economic competition, U.S.-Japan trade friction, and a growing disparity between Japan's economic position and its international profile. Tensions between Americans and Japanese were symbolized, on the one hand, by "Japan bashing" in the United States and, on the other, by certain Japanese industrialists flaunting a Japan that "Can Say No" to the United States. The battle over whaling regulation that began in the 1970s and continues even to this day compounded existing tensions. Japanese resistance to American-led pressure to cease whaling, as well as the international attention that Japan's resistance attracted, created a new international image for Japan: that of an "outcast" whaling nation in an antiwhaling world. Once more, Japan found itself secluded from a Western-based community of "law-abiding" nations. Significantly, Japan's whaling image is disproportionate to the actual importance of whaling and whale meat to the Japanese economy and diet, as whaling actually constitutes only a small fraction of the Japanese fishing industry.[34] International differences regarding whaling also brought forth a two-sided image of Japan, as either a global renegade or a victim of America's cultural imperialism. As in the 1850s, the efforts of Western nations to exert pressure on Japan to adopt their own standards of international behavior fueled the creation of new Japanese identities.

The struggle of Japanese whalers throughout the 1980s to continue their trade in spite of the regulatory trend toward protecting whales inflected Japan's "whaling" identity in a new way. The antiwhaling efforts of the IWC, conservationists, and the U.S. government, combined with Japanese responses to those efforts, hardened evolving images of Japan on both the domestic and the international fronts. In the process, many Japanese came to hold a perception of themselves as victims of international persecution. Abroad, meanwhile, active Japanese opposition to the whaling ban and the ongoing fight to continue whaling created an impression of Japan as an international scofflaw and reinforced the view, particularly widespread in the 1980s, of Japan (Inc.) as an amoral economic machine interested only in profits. It was Japan's near isolation on the issue of the ban that made it a "whaling nation," in spite of the industry's relative insignificance in the economy and the dwindling consumption of whale meat by its population. Because Japan stood out in this particular arena, whaling came to serve as a metonym for the country as a whole. This was true both within the realm of American opinion, which held Japan as a renegade in a cetacean-loving international community, and within Japan, where the threat to whaling created a close identification of the industry with disappearing national cultures and traditions.

The typical conservationist's view, popularized by the American media in the 1980s, is of a sneaky, villainous Japan, pillaging the ocean's endangered creatures behind a flimsy pretense of conservation and research.[35] Although several other countries registered objections to the moratorium, journalistic accounts during that decade generally focused on Japan as the source of opposition. A particularly acerbic example is an article by Andrew Davis, assistant national media director of Greenpeace USA, published in the *Christian Science Monitor* two years after the moratorium went into effect. "Slaughter" and "massacre" were among the words the article used to describe Japanese research whaling. Like most reporters and commentators of the time, Davis depicted Japan as sole culprit in the depletion of the whale population. He and other American opinion-makers voiced doubts about the validity of the research that served as the justification for Japanese whaling under the moratorium.[36] Suggesting that research whaling was simply old-fashioned commercial whaling in a rather transparent disguise, Davis issued a dire warning:

> The [International Whaling] commission cannot remain effective without public vigilance against the transgressions of the few renegade members that threaten its integrity.
>
> The battle to save the whales has not ended, but has opened on a more subtle front. Spurious research whaling must be stopped before these so-called "researchers" exterminate the whales in the name of science.[37]

Although Davis referred to a "few renegade members," he named only Japan explicitly. By denying the validity of research whaling, he suggested that Japan's activities threatened the integrity of the IWC itself, and he adopted a strident military rhetoric in describing Japan as the enemy in a human "battle" over whales. His article neatly captures American attitudes of the 1980s, promoting a negative image of Japan as a "renegade" country of cold-blooded whale exterminators, an image that would worsen as a result of tensions in other areas of U.S.-Japan relations.

On the other side of the Pacific, such pronouncements compounded the sense of victimization and discrimination felt by Japanese because of the process and outcome of decision-making in the IWC. The dominance of nonwhaling nations on the commission created a perception of the international community as "ganging up" on Japan. The U.S. threat to apply sanctions if Japan did not comply with the moratorium, even though the latter had followed IWC rules, was interpreted by many in Japan as discrimination born out of anger and jealousy over their nation's newfound economic prominence.

As in the mid-nineteenth century, Japan's new whaling identity was not simply imposed from the outside but was constructed, with a different inflection, from within. From the standpoint of Japanese whaling advocates, Japan's actions had been not only legal and economically rational, but also ecologically benign. Japanese opinion-makers maintained that there were no ecological reasons to abandon commercial whaling entirely, as scientific reports showed that there were adequately sustainable stocks of certain species of whale. Japanese pundits also argued that the IWC decision was unfair because of the skewed membership of the commission. In fact, changes in the whaling industry had left the IWC composed predominantly of representatives from nonwhaling nations. A Japanese delegate to the IWC complained that some new members were not represented by their own citizens but by the spokespersons of certain "save the whale" organizations.[38] An editorial in the influential Tokyo daily *Asahi shinbun* opined as follows: "[T]his moratorium, even though it is called environmental conservation, is lacking in scientific proof of whale preservation. We cannot agree with the attitude forced onto the IWC by the antiwhaling faction, which is centered around countries that have no relation to whaling."[39]

Whaling advocates also complained that the decision ignored one of the original goals of the 1946 International Convention for the Regulation of Whaling, implemented not only for the purpose of conservation, but for the "orderly development of the whaling industry."[40] Some argued that a total moratorium would deal a fatal blow to that industry, and neglected the important fact that Japanese hunted only the relatively plentiful Minke whales (Lin.: *Balaenoptera acutorostrata*). Japanese practices contrasted with those of the indigenous Inuit of North America, who continued to hunt the most endangered bowhead whale (Lin.: *Balaena mysticetus*) under an exemption from the moratorium.[41] The sense of unfairness surrounding both the IWC decision and the Inuit exception led many Japanese to the conclusion that the moratorium was the result of discrimination: Japan was not a renegade nation, but rather a victim of "Japan bashing."

The image of victimhood was made more powerful by concurrent American pressures in the broader economic arena. Some Japanese laid the blame for what they perceived as discrimination on anti-Japan sentiments engendered by economic tensions between the two North Pacific nations. Furukawa Masafumi, for example, a ship captain on Japan's last commercial whaling trip to Antarctica in April 1985, insisted that the moratorium was "racial discrimination" and that the "United States put pressure on us only because there is this 'hate Japan' feeling over trade friction and other problems."[42] The dispute over whaling did not take place in a vacuum, but rather in the context of strong outside pressures on Japan to change its economic structures, and of more general American anxieties about Japan's economic might supplanting that of the U.S. as "Number One." This larger context conditioned responses in both Japan and the U.S. and colored Japan in conflicting hues on both sides of the Pacific.

Many Japanese whaling advocates saw the American stance on whaling as hypocritical bullying. Even the crew of Japan's last commercial whaler were aware that Americans themselves operated most of the world's whaling ships in the nineteenth century and were thus, presumably, the original culprits in the depletion of whale stocks.[43] In response to the American threat to impose sanctions on countries that did not accept the moratorium, the director of the Japan Whaling Association noted that it was Americans in the first place who had insisted on a clause in the IWC rules that any member country could be exempted from a decision by the commission simply by registering an objection. Since that time, many countries, the United States included, had taken advantage of the clause.[44] This historical record hardened the notion that Japan was being singled out for criticism, especially when coupled with the U.S. insistence that native Inuit be exempt from the moratorium. One writer decried the contradiction he saw in the IWC stance towards whaling by North American Inuit, calling American antiwhaling propaganda "baseless IWC bullying." He wrote, "I cannot understand the illogical idea of unreasonable discrimination between America, on the one hand, and Japan and other whaling countries, on the other."[45] The impression of American hypocrisy reinforced the perception of Japan as the victim of unfair treatment, even racial discrimination.

Japanese critics saw in American pressure a cultural imperialism that assumed that any culture that allowed whales to be killed and eaten was cruel, barbaric, and inferior. Many accused antiwhaling activists of riding roughshod over their "traditional" culture and the unique view of whales that it had shaped. An official at the Japan Whaling Association suggested that Japanese had their own understanding of whales, possibly quite different from popular views elsewhere, but equally valid: "I know that others may have different views toward wild creatures, but in Japan we believe whales are a resource that should serve human beings."[46] Another Japanese commentator similarly appealed to cultural differences: "If you [conservationists] all want to love whales, that's fine, but we have been making food of them since more than a thousand years ago."[47] According to these views, Americans failed to recognize cultural differences—with the all-too-conspicuous exception of Inuit residing within North American borders—and sought to impose their own values and gastronomic ethics on Japanese. The image that was generated cast Japan in the role of beleaguered victim of racial discrimination, its "centuries-old culture"—in this highly emotive context it mattered little that whaling as it was currently practiced was a recent importation from the West—threatened by pressure to conform to the standards of the American cultural superpower and its allies in a global battle over whales.[48] During the nineteenth century, whaling had been both an impetus for and a part of Japanese westernization and internationalization. In the late twentieth century, by contrast, Japanese evoked whaling practices to illustrate the power of ancient traditions and the distinctiveness of Japan's cultural heritage. In both cases, whaling grounds proved a volatile battlefield in the ongoing negotiation and renegotiation of national culture and international identity.

The whaling debate of the 1980s between conservationists and whaling advocates also produced, in addition to the opposing identities of villain and victim, a mutually held view of Japan as a "whaling nation." One line of argumentation against the moratorium presented whaling as an essential aspect of Japan's "traditional" culture, if no longer an important part of its economy. The cultural argument held that whaling was an important element of Japanese tradition in at least two respects: first, in the form of techniques and rituals surrounding the whaling industry and, second, as part of Japan's distinctive food culture, which included whale meat as a symbolically, if no longer quantitatively, important cuisine. By the early 1980s, Japan's whaling industry had greatly contracted from its peak, but more than fifty thousand people continued to depend on it for their livelihoods. For this reason, advocates argued, Japan could not easily break its whaling habits.[49] But the connection was more than economic. After the declaration of the whaling ban, the mayor of Taiji, a western Japanese town known for whaling, warned that the "moratorium not only deprives us of an important part of our livelihood but also destroys the tradition and culture of our community."[50] By assigning to whaling the role of "tradition" and "culture," he raised it above the level of a sunset industry that had anachronistically survived beyond its day. This new role imbued the industry with a cultural meaning that made it worth fighting to preserve beyond the bottom line of profitability.

Whaling advocates also responded to the moratorium with the accusation that the nonwhaling countries of the IWC had imposed their own morality on Japan's food culture. Calling whale meat an essential part of Japan's "food lifestyle" suggested that a moratorium would affect not only members of the whaling industry, but all of the Japanese citizenry as well. Although the consumption of whale meat was limited to relatively rare occasions in a few coastal towns throughout most of Japanese history, a program instituted by the American occupation forces of including it in school lunches throughout the country had made it a familiar (if not necessarily beloved) staple food for a whole generation.[51] As previously noted, in the lean years immediately after the war, whale meat comprised nearly half the total intake of animal protein by the Japanese population.[52] By the early 1980s, falling international quotas had reduced Japan's annual whale-meat consumption to about one tenth of its historical peak, but many Japanese continued to view whale as an important part of the national diet.[53] An *Asahi shinbun* editorial, pointing out the alimentary imperialism of the United States in obliging the rest of the world to adopt its own ideas of which animals were to be used as food and which not, illustrates this point. "The eating culture of Japanese, who use whale meat as a source of animal protein, must be respected. Europeans and Americans are pressing their own food culture and ethical views [on Japan] in saying that it is all right to eat cow meat and pig meat, but unacceptable to eat whale meat."[54] The American position implied that, in the late twentieth century, "civilized" peoples ate the flesh of cattle and swine but not that of cetaceans. Other writers pushed the critique of culinary imperialism even further, claiming that eating whale was so ingrained in Japanese culture that the ability to do so was a matter of human rights.[55] This rhetoric took tactical advantage of a growing discourse on human rights—but obviously not animal rights—of which Americans were often the most vocal proponents.

Another prowhaling argument held up the industry as an important element of Japanese food self-sufficiency, a goal that was simultaneously causing international tensions in connection with Japanese rice policies.[56] The importance of whale meat to the Japanese diet had been decreasing each year due to international whaling regulations, but whale meat had historically played a special role in maintaining Japanese self-reliance on animal foodstuffs, especially in the postwar years when it was relatively plentiful and cheap. Advocates of whaling argued that without whale meat, the Japanese population would be much more vulnerable to external conditions, making the moratorium a major national-security concern in terms of food resources.[57]

By labeling the skills, products, and technologies of the industry as part of Japanese culture and tradition, whaling advocates suggested that the desire to "save" whales was not a universal value, but rather the peculiar quirk of another culture—albeit a globally powerful one. In fact, in the United States, the whale-conservation effort was part of a larger environmental movement that had grown strong in recent decades. There was a century-long lag between the decline of whaling and the rise of conservationism in the United States. It was only since the 1970s "save the whale" campaigns that killing whales had come to be seen as morally wrong. In their 1992 study of Japanese whaling, the Scandinavian scholars Arne Kalland and Brian Moeran expressed sympathy with the viewpoint of many Japanese whaling advocates:

> What we in fact have, then, are at least two distinct value systems, each firmly embedded in and conditioned by historical processes in the cultures where they prevail. It smacks of cultural imperialism, therefore—if not of racism—for one cultural group to impose its values on the other, especially when the latter is seen to be morally inferior to oneself.... In their campaigns against whaling, animal rights groups carry on the dubious western tradition of forcing upon others the values which at any given moment happen to be in vogue at home.[58]

While Kalland and Moeran correctly identified the problem of cultural blindness and self-righteousness, they revealed their own biases in suggesting that efforts to impose one's own values can be limited to a specific tradition.

Not all Japanese believe whaling to be an important part of their culture. Some Japanese scholars have criticized the very notion of a whaling culture that arose in response to the moratorium. Takahashi Jun'ichi, an anthropologist who has researched whaling cultures in Japan and the United

States, has pointed out that, although it is meaningful to talk of a whaling culture in Japan, use of that phrase in popular publications of the 1980s was often tied to an ethnocentric viewpoint.[59] The anthropologist Morita Katsuaki has called the idea of a culture of whaling in Japan a "media culture," or a culture created by the media in response to the international dispute over whaling. He refuted the "whaling culture argument" on the grounds that, while it did have some basis in fact, it twisted a great deal of relevant information. Morita agreed, for example, that the practice of eating whale meat in Japan is very old, but countered that it was historically limited to a few villages and relatively infrequent occasions, not becoming a national or everyday practice until the early postwar years.[60] Regardless of whether whaling had been an integral part of Japanese culture for centuries, or had only recently been awarded the status of national culture, the important point is that many Japanese in the 1980s saw themselves as a part of a whaling culture, thereby redefining their own national identity according to the Japanese government's position in a particular international dispute, and in turn influencing the progress of that dispute.

At the present time, whaling is one of the rare high-profile international issues on which Japanese challenge international trends and U.S. leadership. The Japanese representative to the IWC continues to petition for a repeal of the moratorium at the commission's yearly meetings. Every year, the appeal is rejected. Whale meat is still available in Japan, though it is increasingly expensive and hard to find. The ongoing fight for resumption of whaling maintains Japan's international identity as a whale-eating rather than a whale-saving nation, in spite of the dwindling importance of whaling and whale meat in the economy, lifestyle, and diet of the Japanese people. In this way, Japan continues to be a "whaling nation" in popular consciousness, even if many Japanese have never tasted whale meat.

CONCLUSION: IDENTITIES ADRIFT

In a 1994 study of the cultural history of whaling, Morita Katsuaki expounded what he called a "semantics of whaling" based on Melville's *Moby Dick*.[61] Drawing on characters in the novel, he delineated three levels of meaning assigned to whales in that work. First, the meaning attached to whales by the owners of the whaling ship is no more or less than as barrels of oil; they see the creatures only in terms of the profit to be gained from their carcasses. Second, the ship's captain, Ahab, sees the whale in absolute terms: it is the embodiment of evil. Third, the story's narrator, Ishmael, personifies the semantics of relativism. Ishmael's, and by extension Morita's, insight is that the whale changes shape according to the cultural filter through which it is viewed. According to Morita's schematic, the whalers of the nineteenth and early twentieth centuries shared the industrial outlook of the *Pequod*'s owners, regarding whales as a resource to be exploited to the furthest possible extent to increase the profits of the hunt. Conservationists of the late twentieth century may be seen as having adopted—and adapted—Ahab's perspective, seeing the whale as a good in itself, rather than evil, but in equally absolute terms. Finally, Japanese whaling advocates in the 1980s disputed the IWC moratorium using Ishmael's semantics of relativity, insisting that their disagreement with the conservationist movement was merely the product of viewing whales through two very different cultural lenses.

The fact that both Japanese and Americans shifted, over the course of a century, from sharing the capitalist view of whales as an exploitable resource, to being divided, in broad terms, between absolute and relative stances, shows that there is no single, transhistorical truth about the ethics of whaling. Likewise, as we have seen, national identity and the content of "tradition" are far from permanent entities, but instead undergo constant invention and reinvention in specific historical contexts. National identity is more than just an inanimate portrait. Governments make diplomatic decisions based on dynamic perceptions of their own and other nations' identities. For many people, Japan continues to be defined in part by human relationships to whales. As those relationships change, Japanese identity will continue to be redefined.

NOTES

1. Although American opinions of Japan carried a peculiar historical weight during the two periods examined in this essay, other perspectives warrant further investigation. For English-language histories of whaling in Japan and discussions of the ongoing international dispute over whaling, see Arne Kalland and Brian Moeran, *Japanese Whaling: End of an Era?* Scandinavian Institute of Asian Studies Monograph Series, no. 61 (London: Curzon, 1992); John R. Schmidhauser and George O. Totten, eds., *The Whaling Issue in U.S.-Japan Relations* (Boulder, Colo.: Westview, 1978).

2. Eric Hobsbawm, "Introduction: Inventing Traditions," in *The Invention of Tradition*, ed. Eric Hobsbawm and Terence Ranger (Cambridge: Cambridge University Press, 1983), 1–14.

3. For examples of early Japanese-American contact, see Peter Duus, ed., *The*

Japanese Discovery of America: A Brief History with Documents (Boston: Bedford, 1997).

4. The Japanese scholar Kimura Ki cites *Moby Dick* as the first major work of American literature to mention Japan. See Kimura Ki, *Japanese Literature: Manners and Customs in the Meiji-Taishō Era*, trans. Philip Yampolsky, vol. 2 of *A History of Japanese-American Cultural Relations (1853-1926)*, Centenary Cultural Council Series (Tokyo: Ōbunsha, 1957), 13.

5. The text is available in electronic format at http://www.princeton.edu/~batke/moby/moby.html.

6. Herman Melville, *Moby Dick, or The White Whale* (Boston: Page, 1950), 468.

7. Ibid., 90, 109.

8. Ibid., 468.

9. Ibid., 358.

10. Ibid., 452.

11. Engelbert Kaempfer, "Japan and Foreign Trade," in *The History of Japan, Together with a Description of the Kingdom of Siam, 1690–92* (Glasgow: James MacLehose and Sons, 1906), wherein Kaempfer asks whether it is good for Japan "to keep it shut up."

12. Melville, *Moby Dick*, 479.

13. Ibid., 107.

14. Ibid.

15. Duus, *Japanese Discovery of America*, 72. See also Peter Booth Wiley and Korogi Ichiro, *Yankees in the Land of the Gods: Commodore Perry and the Opening of Japan* (New York: Viking, 1990), 29, 36.

16. Matthew C. Perry, *The Japan Expedition, 1852-1854: The Personal Journal of Commodore Matthew C. Perry*, ed. Roger Pineau (Washington: Smithsonian Institution Press, 1968).

17. Melville, *Moby Dick*, 229.

18. English-language narratives of Manjirō's life may be found in numerous works, including Fumiko Mori Halloran, "John Manjirō: Whaler, Navigator, and Interpreter," in *Nakahama Manjirō's Hyōsen kiryaku: A Companion Book* (Philadelphia: Rosenbach Museum and Library, 1999), 18–24; Kalland and Moeran, *Japanese Whaling*, 73–75; Kimura, *Japanese Literature*, 65–71; Katherine Plummer, *The Shogun's Reluctant Ambassadors: Japanese Sea Drifters in the North Pacific*, North Pacific Studies Series, no. 17 (Portland: Oregon Historical Society Press, 1991), 138–60.

19. Kalland and Moeran, *Japanese Whaling*, 74.

20. Nishiwaki Masahiro, "The Failure of Past Regulations and the Future of Whaling," in *The Whaling Issue in U.S.-Japan Relations*, 45.

21. Kalland and Moeran, *Japanese Whaling*, 71–73.

22. Hattori Tetsu, ed., *Nihon hogei ikō* (Tokyo: Dainihon Suisankai, 1888; reprinted as Meiji kōki sangyō hattatsushi shiryō, no. 102 [Tokyo: Ryūkei Shosha, 1992]), 180. For a modernized version, see Morita Katsuaki, *Kujira to hogei no bunkashi* (Nagoya: Nagoya Daigaku Shuppankai, 1994), 325.

23. See Luke S. Roberts, *Mercantilism in a Japanese Domain: The Merchant Origins of Economic Nationalism in 18th-Century Tosa* (Cambridge: Cambridge University Press, 1998), 1–4.

24. Fukumoto Kazuo, *Nihon hogei shiwa*, rev. ed., Kyōyō sensho, no. 83 (To-

kyo: Hōsei Daigaku Shuppankai, 1993), 206; Kalland and Moeran, *Japanese Whaling*, 75.

25. Lance E. Davis, Robert E. Gallman, and Karin Gleiter, *In Pursuit of Leviathan: Technology, Institutions, Productivity, and Profits in American Whaling, 1816-1906* (Chicago: University of Chicago Press, 1997), 519–20; Kalland and Moeran, *Japanese Whaling*, 75.

26. Kalland and Moeran, *Japanese Whaling*, 75, 84.

27. Ibid., 87–88, 90; Harry N. Scheiber, *Inter-Allied Conflicts and Ocean Law, 1945-53: The Occupation Command's Revival of Japanese Whaling and Marine Fisheries* (Taipei: Institute of European and American Studies, Academia Sinica, 2001), 136.

28. The 1909 regulations may be found in "Shōrei," *Kanpō* no. 7899 (21 October 1909): 571–72.

29. Peter Gidon Bock, "A Study in International Regulation: The Case of Whaling" (Ph.D. diss., New York University, 1966), 77, 156; Larry L. Leonard, "Recent Negotiations toward the International Regulation of Whaling," *American Journal of International Law* 35 (1941): 90–91.

30. Until 1938, Japanese representatives continued to participate in several special committees of the League of Nations, including those dealing with intellectual cooperation, drug trafficking, and the welfare of women and children. Japanese leaders also sought alternative means of international cooperation. For more on this topic, see my Ph.D. dissertation, "Warring Internationalisms: Multilateral Thinking in Japan, 1933-1964" (Columbia University, 2004).

31. "International Convention for the Regulation of Whaling," *American Journal of International Law* 43 (1949): supplement to no. 4, 175.

32. See, for example, Andrew Davis, "Japan's Dubious Campaign to 'Research' Whales," *Christian Science Monitor*, 14 December 1987, 4 (opinion section); Kalland and Moeran, *Japanese Whaling*, 12.

33. Nakamura Takeshi, "Hen na kuni to dantai to daihyōtachi," pt. 2 of series titled "Okashi na okashi na kujira no kokusai kaigi," *Asahi jānaru* 24, no. 38 (17 September 1982): 39.

34. In 1981, whales accounted for less than half a percent of the total take of Japan's fishery industry. See Imai Masaru, "National Sentiment More Than Economics Is at Stake," Kyodo News Service, Japan Economic Newswire release, 2 July 1982.

35. The American media were not alone in presenting negative images of Japanese whaling. Kalland and Moeran (*Japanese Whaling*, 16), for example, cite the following British headline from the 11 May 1991 *Daily Star*: "Sickest Dinner Ever Served: Japs Feast on Whale."

36. Japanese advocates of whaling argued that research was necessary to determine when whale populations had recovered enough to resume commercial whaling.

37. Davis, "Japan's Dubious Campaign to 'Research' Whales."

38. Quoted in "Whaling Ban Called Unjustified by Whaling Industry," Jiji Press Ticker Service release, 2 August 1982.

39. "Dōri ga hikkomu hogei zenmen kinshi," *Asahi shinbun*, 25 July 1982, 5 (morning edition).

40. For examples, see, "Dōri ga hikkomu hogei zenmen kinshi"; "IWC o

seijō na kidō ni modose," *Yomiuri shinbun*, 26 July 1982, 3 (morning edition); "Whaling Ban Called Unjustified by Whaling Industry."

41. See, for instance, "Dōri ga hikkomu hogei zenmen kinshi"; Nakamura, "Hen na kuni to dantai to daihyōtachi," 38; Sugita Eriko, "Chōsa hogei sae mitomenu 'jindōteki' kokusai jōshiki: 'Yaban na Nihonjinron' o hihan shinai Nihon suisan gaikō no fukakai," *Asahi jānaru* 29, no. 44 (23 October 1987): 101.

42. Quoted in Eugene Moosa, "Japanese Whalers Embittered by Moratorium on Hunting," Associated Press release, 28 April 1985.

43. Moosa, "Japanese Whalers Embittered by Moratorium on Hunting."

44. Nagasaki Fukuzō, "Jūgatsu shukkō no Daisan Nisshinmaru ga hogei bosen no saigo no kōkai to naru ka wa Beikoku de no saiban no kekka ikan ni yoru," *Chūō kōron* 101 (1986): 64.

45. Nakamura, "Hen na kuni to dantai to daihyōtachi," 36, 38.

46. Quoted in John Burgess, "Japan Halts Whaling in Antarctica," *Washington Post*, 17 March 1987, A23.

47. Nakamura, "Hen na kuni to dantai to daihyōtachi," 39.

48. Although certain Japanese towns and villages had, in fact, been whaling for centuries, whale meat was not eaten on a regular basis or a nationwide scale until after the Second World War.

49. "Dōri ga hikkomu hogei zenmen kinshi," 5; Imai, "National Sentiment More Than Economics Is at Stake."

50. "Whaling Ban Called Unjustified by Whaling Industry."

51. Scheiber, *Inter-Allied Conflicts and Ocean Law*, 136.

52. Kalland and Moeran, *Japanese Whaling*, 146.

53. "Japan-U.S. Ties Strained by Whaling Problem," Jiji Press Ticker Service release, 30 November 1984.

54. "Dōri ga hikkomu hogei zenmen kinshi," 5. An editorial the following day in the Tokyo daily *Yomiuri shinbun* (26 July 1982, 3 [morning edition]) echoed this sentiment: "The relationship between animals who are used as food and humans differs according to a given country's geographical features, culture, religion, and eating habits. It is outrageous to look disapprovingly at such differences and ... force one's principles on other countries."

55. Nakamura Takeshi, quoted in Imai, "National Sentiment More Than Economics Is at Stake."

56. On Japanese rice policy in the 1980s, see Aurelia George, *The Politics of Liberalisation in Japan: The Case of Rice*, Australia-Japan Research Centre Research Paper no. 188 (Canberra: Australian National University, 1990).

57. Yutaka Hirasawa, "The Whaling Industry in Japan's Economy," in *The Whaling Issue in U.S.-Japan Relations*, 85.

58. Kalland and Moeran, *Japanese Whaling*, 193.

59. Takahashi Jun'ichi, "Geirui no shigen kanri to bunka jinruigakuteki shiten no motsu igi," in *Geirui shigen no kenkyū to kanri*, ed. Sakuramoto Kazumi, Katō Hidehiro, and Tanaka Shōichi (Tokyo: Kōseisha Kōseikaku, 1991), 205–7.

60. Morita, *Kujira to hogei no bunkashi*, 414–15.

61. Ibid., 370–71.

CONTRIBUTORS

JESSAMYN R. ABEL is a Lecturer in the History Faculty at the Massachusetts Institute of Technology. She currently researches the changing meanings of internationalism in transwar Japan and the role of cultural production and exchange in imperialism.

ALEXANDER BAY is a Ph.D. candidate in the History Department at Stanford University. He is completing a dissertation on modern medicine and beriberi. His research interests include the history of science and medicine in early-modern and modern Japan.

MARTHA CHAIKLIN teaches at the University of Wisconsin-Milwaukee. She researches early-modern Japan, in particular, the cultural history of Japanese relations with Europe. She is the author of *Cultural Commerce and Dutch Commercial Culture: The Influence of European Material Culture on Japan, 1700-1850* (2003).

RIA KOOPMANS-DE BRUIJN is East Asian Studies Librarian in the C. V. Starr East Asian Library at Columbia University and specializes in Japanese folklore. She is particularly interested in animal folklore, both within Japan and in comparative contexts. She is the author of *Area Bibliography of Japan* (1998).

HOYT LONG is a Ph.D. candidate in the Department of Asian Languages and Cultures at the University of Michigan. He researches modern Japanese literature. His dissertation examines the geography of cultural and literary production in Japan as shaped by the evolution of print capitalism, focusing in particular on the early twentieth century and the work of Miyazawa Kenji.

DAVID B. LURIE is Assistant Professor of Japanese History and Literature in the Department of East Asian Languages and Cultures at Columbia University. He is an expert on the history of writing systems, especially in East Asia, and on early Japanese philology. He is currently completing a book manuscript titled *Realms of Literacy: Early Japan and the History of Writing*.

IAN MILLER is Assistant Professor of Japanese History at Arizona State University. He is currently working on a cultural history of the Ueno Zoo titled *The Nature of the Beast: The Ueno Zoological Gardens and Imperial Modernity in Japan, 1882-1982*. His research and teaching interests include the cultural history of imperialism, urbanism, and consumerism, and the history of human dealings with the natural world.

GREGORY M. PFLUGFELDER is Associate Professor of Japanese History at Columbia University. He is the author of *Politics and the Kitchen* (in Japanese, 1986) and *Cartographies of Desire* (1999), for which he received the Yamakawa Kikue Prize and Honorable Mention for the John Boswell Prize, respectively.

AARON SKABELUND is a Japan Society for the Promotion of Science Postdoctoral Fellow in the Faculty of Law at Hokkaido University. He is preparing for publication a book manuscript titled *Imperial Dogs: A Canine History of Japan, 1850-2000*. Starting in the fall of 2006, he will be an Assistant Professor in the Department of History at Brigham Young University.

BRETT L. WALKER is an Associate Professor at Montana State University. He is the author of *The Conquest of Ainu Lands* (2001) and *The Lost Wolves of Japan* (2005), and is the recipient of the Leopold-Hidy Award.

INDEX

Note: Italicized page numbers refer to figures and tables